REMAKING URBAN CITIZENSHIP

REMAKING URBAN CITIZENSHIP

ORGANIZATIONS, INSTITUTIONS, AND THE RIGHT TO THE CITY

COMPARATIVE URBAN AND
COMMUNITY RESEARCH, VOLUME 10

MICHAEL PETER SMITH &
MICHAEL MCQUARRIE, EDITORS

Transaction Publishers
New Brunswick (U.S.A.) and London (U.K.)

This book is printed on acid-free paper that meets the American National Standard for Permanence of Paper for Printed Library Materials.

Library of Congress Catalog Number: 2011041495
ISBN: 978-1-4128-4618-9
Printed in the United States of America

Library of Congress Cataloging-in-Publication Data

Remaking urban citizenship : organizations, institutions, and the right to the city /
    Michael Peter Smith and Michael McQuarrie, editors.
        p. cm. -- (Comparative urban and community research ; v. 10)
    Includes index.
    ISBN 978-1-4128-4618-9
    1. Sociology, Urban. 2. Citizenship. I. Smith, Michael P. II. McQuarrie, Michael.

HT151.R386 2012
307.76--dc23

2011041495

Contents

Acknowledgements

We wish to thank the contributors to *Remaking Urban Citizenship* for reflecting upon and carefully revising their original submissions to our call for papers; their efforts have given greater coherence to this book as a whole. We owe a special thanks to our editorial assistant, Robert Saper, for the improvements he has made to each chapter of the book through his insightful editorial comments and for his excellent copy-editing of the entire manuscript. We also wish to thank Andrew McIntosh, Mary Curtis, and Irving Louis Horowitz of Transaction Publishers for their continuing support for the Comparative Urban and Community Research Book Series.

Michael Peter Smith and Michael McQuarrie
University of California, Davis

PART I

CONCEIVING AND LOCATING CITIZENSHIP

1

Remaking Urban Citizenship

Michael Peter Smith and Michael McQuarrie

This volume started with a basic idea. We were interested in the changing shape of citizenship, the role of cities in shaping it, and the struggles that inevitably define it. We were prompted by a growing sense that not only were scholars reassessing the meaning of citizenship in reaction to the changing ways that governance is articulated at different scales and in different institutional settings, but that the claims being made around citizenship were changing. Perhaps most visibly, there is a growing movement that specifically claims a "right to the city" that echoes discussions of critical urbanists like Henri Lefebvre (1996; 2003 [1970]). In this context, the claim to have rights is associated with membership in a city rather than a nation. These claims mobilize people on the basis of propinquity and membership in a more legally amorphous community than the nation-state. They tend to privilege multiple modes of belonging beyond legal citizenship and place of birth—such as work, residence, and civic responsibility—as the bases of claims to rights and citizenship.

While this growing movement has received considerable scholarly attention, along with the increasingly expansive discussion of the connection between citizenship and cities (see Holston, 1999; Holston and Appadurai, 1996), it remains unclear whether these claims are able to gain much traction legally, politically, organizationally, and institutionally. Certainly, the claims are being made. In the US the massive nationwide urban protests against proposed draconian Congressional anti-immigration legislation in May 2006 is merely the most visible example. Dynamics such as changing attitudes about work, migration, and transnational subjectivities go a long way in explaining why such claims are being made. However, for us, the question is whether these changing identities and political claims matter for cities beyond simply being indicative of subjective political views. With this in mind, we decided to edit a book that would assess the degree to which new definitions of citizenship and the claims based on them were actually changing the institutional and organizational fabric of cities. Are cities becoming more inclusive in response to claims of citizenship and rights by people who might not have legal status or who might have legal status but be subjected to institutional closure?

Different nation-states and cities define group membership and exclusion in a variety of ways, and they are varyingly welcoming to strangers. This is often, and probably primarily, understood as an issue of policy. What laws define citizenship? How easy is it to realize that status? How closely is legal citizenship tied to social membership? Luis Guarnizo's chapter on the *longue durée* social construction of citizenship from ancient Greece to today's global system was placed at the beginning of *Remaking Urban Citizenship* because it calls attention to the importance of taking formal-legal citizenship as an analytical category since it is an enduring mechanism against which rights claims are made and by which, under the notion that all are equal before the law, social inequalities can be reproduced. The focal point of his argument is that "citizenship" is first and foremost a formal institution. It is a mechanism used by the state to regulate and govern those whom it includes in or excludes from membership. Much can be gained by thinking through the complexity of this relationship at various scales. As Guarnizo's chapter makes clear, the granting or withholding of citizenship has been as much a tool of state control, discipline, and *governmentality* (Foucault, 1988), including the governmentality of the local state, as it has been a membership institution for gaining access to rights and entitlements. His chapter supports calls for careful theorization of the political obligations as well as the political rights and entitlements of citizenship to provide a more complete picture of the making and remaking of the citizenship contract between states and citizens operating at various scales (see Smith, 2009).

Historically, the way these questions of membership and control have been addressed has had a significant impact on social change. For example, it is a trope that the United States is a nation of immigrants. The US is indeed that, but the trope carries with it the incorrect implication that the US is welcoming to all immigrants equally or that it is welcoming to immigrants at all. Just as deceivingly, it can point in the limiting direction of comparative regimes of legal citizenship as the only appropriate avenue for analysis and policy intervention. This is exacerbated in a moment like the contemporary one when the meaning of citizenship and the policies that define it are hotly contested in the public sphere.

Social scientists have long understood that, with respect to membership, "belonging" goes well beyond the question of formal-legal status. The law is only one institutional arena, albeit a central one, that defines who we are and the status of our membership. Social scientists also study labor markets, residential communities, political representation, educational systems, small businesses, professions, ownership of property, religion, and, of course, civil society. Each of these institutional and organizational settings has dynamics that can enable newcomers, strangers, or the stigmatized to move through them with relative ease, or these contexts can be organized to marginalize and exclude these "others." When many of these settings line up to exclude or include in a given place, we can describe a general circumstance of *social closure* or *social integration* that also has implications for equity, social mobility, and democracy (Kalavita, 1998; Smith, 1995; Wacquant, 2008; Wilson, 1996).

Understanding these dynamics is becoming more important as increasingly we recognize that democracy, equality, and diversity do not always parallel each other (Fainstein, 2010). Institutions that produce diversity might be highly unequal in other ways, and democracy can be an instrument for marginalizing minorities. For example, elected officials in the cities of San Jose and San Francisco, California, both cities with large immigrant populations in the same state, have radically different perceptions of outsiders, their political importance, and the need of political institutions to respond to their needs. (In this volume, compare Bloemraad and Gleeson with de Graauw.) These differences are constituted locally rather than at the national or even the state level. Moreover, the institutional settings discussed in these chapters—the domains of politics and civil society—do not address many other settings. For example, San Jose is characterized by political institutions in which immigrants are relatively invisible, but immigrants might not be nearly as invisible in its labor market. We are talking about Silicon Valley, after all.

The premise of this volume is rooted in organizational sociology, yet many contributions take us well beyond a focus on organizations. Indeed, the outcome of the authors' combined efforts is something other and something better than the volume's original question could have anticipated.

For organizational sociologists, institutions and organizations can be read off of one another, making both of these objects central for understanding social change in organizational societies like ours. As such, organizations can become privileged sites for institutional analysis. If the claim to a "right to the city" does indeed matter, it should be visible in organizational populations and new institutional arrangements. Some of the contributors to *Remaking Urban Citizenship* have indeed gone down the organizational path in answering the question posed by the volume. We were pleasantly surprised, however, by a number of essays that resisted viewing the "right to the city" phenomenon through a strictly organizational lens. Some contributors questioned whether the focus on formal organizations as hard measures of power, inclusion, and urban citizenship might actually obscure important dynamics of social change produced by the "soft" power of everyday practices by which subaltern populations appropriate and use urban space. Other contributors argued that particular organizations, organizational populations, and institutional settings are best understood when viewed not in isolation but in the broader context of the distinctive *local civil societies* that characterize different cities.

There are three surprising ways in which the contributions to this volume are distinctive and mutually reinforcing. First, the chapters collected here come from scholars who primarily identify with different disciplines, different theoretical questions, and different methodological approaches. Yet, despite these distinctions, the commonalities and differences among these chapters do not, for the most part, fall neatly along the lines one might expect. In the section on organizations and institutions, for example, we have placed scholars who are primarily known as critical urbanists along with sociologists of migration; the analyses they present share far more in common with that of the accompanying sociologists than they do with some of the critical urbanists in other sections. Of course, there are differences in tone, styles of presentation, and theoretical orientation. However, we have endeavored to organize the contributions so that the reader can appreciate the broader pictures that emerge from these sections, pictures that are visible using multiple approaches but which gain depth and richness because they are presented utilizing different interpretive frameworks and analytical procedures.

Second, these chapters are also suggestive of some important things about cities today, which, again, do not map simply onto theoretical orientation or fall neatly into disciplinary domains. For example, collectively, these contributions argue for a return of "the local" as a relevant site of analysis. While we have long known that wider flows of people, capital, and resources affect cities, it is how these extra-local flows come together and interact in local institutional contexts in specific places that really matters. What we see in these contributions is that different cities contain very different avenues of mobility and marginalization, integration and closure, membership and exclusion. There is no single institutional setting in which these processes can be measured. These chapters give a sense of the variability of local institutions and the ways in which they overlap, fold over one another, and create different interstices that make action possible—even by the marginalized. Of course, this does not mean that more distant, systemic, transnational, or global processes do not matter; they most certainly do, as demonstrated by Luis Guarnizo's theoretical essay on the social construction of citizenship, Sites and Vonderlack-Navarro's empirical study of Chicago's Mexican hometown associations, and Miraftab's analysis of the appropriation of public space in Beardstown, Illinois. However, such wider-scale processes are always articulated through local institutions and organizations in place-specific ways. The result of this variability is that cities provide very different structures of opportunity and marginalization even when basic legal definitions of membership and exclusion are consistent.

Third, the contributions to *Remaking Urban Citizenship* share a common orientation that politics and civil society clearly matter. Political engagement and action in the public sphere, even when they are about relatively mundane issues like access to a public park to play a game of soccer, contain possibilities that cannot be abstractly or objectively defined. Of course, the organization of governance, formal politics, and civil society can have a huge impact on the possibility of politics, as many of these contributions make clear. One also gets the sense from a number of these contributions that political engagement itself matters. Some have taken up the question of the possibility of politics itself, particularly the essays in the last section, while others examine how these possibilities are shaped by focusing on political representatives or the organization of civil society in different places and/or at different scales.

*****

What has been produced collectively and inadvertently by the essays gathered here is a three-dimensional picture that operates at different scales and with different conceptions of political possibility. As a result, the product of the collected essays is considerably more than the sum of its parts. Many chapters offer insights on more than one of the three key dimensions informing this book—cities, organizational and institutional structures, and the political sphere itself. Thus our division of them along these lines is a bit of an editorial imposition. However, we believe that the different emphases placed on these dimensions in the volume's chapters is indicative of distinct but mutually reinforcing perspectives. Notably, the commonalities and differences among the chapters along these axes of distinction bridge more conventional distinctions between urbanists, social movement researchers, immigration scholars, pluralist and critical theoretical perspectives, scholars of the US and scholars of Europe and China, and so on. The result is a truly interdisciplinary intervention that bridges discussions that normally take place more or less in isolation from one another. The unique conversation that emerges in this volume thus reflects the significance and complexity of the issue, the need to marshal multiple types of scholarly resources to properly understand it, and, quite importantly, the insights and knowledge of the excellent scholars who are contributing to our understanding of it.

The first dimension of analysis is cities themselves rather than particular organizational populations or institutional settings. Cities have distinctive *civil societies*. This is often commented on as a distinctive *culture*, but the fabric of culture is stitched together by different venues, associational practices, and organizational ecologies. This connection between cities, civil societies, and urban citizenship is explicitly enunciated in Tony Roshan Samara's essay. Samara's contribution is based on his direct involvement in the US-based Right to the City Alliance (RTTCA), a national urban movement with grass-roots organizations in several major US cities that seeks to remake urban civil societies and produce more democratic urban polities. Samara's study gives voice to the coalition's quest to rescale citizenship downward by focusing on the relationship between urban citizenship and the meaning of "home." Although he is a forceful advocate of RTTCA political practices, Samara is also aware of the challenges faced by their campaigns. Particularly intriguing is his observation that the Alliance's very discourse on "home" and "belonging" can be used to exclude newly arrived urban neighborhood residents.

Scholars are increasingly aware that distinctive urban cultures and civil societies can produce exclusionary as well as inclusionary effects—such as greater or lesser tolerance, greater or lesser equality, and so on—that directly impact the nature of day-to-day life for urban residents. However, studying the character of this fabric itself is not often undertaken, particularly in a comparative fashion. Other chapters in this volume by Ernesto Castañeda and by Walter Nicholls and Floris Vermeulen take up this analytical challenge directly, in addition to making their own distinctive contributions to understanding the relationship between "strangers" and the city. Castañeda utilizes interview data with different migrant populations in Barcelona, New York, and Paris in order to uncover the distinctive ways that the civil societies of those cities are organized to shape urban living for migrants. Nicholls and Vermeulen use a comparative analysis of struggles over land use that involve "outsiders" in Paris and Amsterdam to address a similar question. The unavoidable implication is that the organization of civil society in cities matters and is worth analyzing in its own right in order to shed light on the distinct challenges and opportunities for reimagining citizenship in different cities.

The second dimension is organizational and institutional structures and practices. In many ways, this is the easiest to investigate. Locating and studying organizations is relatively straightforward; they can be readily compared across both organizational populations and cities; and they often and effectively reveal much about the priorities and interests of many actors beyond the organizations themselves. This is the lens utilized by Xuefei Ren, Irene Bloemraad and Shannon Gleeson, Els de Graauw, and William Sites and Rebecca Vonderlack-Navarro. The general picture that emerges from these essays is that the basic instinct of the volume is correct. The changing nature of citizenship, while not always articulated as a claim to a right to the city, is playing an increasing role in the way that organizational populations, institutions, and urban civil societies are generally organized.

The first contribution in this section by Xuefei Ren takes seriously the idea that organizations mediate between people and institutional settings. Looking through the lens of NGOs, Ren is able to describe both the distinctive institutional environment in China that enables the social marginalization of migrants from rural areas and the ways in which that environment produces a logic of organizational practice that is likely to lead to expanding political and legal rights. Ren suggests this outcome is likely even despite serious constraints on NGO activity that are rooted in the tight relationship between state and civil society in China. The case is instructive more generally. The processes Ren describes and the framework of analysis she provides are salient beyond the borders of the People's Republic of China. In particular, while the laws are distinct and the civil society is distinct, the problem of institutional marginalization is by no means exclusively an issue of race, ethnicity, or national citizenship. Efforts to overcome that marginalization in China also share many of the constraints and possibilities described in other chapters in this section.

Irene Bloemraad and Shannon Gleeson operate with some similar assumptions about the role of organizations as mediators in their examination of immigrant "visibility" in San Jose, California. However, they are especially concerned with the underrepresentation of immigrant and ethnic organizations in San Jose's civil society. They argue that visibility is effectively gated behind formal organizations and, as a consequence, that underrepresentation is a mechanism of marginalization. They note, despite these constraints, that activists from immigrant and ethnic communities have at times figured out ways to make their voices heard in San Jose politics, such as during the 2006 immigrants' rights protests. However, this sort of activity is difficult to sustain without formal organizations.

Using data that is similar to Bloemraad and Gleeson's, Els de Graauw's analysis of San Francisco is able to gain a more empirical handle on the possibility of integration and inclusion via civil society organizations. San Francisco is a diverse city that is, compared to many cities, very accommodating to new arrivals from other countries. Its contrast to San Jose in this respect can be explained, in part, by historical factors and differences in each city's respective location in the flows of resources and people. But these do not explain enough. De Graauw's contrast with both Bloemraad and Gleeson and Ren is instructive, making it clear that local institutions and organizations can be decisive in determining the degree to which a city is accommodating to different groups of people. Like many contributors to this volume, De Graauw also focuses on the relationship between civil society organizations and elected representatives, emphasizing that this as a strategically important analytical site for understanding the relationship between cities and their more marginalized populations, such as recent immigrants.

In their multi-scalar analysis of immigrant politics in Chicago, William Sites and Rebecca Vonderlack-Navarro seek to explain why Mexican hometown associations (HTAs)—the transnational organizations formed by migrants and active in many US cities—have evolved from a coalition of inter-local civic associations focused on their Mexican hometowns to an organizational alliance focused increasingly on US-based interest-group activity. Central to their analysis is the surprising finding that state-led rescaling on both sides of the US-Mexican border has tended to facilitate *localist* forms of US political incorporation for the HTAs. Sites and Vonderlack-Navarro show that this HTA scale-shift in Chicago has been shaped by a powerful set of contextual incentives and changing political opportunity structures operating on both sides of the US-Mexican border. Their analysis of multi-scalar political organizations and practices demonstrates the fruitfulness of examining a broader array of political actors and institutional fields, and of employing a longer-term historical focus, than is common in studies of urban civil society and migrant political activism. This attention to the long-term multi-scalar political practices of global migrants is also a key strength of the case study of the multiple national, local, and supranational memberships successfully claimed by Colombian migrants in Madrid that is used to anchor Luis Guarnizo's theoretical argument in Chapter 2.

This brings us to a third analytical dimension of the remaking of urban citizenship—the political itself. The contributions to the final section of our book each resist the premise that the possibilities for gaining "urban citizenship" are best measured through organizational and institutional articulation. These authors resist the assumption that success is best measured through the institutionalization of voice in organizational and institutional settings. Their reasoning is instructive. Governance is rarely totalizing, even if the patterns of access and closure shift or privilege different practices. Actors and groups can make good choices given certain political circumstances or not. Organizations can sometimes facilitate success in the inherently indeterminate nature of political engagement, but they do not always do so. Sometimes other tools for realizing strategic goals are necessary.

Mark Purcell opens this section with a very useful examination of the case of the cleanup of a Superfund site in Seattle. He pushes back against a narrative that assumes that neoliberal institutions will always curtail opportunities for political involvement by non-market actors. Purcell argues that environmental law suggests that neoliberal governance is a "palimpsest" of layered institutions that do not share a singular logic. As a result, neoliberal governance is certainly different, but it is also fractured. Aspects that are designed to limit government authority over private actors and enable more flexible responses can also create space for mobilized citizens to influence policy outcomes. At the same time, it seems that in order to be successful in this setting, citizens must increasingly become their own experts; they cannot simply rely on inhabitance as the basis for their authoritative interventions. Of course, not all citizens can adapt as effectively as the Duwamish River Cleanup Coalition described by Purcell, but the point stands: political engagement has its own internal possibility, even in the neoliberal era.

Faranak Miraftab takes a different tack in her examination of Togolese and Mexican migrants in the small meatpacking town of Beardstown, Illinois. She argues that change is not necessarily manifested in organizational representatives or new institutional access; in fact, change often comes about through "informal politics" and "everyday practices" that appropriate urban space. In Beardstown, many formal local institutions and organizations are largely organized to exclude the immigrant population. However, migrants do achieve a degree of inclusion in public space, real estate markets, public education organizations, and in religious organizations. These appropriations then become venues for building relationships across lines of difference on terms that are not simply imposed by the receiving culture. The "right to the city" is claimed, but not in formal, legal, or political terms. Rather, it is claimed in terms of gaining access to the use values of public and private urban spaces.

The volume concludes with a stimulating chapter by Debbie Becher that is reminiscent of William Sewell's work on the "event," but without the same sense of permanence (1996). Becher attempts to harness and stabilize the indeterminacy and possibility of "political moments" for use in social scientific analysis. It quickly becomes clear that this is a tricky category. It is, first of all, difficult to use; the insights we might gain from it, though, certainly suggest that we should try. Second, Becher takes us down a road that leads away from understanding politics in purely instrumental and strategic terms and, therefore, away from many of the dominant social-scientific understandings of politics. This is not a bad thing. Our understanding of politics suffers when it brackets out the meaningful, the possible, and the temporary. The "political moment" is never intended by actors to be formalized or institutionalized. It is not meant to be permanent. Political moments, moreover, can organize and mobilize citizens around immediate and pressing concerns instead of abstract ideologies or principles. Using a case of conflict over land use in Philadelphia, Becher demonstrates how realizing the right to the city is not necessarily accomplished through formal organizations or institutionalized access but through effective mobilization at moments of opportunity, even reactive ones.

Taken together, the chapters comprising *Remaking Urban Citizenship* give a fascinating picture of the possibilities and constraints that operate when city-dwellers attempt to make claims based on "belonging" to a given place. The "right to the city" is now a slogan for a movement, but it is more than that. It is a process of redefining the shape and meaning of citizenship through everyday practices, association, and political contention. The changing nature and extension of flows of material and interpersonal exchange, enabled by processes like the globalization of economic activity and migration, facilitate this process and also confront urban residents, organizations, and governors with a series of challenges and opportunities. These challenges and opportunities do not exist simply because the flows exist. They are shaped and articulated in the highly varying institutional and organizational landscape of cities. This fact of variability carries with it political possibility by providing more points of engagement. Variability, however, also constrains and limits the extent of any particular reform or outcome of contention. Finally, these chapters make clear that an organizational focus can be both useful and limiting. Organizations enable collective action by many—action that can and does enable recognition of the marginalized—but they also carry with them a host of undesirable limitations. The "right to the city" is alive and well as a movement and as a point of widespread engagement and contention. Claims for a "right to the city" are making a difference in various settings, even being institutionalized if the local configuration of civil society permits. However, it is not yet clear whether these promising local developments will lead to a more widespread transformation in the institutional organization of cities or a more generalized remaking of urban citizenship. The future course of the "right to the city" remains to be seen.

References

Fainstein, S. (2010). *The Just City*. Ithaca: Cornell University Press.

Foucault, M. (1988). "Techonologies of the Self." In L. H. Martin, H. Gutman, and P. H. Hutton (Eds.), *Technologies of the Self: A Seminar with Michel Foucault* (pp. 16-49). Amherst: University of Massachusetts Press.

Holston, J. (Ed.) (1999). *Cities and Citizenship*. Durham and London: Duke University Press.

Holston, J. and A. Appadurai. (1996). "Cities and Citizenship." *Public Culture*, 8, 187-204.

Kalavita, K. (1998). "Immigration, Law and Marginalization in a Global Economy: Notes from Spain." *Law & Society Review*, 32(3), 529-66.

Lefebvre, H. (1996). *Writings on Cities*. E. Kofman and E. Lebas (Eds. and Trans.). Malden, MA/Oxford: Blackwell.

_____. (2003 [1970]). *The Urban Revolution*. Minneapolis: University of Minnesota Press.

Sassen, S. (1998). *Globalization and its Discontents*. New York: New Press.

Sewell, W. (1996). "Historical Events as Transformations of Structures: Inventing Revolution at the Bastille." *Theory and Society*, 25, 841-81.

Smith, M. P. (1995). *Marginal Spaces*. New Brunswick and London: Transaction Publishers.

_____. (2009). "The Incompleteness of Rights-bearing Citizenship: Political Obligation and Renationalization." *Political Power and Social Theory*, 20, 275-80.

Wacquant, L. (2008). *Urban Outcasts: A Comparative Sociology of Advanced Marginality*. Cambridge: Polity.

Wilson, W. J. (1996). *When Work Disappears: The World of the New Urban Poor*. New York: Vintage.

2

The Fluid, Multi-scalar, and
Contradictory Construction of Citizenship*

Luis Eduardo Guarnizo

Citizenship has existed for nearly three millennia. Throughout its long history, it has been the main institution regulating membership in political communities and has provided the philosophical rationale and quotidian structure for the sociopolitical organization of societies and legitimate systems of governance.[1] In the twentieth century, the age of the nation-state, citizenship became the institutional building block of national membership and international relations. By the early twenty-first century, however, the everyday practices, as well as theoretical and legal meanings of citizenship had experienced considerable transformations. Most scholarly research has concluded that these changes have in great part been fueled by an intricate and intertwined host of global processes ranging from the hyper-mobility of capital and people to the introduction and use of universal rights, to the expansion of transnational grassroots networks. Ensuing academic debates on the implications of citizenship transformation have generated the emergence of multiple new types of citizenship, which are often used to represent contemporary changes. Urban, international, transnational, cosmopolitan, nested, global, and environmental are among the copious types of new citizenships recently coined by social scientists.

While it is useful to describe specific manifestations of contemporary sociopolitical membership, the labeling of such manifestations as different kinds of citizenship has limited analytical purchase. To be sure, descriptive labels (e.g., "urban citizenship") could become practical dictums around which political vindications could be articulated—such as in the right to the city movement (see for example, Purcell, 2003; Tides Foundation, 2007). The low epistemological power of such labeling is due to the fact that it elevates particular dimensions of citizenship to the level of discrete 'types' separated from, or even opposed to, any general concept and everyday shared practices of citizenship. By doing so, this epistemic turn actually misconstrues the peculiar complexities of contemporary citizenship, assuming either its devaluation, erosion, withering away, or decomposition into multiple different types. I posit, instead, that the logic, practices, and meaning of contemporary citizenship have become pluri-dimensional, multi-scalar, and fluid. These features of citizenship result from grassroots practices and state policies, which are embedded in a rapidly changing and increasingly unequal world political economy dominated by a dual discourse centered on liberal democracy and market-fundamentalism.

One of the central arguments of this chapter is that instead of conceiving of contemporary citizenship as a totally new version of citizenship, we should see it as a sort of synthesis of the long history of citizenship as determined by three factors that have shaped citizenship since its inception in ancient Greece, namely: *scale, mobility*, and *inequality*. Today's citizenship is best conceived not as an assemblage of diverse and discrete 'types' of citizenships, nor as a hodgepodge of mono-scalar citizenships (e.g., global or urban). Rather, contemporary citizenship is a means of both multilevel membership and global control that recombines multiple geopolitical memberships that are related to different scales (i.e., local, trans-local, national, regional, supranational, transnational). This recombination has been induced by increasing global mobility (most commonly capital investments and disinvestments, free trade, international migration, and transnational grassroots engagement) in a global order characterized by historic levels of socioeconomic polarization.

While citizenship is fundamentally a mechanism of state control and rule, both analysts and activists tend to emphasize its role as a membership institution and thus see it as a ticket to gain access to rights and entitlements. This tendency, paradoxically, obscures the significance of today's citizenship as a tool of *governmentality* (Foucault, 1988), behind which socioeconomic inequality is reproduced and maintained. By emphasizing rights and entitlements without addressing the power relations mediated by the institution of citizenship, activists and analysts have, however inadvertently, displaced the focus of their advocacy.

Scale, inequality, and mobility are the dimensions shaping citizenship as it is addressed here. I offer a *longue durée* overview of citizenship's history from ancient Greece to today's global system of nation states to analyze the dialectics of inclusion-exclusion and sociopolitical control of citizenship as it is structured by socioeconomic *inequality*, geopolitical *scale*, and people's spatial *mobility*. This examination will help us see how citizenship has historically been transformed to become what it is today: a key tool to govern under conditions of high global mobility and acute inequality.

My intention is to contribute to contemporary scholarly debates by casting a historically informed analytical light on current practices, legal redefinitions, and scholarly conceptualizations of citizenship. This should prove a useful endeavor, for most recent studies tend to be dominated by the dictatorship of the present—that is, the tendency to see present situations as being dictated solely by current conditions and detached from historical influences. Few recent studies of contemporary citizenship are historically informed. And when some historical concerns are included, often the historical framework goes back to periods as recent as the mid-twentieth or mid-nineteenth centuries, or, alternatively, it simply refers to ancient Greece (for significant exceptions see Bauböck, 1994; Ignatieff, 1995; Pocock, 1995). There is a strong penchant to privilege what is perceived as unique and to explore novel transformations in contemporary citizenship.

However, emphasizing the historical uniqueness of present conditions inevitably neglects historical continuities that could help us to gain a better understanding of the practical and theoretical implications of today's practices, formal definitions, and everyday meanings of citizenship. Many of the arguably novel practical and theoretical features of today's citizenship already emerged and waned earlier in history. Thus, rather than being historical ruptures, current changes represent the confluence, recombination, and effects of inequality, scale, and mobility, which are dimensions that have persistently shaped citizenship across time and space. This does not mean, however, that contemporary citizenship does not present features that are new or unprecedented. Rather, it means that incorporating the 'old' allows us a better grasp of the significance of the 'new' in today's reconfigured citizenship—and it could also help us formulate more nuanced predictions of the future.

The argument is divided into four sections. The first presents a brief summary of the current global context in which citizenship is being reconfigured and the academic debates generated by its transformation. This is followed by an historical overview of citizenship, which in turn is divided into three parts discussing, respectively, the relationship between citizenship and socioeconomic inequality, geopolitical scale, and human mobility. A case study that illustrates the way in which citizenship has become a dialectical double-edged tool of inclusion and exclusion, empowerment, and rule operating at multiple scales will follow. Closing the argument is a general analytical discussion and conclusion addressing the practical and theoretical implications of contemporary citizenship, particularly urban citizenship, in a globalized world.

The Contemporary Global Context

Scholars broadly agree that contemporary globalization has transformed practices and conventional understandings of national citizenship. Global processes include the increasing mobility of capital (Held and Kaya, 2007; Stiglitz, 2007) and labor (Castles and Miller, 2009; Jacobson, 1997; Soysal, 1994), the expansion of transnational grassroots and non-governmental activism (Keck and Sikkink, 1998; Tarrow, 2005), and the consolidation of systems of governance with a planetary or regional reach (Jupille and Jolliff, 2011; Rosenau, 1997). People's global mobility, most especially labor migration, is consistently seen as a chief factor explaining the transformation of citizenship.[2] International migration, given its absolute size, multidirectional patterns, and heterogeneous socio-cultural and national composition, has become the most visible global force transforming citizenship regimes throughout the world.

It is within this rapidly changing context that an intense scholarly debate on citizenship has emerged, particularly in European countries. Following the end of the Cold War and the formal establishment of the EU, many state members saw a steep increase in the arrival of foreign laborers and refugees fleeing conflicts nearby (e.g., in the former Yugoslavia) or farther away, especially from former colonies (e.g., from Sub-Saharan Africa, Latin America). This dual process of supranational integration and rising large-scale immigration has had an important impact on Europe's citizenship regimes and national identities. The United States also saw a dramatic increase in immigration pressures by a growing number of Latin American and Caribbean people displaced by the neoliberal storm sweeping their countries since the mid-1980s. The ensuing tightening of US borders, as a balloon effect, redirected many of those rejected by US immigration officers to the European continent (Castles and Miller, 2009; Guarnizo, 2009).

The contextual situation affecting citizenship in the global North became more complicated after the terrorist attacks in the United States on the morning of September 11, 2001 and the subsequent bombings of trains, buses, and airports in Spain (March 11, 2004) and the United Kingdom (London on July 7, 2005, and Glasgow on June 30, 2007). These and other similar attacks brought national security concerns into discussions about stricter immigrant and immigration policies and access to citizenship in the global North. These concerns fueled the approval of restrictionist policies at the supranational (i.e., the EU), national, and local levels. Such policies, including the militarization of international borders and the establishment of ever more stringent immigration controls curtailing the mobility rights of most people from the South, have severely limited or outright prohibited immigrants' access to social rights and restricted their path to naturalization. Moreover, rich countries drastically reduced the approval rate of asylum petitions to the point of rendering asylum seeking (until recently considered a sacred universal right) almost illegal (Flynn, 2004; 2005; Geddes, 2003; Guarnizo, 2009; Lewis and Neal, 2005).

How have countries of origin responded to the increasing emigration of their citizens, especially to the global North? How has this increased exodus affected national regimes of citizenship and social organization in labor-exporting southern countries? While strong restrictionist winds are sweeping across the global North, cosmopolitan breezes are crisscrossing the global South. In effect, many migrant-sending countries in the South are redefining citizenship by expanding its territorial scale in order to incorporate their nationals abroad into new trans-territorial and even global national projects. Departing from the received principle that every person should have only one citizenship and one national identity as recommended by The Hague Convention of 1930, an increasing number of southern states have reformed their national constitutions to grant their citizens the freedom to acquire other citizenships without losing their original one (Faist and Kivisto, 2007; Guarnizo, Sanchez, and Roach, 1999; Herrera and Ramírez, 2008; Smith and Bakker, 2008; Smith, 2006; Yeshayahu Gonzales-Lara and Santome, 2007).[3] In some cases, the reconfiguration of citizenship in the South has gone beyond just granting dual citizenship rights. For example, the new Ecuadorean constitution, approved in 2008, redefines Ecuadorean citizenship as universal citizenship (Gobierno Nacional de la República del Ecuador, 2008). According to the constitution, Ecuador "recognizes and guarantees to every person...[t]he right to freely transit across the national territory and choose his/her place of residence, as well as to freely enter and exit the country, according to the law" (Article 66). Moreover, the new constitution establishes that 'all the foreigners in the Ecuadorean territory will have the same rights and duties that Ecuadoreans have' (Article 9). It also recognizes that 'people have the right to migrate'; so the constitution determines that Ecuador will not 'identify nor will [it] consider any human being as illegal due to his/her migratory condition' (Article 40). These various reconfigurations of citizenship aimed at incorporating nationals abroad into their homeland's national project has resulted in, among other things, higher rates of naturalization of southern nationals in the North (Mazzolari, 2005).

How have scholars interpreted these transformations of citizenship? A very rich and complex body of literature has recently emerged addressing this question. The succinct review that follows is limited to the most influential contributions. Discussions on citizenship abound not only in academic circles, but also among politicians, policy-makers, grassroots activists, international migrants, and many other members of global civil society. This renaissance of citizenship has resulted in mounting confusion, as the term is often used to describe many disparate processes. It has come, variously, to mean:

> the nationality indicated by a passport, participation rights in various public and private contexts, entitlement to benefits, commitment to a particular political or social order, [and] even decent behavior towards one's colleagues on university campuses (Fahrmeir, 2007).

Evidently, this calls for more rigorous analyses in order to keep citizenship a more precise and useful analytical category for understanding contemporary society.

Many scholars have undertaken this task. A significant result of these efforts has been the introduction of multiple 'types' of citizenship. Several common themes pervade these new typologies. Perhaps the most salient common feature is a concern with the *changing scale* under which citizenship seems to operate today. The newly labeled citizenships are based on the scale of the political community they tend to be associated with. The diverse types of citizenship fall onto a continuum that includes, in ascending size, urban and municipal (Purcell, 2003; Tides

Foundation, 2007), national (Marshall, 1992), transnational (Smith and Bakker, 2008), regional (Faist, 2001), world, and cosmopolitan scales (Habermas, 1995; Held, 2010; Linklater, 1998). Some analysts declare with enthusiastic optimism that "The arrival of world citizenship is no longer merely a phantom. [...] State citizenship and world citizenship form a continuum that already shows itself, at least, in outline form" (Habermas, 1995, p. 279). In a similar Kantian vein, David Held sees the global interconnectedness generated by the mobility of people and capital as engendering a multilayered "political order of transparent and democratic cities and nations as well as of regions and global networks within an overarching framework of social justice." Accordingly, it is within such global political order that "the puzzling meaning of cosmopolitan or global citizenship became clearer." Fifteen years after Habermas, Held wishfully hopes that such global cosmopolitan governance will eventually materialize "even though now it seems remote!" (Held, 2010, pp. 178-81).

From a somewhat different perspective, Yasemin Nuhoglu Soysal points to the extension of political rights to guest workers in Europe and argues that citizenship has moved up well beyond the scale of the nation state. "A new and more universal concept of citizenship has unfolded in the postwar era," she argues; it is one that is "based on universal personhood rather than national belonging...," which thus "...[undermines] the national order of citizenship" (Soysal 1994, p. 1). She calls this model—which is "anchored in deterritorialized notions of persons' rights"—"postnational" (p. 3). The postnational citizenship argument, however, overlooks the racialized imaginary around which a common European identity is currently being constructed and the entrenched sociocultural marginalization and disempowerment this entails.

In this same vein, analysts like Bhabha (1990) go further, depicting global migrants as new nomads, as hybrid social actors whose identities have been freed from the siren calls of national identity formation promoted either by their countries of origin or state-centric discourses in their new destinations. Others seek to solve the apparent tension created by the construction of a citizenship that combines a large supranational scale (i.e., European citizenship, Andean citizenship) with a smaller scale (i.e., national and local citizenships). Thomas Faist, for example, introduces a concept of 'nested citizenship,' which, like a Russian doll, smoothly incorporates these separate scales into the new type of citizenship generated by the formation of the European Union (Faist, 2001). Still other analysts have dealt with the new recombination of scales generated by the responses of sending countries to increasing global mobility by introducing new types of citizenships, including transnational and trans-local citizenships (Besserer, 1999). On the low end of the scalar continuum, revisiting the 'right to the city' concept introduced by the influential urban sociologist Henry Lefebvre (1973), some analysts and activists have introduced 'local' and 'urban' citizenship as inclusive responses to neoliberal globalization (Harvey, 2008; Purcell, 2003; Smith, 2006). It is this mode of urban citizenship and its relationship to the practices of citizenship at wider scales that forms the central concern of the remainder of this essay and the core theme of this book.

This development of demands for local incorporation highlights a second common characteristic in the current literature on citizenship, namely a strong emphasis on *inclusion*, as represented by the rights associated with citizenship. This indicates a significant departure from classical citizenship, which almost exclusively focused on defining the ideal citizen and *his* civic obligations (at the time there were not active female citizens). The focus on inclusion seems to assume that by gaining formal inclusion in the political urban community, immigrants will automatically gain socioeconomic equality, overcoming their sociopolitical marginalization and economic exploitation.

A third common dimension of contemporary analyses of citizenship emphasizes the social construction and everyday practices of citizenship, rather than the political or legal construction of it. The tendency here is to privilege description over analysis, immediate experiences over larger, historically informed trends. Such empirical presentism leads analysts to end up labeling such practices as singular, novel processes departing from, or even standing in opposition to, historical trends, practices, and definitions of citizenship.

This leads me to the next dimension shared by many current analyses of citizenship, namely, the tendency to define citizenship practices in normative terms. By focusing on what appears to be new practices, scholars fall into the analytical trap that is inherent to sampling on the dependent variable. This methodological bias tends to blind analysts to instances in which the observed practice does not occur. Logically, such an approach leads the analyst to exaggerate the incidence and sociopolitical implications of the observed practice, which then may be perceived as a prevailing norm or as an outcome that can be reproduced in other places.

The analytical historical rupture is forming a new consensus according to which national citizenship is being eroded, devalued, or even made irrelevant, by a fragmented panoply of new, discrete types of citizenship operating at different scales. Some of these emerging citizenships are becoming effective symbols around which emerging grassroots movements seek to coalesce. However, as formulated, the analytical purchase of these new citizenships is often limited.

A consideration of the long past of citizenship will place in historical perspective the multi-scalar, fluid, and cyclical construction and reconstruction of the everyday and formal meanings and implications of citizenship. As we will see, this long-term historical turn is necessary because "citizenship" has become a conflated analytical homonym, which variously refers to political membership, cultural belonging, access to rights, and duties, as well as to heterogeneous everyday practices in social, political, civic, cultural, and economic domains.

Socioeconomic Inequality and Citizenship

From ancient Greece to the early 18th century, defining the ideal citizen and his duties were the main concerns in the analytical and political definition of citizenship. According to Plato, the perfect Athenian citizen was one 'who knows how to rule and be ruled as justice demands' (Plato, 1970, I.643). For him, the ultimate goal of citizenship was to produce a harmonious and stable polity. His disciple Aristotle, who actually was a foreigner, a non-citizen resident of Athens, went beyond Plato's normative approach and analyzed the state and citizenship practices of his time. According to Aristotle, "[t]he citizen in [...] the strict sense is best defined by the one criterion, 'a man who shares in the administration of justice and in the holding of office.'" (Aristotle, 1952, 1274b 32-6). For him, the citizen was endowed with the intelligence and rational capacity to decide about and pursue the common good through his active engagement as ruler. For Aristotle, the qualities and conditions of citizenship were given, not freely chosen; the citizen must be a free, native-born man whose parents were citizens, a patriarch, a warrior, and a master of slaves.

Athenian citizenship was based on the separation between the *polis* (state) and the *oikos* (household), between the public and the private spheres. Citizens would discuss the affairs of the *polis*, not those of the *oikos*; the issues of war and commerce, not those of household management. As such, the citizen was a *zoon politikon*, a rational political animal, and the *polis* was the unique site for the development of his human capacities. The capacity to rule over things, slaves, women, temporary and permanent immigrants *(metics),* and their own fellow citizens made the citizen "the highest order of being [...] and it follows that rule over one's equal is possible only where one's equal rules over one" (Pocock, 1995, p. 31). Citizenship equality included only a small minority and was based on the political exclusion of the vast majority.

Athenian citizens related directly to each other as equals, regardless of the size or quantity of their possessions; citizens' property was taken for granted and not discussed. In Rome, however, a person became a citizen through the combination of economic power and law; Romans became citizens through the possession of things and jurisprudence. Roman jurisprudence regulated and protected property and as such promoted 'possessive individualism' before market supremacy took hold as the main mechanism of social stratification (Pocock, 1995, p. 35). A citizen became a person free to act by law *(legalis homus)*; in this sense, citizenship became a legal status. Legal citizenship status thus denotes membership in a community of shared law, which is not necessarily identical to a territorialized community. In contrast to citizenship in Greece, ancient Roman citizenship was as stratified as Roman society. Political participation, or 'ruling' as the Greeks would have it, was exclusively limited to male citizen members of the small Senatorial class. Female citizens, regardless of their class position, were not allowed to participate in politics (i.e., did not have voting rights) or take public office, although they were free to possess property and engage in economic, social, and cultural activities (Burns, 2007).

The 'classical' definition of citizenship unequivocally implies that only a very small number of human beings in the history of humankind have been in a position to realize their full humanity because they happen to have been members of a kind of political community that uniquely gives play to their political human capacities. In Athens, it was precisely because of the political exclusion of women, slaves, and foreigners that the citizen minority was able to exercise its citizenship as a full-time activity; it is only in this way that citizens were able to develop and apply their 'human capacities' to rule. In Rome, the legal status of citizenship was possible because of the political exclusion of women, foreigners, and slaves. Here too, citizenship was not only a legal status vis-à-vis the state, but a tool in the hands of the state to govern.

In medieval Europe, influential analysts such as Niccolò Machiavelli (1469-1527), regarded as the most famous defender of citizen liberties, were inspired by the ideal of civic virtue as practiced by the Romans and the Greeks. While he called for a new ethos of devotion to the political community sealed by a practice of collective self-rule and self-defense, his conception of the citizen-body remained staunchly patriarchal. Only beginning in 17th century England did citizenship start to be spoken of more in terms of rights than duties. This trend was consolidated by the mid-20th century.

A glance at the historical record reveals a close connection between citizenship and property. In Greece citizens were property owners. In fact, Aristotle insisted that property ownership be a precondition for citizenship. Throughout the centuries, the idea that citizens should be property owners has been persistently argued. It was only during the 20th century that this association was formally eliminated in most polities (Marshall, 1992). According to the argument, a person (usually a man) without property would have neither freedom or free time or resources to get involved in public affairs. More importantly, ownership of property would be indicative of 'virtue' since it represents strong abilities to rationally use skills and moral values to accumulate. A further moral justification claimed that a man with property would be less likely than a man without property to be bribed; thus, he would be more able to govern well. For Locke, the propertied would be endowed with the right to preserve his life, liberty, and estate. During the Middle-Ages and in the city-states of the Renaissance, property and citizenship were two sides of the same coin, and in the late 18th century, the French Declaration of the Rights of Man and the

Citizen (1789) declared that there was a virtuous relationship between "liberty, property, security and resistance to oppression."

These exclusive characteristics of citizenship remained the norm for over two millennia. Throughout the long history of citizenship, class, gender, immigration, and ethno-racial categorization and stratification have always been central to its constitution. This formal understanding seems to be coming back not only among some anti-immigrant social segments but also among politicians in local and sub-national governments in the global North today. In a way that is reminiscent of Aristotelian citizenship, some northern citizens and local governments argue that southern foreigners do not have what it takes to become citizens; this argument is often backed by either culturalist (i.e., ethnic) or racialized arguments, rather than by social or economic ones.

In the wake of World War II, T. H. Marshall argued that the equality of citizens before the state and the law could be constructed despite socioeconomic inequality in civil society (Marshall, 1992). Although Marshall sought to bridge this gap between political equality and social inequality, the disjuncture he identified nevertheless became the dominant normative definition of citizenship in the second half of the 20th century. Concomitantly, citizenship was conceived as legal membership in the national political community. The emphasis, then, was placed not on the exclusive characteristics of the ideal citizen and his duties but on the inclusive rights and entitlements associated with citizenship. Citizenship, however, is certainly much more than membership, for it is a key instrument for the state's control, rule, and discipline over the national population. As such, citizenship determines the boundaries of everyday behavior and access to opportunities and societal rewards. In sum, citizenship has become a crucial instrument that bridges and legitimizes civic equality and social inequality, and it is used as a means of governing in a globalized world.

Historically, the definition and exercise of citizenship both as membership and as a ruling tool, has been shaped by, closely linked to, and dependent on the specific geopolitical scale of the polity. I turn now to an examination of this relationship.

Scale and Citizenship

Geographic scale refers to the socially constructed hierarchy of bounded spaces of different sizes, such as the local, regional, national, and global. Scale is not fixed, static, or given, but is a malleable and flexible political and social construction of place that is periodically transformed (Miller, 1994; Smith and Dennis, 1987). In this sense, scale is both the arena and outcome of contested social and political action (Weller, 2007). We can also understand scale in relational terms, as comprising dense networks of interpersonal and inter-institutional relationships that span and interpenetrate from the local to the global (Herod and Wright, 2002). Scale matters for understanding the changing nature of citizenship because social actors are agents engaged in social interactions that shape the spaces and institutions in which they interact. The power relations among social actors incessantly construct and re-construct scale. From this perspective, the arena in which contested political struggles are played out (i.e., the polity and the boundaries of citizenship) is as malleable as scale. This does not mean, however, that scale is just an epistemic, subjective dimension of social life. For in addition to this epistemic dimension, scale is also an ontological reality (Sayre, 2005): international borders and territories do exist and are enforced, no matter how porous they may be.

Scale has always been at the core of the normative definition and everyday experience of citizenship. So when analyzing citizenship, one of the first questions to ask is to what sociopolitical space does citizenship refer? More precisely, in what sociopolitical spaces are specific citizenship rights and duties (political, economic, social, and cultural) actually applicable, achievable, redeemable, and enforceable? The issue is determining the scale of the state's jurisdiction at which citizens and non-citizens are subjected to its rule.

Most contemporary references to classical Greek citizenship see it as an ideal category but do not consider the issue of scale, which was fundamental for classical scholars such as Plato and Aristotle. Plato's ideal of the perfect state included a very specific size of the *polis*, namely, 5,040 citizen households (Plato, 1970). The actual number of Athenian citizens during the 5th and 4th centuries BC, however, is estimated to have been around 30,000 (a number which has to be multiplied several times to include all the women, children, slaves, and *metics* that formed the total population) (Heater, 2004, p. 26). For Aristotle, this was too big a *polis*. He argued that

> [w]e cannot overlook the fact that such a number will require a territory of the size of Babylon or some such space which is similarly unlimited in extent. It will need all that to support 5,000 persons in idleness, especially when we reflect that they will be augmented by a crowd of women and attendants many times as great as themselves (Aristotle, 1952, 1265a 6).[4]

This concern with scale had to do with several central issues, including security against external enemies, self-sufficiency, and most, especially political, control over the population.

In ancient Greece, the state's ability to exercise control over the population was paramount. As such, this ability was closely related to the *polis*' scale. Aristotle, contrary to an apparently dominant view at the time, considered that "[a]ny object will lose its power of performing its function if it is either excessively small or of an excessive size" (Aristotle, 1952, 1326a 10). Size was crucial for governing, for in order for the state to rule well, "the citizens of a state must know one another's character" (1326b 13). Moreover, if the state is too big and the population too large, immigrants could illegally abrogate the exclusivity of citizenship rights, for "[f]oreigners and resident aliens [*metics*] readily assume a share in the exercise of political rights: it is easy for them to go undetected among the crowd" (1326b 14).

Medieval municipal citizenship emerged in Europe following the urban revolution of the 12th century. Although in medieval Europe citizenship was of relatively marginal significance, when it was used, it was closely related to Aristotle's conception. In everyday practice, citizenship signified a privileged status in a city or a town, not in a large territorial state. Citizenship, then, was the assertion of juridical identification against the domination by, personal submission to, and identification with a lord, rather than identification with a territory or community. In a way that is reminiscent of classical citizenship, the inhabitants of the newly liberated cities and villages "became both members and subjects at the same time" (Rigaudiere, 2002, p. 1). The citizen was thus seen as circumscribed to a specific city-state's "territorial and juridical space where he has elected to establish domicile and where he resides." Again, the scale of the polity is central to defining the space of citizenship. In this case, it was a space not only of juridical protection, but where power was exercised. Boundaries delimited the scale of the polity and, while being defined by the competitive powers surrounding the polity, they also "mark[ed] at the same time the frontiers of other citizenries" (p. 24). The bond inherently tying each new arrival to the other citizens implies not only accessing the common goods of the city (freedom, safety, 'securing his domicile') but also assuming responsibilities (taxation, political participation). Although political participation remained optional, control over taxation, which was connected to security and basic infrastructure of the city-state, remained a central tool of municipal governance.

Overall, municipal citizenship flourished during the Medieval period due to a combination of factors, including its separation from the inhibitions and control of Christianity, the strengthening of Roman law that gave citizenship its official legal status, and the liberation of cities and towns from the powerful control of the church and feudal lords who prevented the realization of civic freedom. Scale remained a key feature of both state and citizenship during this period.

By the 18th century, Jean-Jacques Rousseau, who was a proud citizen of Geneva, a small city-republic of around 25,000 inhabitants, considered that a state must be neither too large nor too small in order to provide good government. In fact, he believed that Geneva represented the ideal size for a modern state, this despite the fact that it was a highly stratified society in which a small elite—around 5 percent of the total population—qualified as citizens with full political rights. He believed that the equality provided by citizenship was best achieved in a small, tight-knit community that was as large as his native Geneva. If a state was too large, he thought, people would develop little affection for rulers they never saw, which would in turn engender their alienation. He thought, as Aristotle did two millennia earlier, that too little land and too small a population would make the state vulnerable, unstable, and dependent upon its neighbors, and would soon give rise to internal conflicts and wars. Analysts' concern with the scale of the polity for defining citizenship was forgotten in later analyses as the normative size of the polity grew from city-state to nation-state. What remained, however, was the abstract meaning of citizenship as political membership.

The 1648 Westphalian model of political organization presupposes a unified, dominant, and central political authority that exercises supreme and autonomous governing power over a specific population living within the borders of a clearly demarcated national territory. Such territory is at the same time both the container of state power and the limit of the state's political jurisdiction. According to Marshall, the progressive evolution of citizenship rights was closely associated with freedom, so '[w]hen freedom became universal, citizenship grew from a local into a national institution' (Marshall, 1964, p. 84). While some analysts have doubted the historical dominance of the nation-state model, there is no doubt that it has been the dominant normative principle guiding global political and national organization for the last two centuries. However, questions of political boundaries and membership that had been settled at the national level are now contested. The efficacy and sovereignty of this system is now being challenged by increasing mobility and promulgations and discourses of universal rights and transnational citizenship.

With the emergence of industrial capitalism in the 18th and 19th centuries, the world was drastically reconstructed, not only economically but also socially and politically, as a global puzzle of national pieces. Until then, the world's geographical divisions had been highly non-uniform, ranging from ancient city-states to regional states, to fiefdoms, to provinces, to kingdoms, and to empires, each one often incorporating a distinct national group. The world today is more clearly divided than it ever has been before, and this has been done on the basis of a common scale: namely, the system of discrete nation states (Smith and Dennis, 1987, p. 160). As a prelude to the rebirth of local/municipal citizenship in the early 21st century and in reminiscence of Aristotle's concern with the size of the polis, by 1949 Marshall argued that trying 'to revive the sense of the personal obligation to work [in a form that it is] attached to the status of citizenship,' was not possible due to the scale of the national community, which he considered 'too large and remote to command this kind of loyalty.' The solution, he thought, 'lies in the development of more limited loyalties, to the local community and especially to the working group' (Marshall, 1964, pp. 130-1). Apparently, the tension between free market and workers' civic engagement required the rescaling of citizenship.

The granting, meaning, and reconfiguration of citizenship, as we have seen, are all very old processes that have affected society since antiquity. The intrinsic connections between geography and power, between space and state, and between territory and rights have existed as long as citizenship itself. The largest scale that citizenship has ever reached is associated with imperialism (one might consider the granting of "universal" citizenship by Rome in the 3rd century and by England in the 19th and early 20th centuries), yet through history the spatial limits of citizenship have varied from the local to the imperial to the national to the local and back again. For the sake of the present argument, it is important to keep in mind the relationship between local and universal citizenship, for, as we have discussed earlier, it should shed some light on current arguments related to post-national, cosmopolitan, and global citizenship—even though none of the proponents of these perspectives seems to be aware of the historical precedent.

The "universal" extension of citizenship can be related to current southern states' discourses and grassroots practices of citizenship operating within a trans-territorial space that transcends, while at the same time is included within, different scales. Perhaps the most tangible consequence of increasing global human mobility today has been the sociocultural, economic, and geospatial reconfiguration of receiving northern cities, as the vast majority of migrants from the global South settle there. Newcomers transform local systems of social inequality and stratification (Castles and Miller, 2009; Smith, 2001). In addition to transforming the ethno-racial composition of migrant-receiving cities, the newly-arrived also help transform local labor markets, social and ethno-racial structures, and the local physical and sociocultural geography. Large-scale migration alters the spatial distribution of the population (via segregation as well as social networking), the everyday practices of cities (spatial concentration of businesses and use of public space), and the composition of local institutions and services such as education, health care, and housing. These changes in turn have challenged receiving societies' accepted representations of local and national identity and, more importantly for the present argument, the formal definitions of who belongs to the nation-state, who is and who is not a citizen, and who deserves to become one and who does not.

Historically, the city has been the epicenter of the construction and practice of citizenship. Today's city is the quintessential place of global engagement (McNeill, 2002). It is the scale at which excluded migrants and their advocates and allies seek a particular form of justice: the scale in which excluded migrants and their advocates and allies seek *civic empowerment* (as opposed to fair economic redistribution) via the granting of citizenship rights—a matter discussed throughout the case studies in this volume. The Right to the City movement, centered on the mobilization of urban or municipal citizenship, as these studies make clear, is a clear expression of this development (Purcell, 2003; Tides Foundation, 2007).

An integral element in the politics of creating places is the divergent understandings of contending constructions of scale and ideology that define social life and the normativity of how humans should relate to one another. These arguments have been complicated by the increasing mobility of people across and within national borders, a process that subverts one of the central tenets of classical citizenship: namely, that citizens are settled residents. What differences does scale make in a mobile world? The answer to this question is linked to conceptions of locality, identity, and the legitimacy of state rule. As we will see in the case study presented further below, the politics of scale involve the politics of interests and consciousness of mobile subjects, and they implicate the simultaneous intervention of different levels of state control (local, national, transnational, supranational) emanating from different countries. Finally, despite the multiple efforts by states to rule and control mobile populations, global mobility operating at multiple scales creates alternative spaces of resistance and evasion, which migrants use to escape or bypass state control altogether.

Spatial Mobility and Citizenship

Historically, theorizing citizenship has been done from the perspective of the local residents, variously called natives, naturals, nationals, and subjects, in relation to the state as a way to exercise control and rule over a given, emplaced population. Normative definitions and analyses of citizenship have, almost exclusively, been constructed from this perspective. Discussions about the inclusiveness/exclusiveness of citizenship and the opportunities, rights, and obligations associated with it are framed, for the most part, in relation to the natives residing within the polity. When strangers, foreigners, or aliens are included in the analysis, they are seen in relation to their level of access to existing paths of socioeconomic incorporation, naturalization, and general accommodation as afforded to them by the state. In other words, rights associated with citizenship are geographically bounded to the scale of the polity, whether it is a city, a region, a nation, or an empire, and in relation to people's emplacement and displacement. The geography of rights such as equality, liberty, and democratic participation assumes that the subjects endowed with these rights are localized inhabitants rather than mobile subjects. In effect, mobility is seldom part of the discourse of citizenship rights; similarly, most analyses and definitions of citizenship seldom are constructed from the point of view of the outsider, the newly arrived, or the mobile denizen.

Yet, the foreigner has always been at the center of citizenship inclusion/exclusion. More generally, citizenship has closely been related to issues of residence (emplacement) and the ability to move freely into or out of a community. Usually, this construction has directly been linked to access to economic rights and political participation. Assigning limits to the access to local economic opportunities has constituted one of the most powerful mechanisms of control and disciplining, for it determines what kind of occupations and economic activities citizens and non-citizens can have access to. In ancient Greece, *metics'* economic participation was limited to merchants. In 17th and 18th century Spain, foreigners were not allowed to be merchants, for commerce was ruled as the exclusive domain of Spanish citizens (Herzog, 2003). The relationship between people's spatial mobility and citizenship rights remains effective in today's global nation-state system. In effect, differences in citizenship status between documented, undocumented, and national (i.e., citizen) workers differentiate labor market participants, affecting their position in labor processes and also allowing both employers and the state to control labor processes and workers (Thomas, 1982). Controlling people's mobility became one of the central concerns of the modern nation-state as a key mechanism of governing. Indeed, as John Torpey recently put it,

> modern states, and the international state system of which they are a part, have expropriated from individuals and private entities the legitimate 'means of movement,' particularly, though by no means exclusively, across international boundaries. The result of this process has been to deprive people of the freedom to move across certain spaces and to render them dependent on states and the state system for the authorization to do so (Torpey, 1998, p. 239).

Part of the state's control over people's mobility relates to the connection between mobility and property and thus socioeconomic and political inclusion/exclusion; presently, for example, foreigners are not allowed to own certain types of businesses considered strategic for national security or properties located in border areas in countries like Mexico and the United States. Concomitantly, the inability of certain mobile people to be able to own property prevents them from not only improving their own lives but from realizing their personal and human capabilities.

Multiple mobilities (Urry, 2007) are now understood to be central to the structuring of inequality within contemporary societies. Mobility has become a central factor shaping contemporary social structures as well as the relationship between state and society. As Bauman has put it:

> Mobility climbs to the rank of the uppermost among the coveted values—and the freedom to move, perpetually a scarce and unequally distributed commodity, fast becomes the main stratifying factor of our late-modern or postmodern times (Bauman 1998, p. 2).

Evidently, citizenship is most significantly affected by these mobilities.

Global migration is a key manifestation of this mobility. In 2010 official estimates put the total number of international migrants at 214 million and that of forced international refugees at 16 million (UN Population Division, 2011). While the UN figures represent the largest absolute amount of international migrants ever registered, experts estimate that the actual figure could reach some 300 million. Yet, even this latter figure represents a very small fraction of the world's population (around 4 percent). However, the sociopolitical and economic impact of international migrants cannot be simply measured by their absolute size on the global scale. Rather, their impact should be measured in relative terms vis-à-vis the populations affected and in terms of the sociocultural, political, and economic effects their mobility engenders.

International migrants and refugees have dispersed across the world, generating variegated effects at multiple scales. In a patterned manner, they have formed critical agglomerations in certain countries and places of reception, where they now represent a significant proportion of the population. The foreign-born have indeed reached high proportions in settler countries such as the United States (12.4 percent), Canada (18.8 percent), and Australia (23.9 percent), as well as in countries with a newer, yet strong, immigration history, such as Switzerland (22.9 percent), Germany (8.9 percent), and the UK (5.2 percent),[5] and in the newest immigrant-receiving countries, such as Spain (12 percent)[6] and Italy (6.5 percent).[7] The transformative effects of migrants and refugees are especially noticeable in urban areas, where the vast majority of migrants tend to settle (Castles and Miller, 2009; Smith, 2001). The conspicuous presence of migrants from the global South in northern cities has triggered tangible effects in urban texture, labor markets, and identity, and more generally has impacted the meaning, definition, and enforcement of citizenship. By 2005, foreign-born people accounted for 36.5 percent of Miami's metropolitan residents and 29.5 percent of both San Francisco's and New York's. This proportion reached 42.6 percent in Hong Kong,[8] 31 percent in Sydney, 27 percent in London, 18 percent in Paris (Migration Policy Institute, 2011), and 16.8 percent in Madrid (Comunidad de Madrid, 2011).

The spatial concentration of migrants in northern cities has introduced high levels of ethno-racial diversity, which has impinged on national discourses of national homogeneity and unity and has forced receiving states to further regulate access to the rights reserved exclusively to national citizens. Among the newest responses to the diversity and alienating effects of globalization and hypermobility has been the introduction of urban or municipal citizenship. In its new reincarnation, local citizenship seeks to incorporate and empower those segments of society that have been alienated, marginalized, or disposed of by global neoliberal processes—the poor, the unemployed, the foreigner—regardless of their legal status vis-à-vis the national state. This move, proposed by some analysts as well as by urban political activists and even some local governments, apparently seeks to trump the role and power of national citizenship, jumping from the global to the local scale and dismissing the national scale in the process (Purcell, 2003; Tides Foundation, 2007). The rationale behind this move shares some common elements with urban and municipal citizenship of the past. It involves changing the scale of the polity as a subversive act against and as refuge from larger dominant powers, and it involves a dramatic increase of mobility from the countryside to the emerging urban centers. At the same time, however, the new urban/local turn is mostly informed by a combination of factors including the hypermobility of labor and capital, as well as the means of production, distribution, and representation. This answer—in the face of a global, borderless process that has worked contrary to the cosmopolitan integration that its proponents have trumpeted—appears to essentialize the local in the name of resisting the global. A closer, critical look at this approach, however, reveals serious epistemological and ontological limitations of urban/municipal citizenship as a viable answer to the present global predicament (Smith and Guarnizo, 2009).

Regardless of the factors motivating it (cultural, social, economic, or political), global human migration affects not only those who move, but also the institutions and societies in places of origin and reception, as well as those that are crisscrossed by the paths of mobility. Increasing global human mobility has significantly affected citizenship. But such effects have not always been direct, singular, and immediate. Rather, it has been a very complex and uneven process. Labor migration and refugee populations have had a significant impact on the allocation of rights to both natives and newcomers in the global North. From the outset, such re-allocation of rights has not been homogeneous and has resulted in a mix of inclusionary and exclusionary policies that often contradict each other.

Despite the latest anti-immigration concerns and controls, large-scale migration has become a structural process rather than a circumstantial event. For rich countries, relatively high levels of steady immigration flows are now indispensable for demographic reasons (to avoid population reductions) and for economic and fiscal reasons (to maintain national productivity levels and to support expanding retirement systems) (Boswell, 2003; Lewis and Neal, 2005). Immigrant labor has become fundamental for key economic sectors of northern countries' economies, which range from high tech to agriculture, to construction, to domestic work. Within this context, issues of membership have become increasingly complex and highly contested (Aleinikoff, 2002; Calavita, 2005).

It is not surprising then to find that responses to the influx of foreign residents are more intricate than simply restrictionist or inclusive, chauvinist or cosmopolitan. The national and supranational dialectics of inclusion/exclusion have gained particular intensity as they operate simultaneously at different geopolitical scales. For example, while national or even supranational policies seek to exclude immigrants, some places with significant foreign-born populations have introduced ordinances to grant local membership to people that would otherwise be considered 'illegal' residents or aliens. Meanwhile, other places have passed local ordinances imposing restrictions that are far more stringent than those existing at the national level.

In the United States, for example, cities such as San Francisco, Oakland, and New Haven have issued municipal identity cards to all their residents as a mechanism to incorporate their foreign residents, and they have instructed their police departments not to cooperate with federal migration authorities to persecute the undocumented (see DeStefano Jr., 2007; Oakland City Council, 2007). On the other side of the political spectrum, many cities and states have passed draconian anti-immigration laws. In 2010, Arizona's state legislature introduced one of the most restrictionist of these bills, SB 1070, which makes it a misdemeanor for non-citizens to be in the state without proper documentation. This law also makes it a crime to shelter, hire, or transport undocumented immigrants and requires local police to check the immigration status of anyone suspected of being undocumented. Since then, a host of similarly crafted, and in many cases more extreme, bills have been proposed all over the country. As of this writing, at least 14 state legislatures had introduced bills similar to Arizona's. These policies, however draconian, represent sub-national states' efforts to rule and discipline societal interaction via citizenship.

This inauspicious context forces southern nation states to respond in defense of their citizens abroad. Their responses, however, must be carefully calibrated because of their increasing macroeconomic dependency on their migrants' remittances and on their demand for national goods and services from abroad (Guarnizo, 2003; Ratha, 2003; Smith and Bakker, 2008). The responses of states of origin are also mediated by geopolitical considerations, as their nationals abroad have the potential to become political advocates for state interests before powerful foreign governments. This contradictory set of considerations has led labor exporting countries to implement a variegated array of constitutional reforms, as well as programs and rhetorical expressions of inclusion, that are designed in part to strategically position nationalist interests vis-à-vis the complex political and economic configurations presented by outmigration. The result has been the expansion and flexibilization of citizenship regimes in the South and the deployment of rhetorical discourses that encourage discipline and good behavior of emigrants as representatives of their nation abroad.

Policies of inclusion have also been recently introduced in European countries that have an old tradition of emigration, such as Spain and Italy. Here, nationals residing abroad have been granted not only the right to maintain their citizenship but also voting rights and representation in national legislative bodies. These policies have helped to formalize migrants' membership ties to the state of origin and to facilitate the performance and expansion of transnational ties linking these populations to their homelands. So now it is not only migrants like Mexicans and Colombians who are authorized to engage in electoral processes in their respective homelands; overseas Spaniards and Italians can also participate in national elections even though they are thousands of miles away from 'home.'

Despite their inclusionary moves, structural and geopolitical constraints limit southern sending states' ability to deliver promised rights and special entitlements to their overseas populations. In this sense, citizenship reforms in the South end up being as mixed and contradictory as those put forth by their northern counterparts. Southern states have to be mindful of their own geopolitical positionality vis-à-vis the rich countries where their co-nationals—on whom, more often than not, they depend economically, politically, and even militarily—reside. Their responses are further complicated as national elites obstinately try to protect their privileged access to power and wealth, while simultaneously substantial proportions of their non-migrant population face poverty and exclusion within national borders, and those living abroad undertake political practices and transmit social and political values that defy the existing *status quo* at home (Glick-Schiller and Faist, 2010; Guarnizo and Diaz, 1999; Levitt,

2001; Smith and Bakker, 2008). Dynamics are complicated yet again when nationals residing abroad try to exert oppositional political influence on national regimes in their homeland (Anderson, 1994).

The upsurge in the international mobility of labor from poor countries is strongly associated with the increasing inequality that is generated by the hypermobility of capital across the world. The evidence shows that capital mobility has significantly deepened global inequality, separating not only the South and the North at a global scale but also the rich from the poor at the national and local scales (Held and Kaya, 2007), which in turn induces specific patterns of mobility (Castles and Miller, 2009). Indeed, the evidence indicates that growing poverty and inequality is no longer confined to the global South, for it is also growing in the affluent North. More importantly, though, the explosive increase in labor migration from poor countries is exacerbating growing inequality in the North. Global migration is thus both a result of socioeconomic changes that increase inequality and a cause of its expansion and deepening.

Madrid at the Crossroads: A Case Study of Multi-Scalar, Fluid, and Contested Citizenship

At a recent two-day public meeting in Madrid, grassroots community leaders and high-level government officials exchanged arguments about public policy issues in a lively and heated discussion. The event was an example of contemporary engaged citizenship in action. While some participants asked officials to extend state services to their localities, others denounced recently introduced local laws for discriminating against their communities and demanded that the central government address their concerns. Specific petitions were formulated. Some leaders requested that new branches of the national vocational training service be created in their cities; others asked that a national subsidized loan program for small entrepreneurs be extended to their communities; and others proposed the creation of a new, inter-governmental program to help homeowners cope with the devastating effects of the current mortgage crisis.

While held in Spain, this apparently conventional meeting actually took place thousands of miles away from the country of origin of most of its participants. The petitions and proposals, couched in terms that bespeak the obvious obligations of the state toward its citizens, actually referred to the extension of official state services, programs, and protection to Colombian citizens residing on a different continent. Organized by the Colombian Ministry of Foreign Relations' *Colombia Nos Une Program* (CNUP), the meeting was held at an elegant hotel in an exclusive zone of Madrid in late November, 2009.[9] The top leadership of the CNUP and members of the Colombian diplomatic corps in Spain, including the Colombian ambassador, were accompanied by high-ranking officials from various Colombian national agencies, including the National Technical Training Service (SENA) and the Colombian Bank for the Promotion of Entrepreneurship and Foreign Trade (BANCOLDEX). Representatives of the Spanish government and the director of the International Organization for Migrations (IOM) office in Colombia (which is the IOM's largest national office in the world) were also present.

The transnational inclusiveness being expressed in the debate suddenly changed when an official from the recently renamed Spanish Ministry of Labor and Immigration (formerly Ministry of Labor and Social Affairs) introduced the newly approved Assisted Voluntary Return Program (AVRP). The program, created after a European Union directive, is allegedly aimed at reducing some of the socioeconomic tensions generated by the global recession, which are particularly acute in the national labor and housing markets, by promoting the massive return of "extra-communitarian" migrants back to their countries of origin. This presentation provoked a bitter reaction among community leaders, who saw the program as the latest expression of official attempts to exclude the migrant (i.e., the non-European and, more often than not, non-white) population of the global South in violation of their human and citizenship rights. The leaders' denunciation of the return program was accompanied by their petition to the Colombian government to intervene on their behalf.

The strong reaction against the Spanish AVRP sharply contrasted with the leaders' enthusiastic response when, earlier in the meeting, the Colombian ambassador announced the signing of a bilateral agreement granting Colombian citizens residing in Spain the right to vote in local Spanish elections.[10] While the AVRP was seen as a blatant, unilateral act of national exclusion, this bilateral agreement was praised as a positive mechanism for facilitating local integration and as an official recognition of the historic ties linking both societies across the Atlantic. While the voluntary return program has been solely a European idea promoted by the IOM among extra-communitarians residing in Europe, as well as among their countries of origin, the local voting rights agreement was the result of bilateral Spanish-Colombian consultations that sought to promote '*una mayor participación social y política de los nacionales de ambos países en* su lugar de residencia' (*Acuerdo*, 2009, p. 5590, emphasis added).[11]

The over 100 Colombian migrant leaders, originally from many different regions of their country, came to the event from every corner of Spain to represent their co-national migrant communities. The Colombian government paid the travel expenses of the majority of these leaders to participate in the event following an open call put forth by the Colombian Embassy. Most of these leaders were documented residents, many of whom were also naturalized Spanish citizens. As a direct result of recent national and supranational constitutional and political reforms, these naturalized Spanish citizens actually possessed multiple citizenship statuses since they also were European and Colombian citizens.[12] So while most of the meeting centered on issues related to their relationship as Colombian citizens with the Colombian state, the participant leaders 'legitimized' their arguments by variously deploying their Colombian citizenship (i.e., "As Colombian citizens we have the right of...") or universalistic principles (i.e., "*No somos máquinas productivas, somos personas!*")[13] or their Spanish or European citizenship (i.e., "As Spanish citizens, we...").

This event illustrates the fluid and contradictory construction of today's citizenship. The complex theoretical and practical implications of this process are multiple. What the participants saw as a normal way to relate to 'their' government seriously questions basic theoretical and political tenets of conventional national citizenship. This kind of citizenship practice is trans-territorial and multi-scalar. While it points out the continuous significance of citizenship as political membership associated with rights and entitlements, it also emphasizes the role of citizenship as a tool of simultaneous control by states ruling at different scales: the supranational European Union, the Colombian and Spanish national states, and the local state of the cities in which Colombians are now allowed to vote in municipal elections. Initially prompted by the increasing economic and sociopolitical importance of their international migrants, the Colombian and Spanish states have rapidly been accommodating their apparatuses at different scales to this new way of governing transnationally. To be sure, this case is not an exclusive Colombian or Spanish experience. As indicated earlier, many other national states of origin, which account for millions of international migrants, also have recently implemented similar, and even more far-reaching and complex, institutional arrangements (Guarnizo, 2009; Rodriguez, 2010; Salazar Parreñas, 2005; Smith and Bakker, 2008; Smith, 2006).

Some reforms, programs, and policies aimed at incorporating Colombians abroad into the national project date back to the early 1990s when the Colombian government adopted deep neoliberal reforms that, among other things, helped to trigger a historic exodus of Colombians to the global North as well as to neighboring countries. However, the most coherent and steady initiatives in this direction started in 2003 when the CNUP was first created. Since then, the government has organized multiple events abroad and in Colombia that seek to open up new commercial channels for Colombian businesses to penetrate the market for "things Colombian" generated by co-nationals residing abroad; at the same time, the government has promoted the continuous and steady flow of migrant remittances and investments into the migrants' homeland.[14] This 'extractive' approach to the overseas population has only very recently included the extension of some social entitlements and state services to overseas nationals. In 2008, for example, a bilateral agreement signed between Colombia and Spain came into effect, allowing Colombians to transfer the pensions earned in either country to the place where they reside and to their descendants.[15] That same year, SENA opened up its newest 'regional' branch—the first ever to be located outside Colombia—in Valencia.[16] According to its director, at the time of the meeting, SENA Valencia had already granted some 1,200 diplomas to Colombian migrants and was also offering some courses in Madrid, Barcelona, and Alicante. Moreover, the institutional significance of Colombians residing abroad for the Colombian state was deepened in August 2009 when, for the first time ever, an integral migration policy was approved by the Colombian government. As part of this new policy, an interagency body was created in order to devise and implement programs aimed at the migrant Colombian population and their relatives still in the country. More interestingly, perhaps, is the fact that the new integral migration policy relates not only to Colombians residing abroad but also to foreigners residing in Colombia; this dual consideration is part of what the government has presented as a symmetrical, balanced approach to provide rights, entitlements, and protection to mobile national and non-national populations. The Director of the CNUP officially presented this policy at the Madrid event.

This multi-scalar, fluid, and contradictory meeting-ground of citizenships in Madrid clearly illustrates the fluidity of citizenship boundaries, citizenry participation, and the applications of new governmentality techniques in the early 21st century.

Discussion and Conclusions

For the past three decades or so, global processes have drastically transformed received definitions and normative practices of citizenship. The century of the nation-state ended with what some scholars, informed by some of the biases of methodological nationalism (Wimmer and Glick-Schiller, 2002), called the crisis of citizenship. Alternative interpretations soon emerged identifying some particular dimensions or practices of citizenship as actually constituting a new set of citizenships. A different interpretation is offered here. Accordingly, the so-called crisis of citizenship is such only if we decide that citizenship refers to membership in a singular political community. If this is the way we understand citizenship, then the institution is indeed in a very serious and lethal crisis. However, if we understand it not just as an institution granting membership, but as a way for the state, or states, to rule, control, and discipline individuals in particular and society in general, then citizenship *qua* citizenship is far from being in crisis. From this perspective, citizenship has been reconfigured as a multi-scalar (as opposed to a singularly scaled) and fluid (as opposed to 'established') mechanism of governance resulting from dynamic and multifarious grassroots practices and state responses to a hypermobile global society. Overlapping scales of excluding, controlling, and ruling dialectically intersect with new ways of belonging, participating, and resisting. These dialectic relations are often expressed by the exercise of substantial citizenship rights (including mobility) by people who have been nominally barred from having any formal rights.

Labeling the particular practices of contemporary citizenship that take place at different scales as discrete 'citizenships' is analogous to undertaking a topographical or external morphological analysis of a given complex process and then identifying each of its components as new and independent expressions that are separate from the whole. I argue instead that what is required to better understand contemporary citizenship is a deeper, historical analysis, as it were, that seeks to uncover its complexities as it operates *simultaneously* at multiple scales, crisscrossing formal political boundaries that range from the local to the national to the transnational to the global. Given its multi-scalar character, legal reconfiguration, and new quotidian practices, today's citizenship has become more salient as a means for regulating, controlling, and disciplining than as an institution whose role is to assign political membership and grant rights to people vis-à-vis a particular polity. Citizenship has become a crucial instrument in the constitution and reconstitution of place and rights (particularly the right to free movement and the free access to economic rights) and of the duties and limitations of foreigners. By so doing, it provides the legal argumentation that legitimizes discourses and practices establishing borders that separate those who are seen as deserving members from those who are seen as undeserving non-members, effectively normalizing the former by criminalizing the latter.

Having been displaced as a direct or indirect consequence of the increasing global mobility of capital, the global labor force from the global South encounters the everyday contradictory practice of citizenship exclusion; they are treated as undeserving of being granted national citizenship or any formal sociopolitical rights (i.e., "illegal aliens," "false refugees") while also being actively recruited and incorporated as a cheap and pliable structural resource that is fundamental for the stability and growth of the economy in receiving societies. Othered individuals tend to be granted some modicum of 'economic' citizenship as workers, though often such citizenship has no substantive legal counterpart. They are simply seen as workers, not citizens (Calavita, 2005). Yet because the relationship between governmentality and resistance is dialectical and citizenship is multi-scalar, cases of exclusion are often met by the novel initiatives of migrants promoting their political inclusion (as was illustrated in the case study above).

While migrants are often economically included and socio-politically excluded in the North, many are nevertheless included by states of origin (e.g., via dual and multiple citizenships), which seek to maintain the loyalty of their diaspora. As part of this effort, policies of long-distance national integration have been introduced by many national states (e.g., voting rights and co-development initiatives). A symbolic politics of inclusion has been accompanied by normative discourses of national identity and behavior as migrants are portrayed not only as heroes working hard to help their homeland but as ideal citizen ambassadors of their nation abroad (Rodriguez, 2010; Smith and Bakker, 2008; Smith, 2006).

The inclusion of global migrants, however, is not only transnational; for local initiatives of inclusion are being spearheaded by grassroots movements, by local states, and even by national governments pursuing the wholesale inclusion of migrants (as demonstrated by the Spanish-Colombian agreement granting electoral rights to each country's respective citizens who legally reside in the other's territory and by Ecuador's universal citizenship). Here we see how global mobility has reconfigured the everyday practices and legal understandings of citizenship, effectively recombining local, national, and transnational scales of belonging.

Contemporary citizenship, therefore, has become a flexible, legitimate, and effective tool of global governmentality in the hands of states in a globalizing world.[17] Furthermore, citizenship refers not only to the way states rule but also to the way in which individuals relate to each other (who is and who is not a citizen), define themselves ("I'm a citizen of such and such place/country.") and shape the conditions under which they are ruled wherever they are located. That is, citizenship operates at multiple spatial levels. This makes it possible for migrants and their organizations to exercise agency by finding access to the right legal/institutional articulations in a world where overlapping multi-scalar constructions are increasingly part of the social fabric.

Indeed, contemporary citizenship, as a hegemonic mechanism of sociopolitical power and control, discipline, and normative regulation, has dialectically created new opportunities for contestation, evasion, and creative resistance by those deemed unworthy to accede to it. A prime illustration of this resistance was the "Day Without Immigrants" that occurred on May 1, 2006. Millions of mostly Latino immigrants and their US supporters, in showing their opposition to draconian immigration reforms being discussed in the US Congress, skipped work and took to the streets; they flexed their economic muscle in a nationwide boycott that succeeded in slowing or shutting down many farms, factories, markets, and restaurants across the United States (Fox, 2010a; 2010b). While officially excluded from the right to possess formal political rights and even from the very right to move to the United States, millions of undocumented migrants publicly demonstrated that they could and indeed do have the ability to exercise substantial political rights. Migrants' public repudiation of their own criminalization by some sectors of US society showed how the very denial of citizenship rights creates dialectical spaces of resistance and, thus, inclusion of the excluded. Efficacy of the protest is not the primary intellectual concern here. Rather, it is important to recognize that citizenship, as a mechanism of discipline and control—of governmentality—thus dialectically engenders its opposition and resistance and demands for a reconfiguration of its content.

While global factors affect every world polity, the actual effects on citizenship are highly contingent on the specific local and historically-determined conditions. These processes, while identifiable as discrete dimensions, are dialectically interrelated and affect each other in complex and dynamic ways. In that sense, I argue that the general premise about the transformative effect of globalization on citizenship must be qualified. In a multi-scalar world, there is significant variation in the direction, scope, and depth of the transformation across national polities and localities. Nevertheless, it is remarkable to find significant historic continuities in the construction of citizenship. On the one hand, xenophobic, chauvinist movements use neo-Aristotelian arguments to justify the civic, political, and social exclusion of immigrants from the global South, who are only included as cheap and pliable workers undeserving to become citizens. On the other, progressive movements promote the inclusion of these immigrants into post-modern city-states under premises of freedom similar to the ones deployed four hundred years ago, although this time such liberating inclusion is justified by a neo-Kantian, cosmopolitan discourse. Assessment of the current and future consequences of globalization on citizenship must therefore be more circumspect in the elaboration of its analytical apparatus and aware of the present contingencies and historical continuities with which global processes are variously manifest in space, place, and time.

Notes

The author is indebted to Michael Peter Smith, Michael McQuarrie, Krystyna von Henneberg, and Robert Saper for their detailed editorial suggestions and comprehensive, valuable, and incisive comments that immeasurably improved the original manuscript.

1. Citizenship has not been the only institutional form of sociopolitical membership and identity. Analytically, however, it is the only one that has historically been associated with notions of individual autonomy, equality of status, and political participation vis-à-vis the state.

2. Global human mobility includes not only economic migrants and refugees, but also tourists, business people, and other types of globetrotters who move across geographies at a faster pace and travel longer distances than ever before (Urry, 2007). For instance, the number of international tourists worldwide has reached record levels. By 2010, the total official number of international tourists reached almost 1 billion (935 million); this figure is up 58 million from 2009 and represents 22 million more than the peak level preceding the 2008 global financial crisis (UN World Tourism Organization, 2011).

3. The Hague Convention stated that "it is in the general interest of the international community to secure that all its members should recognize that every person should have a nationality and should have one nationality only." Moreover, "the ideal towards which the efforts of humanity should be directed in this domain is the abolition of all cases both of statelessness and of double nationality" (League of Nations, 1930).

4. Aristotle was thinking in terms of a general Greek *polis*, not just Athens. Most Greek city-states were rather small with an average territory of about 70 square miles. Athens was exceptionally large, having a territory of 1,000 square miles (see Aristotle, 1952, translator's comment, no. 1, p. 57).

5. Migration Policy Institute (n.d.).

6. Instituto Nacional de Estadística (Retrieved Mar 6, 2011, from http://www.ine.es/).

7. Instituto Nazionale di Statistica. (2009). *Rapporto Annuale—La situazione del Paese nel 2008.* Sistema Statistico Nazionale. Rome.

8. According to UN Population Division estimates, the foreign-born in Hong Kong reached 2,998,686 in 2005 (UN Population Division. (2006). *Trends in Total Migrant Stock: The 2005 Revision.* POP/DB/MIG/Rev. 2005).

9. V Seminario Internacional de Colombia Nos Une, Madrid, Nov 28-29, 2009.

10. Signed in January, 2009, this agreement entered into effect in January 2010. Local voting rights are granted to Colombian citizens who reside legally in Spain. In reciprocity, Colombia grants the same voting rights to documented Spanish citizens residing in Colombia (*Acuerdo*, 2009).

11. 'A higher social and political participation of the nationals of both countries in their *place of residence.*'

12. The 1991 Colombian Constitution approved the right for Colombians to have more than one citizenship. According to Chapter I, Article 96, "*Ningún colombiano por nacimiento podrá ser privado de su nacionalidad. La calidad de nacional colombiano no se pierde por el hecho de adquirir otra nacionalidad.*" On the other hand, Spanish citizens, as members of a signatory state of the European Union's 1992 Maastricht Treaty, are also European citizens (see *Consolidated Version of the Treaty on the Functioning of the European Union*, 1957; *Maastricht Treaty*, 1992).

13. "We are not productive machines, we're human beings!"

14. The CNUP, for example, has organized, since its creation, dozens of so-called housing fairs to promote the sale of urban housing and lots among Colombians throughout the Colombian overseas geography, including in cities such as Madrid, New York, Miami, and London. It has also created several websites to promote business and communication among migrants abroad and between migrants and their homeland.

15. See *Convenio*, 2008.

16. The Valencia branch was opened in collaboration with the Universidad Politécnica de Valencia (UPV). The courses and graduation ceremonies are held on the UPV campus. While SENA Valencia offers some courses in other cities, Colombian leaders participating in the Madrid event wanted to have similar physical branches opened in their own regions, as SENA has done in Colombia. Technical training courses in Spain are for Colombian citizens residing in Spain and who hold a high school diploma only (see http://senavalencia.com).

17. I use *governmentality* as Foucault (1988, p. 19) defined it: "This contact between the technologies of domination of others and those of the self I call governmentality." This conception of governmentality reflects Marx's argument, according to which every production technique requires not only a modification in an individual's skills but also of their attitudes.

References

Acuerdo entre el Reino de España y la República de Colombia, sobre participación en las elecciones municipales de los nacionales de cada país residentes en el territorio del otro. (2009).

Aleinikoff, T. A., and D. Klusmeyer. (2002). *Citizenship Policies for an Age of Migration*. Washington, DC: Carnegie Endowment for International Peace/Migration Policy Institute.

Anderson, B. (1994). "Exodus." *Critical Inquiry*, 20(2), 314-27.

Aristotle. (1952). *Politics*. E. Barker (Trans.). London: Oxford University Press.

Bauböck, R. (1994). *Transnational Citizenship: Membership and Rights in International Migration*. Aldershot: Edward Elgar.

Bauman, Z. (1998). *Globalization: The Human Consequences*. New York: Columbia University Press.

Besserer, F. (1999). "Estudios transnacionales y ciudadanía transnacional." In G. Mummert (Ed.), *Fronteras fragmentadas* (pp. 215-38). Zamora, Michoacán, Mexico: El Colegio de Michoacán.

Boswell, C. (2003). *European Migration Policies in Flux: Changing Patterns of Inclusion and Exclusion*. Oxford: Blackwell.

Burns, J. (2007). *Great Women of Imperial Rome: Mothers and Wives of the Caesars*. London: Routledge.

Calavita, K. (2005). *Immigrants at the Margins: Law, Race, and Exclusion in Southern Europe*. Cambridge: Cambridge University Press.

Castles, S., and M. J. Miller. (2009). *The Age of Migration: International Population Movements in the Modern World* (4th ed.). New York/London: The Guilford Press.

Comunidad de Madrid. (2011). *Informe de la población extranjera empadronada en la Comunidad de Madrid, enero de 2011*.

Consolidated Version of the Treaty on the Functioning of the European Union. (1957). C 83.

Convenio de Seguridad Social entre el Reino de España y la República de Colombia. (2008). 54.

DeStefano, J., Jr. (2007). *Statement of Mayor John DeStefano, Jr. to Board of Aldermen Finance Committee on Municipal Identification Program*.

Fahrmeir, A. (2007). *Citizenship: The Rise and Fall of a Modern Concept*. New Haven: Yale University Press.

Faist, T. (2001). "Social Citizenship in the European Union: Nested Membership." *Journal of Common Market Studies*, 39 (1), 37-58.

Faist, T., and P. Kivisto (Eds.). (2007). *Dual Citizenship in Global Perspective: From Unitary to Multiple Citizenship*. New York: Palgrave MacMillan.

Flynn, D. (2003, Nov). "'Tough as Old Boots?' Asylum, Immigration and the Paradox of New Labour Policy." Dicussion paper presented at the Joint Council for the Welfare of Immigrants, London.

_____. (2005). "New Borders, New Management: The Dilemmas of Modern Immigration Policies." *Ethnic and Racial Studies*, 28(3), 463-90.

Foucault, M. (1988). "Techonologies of the Self." In L. H. Martin, H. Gutman, and P. H. Hutton (Eds.), *Technologies of the Self: A Seminar with Michel Foucault* (pp. 16-49). Amherst: University of Massachusetts Press.

Fox, J. (2010a). "Coalitions: Translating Engagement into Empowerment." In X. Bada, J. Fox, R. Donnelly, and A. Selee (Eds.), *Context Matters: Latino Immigrant Civic Engagement in Nine U.S. Cities* (pp. 13-17). Washington DC: Woodrow Wilson International Center for Scholars.

_____. (2010b). "Understanding Latino Immigrant Civic Engagement: Context Matters." In X. Bada, J. Fox, R. Donnelly, and A. Selee (Eds.), *Context Matters: Latino Immigrant Civic Engagement in Nine U.S. Cities* (pp. 7-12). Washington, DC: Woodrow Wilson International Center for Scholars.

Geddes, A. (2003). *The Politics of Migration and Immigration in Europe*. London: Sage Publications.

Glick Schiller, N., and T. Faist. (2010). *Migration, Development, and Transnationalization: A Critical Stance*. Oxford: Berghahn Books.

Gobierno Nacional de la República del Ecuador. (2008). *El texto de la Nueva Constitución— Grandes pasos para garantizar los drechos de las personas migrantes*.

Guarnizo, L. E. (2003). "The Economics of Transnational Living." *International Migration Review*, 37(3), 666-99.

_____. (2009). *Londres Latina: La presencia colombiana en la capital británica*. Mexico City: Miguel Angel Porrúa.

Guarnizo, L. E., and L. M. Diaz. (1999). "Transnational Migration: A View from Colombia." *Ethnic and Racial Studies*, 22(2), 397-421.

Guarnizo, L. E., A. I. Sanchez, and E. M. Roach. (1999). "Mistrust, Fragmented Solidarity, and Transnational Migration: Colombians in New York City and Los Angeles. *Ethnic and Racial Studies*, 22(2), 367-96.

Habermas, J. (1995). "Citizenship and National Identity: Some Reflections on the Future of Europe." In R. Beiner (Ed.), *Theorizing Citizenship* (pp. 255-81). Albany: State University of New York Press.

Harvey, D. (2008). "The Right to the City." *New Left Review*, 53(Sep/Oct), 23-40.

Heater, D. (2004). *A Brief History of Citizenship*. New York: New York University Press.

Held, D. (2010). *Cosmopolitanism: Ideals and Realities*. Cambridge, UK: Polity Press.

Held, D., and A. Kaya (Eds.). (2007). *Global Inequality*. Cambridge, UK: Polity Press.

Herod, A., and M. W. Wright (Eds.). (2002). *Geographies of Power: Placing Scale*. Malden, MA: Blackwell.

Herrera, G., and J. E. Ramírez (Eds.). (2008). *América Latina migrante: Estado, familia, identidades*. Quito Ecuador: FLACSO.

Herzog, T. (2003). *Defining Nations: Immigrants and Citizens in Early Modern Spain and Spanish America*. New Haven: Yale University Press.

Ignatieff, M. (1995). "The Myth of Citizenship." In R. Beiner (Ed.), *Theorizing Citizenship* (pp. 53-78). Albany: State University of New York Press.

Jacobson, D. (1997). *Rights Across Borders: Immigration and the Decline of Citizenship*. Baltimore: The Johns Hopkins University Press.

Jupille, J., and B. Jolliff. (2011). "Regionalism in the World Polity." Paper presented at the European Union Studies Association 2011 Biennial Meetings. Retrieved Jun 17, 2011, from http://euce.org/eusa/2011/papers/11g_jupille.pdf.

Keck, M. E., and K. Sikkink. (1998). *Activists Beyond Borders: Advocacy Networks in International Politics*. Ithaca: Cornell University Press.

League of Nations. (1930, 13 Apr). *Convention on Certain Questions Relating to the Conflict of Nationality Law*. Retrieved Jun 17, 2011, from http://www.unhcr.org/refworld/docid/3ae6b3b00.htm.

Lefebvre, H. (1973). *El derecho a la ciudad*. Barcelona: Ediciones Península.

Levitt, P. (2001). *The Transnational Villagers*. Berkeley: University of California Press.

Lewis, G., and S. Neal. (2005). "Introduction: Contemporary Political Contexts, Changing Terrains and Revisited Discourses." *Ethnic and Racial Studies*, 28(3), 423-44.

Linklater, A. (1998). "Cosmopolitan Citizenship." *Citizenship Studies*, 2(1), 23-41.

Maastricht Treaty. (1992).

Marshall, T. H. (1964). *Class, Citizenship, and Social Development*. Chicago: University of Chicago Press.

_____. (1992). *Citizenship and Social Class*. London: Pluto Press.

Mazzolari, F. (2005). "Determinants of Naturalization: The Role of Dual Citizenship Laws." *Working Papers*, 117. The Center for Comparative Immigration Studies, University of California San Diego.

McNeill, D. (2002). "Barcelona as Imagined Community: Pasqual Maragall's Space of Engagement." *Transactions of the Institute of British Geographers*, 26(3) [article first published online].

Migration Policy Institute. (n.d.). "Data Hub." Retrieved Mar 6, 2011, from http://www.migrationinformation.org/datahub/northamerica.cfm.

Miller, B. (1994). "Political Empowerment, Local-central State Relations, and Geographically Shifting Political Opportunity Structures: Strategies of the Cambridge, Massachusetts, Peace Movement." *Political Geography*, 13(5), 393-406.

Oakland City Council. (2007). *Resolution No. 80584 CMS*. Retrieved Jun 17, 2011, from http://clerkwebsvr1.oaklandnet.com/attachments/16374.pdf.

Plato. (1970). *Laws*. T. J. Saunders (Trans.). Harmosndsworth, UK: Penguin.

Pocock, J. G. A. (1995). "The Ideal of Citizenship Since Classical Times." In R. Beiner (Ed.), *Theorizing Citizenship* (pp. 29-52). Albany: State University of New York Press.

Purcell, M. (2003). "Citizenship and the Right to the Global City." *International Journal of Urban and Regional Research*, 27(3), 564-90.

Ratha, D. (2003). "Workers' Remittances: An Important and Stable Source of External Development Finance." In The World Bank (Ed.), *Global Development Finance* (pp. 157-75). Washington, DC: Editor.

Rigaudiere, A. (2002). "Municipal Citizenship in Pierre Jacobi's *Practica aurea livellorum* (ca. 1311)." In J. Kirshner and L. Mayali (Eds.), *Privileges and Rights of Citizenship: Law and the Juridical Construction of Civil Society* (pp. 1-25). Berkeley: School of Law (Boalt Hall), University of California at Berkeley.

Rodriguez, R. M. (2010). *Migrants for Export: How the Philippine State Brokers Labor to the World*. Minneapolis: University of Minnesota Press.

Rosenau, J. N. (1997). *Along the Domestic-Foreign Frontier: Exploring Governance in a Turbulent World*. Cambridge: Cambridge University Press.

Salazar Parreñas, R. (2005). *Children of Global Migration: Transnantional Families, and Gendered Woes*. Stanford: Stanford University Press.

Sayre, N. F. (2005). "Ecological and Geographical Scale: Parallels and Potential for Integration." *Progress in Human Geography*, 29(3), 276–90.

Smith, M. P. (2001). *Transnational Urbanism: Locating Globalization*. Malden, MA: Blackwell Publishers Ltd.

Smith, M. P., and M. Bakker. (2008). *Citizenship across Borders: The Political Transnationalism of El Migrante*. Ithaca, NY: Cornell University Press.

Smith, M. P., and L. E. Guarnizo. (2009). "Global Mobility, Shifting Borders and Urban Citizenship." *Tijdschrift voor Economische en Sociale Geografie*, 100(5), 610–22.

Smith, N., and W. Dennis. (1987). "The Restructuring of Geographical Scale: Coalescence and Fragmentation of the Northern Core Region." *Economic Geography*, 63(2), 160-82.

Smith, R. C. (2006). *Mexican New York: Transnational Lives of New Immigrants*. Berkeley: University of California Press.

Soysal, Y. N. (1994). *Limits of Citizenship: Migrants and Postnational Membership in Europe*. Chicago: University of Chicago Press.

Stiglitz, J. E. (2007). *Making Globalization Work*. New York: W.W. Norton & Company.

Tarrow, S. (2005). "The Dualities of Transnational Contention: 'Two Activist Solitudes' or a New World Altogether?" *Mobilization: An International Journal*, 10(1), 53-72.

Thomas, R. J. (1982). "Citizenship and Gender in Work Organization: Some Considerations for Theories of the Labor Process." *American Journal of Sociology*, 88(Splmt.), S86-S112.

Tides Foundation. (2007). "The Right to the City: Reclaiming Our Urban Centers, Reframing Human Rights, and Redefining Citizenship." Retrieved Jun 17, 2011, from http://www.tides.org/fileadmin/tf_pdfs/TheRightToTheCity.pdf

Torpey, J. (1998). "Coming and Going: On the State Monopolization of the Legitimate 'Means of Movement'." *Sociological Theory*, 16(3), 239-59.

United Nations Population Division. (2011). *International Migrant Stock: The 2008 Revision*. Retrieved Jun 17, 2011, from http://esa.un.org/migration/p2k0data.asp.

United Nations World Tourism Organization. (2011). *International Tourism: First Results of 2011 Confirm Consolidation of Growth*. Madrid: *Author*.

Urry, J. (2007). *Mobilities*. Cambridge, UK: Polity Press.

Weller, S. (2007). "Power and Scale: The Shifting Geography of Industrial Relations Law in Australia." *Working Papers*, 28. Centre for Strategic Economic Studies, Victoria University.

Wimmer, A., and N. Glick Schiller. (2002). "Methodological Nationalism and Beyond: Nation-state Building, Migration and the Social Sciences." *Global Networks*, 2(4), 301-34.

Yeshayahu Gonzales-Lara, J., and D. Santome. (2007). "El voto transnacional: La diaspora peruana y el voto en el exterior." Retrieved Jun 17, 2011, from http://www.facebook.com/topic.php?uid=129372253763836&topic=135.

PART II

THE RIGHT TO THE CITY:
POLITICAL PROJECT AND URBAN CHARACTERISTIC

3

Citizens in Search of a City:
Towards a New Infrastructure of Political Belonging

Tony Roshan Samara

In May of 2010 the Right to the City Alliance released a provocative report entitled *We Call These Projects Home: Solving the Housing Crisis from the Ground Up*. Drawing from interviews, focus groups, and workshops with residents from seven cities in six major metropolitan areas, the report delivers a series of findings that contradict much of what is said about public housing in the media and much of what many researchers take as an article of faith: despite almost uniformly negative portrayals of public housing, it works—and many people would prefer to stay rather than be dispersed. The report marks a direct challenge to the 'concentrated poverty' narrative and the deconcentration policies that have framed urban anti-poverty strategy for decades. Indeed, the report takes aim at the eviction of low income people of color from their neighborhoods by a combination of state policy, market pressures, and other forces operating inside, across, and at the edges of licit institutions, and it critiques the associated dismantling of the social and political institutions they have built.

Twenty years of housing policy guided by the principle of deconcentration have generated a sometimes contentious debate about the record of moving people to opportunity and the broader social consequences of dispersing the poor (Briggs, 2008; Goetz and Chapple, 2010; Imbroscio, 2008; Popkin, Levy, and Buron, 2009; Steinberg, 2009). The political dimensions of displacement are often overshadowed by research attempting to capture the costs and benefits of deconcentration for those who moved (either by choice or by force) and those who returned or were left behind. The more critical contributions to this literature do raise important concerns regarding the ideological underpinnings of the "dispersal consensus" and what some see as continuities between the era of urban renewal and more recent policy (Crump, 2002; Goetz, 2000; 2010; Lipman, 2009; Steinberg, 2009). Most of these concerns underscore the injustices of federal policy and market practice that have the effect, intentionally or not, of displacing low income populations when they inconveniently occupy newly desirable spaces. They also draw attention to the concurrence of this process with a newly rescaled global economy that operates through certain cities or certain areas within cities.

Less attention, however, has been given to the resistance to this new urban politics, in which the poor are often moved along to make way for "redevelopment" or, as in the case of housing policy, "for their own good" (for two notable exceptions see Hackworth, 2005, and Goetz, 2000). Few have gone as far as the Alliance's report in documenting the extent to which policy and its intellectual architecture are at odds with what substantial numbers of public housing residents think and want. This neglect demands attention because, in addition to what can, at best, be described as a mixed record on social and economic measures, deconcentration is a direct cause of the destruction and degradation of political spaces that the urban poor have struggled to construct over decades, often despite their *de facto* disenfranchisement and the shifting dynamics of state and public hostility, paternalism, and apathy. The shift from generalized abandonment of ghettos to a more proactive posture towards the urban poor by the state, private interests, and certain elements of the non-governmental sector has generated a renewed urban resistance to displacement and deconcentration. This resistance is at once a straightforward defense of poor people's housing and a deeper, nascent challenge to neoliberal urban governance. A successful challenge will eventually require the institutionalization of political forms and forces emerging to protect home and political spaces.

This chapter addresses this political challenge directly by focusing on the US-based Right to the City Alliance (RTTCA) as a movement with the potential to remake citizenship and to produce a new urban polity, both of these tasks being key components of institutionalizing a democratic form of counter-governance. "Right to the city" as a theory represents a new, if still ill-defined, articulation of citizenship that speaks to the crisis of traditional nation-state citizenship in an era of transnationalism and globalization. While drawing on data from RTTCA campaigns, interviews, and movement literature, this chapter attempts to identify the central strategic moves of this still emerging articulation of citizenship as it relates to the issue of housing.

Housing is an issue that concerns all of the RTTCA member organizations, making it a useful lens through which to develop an overview of the right to the city movement as a whole. The prominence of the issue for over forty organizations spread over eight metropolitan regions lends support to the argument that there is a generalized housing crisis for the urban poor, one that has long preceded the officially recognized recent housing crisis associated with the 2008 meltdown of the financial sector. According to the United Nations Human Rights Council (2009) the enduring housing crisis for the urban poor may represent the most pressing human rights issue facing the entire country. Housing, and the crisis associated with it, is also linked directly to the issue of citizenship, making it an important entry point into the new political forms that "right to the city" is generating as a movement and a theory.

A central idea animating this investigation of the relationship between housing and citizenship is that spatial deconcentration may not only be flawed as an anti-poverty strategy—resulting in a net loss of affordable housing for low income urban residents—but may also represent a destruction of the political home spaces, or polities, within which residents can aggregate and mobilize their political power. Deconcentration in this view represents an act of spatial governance that overlaps neatly with the geographic, economic, and racial politics of a broader urban governmentality in which interlocking institutions, individual processes, and organizations function as an exclusionary polity through which urban spaces are made/destroyed and lower income urban residents are effectively disenfranchised (Foucault, 1991; Goetz, 2010; Samara, 2007). The social crisis of affordable housing is therefore at the same time a political crisis for marginalized urban populations and a crisis for democracy. The systematic and anti-democratic demolition of public housing (over 200,000 public housing units have been demolished since 1995 and another 230,000 are currently on the chopping block) is only the most extreme case of policies and practices which are steadily chipping away at the power bases of marginalized urban residents and further undermining their ability to participate effectively as individuals and as communities in the governance of the places they call home (Right to the City Alliance [RTTCA], 2010).

Here I attempt to describe the conceptual landscape of the political subjectivity emerging in this context. The rest of the chapter is divided into six sections. The first section is a discussion of the crisis of citizenship and "right to the city" as a response to this crisis. The following four sections outline the key strategic moves that position "right to the city" as an incubator for new citizenship; they are, respectively: the rescaling of citizenship, the focus on the relationship between citizenship and home, the rejection of individual and market-centered citizenship, and the assertion of a right to place as a distinctive feature of the right to the city. The chapter ends with a brief reflection on both the promises and perils of this particular political mobilization.

Citizenship as an Institution in Crisis

Before we consider the crisis of citizenship and the city, some broader context is necessary. Citizenship more generally has been in crisis for some time due to weaknesses intrinsic to the modern institutions through which democracy and liberty were to be constituted as material realities: namely, the citizen (political subject), the nation (territory/polity), and the people (population). Citizenship has been made and remade as these categories and the relationships between them have been configured and reconfigured in response, for instance, to new rights claims or demands for membership. Consequently (at least in modern times) citizenship has never been stable. Rather, it has exhibited a consistent precariousness that has always threatened to derail the entire liberal democratic project and the spirit of progress that animates it: defined too narrowly it undermines legitimacy and provides purchase for resistance, too broadly and it loses its utility as a mechanism of modern governance through inclusion (Holston, 2008; Mamdani, 1996).

In *Fear of Small Numbers*, Arjun Appadurai (2006) refers to Samuel Huntington's fear of Latino cultural "contamination" of the United States as a means of illustrating the observation made by Hannah Arendt in *Eichmann in Jerusalem* that the Achilles heel of modern liberal societies is the idea of a national peoplehood. This notion, of course, has long been a central theme of the scholarship on race, nationalism, and post-colonialism (Mamdani, 1996; Marx, 1998). The nation was constructed as exclusive, and this exclusivity has scarred the domestic terrain along the axes of race and gender in particular. Various mechanisms of exclusion produce tiered citizenship, wherein the formal borders of citizenship expand even as access to power within those borders becomes more restricted, as captured in the notions of "second class" and "differentiated" citizenship (Holston, 2008; Somers, 2008). As national inclusion has expanded, exclusion has been rescaled and reconfigured. Today, it may be argued that we are witnessing the end of that project as a viable form of governance.

The structural weaknesses of the institution of citizenship could be masked, ignored, or suppressed for a brief moment of time that has long since passed. When structural weaknesses did surface the damage was often localized or limited to geopolitical peripheries, where they could be explained away by reference to external forces—whether deficient social formations (e.g. cultural interpretations), weak implementation (e.g. corruption), or some combination of the two—or defused for a time by accommodating new rights claimants without ceding to them any real power to rearrange social hierarchies. Today, however, the crisis is systemic and acute, apparent globally and in the political centers from which the citizenship project was first launched.

Paradoxically, the weakening of citizenship's political power as an entry point to more formal governance has fueled a strengthening of its symbolic power or its power as a mechanism of informal governance. Migration dynamics provide one of the most visible expressions of this as states respond to the increasing number of immigrants, in many cases, through some form of banishment or expulsion from the polity. To be sure, this particular politics of citizenship is not merely symbolic. To deny citizenship, whether by banishment or socio-political marginalization, is to deny rights or, more specifically, the right to have rights (Bellamy, 2008; Somers, 2008). If we think of citizenship as a container for the bundle of rights that comes with political membership, then to strip an individual or group of citizenship is to leave them without the rights that are fundamental to the liberal democratic project (Leary, 2000).

The crisis of citizenship can be read in one of two ways, both of them being linked to processes of denationalization (Sassen, 2006). First, we might take the crisis as representative of a generalized collapse, wherein the liberal democratic project has reached a terminal stage precipitated by the somewhat unexpected consequences of globalization. Citizenship in this perspective is a fairly rigid institution, one incapable of adapting to the realities of "multiculturalism" in previously imagined, mono-cultural societies (Huntington, 2005). This results in searching for the definition and meaning of citizenship's core categories since the referents for the citizen—the people and the nation—can no longer be taken for granted or be asserted without challenge. The polity itself is faced with the mortal danger of fragmentation. Politics in this approach is primarily defensive if not aggressive, particularly in its later stages.

A second, more historically-grounded reading discerns a more cunning and adaptive citizenship, one that draws in difference so that difference may be rendered powerless and be overwhelmed in the end. In contrast to previous eras, when exclusion rather than inclusion was the central element of citizenship, the near universal extension of citizenship as the primary form of political subjectivity now produces a crisis for the governed and for those who govern. For the latter, mass inclusion has blunted demands for an actual democratization of power, but in the absence of social justice this has been, at best, a temporary victory with its own political costs. The near universality of citizenship has made its limits as a form of political subjectivity more clear, even as struggles over membership continue to erupt. History does not break at neat, convenient intervals; rather, new struggles emerge even as old ones remain ongoing and unresolved, often raising difficult questions for social movements about strategy and the allocation of resources. There is undoubtedly still much life in the various projects to engineer inclusive if disempowered forms of citizenship (Holston, 2008; Wacquant, 1996). However, despite these ongoing struggles, citizenship is no longer a site of decisive political power; this power has migrated elsewhere.[1]

The relationship between democracy and citizenship is complex but for my purposes it is useful to think of the crisis of citizenship in terms of disenfranchisement: not disenfranchisement through formal exclusion but through inclusion. National citizenship has become increasingly ineffective as a form of political subjectivity. This crisis has been imminent, perhaps for as long as there has been citizenship, but we are currently in a period where efforts to reform or expand national citizenship appear inadequate solutions to the democracy deficit that is now global in nature (Varsanyi, 2006). In response we have witnessed arguments for universal citizenship (often linked to the movement around human rights) as well as transnational, cosmopolitan, and local citizenships. Whatever their relative merits, these proposals underscore the depth of the crisis we face. The emergence of "right to the city" suggests that social formations organized around new forms, new sites, and new productions of power are now an important feature of the political landscape.

The Rescaling of Exclusion: The Infrastructures of Making Aliens in the City

Traditionally, inquiries into the crisis of citizenship were pitched at the national and global scales. More recently, however, urban scholars have begun to explore this terrain as well, partly in response to new circuits and practices of governance that operate in and through city spaces. Framing these explorations is the potential for new political spaces and political subjects to emerge as the relationship between nation and citizen becomes destabilized, particularly at the urban scale (Sassen, 2002). The city as a site for renewed battles over political inclusion makes sense because cities have become places of concentrated power from which global processes are commanded and nodes through which central transnational networks run. This makes cities ideal candidates for the production of new polities and new politics.

Urban areas are currently dominated by forms of governance, whether we identify these as forms of gendered capitalism, racial neoliberalism, or similar hybrid systems in which market principles infuse not only economic relations but also social and political relations. These dominant forms constitute an architecture of exclusion in political terms. They form a dynamic infrastructure of urban governance that leaves some legal residents—in many cases most legal residents—effectively outside of the *de facto* polity through which urban space is produced. In practice, this exclusion functions in a number of related and often mutually reinforcing ways, which may range from the quasi-privatization of central city areas to the dispersion of power through opaque, decentralized governance networks that are difficult for most citizens to access (Purcell, 2002; Samara, 2010).[2] A defining consequence of these shifts is that the link between citizenship and rights becomes destabilized: while the *de jure* relationship remains, the power of citizenship rights dissipates.

Economically and politically marginalized residents banished from urban spaces in the United States are not cast out because they have lost their citizenship or the bundle of formal rights which it contains, but because their position within the networks of urban governance leaves them relatively powerless to enact policies that would allow them to stay. They are also priced out of the other means of entry: the market. Thus, they have rights, though not necessarily all those they demand, but they cannot leverage them to mobilize the necessary power to remain in their homes. In this process of displacement, a loss of both home space and political space occurs. They remain citizens within the context of the national polity, yet they are without a polity in those spaces in which they actually live.[3] They have the right to remain in the country, but not in their neighborhoods or cities, which is often where inequality is organized and can be most effectively challenged (Lalloo,1998).

One useful way to characterize "right to the city" is as a new political vocabulary for contemporary democratic struggles and as an expression of the need to revisit, and perhaps reconfigure, basic, often taken-for-granted democratic principles and practices (Purcell, 2008). As such, "right to the city" can be viewed as part of a broader, renewed focus on the local that sees the city as a site of control and of resistance (DeFilippis, 2003). If the modern project of citizenship represented an attempt to scale up citizenship to the national, then "right to the city" may represent, in the wake of the failure of that project, a return to its origins.

A Return to Origins: Rescaling Political Subjectivity

Citizenship began in the city, so perhaps it is fitting that in a time of crisis it returns to its origins in an attempt to rebuild. It returns, however, not only as an institution battered and bruised by centuries of political conflict but also, more immediately, to a city that is dramatically different than the one from which it originally grew. Still, the historical link remains significant because of the privileged position the city has held in the context of citizenship; the city is the preeminent site of the social and, more specifically, the most fertile terrain upon which a politics of 'citizens-as-rights-claimants' can grow (Holston, 2001; Isin, 2008). I would stress that fundamental inequalities shape the emergence of the discourse on the "right to the city" and that this return to the city holds many possibilities but offers no easy victories.

The rescaling of political subjectivity to the city is perhaps the most remarked-upon aspect of "right to the city" as it pertains to citizenship. The intensification of urban inequality combined with a crisis of citizenship and democracy at the national scale helps to explain the emergence of the right to the city discourse over the past decade. The city stands in distinction from the nation and the global, and it asserts a distinct socio-spatial referent for politics and for a new political subject, the inhabitant, or put another way, the urban citizen. In Henri Lefebvre's original formulation, the citizen is the urban inhabitant and the urban inhabitant is the citizen; the fusion of these two, encapsulated by the term *citadin*, meaning city dweller or resident, is a response to the traditional social, spatial, and political exclusion of the urban poor and working class (Purcell, 2002). While in Lefebvre's formulation the politics of the *citadin* is a response to an exclusion that was organized locally and nationally, citizenship at the scale of the city today is much more a response to an exclusion that is organized by a vastly more expansive, transnational network of urban governance (Samara, 2011).

A fully formed urban citizenship would require an institutionalization of political power and subjectivity in which political participation and the belonging it implies are not embedded with membership in the national polity. This would address directly one of the most vexing challenges posed by globalization: the transnational movement of people and the question of the political rights of mobile populations and people who reside, legally or otherwise, in nations outside their nation of citizenship. More generally, it would open up space for new political subjectivities that respond to the crisis of citizenship, provide new forms to contain old and new rights, and allow for new approaches to effecting rights claims.

It goes without saying that the rescaling of citizenship to the urban is central to the formulation of citizenship emerging from the right to the city movement, including RTTCA. This centrality, in turn, clarifies the importance of housing and anti-displacement not only to urban social movements in general but to urban citizenship in particular. The concepts of residence and inhabitance imply a relative permanence or security of tenure, for which secure housing is a requirement, and they link citizenship intrinsically to a politics of home. This connection is explored in more detail below. However, before moving on to that, it is worth elaborating how RTTCA gives a particular form to this rescaled political subjectivity.

As RTTCA co-founder Gihan Perera has pointed out, the organizations involved in the RTTCA are all from so-called "hot market" cities that have experienced a dramatic intensification of the local real estate market in the 1990s, which has adversely impacted low income residents and their communities (Tides, 2007). This context explains the focus on resisting displacement and the development of a political approach that goes beyond making demands for specific social reforms (housing support, living wages, etc.). Instead, what emerged was a broader and deeper demand for political transformation in the context of a rapidly changing and increasingly complex—and some would say inaccessible—governance structure that put into stark relief the enduring reality that the urban poor have been effectively shut out of participating in the reshaping of their own cities and communities. "Right to the city"" was adopted as a framework to give conceptual coherence to disparate campaigns, organizations, and struggles in a wide range of cities experiencing similar transformations that were already, in a sense, engaged in right to the city mobilizations.

RTTCA has fixed the urban/the city as the conceptual political space as a means of networking these mobilizations ideologically and organizationally. Combining the spatial analysis of transnational processes with an explicit focus on the struggle over power situates RTTCA as a familiar, if differently scaled, model of democratic struggle, one in which a different citizen is required to address a range of challenges that are urban in form and for which national citizenship is inadequate. The agendas that various RTTCA organizations put forward, being organized around anti-displacement and decision-making about the production of urban space, suggest a far more radical program than one organized around specific social demands or having a place at the decision-making table. Instead it is an attempt to wrest decisive political power away from those who currently wield it and to produce a dramatically different city than the various market regimes are currently producing.

Finally, RTTCA as an expression of "right to the city" represents not only a scaling down from the global but also a scaling up from the intra-urban. All of the movements within the Alliance, even if they articulate demands at the city-wide scale, operate only in parts of the city; all are neighborhood- and community-based, not city-based. Given the role of cities—particularly hot-market US cities—in transnational processes, this scaling up can be viewed as a strategic attempt to operate at the interface of the neighborhood and the global while simultaneously adding to the importance of the urban polity. In other words, RTTCA both acknowledges and reinforces the centrality of the city as a primary place of politics. While on the one hand this represents a potentially powerful move, it also treats the city as a somewhat abstract place precisely because the city is not the scale of everyday life for the communities these organizations represent; nor is it at all clear whether operating at the scale of the city is in the interests of these communities or whether they would even be capable of doing so under even the best circumstances. This tension within a rescaled politics reminds us that the city itself is a differentiated space of highly unequal places. Understanding urban citizenship requires that we take a more fine-grained look at the relationship between political subjectivity and place than the perspective afforded by that of the abstracted city.

The City as Home: Citizenship, Place, and Belonging

Citizenship has historically been linked to place in ways that modern regimes and conceptions of citizenship still may not fully appreciate. The significance lies in the concept of belonging; citizenship implies belonging to a particular place. Remarking on this relationship from ancient Greece to early modern times, Engin Isin writes that, "citizenship was articulated as belonging to the city and the social and political rights that derived from that belonging" (2008, p. 267). It was only in belonging to the city, he continues, that citizenship was acquired; this belonging was the basic condition of citizenship (p. 268). As we know, the city's role as this privileged place of citizenship eventually came to an end, marking the beginning of the modern age proper and the rise of a new "place"—the nation—which required new measures of belonging and new forms of citizenship (Anderson, 1991).

The notion of belonging to a place as a foundation upon which citizenship is based has both social and political dimensions. Socially, belonging refers to a range of social ties that have meaning for those involved and that define the group, be it a family, community, or nation. Politically, it refers to those who have a right to be and participate in the political life of that group and its governance. Historically, the link between the social and the political has always been evident, and the citizen has been understood as belonging in both senses of the word. In practice, however, the relationship has been and continues to be a source of tension and conflict. Debates about gentrification, for example, explicitly or implicitly involve a discourse on who has a right to be in particular spaces. Though this particular discourse often limits rights to those associated with ownership or control of property, the tension between the political and social meanings of belonging are fundamentally what is at stake.

This recurring theme is emphasized in the RTTCA founding conference report, which states that, "the struggle over right to the city is not only about land and housing but also about community and how our communities are governed and by whom" (Samara, 2007b, p. 7). Here, community is not coterminous with the city. It refers instead to specific social and political spaces called home spaces; they are the places to which people, individually and collectively as a community, feel they belong. The concentration and segregation of poor people of color in urban ghettos has been a source of deprivation and marginalization, but from within that context, these communities have been able to mobilize considerable political power relative to their socio-spatial position. The nature of these struggles has varied, but in general they have been centered on the defense of home spaces.

The concept of home is important for understanding citizenship and the focus of RTTCA groups on housing. It makes more concrete the relationship between citizenship and place and acts as a mediating concept between this relationship and actual campaigns for housing. RTTCA housing campaigns, as indicated in the quotation above, are not simply campaigns about affordable housing; they are also concerned with a broader agenda of anchoring and securing social and political spaces to which their residents belong but over which they may have little control or ownership in the legal sense. These political spaces represent the polities in which a rescaled urban citizenship ultimately takes root. They are the social and political homes or places of belonging from which the political power of the urban poor springs, and these polities disappear when housing disappears.

Historically, housing, including public housing, has been central to the story of citizenship and exclusion in the United States. Opponents of public housing in the first half of the 20th century linked race and nationalism to counterproposals for public housing, claiming it was un-American and promoted racial integration. Homeownership, on the other hand, resonated with ideals of the market and democracy; it also provided whites with an escape route from the growing black urban population (Argersinger, 2010). White flight and black segregation in the emerging ghettos after World War II led to the creation of new political spaces as exclusion was rescaled and reconfigured across the national and urban landscape (Self, 2003). Political power absconded to the newly formed suburbs along with the suburban voter, a new citizen, so to speak, in the postwar political landscape. The links between housing and citizenship further detail the nature of political subjectivity emerging from RTTCA mobilization in terms of its relationship to place. Public housing, for example, has traditionally been both a site at which poor people's power has been mobilized and a target of this power by residents, particularly black women (Williams, 2005). Public housing thus demarcates a polity, which, despite often overwhelming odds, has empowered low income and politically marginalized women of color in ways that tend to be overlooked or ignored. Deconcentration through federal policy or gentrification produces disorganization; it destroys the polity, therefore disorganizing the political community through dispersion and constituting acts of spatial governance. The RTTCA report on public housing, taking perhaps the most forceful position, makes clear that one of the most important functions of public housing has been and continues to be to provide a physical infrastructure for communities and to provide a sense of stability. In the view of the report's authors, a direct consequence of current federal policy, which is essentially a policy of demolition, is the disruption of this stability. One resident of public housing in New Orleans explains the effects of disorganization this way:

> It affected my life a lot moving from St. Thomas…after they tore it down we moved into the Lafitte housing development. They had us mixed up in a lot of situations. It was hard living in this place…. You split up people from all kinds of generations, all kinds of public housing and you made it bad for us to live…it is very stressful, it is hard for us. Especially young Black women (RTTCA, 2010, p. 37).

Gentrification and other forms of displacement are threats to home precisely because they break the relationship between people and place; they banish the citizen who finds (if she did not already suspect) that her citizenship counts for less than we are typically led to believe. Citizenship is, it seems in many cases, only indirectly related to the power that displaces inhabitants from their homes, unless of course, they are private homeowners. Below the national scale, there is in practice very little an individual or community can do through their identity as citizens to protect their status of belonging to a neighborhood to which they have laid claim or feel a part. As we see in the next section, much of this disempowerment can be traced to the rights regime of liberal democracy. Citizenship emerging from RTTCA challenges this regime, since even in those cases where residents are able to obtain new housing, they are rarely able to rebuild a home.

Return of the Social: Challenging Individual- and Market-centered Conceptions of Citizenship

The liberal democratic model of citizenship revolves around an abstract individual in whom certain political rights, inalienable or otherwise, are vested. This model has been married with a market-driven individualism to create a modern political subjectivity that is empowered and disciplined more through markets than through formal participation in electoral politics. The emergent neoliberal citizenship we have been discussing here is defined by its distinction from and opposition to this conception of rights. In response, "right to the city" offers a broader, socially grounded vision of rights, one in which the social spaces and social networks that underpin the political power of urban populations are protected with at least the same force as the political rights of the individual.

In the realm of social policy, neoliberalism explicitly addresses itself to inequality and poverty, and it seeks to bring the power of the unfettered market to bear upon them. That is, in its own view it is not a retreat of the state from the social as much as it is a reorientation from 'direct provider' to 'facilitator' or 'enabler' (Rose, 2000). As a form of governance it reduces the actual power of the citizen to make social claims on the state and replaces this with the potential access (opportunity) of the citizen to social goods and rights through the market, as in the case of housing. Underpinning both these dimensions of citizenship is the individual, as voter (political rights) and consumer (social rights) (Dodson, 2006; Peck and Tickell, 2002; Purcell, 2008).

One important aspect of neoliberal governance in this context is the creation of populations. Colin Gordon, in discussing Foucault's work on governmentality, refers to the importance of producing populations at the level of representation so as to make certain things socially possible

(Gordon, 1991). Social policy, for example, always has a target population and this population must be made. Within the context of urban poverty there has been a long-running and newly-resurgent debate on culture and poverty that in many ways revolves around contested representations of the poor. Numerous observers, for example, have tied the rise of Third Way social policy to the overwhelmingly negative portrayals of the black urban poor during the 1970s and 1980s (O'Connor, 2001; Steinberg, 2011).

Neoliberal social policy emerges in this context to offer solutions at the level of populations, but targets individuals through the medium of market-driven policy that can separate or free 'good people' from 'bad communities.' Central to this strategy is the concept of individual choice, through which the social generally, and the community more specifically, are rendered either invisible or are reconstituted as backdrop. Presented as a widening of opportunity, choice becomes the basis of social policy and the realization of social rights or goods, but it also becomes a means through which the morality of marginalized citizens and their deservingness can be measured. As stated well by Nikolas Rose: "Those who refuse to become responsible and govern themselves ethically have also refused the offer to become members of our moral community. Hence, for them, harsh measures are entirely appropriate.... Citizenship becomes conditional on conduct" (Rose, 2000, p. 1407).

This approach to governance through discipline of populations is a defining feature of federal housing policy in the United States. Although the dismantling of the welfare system is the most well-known application of neoliberalism to US social policy, its role in shaping housing policy is equally important, and perhaps more so from the perspective of political power. Not only has policy steadily introduced the private sector into the provision of public housing over recent decades, but, through the HOPE VI program, it has also further institutionalized a discourse of individual choice that was originally introduced through the Section 8 housing voucher program. The key difference is that HOPE VI involves the deconcentration of the urban poor through the demolition of public housing rather than through individual vouchers alone; it is a more direct attack on the social and political spaces that residents call home by means of deconcentration.

It is in the rejection of this individualized and market-mediated citizenship that advocates of "right to the city" and the RTTCA make an additional contribution to our thinking about citizenship and the city. The expressions of political subjectivity that emerge from campaigns and movement literature suggest both a less abstract citizen/individual—i.e., one who is rooted in specific places—and an insistence on a conception of citizenship that challenges current market linkages and that reintroduces the struggle for social rights and the defense of social spaces through anti-displacement campaigns. A small but growing literature has begun to document the loss of social support networks—of home and community—that deconcentration produces, whether through market displacement or through federal policy (Gibson, 2007; Keene, Padilla, and Geronimus, 2010; Manzo, Kleit, and Couch, 2007). This important research provides support for the long-standing claims made by urban residents and community organizations that anti-poverty and housing policy often have undermined relatively fragile communities and the political bases which protect them against a hostile state and broader society.

More specifically, the RTTCA articulates demands for citizenship based on three rejections. First is the rejection of the representations of the urban poor which underpin the moral dimension of social policy that centers on providing 'good individuals' with the choice to escape 'bad communities.' *We Call These Projects Home* and *Displacing the Dream*, a report by the Youth Media Council with contributions from RTTCA members in the San Francisco/Oakland region, document the overwhelmingly negative portrayals of public housing residents in the media and the ways coverage of housing and gentrification have downplayed displacement and racism, highlighted market based solutions, and lacked input from residents themselves (RTTCA, 2010; Youth Media Council, 2008). These reports not only expose and reject existing media portrayals, but in the process they present a different subject, one whose new representation implies a different politics. Speaking about this dynamic, Rob, an organizer with Picture the Homeless, an RTTCA member organization from New York, says:

> They don't listen to us. People need to listen to homeless people. Listen to people who are disenfranchised. Listening to people who are poor is not part of the bureaucratic strategy. [...] Bureaucracy means that you sit down with the experts and the officials, you don't sit down with people in need. [...] Now, one of the things Giuliani was successful in is stereotyping homeless people. 'They're bums, they lack knowledge, they can't do this, they can't do that.' Giuliani spent a lot of time stigmatizing homeless folks in the city and anointing them as 'lacking knowledge.' (personal interview, 2008).

As Rob's testimony indicates, one aspect of the work Picture the Homeless is doing is reframing the meaning of homelessness as a political identity that demands recognition. The act of speaking back to misrepresentations suggests an attempt to claim recognition as citizens through a contestation of the meaning and morality of the marginalized *citadin*. This struggle for recognition underpins the different struggles for rights emerging from the right to the city discourse; RTTCA groups represent communities that, even if they do have citizenship in the formal sense, are not recognized as part of the political process.

The second rejection is that of market-mediated property relations, which commodify urban land, treat the individual as the primary target of housing policy, and posit individual ownership as the goal of that policy. In its 2009 policy platform, Right to the City—New York City, a coalition of more than twenty New York City RTTCA member organizations and allies, explicitly rejected the model of housing reform captured in HOPE VI and other policies:

> All NYC housing policy must be based upon the idea that land belongs to the people who live in a community. We believe in the investment of alternative community-based housing forms, such as community land trusts, housing cooperatives, and mutual housing associations (Right to the City—NYC, 2009, p. 13).

This vision of ownership and the policies that would emerge from it diverge greatly from current policy. In articulating a subject of policy reference that is broader than the individual, the call for community-oriented ownership and housing goes against the historical grain of housing discourse in the US and seeks to reconfigure the relationship between housing and citizenship by rejecting the alleged connection between individual (male) home ownership and the moral citizen as the foundation of democracy.

This leads directly into the third and final rejection. RTTCA rejects the invisibility or marginalization of the social—of home spaces—in current policy. Rather than serving as a backdrop, social spaces become central to what RTTCA organizations defend. Whereas HOPE VI elides any meaningful engagement with communities, RTTCA campaigns acknowledge the centrality of social networks of support and the social spaces that underpin political power. Whereas deconcentration policies encourage escape from the social and the dismantling of existing communities, these campaigns are organized around their defense. As discussed earlier, while struggles for actual housing are of course important, the anti-displacement nature of all RTTCA housing struggles indicates that more than housing is at stake. Here a different citizenship emerges, expressed not through an abstract individualism detached from place but through the networks of place-based social ties that make the mobilization of residents' political power possible. The significance of all these rejections for citizenship and democracy is that the community, as much as the individual, serves as a reference point for policy and politics.

The Right to Place

The final component of this new citizenship is the right to place. While the right to place may not be unique to RTTCA, this claim is arguably its most defining feature at present and the one that most distances the movement from a liberal democratic tradition of rights claims (even the more progressive iterations of that tradition that include social rights). Many of the rights associated with "right to the city" are fairly straightforward social, political, and civil rights: to housing and other basic needs; to meaningful participation in the democratic process; and to freedom from harassment by the state and its agents, primarily the police and immigration authorities. Other rights, such as the right to shape urban spaces, are potentially more radical, though they are often also more abstract (Leavitt, Samara, and Brady, 2009; Purcell, 2002). While some rights claims are foreign to the US context—social rights in particular—they are more common in other national contexts and in the international arena. Thus, most of the rights demands of "right to the city" do not reject or transcend traditional liberal democracy; rather they can be read as an attempt to press states into enforcing or expanding existing rights.

The claim of spatial rights, however, exists separately from the liberal democratic tradition, and it is this difference more than anything that gives "right to the city" its political distinctiveness. The right to place may be closely bound up with the social demand for security of tenure and decent housing, but it cannot be reduced to these. The right to place should be understood instead as the formalized political articulation of the social demand for housing and home: a right to reside in a particular place. It is what can transform the social demand explicitly into a political demand for governance power. It is not just an attempt to redistribute resources or change policy, though it may do either without going further. It is an attempt to redistribute political power and to provide both a political and spatial anchor for the other components of citizenship. The right to place appears to imply a protection of home spaces, meaning both shelter and community, but also it is a defense of an alternative or counter polity. It is arguably the most important right out of the bundle of rights that this new citizenship contains; for, without a right to place, the very presence of those who claim it within the city is threatened.

It is appropriate to frame this political demand as a rights claim because, following from the discussion throughout the chapter, a secure place is essential for the proper functioning of democracy for marginal communities and the individuals who constitute them, not least because the right to place secures the polity within which urban citizens can be enfranchised. The right to place is essential to what makes "right to the city" a compelling response to the crisis of citizenship and democracy, in addition to whatever value it may have in delivering actual social demands/rights and civil rights. Indeed, given the foregoing discussion, we could even refer to this right as a right to a polity.

To elaborate further, the right to place shapes emergent citizenship in at least three important ways that will play out differently and unevenly across different terrains. First, it gives political expression to the relationship between political subjectivity and home space, and in doing so it constitutes the latter as a polity as well as a social space. It seeks to protect home space not only as a site of the social or of community but as a site of the political, within which urban political actors can emerge and mobilize their collective power. The right to place links the citizen not to an abstract polity—neither to the nation nor even to the city—but to home space or community, to a place where one belongs, while recognizing that this is where the power of these citizens resides.

Second, the right to place directly challenges the current rights regime of land ownership, which is guaranteed primarily through market-mediated, legal property ownership by a legally constituted individual (i.e., a person or a corporate body). In its place, the right to place widens the concept of ownership to include communities and to be based on other forms of possession, such as occupancy. Given the role that the private property regime has played and continues to play in displacement, such a challenge is absolutely crucial. In this sense, the right to place provides a mechanism through which other forms of ownership—many of them in practice today as efforts to preserve affordable housing—can be strengthened and made more politically possible through a different property regime.

Finally, this right can alter dramatically the meaning of other, more well recognized social rights (e.g., the right to housing) by grounding these in a spatial politics and, more specifically, in an urban polity/political space. In fact, a right to housing appears inadequate in many ways absent the right to place. Currently, housing rights do not protect against tenure insecurity, as one could conceivably be moved from adequate house to adequate house. More importantly, the right to housing in and of itself does not imply anti-displacement, and therefore, as mentioned above, it cannot protect home spaces or polities.

The right to place appears to grow naturally from the RTTCA under the banner of anti-displacement. The concrete expression of this right within RTTCA is primarily in the form of the 'right to stay,' indicating the extent to which displacement is an overarching feature of contemporary urban struggles. RTTCA has identified the right to stay in the city as one of the two core principles underpinning its formation (the other being the right to participate in the production of urban space, which clearly implies the first) (Tides, 2007). The right is expressed explicitly and implicitly in a number of campaigns waged by RTTCA at the national, regional, and local scales, and it forms a principle around which campaigns are formed. It was perhaps most evident in the support for and mobilization around a right to return for displaced residents of New Orleans in the aftermath of Hurricane Katrina and the subsequent social disaster of affordable and public housing demolition (Center for Media Justice, 2007).

Other campaigns also indicate that the right to stay is a central tenet of RTTCA organizing. Eviction blockades, carried out by organizations such as the Boston-based organization City Life/Vida Urbana, are attempts to keep people in their homes not only as a housing strategy but as a strategy to keep neighborhoods and communities intact. They are strategies of spatial governance. In interviews conducted with members of the organization, the linkages between physical space, social networks, and political power were made quite clear, and it was through these interconnections that individual residents were able to become empowered citizens. Here, Steve, who is an organizer with City Life, discusses the right to resist displacement and the role of a place-based polity in fostering what may be an emergent citizenship:

> People have not heard anybody say that they have the right to resist. So their natural position is that they don't have the right to resist, because who has ever said that they do[?]. But they get to us and we say they do and if they come to a couple of our meetings, they really—that is their natural position. They kind of start smiling really literally and they say, 'Wow, yeah. Yeah that's right.' And so what they think they have—what they think they want is really different after they come to a couple of our meetings than what they thought they wanted, because now they think

they have more options and so people are gravitating towards the radical position. It's really broad, I think, but they'd never heard it before until they get to us (personal interview, 2008).

While it is still too early to tell what will develop from the right to the city movement, it is certainly of some significance that it is a national mobilization around anti-displacement as both a political and a social right.

Conclusion: The Razor's Edge of Marginal Politics

Gentrification and federal housing policy in the United States are generally—and incorrectly—excluded from the discussions of the global phenomenon of displacement in urban settings. Situating RTTCA and its anti-displacement campaigns within the context of rights, citizenship, and democracy can not only correct this error, but can also advance an anti-displacement agenda by contributing to the focus on local polities in a time when the national and the global scales are in crisis. In an era when the discourse of placelessness is ascendant, it is perhaps fitting that so many new poor peoples' movements are re-centering the importance of "place."

It remains to be seen what will come of the political spaces RTTCA is currently constructing. As others have cautioned, "right to the city" is still new, and even under the best circumstances its outcome will be contingent. To close, therefore, I offer some thoughts on a number of challenges I see for this project.

Indeterminate outcomes. Purcell points out that the most "right to the city" can provide is opportunity; it cannot guarantee outcomes. We do not know, under even the most optimal circumstances, what kinds of citizens and citizenship practices will be produced by right to the city approaches or whether these will be able to substantially change the current balance of power in cities and neighborhoods. We might imagine they will be more just, more democratic, and more secure, but this cannot be assumed. We also cannot know whether they can avoid being appropriated by middle classes (Baviskar, 2011), affluent expatriates (Smith and Guarnizo, 2009), or even street gangs (Holston, 2009).

Ambiguity of principles. I think there is significant ambiguity and lack of clarity within the campaigns, the organizations, and the broader right to the city movements. Contained within the discourse of rights is a clear tension between a democratic impulse that would expand liberal democratic rights and another impulse directed toward a kind of autonomy.

Network power in transnational cityscapes. The urban world increasingly takes the form of transnational cityscapes. These are highly connected and easily traveled by elite actors, or the cosmopolitan citizens, who are responsible for shaping them; however, they are more difficult to form and maintain for citizens located in marginal spaces. Opposition to public housing policy, for example, tends to be highly localized, although many locales may experience protest (Hackworth, 2005). To be sure, there are efforts underway (in the international movement of slum dwellers, for example), but these are weak networks relative to the strong elite networks that must be confronted on economic, political, and cultural grounds. Efforts within and beyond RTTCA to build power regionally and nationally are necessary steps, but the real challenge will be in converting these efforts into effective mobilizations of power that can outmaneuver much larger and better resourced coalitions.

Cooptation of discourse. The theme for the recently concluded World Urban Forum was "Right to the City." While this signifies an important ideological victory for marginal urban residents around the world, it also raised the specter of cooptation of radical discourse by conventional institutional actors embedded in hegemonic governance networks. This danger exists at other scales and in smaller spaces as well, as local elites seek to absorb and deflect the radical push of right to the city demands, thus creating new governmentalities that employ the discourse and even institutions of the oppressed (Roy, 2009).

Problem of inclusion-exclusion. It is unclear how new polities and new infrastructures of inclusion can avoid replicating mechanisms of exclusion. The concept of belonging, for example, can be used to exclude rather easily, and this is a very real danger conceptually and in practice. It is a peril that can be manipulated by opponents. The long-term-versus-newcomer dichotomy, for example, may be easy to support when newcomers are gentrifiers, but what about when newcomers are from similar social circumstances as long-term residents? In South Africa some of the most bitter conflicts in townships are expressed in stark xenophobic terms that make use of right to the city claims. In Shanghai and New Delhi, established and often more affluent residents deploy right to the city discourse against the 'predations' of newly-arrived, often destitute migrants who for the most part share the same national origin as long-term residents.

Despite these dangers and uncertainties, we should take seriously the potential in the right to the city movement and engage it and work with it to navigate the opportunities as well as the traps that lie ahead. Certainly a renewed commitment to democracy and a concerted effort to dismantle ossified, inflexible, and ineffective political subjectivities and structures are needed. The weaknesses of these should be taken as an opportunity to build new infrastructures from the ground up, and in that sense the right to the city movement may represent something truly historic.

Notes

1. A third read, generally associated with political liberalism, sees citizenship as flexible enough to adapt to difference with each form of difference being able to maintain its essential integrity. This read, I would argue, was operative for much of the 20th century, and it is in the wake of its collapse that the current crisis has emerged. Some would argue it is still a viable political project or that it can be rehabilitated. These are contentions with which I would disagree, but this matter is not my focus here.

2. Of course, this applies only to legal residents. There is an equally important and related discussion to have regarding "right to the city" and undocumented residents. See Varsanyi (2006).

3. Of course, they may become members of new polities in new neighborhoods (or they may not). However, this does not speak to the issue of the original physical and political displacement, nor does it in any way justify it.

References

Anderson, B. (1991). *Imagined Communities: Reflections on the Origin and Spread of Nationalism.* New York: Verso.

Appadurai, A. (2006). *Fear of Small Numbers: An Essay on the Geography of Anger.* Duke University Press.

Argersinger, J. A. E. (2010). "Contested Visions of American Democracy: Citizenship, Public Housing, and the International Arena." *Journal of Urban History*, 36(6), 792-813.

Baviskar, A. (2011). "Cows, Cars and Cycle-rickshaws: Bourgeois Environmentalism and the Battle for Delhi's Streets." In A. Baviskar and R. Ray (Eds.), *Elite and Everyman: The Cultural Politics of the Indian Middle Classes.* Routledge India.

Bellamy, R. (2008). *Citizenship: A Very Short Introduction.* New York: Oxford University Press.

Briggs, X. de S. (2008). "Maximum Feasible Misdirection: A Reply to Imbroscio." *Journal of Urban Affairs*, 30(2), 131-7.

Center for Media Justice. (2007). "As Holidays Approach, Bulldozers Descend on New Orleans Poor." Media Advisory. Retrieved May 5, 2011, from http://centerformediajustice.org/wp-content/files/SavePublicHousingKit.pdf.

Crump, J. (2002). "Deconcentration by Definition: Public Housing, Poverty, and Urban Policy." *Environment and Planning D: Society and Space*, 20, 581-96.

DeFilippis, J. (2003). *Unmaking Goliath: Community Control in the Face of Global Capital.* New York: Routledge.

Dodson, J. (2006). "Rolling the State: Government, Neoliberalism and Housing Assistance in Four Advanced Economies." *Urban Research Paper*, 7. Griffith University, Brisbane.

Foucault, M. (1991). "Governmentality." In G. Burchell, C. Gordon, and P. Miller (Eds.), *The Foucault Effect: Studies in Governmentality* (pp. 87-104). Chicago: University of Chicago Press.

Gibson, K. J. (2007). "The Relocation of the Columbia Villa Community: Views from Residents." *Journal of Planning and Education Research*, 27(5), 5-19.

Gordon, C. (1991). "Governmental Rationality: An Introduction." In G. Burchell, C. Gordon, and P. Miller (Eds.), *The Foucault Effect: Studies in Governmentality* (pp. 1-52). Chicago: University of Chicago Press.

Goetz, E. G. (2000). "The Politics of Poverty Deconcentration and Housing Demolition." *Journal of Urban Affairs*, 22(2), 157-73.

———. (2010). "Gentrification in Black and White: The Racial Impact of Public Housing Demolition in American Cities." *Urban Studies*. Advance online publication. doi:10.1177/0042098010375323.

Goetz, E. G. and K. Chapple. (2010). "You Gotta Move: Advancing the Debate on the Record of Dispersal." *Housing Policy Debate*, 20(2), 209-36.

Hackworth, J. (2005). "Progressive Activism in a Neoliberal Context: The Case of Efforts to Retain Public Housing in the United States." *Studies in Political Economy*, 75, 29-51.

Holston, J. (2001). "Urban Citizenship and Globalization." In A. J. Scott (Ed.), *Global City-Regions: Trends, Theory, Policy* (pp. 325-48). New York: Oxford University Press.

———. (2008). *Insurgent Citizenship: Disjunctions of Democracy and Modernity in Brazil.* Princeton, NJ: Princeton University Press.

———. (2009). "Dangerous Spaces of Citizenship: Gang Talk, Rights Talk and Rule of Law in Brazil." *Planning Theory*, 8(1), 12-31.

Huntington, S. (2005). *Who Are We?: The Challenges to America's National Identity.* New York: Simon and Schuster.

Imbroscio, D. (2008). "'[U]nited and Actuated by Some Common Impulse of Passion': Challenging the Dispersal Consensus in American Housing Policy Research." *Journal of Urban Affairs*, 30(2), 111-30.

Isin, E. F. (2008). "The City as the Site of the Social." In E. F. Isin (Ed.), *Recasting the Social in Citizenship* (pp. 261-80). Toronto: University of Toronto Press.

Keene, D. E., M. B. Padilla, and A. T. Geronimus. (2010). "Leaving Chicago for Iowa's 'Fields of Opportunity': Community Dispossession, Rootlessness, and the Quest for Somewhere to 'Be OK'." *Human Organization*, 69(3), 275-84.

Lalloo, K. (1998). "Citizenship and Place: Spatial Definitions of Oppression and Agency in South Africa." *Africa Today*, 45(3-4), 439-60.

Leary, V. (2000). "Citizenship, Human Rights, and Diversity." In A. C. Cairns, J. C. Courtney, P. MacKinnon, H. J. Michelmann, and D. E. Smith (Eds.), *Citizenship, Diversity, and Pluralism: Canadian and Comparative Perspectives* (pp. 247-64). Montreal: McGill-Queen's Press.

Leavitt, J., T. R. Samara, and M. Brady. (2009). "Right to the City: Social Movement and Theory." *Poverty & Race Research Action Council*, Sep/Oct. Retrieved May 5, 2011, from http://www.prrac.org/full_text.php?text_id=1238&item_id=11801&newsletter_id=107&header=Community+Organizing&kc=1.

Lipman, P. (2009). "The Cultural Politics of Mixed-income Schools and Housing: A Racialized Discourse of Displacement, Exclusion and Control." *Anthropology and Education Quarterly*, 40(3), 215-36.

Mamdani, M. (1996). *Citizen and Subject: Contemporary Africa and the Legacy of Late Colonialism.* Princeton, NJ: Princeton University Press.

Manzo, L. C., R. G. Kleit, and D. Couch. (2008). "'Moving Three Times Is Like Having Your House on Fire Once': The Experience of Place and Impending Displacement among Public Housing Residents." *Urban Studies*, 45(9), 1855-78.

Marx, A. (1998). *Making Race and Nation: A Comparison of the United States, South Africa and Brazil.* New York: Cambridge University Press.

O'Connor, A. (2001). *Poverty Knowledge: Social Science, Social Policy, and the Poor in Twentieth Century U.S. History.* Princeton, NJ: Princeton University Press.

Peck, J., and A. Tickell. (2002). "Neoliberalizing Space." *Antipode*, 34(3), 380-404.

Popkin, S. J., D. K. Levy, and L. Buron. (2009). "Has HOPE VI Transformed Residents' Lives? New Evidence from the HOPE VI Panel Study." *Housing Studies*, 24(4), 477-502.

Purcell, M. (2002). "Excavating Lefebvre: The Right to the City and Its Urban Politics of the Inhabitant." *Geojournal*, 58(2-3), 99-108.

_____. (2008). *Recapturing Democracy: Neoliberalism and the Struggle for Alternative Urban Futures.* New York: Routledge.

Rose, N. (2000). "Community, Citizenship, and the Third Way." *American Behavioral Scientist*, 43(9), 1395-411.

Roy, A. (2009). "Civic Governmentality: The Politics of Inclusion in Beirut and Mumbai." *Antipode*, 41(1), 159-79.

Right to the City Alliance (RTTCA). (2010). *We Call These Projects Home: Solving the Housing Crisis from the Ground Up.* Retrieved July 2010 from http://www.righttothecity.org/we-call-these-projects-home.html.

Right to the City—New York City. (2009). *Policy Platform 2009.* Retrieved May 5, 2011, from http://urbanjustice.org/pdf/publications/RTTC_16july09.pdf.

Samara, T. R. (2007a). "Development, Social Justice and Global Governance: Challenges to Implementing Restorative Justice and Criminal Justice Reform in South Africa." *Acta Juridica*, 2007, 113-33.

_____. (2007b, Jan). "Right to the City: Notes From the Inaugural Convening." Los Angeles, CA: Strategic Actions for a Just Economy.

_____. (2011). "Transnational Urban Governance and the Mega-Event: A Comparative Study of Cape Town, New Delhi and Shanghai." *China Urban Studies*, 3, 289-303.

Sassen, S. (2001). *The Global City.* Princeton, NJ: Princeton University Press.

_____. (2002). "The Repositioning of Citizenship: Emergent Subjects and Spaces for Politics." *Berkeley Journal of Sociology*, 46, 4-25.

_____. (2006). *Territory, Authority, Rights: From Medieval to Global Assemblages.* Princeton, NJ: Princeton University Press.

Self, R. O. (2003). *American Babylon: Race and the Struggle for Postwar Oakland.* Princeton, NJ: Princeton University Press.

Smith, M. P., and L. E. Guarnizo. (2009). "Global Mobility, Shifting Borders and Urban Citizenship." *Tijdschrift voor Economische en Sociale Geografie,* 100(5), 610-22.

Somers, M. R. (2008). *Genealogies of Citizenship: Markets, Statelessness, and the Right to Have Rights.* Cambridge, UK: Cambridge University Press.

Steinberg, S. (2009). "The Myth of Concentrated Poverty." In C. Hartman and G. D. Squires (Eds.), *The Integration Debate: Competing Futures for American Cities* (pp. 213-28). New York: Routledge.

————. (2011, Jan 13). "Poor Reason: Culture Still Doesn't Explain Poverty." *Boston Review.* Retrieved May 5, 2011, from http://www.bostonreview.net/BR36.1/steinberg.php.

Tides Foundation. (2007). *The Right to the City: Reclaiming Our Urban Centers, Reframing Human Rights, and Redefining Citizenship: A Conversation Between Donor Activist Connie Cagampang Heller and Gihan Perera of the Miami Workers Center.* Retrieved May 5, 2011, from http://www.tides.org/fileadmin/user/pdf/TheRightToTheCity.pdf.

United Nations Human Rights Council. (2009, Feb 4). "Report of the Special Rapporteur on Adequate Housing as a Component of the Right to an Adequate Standard of Living, and on the Right to Non-discrimination in this Context, Raquel Rolnik." A/HRC/10/7. Retrieved May 5, 2011, from http://www.unhcr.org/refworld/docid/49a54f4a2.html.

Varsanyi, M. W. (2006). "Interrogating 'Urban Citizenship' *vis-à-vis* Undocumented Migration." *Citizenship Studies,* 10(2), 229-49.

Wacquant, L. (1996). "The Rise of Advanced Marginality: Notes on its Nature and Implications." *Acta Sociologica,* 39(2), 121-39.

Williams, R. Y. (2005). *The Politics of Public Housing.* New York: Oxford University Press.

Youth Media Council. (2008). *Displacing the Dream: A Report on Bay Area Newspaper Coverage of Development and Gentrification.* Oakland, CA: *Author.* Retrieved May 5, 2011, from centerformediajustice.org/download/40/.

4

Urban Citizenship in New York, Paris, and Barcelona: Immigrant Organizations and the Right to Inhabit the City

Ernesto Castañeda

Building on ethno-surveys and multi-sited ethnographic fieldwork conducted in New York, Paris, and Barcelona, this chapter discusses immigrant representation, ethnic organizations, urban citizenship rights, and minority political participation in these cities. It describes how organizations and institutions differently mediate immigrant political incorporation, social integration,[1] and structural assimilation given the different social, political, and institutional contexts of each city. Structural assimilation is defined by Milton Gordon as the moment when immigrant groups enter "fully into the societal network of [mainstream and powerful] groups and institutions" (Gordon, 1964, cited in Jiménez, 2010, p. 71). This would include the opportunity for upward social mobility, the lack of residential segregation, intermarriage, and the potential for participation in politics and public activities as equals (Gordon, 1964). The prospect of structural assimilation is important to understand the immigrants' objective and subjective belonging to the cities where they live. For undocumented immigrants, establishing their collective right to inhabit a new city first and foremost is crucial in opening the door for a further "right to the city," which entails the ability to fully participate and transform the cities where they live to the benefit of its inhabitants over that of capital (Lefebvre, 1968). Different ideas of what constitute legitimate political and cultural organizations provide distinct avenues to participate politically in urban life.

After comparing organizational fields in different countries, I find that while most immigrants are not members of neighborhood, city-wide, national, ethnic, or hometown associations, the mere possibility of existence and survival of these organizations explains much about the context of immigration and the relationship that individuals have with the state. Immigrant associations help newcomers integrate through language, vocational and cultural workshops, and legal advice. They also help with practical issues of labor, food, housing, education, and self-esteem. But immigrant and minority organizations also play a key role in mobilizing dispersed immigrants with common origins and cultural backgrounds to make claims upon the state by engaging in contentious politics in the public arena or by lobbying and meeting with politicians and city officials at private events. Associations can be crucial in channeling immigrant discontent by voicing immigrant needs, making collective political claims, combining efforts, and dissipating discontent and alienation—even when they fail to obtain all of their explicit demands (Castañeda, 2010).

Despite the commonly observed organizational shortcomings, budgetary dire straits, internal divisions, inter-organizational competition, and the rise and disappearance of ethnic associations, the mere existence of these organizations is an indicator of the degree of political voice of minorities and immigrants in a city regardless of formal citizenship. Associations can only thrive in a welcoming cultural and institutional environment (thus, their partly derivative nature), but once associations are taken seriously by city governments, they have important effects that cannot be reduced to individual actions. Minority associations, then, are socially productive actors with emergent properties (McQuarrie and Marwell, 2009).

Institutional Fields and Contexts of Reception

Organizations' actions and campaigns matter, but the legal and cultural frameworks that regulate them may matter even more since organizations are interested in achieving legitimacy by looking like other organizations in their field (DiMaggio and Powell, 1983; McQuarrie and Marwell, 2009; Powell and DiMaggio, 1991). Immigrant organizations are rendered more or less legitimate by types of citizenship regimes, legal and bureaucratic precedents and procedures, official immigration histories, and mythologies. While these organizational fields are very dense in New York and Barcelona where undocumented immigrants can sometimes act as *de facto* urban citizens, this does not happen so easily in Paris where new ethnic organizations are viewed as threatening and as antithetical to the French republican model of theoretical ontological individual equality and homogeneity (Bowen, 2007). More surprisingly, the weakness of ethnic associations in the Parisian metropolitan area ends up reducing the right to the city of descendants of immigrants, who, despite being legal French citizens, suffer high levels of discrimination, racial profiling, and unemployment (Silberman, Alba, and Fournier, 2007).[2] The comparison between these cities shows that the right to the city goes beyond legal citizenship binaries. A collective right to the city is more empowering and self-fulfilling than an individualized, neo-liberal matching of resident and neighborhood based on income and cultural taste, or the price of real estate, restaurant menus, and entertainment venues.[3]

In the formation of local organizational fields, historical precedence, international emulation, and diffusion matter (Longhofer and Schofer, 2010; McAdam, Tarrow, and Tilly, 2001; Tilly, 1984). The model and watershed moment for ethnic organizations is the American civil rights movement. In the United States the civil rights movement was to a certain degree successfully institutionalized into law, collective memory, and social and political organizations. The US has historically emphasized race in talking about social differences, while historically class and religious differences have been more salient in France and Spain (Fassin and Fassin, 2006). Immigrants thus move into different contexts of reception with different possible avenues for political voice.

Ethnic and immigrant organizations play key roles by providing personal and institutional intermediaries, leaders, spokespeople, and even token minorities and successful immigrant stories for public consumption, while also tackling some of the many thorny issues faced by this underpaid and vulnerable population. Following a long tradition of urban ethnic politics formerly controlled by Irish, Italians, and others, Latino immigrant elites in New York have employed ethnic politics and local patron-client relations. Puerto Ricans and Dominicans have done so successfully in New York (Marwell, 2004; 2007) and Mexicans are increasingly trying to do so (Dávila, 2004; R. C. Smith, 2006). French citizens of color have taken note of the American context (often idealizing it) and have tried to borrow many of the organizational forms of American ethnic politics; yet, lacking a similarly deep institutional supporting infrastructure, they are perceived by outsiders in a very different manner. While the NAACP, the National

Council of La Raza, the American Civil Liberties Union, Congressional Caucuses, and other organizations may receive some federal, state, and local funds or tax breaks—often in combination with private donations—they are often seen by their members and by third parties as independent. In contrast, equivalent organizations created or supported by the French state are seen as direct agents of the state; they are to be distrusted as neutral bodies. The government of Barcelona, even though it lacks an experience parallel to that of New York, has been successful to a great degree in implementing policies that give economic support for immigrant clubs. These official clubs have allowed immigrant participants to shape organizational activities and programs in a way that involves their communities and makes them feel like they have a right and place in the city.

McQuarrie and Marwell (2009) call for a more careful look at organizations when studying urban issues. They write:

> [O]rganizations look and act the way they do because of the pressure for conformity to or legitimacy in a wider institutional field. [...] Considering the dynamics of the communities and cities in which organizations are situated could yield positive contributions to organizational theory and urban sociology (pp. 259-60).

It is indeed fruitful to focus upon immigrant and transnational organizations *per se*, and this chapter adds to this research agenda.

Data and Methodology

This chapter raises an important caveat for migration scholars: when looking at the immigrant experience only through the statements of the spokesmen and leaders of community based organizations (CBOs), consular offices, non-governmental associations (NGOs), or hometown associations (HTAs), one cannot comprehend the perils and daily life experiences of regular immigrants in the way that one can by conducting in-depth interviews or engaging in non-participant observation with immigrants themselves (whether or not they engage in collective action or participate as members of immigrant associations). Unfortunately, when looking for "representative immigrants" to interview, journalists and new researchers of immigration are often tempted to contact immigrant associations and those non-governmental organizations whose explicit purpose is to support or oppose immigration. By doing this, one gets a polarized and politicized perspective while missing much of the action in the middle. This is the case because, as with the general population, most people are not active members of voluntary organizations. This, however, does not mean that the existence—or lack thereof—of ethnic associations is irrelevant to the right to the city and general life chances of immigrants and minorities.

This chapter proposes that one should simultaneously study both immigrant organizations and relatively isolated immigrants in order to better assess the effects and limitations that immigrant organizations have on polity and community. The chapter thus draws on ethno-surveys, in-depth interviews, and non-participant (or direct observation) conducted between 2003 and 2010 in the cities of New York, Paris, and Barcelona, as well as in three migrant-sending countries: Mexico, Algeria, and Morocco (Castañeda, 2010). The samples are purposive, seeking to include individuals who differ along lines of occupation, neighborhood, gender, class, race, generation, and political orientation. Many of the immigrants in the sample are first generation economic migrants working low skilled jobs. To get at processes of racialization and systematic exclusion, the samples in New York, Paris, and Barcelona also include second- and third-generation immigrants. To control for class I have also surveyed professional, highly skilled Mexican migrants living in the United States and Europe. The samples were not randomly generated from a general directory or a census of minorities, since the latter does not exist in the Parisian case.[4] The samples used are small, and thus, their generalizability is limited. The percentages shown in the tables below should not be taken as precise or absolute. Yet the trends are robust across cities and are similarly reported from both the sending and receiving communities. The trends discovered follow a social-class logic; that is, the higher the education level, the higher the participation in civil life and civil associations and politics in general. This coincides with traditional findings of voting and political behavior (Verba and Nie, 1972; Wolfinger and Rosentone, 1980, cited in Jones-Correa, 1998, p. 53).

Table 1. Demographic Characteristics of Purposive Samples Surveyed

	Receiving Cities			Mexican Professionals Living Abroad			Sending Countries			Total
Location	Paris	Barc	NYC	USA	Spain	France	Algeria	Morocco	Mexico	
Population	N Afr	N Afr	Latinos	Mx Pro	Mx Pro	Mx Pro	Algeria	Morocco	Mexico	
n	65	33	373	27	18	12	63	9	49	**457**
Av Age	32	30	32	36	34	34	29	38.2	45.8	**35**
Men	75%	85%	49%	66.7%	72.2%	41.7%	71%	100%	90%	**72%**
Women	25%	15%	51%	33.3%	27.8%	58.3%	29%	0%	10%	**28%**

The ethno-survey results are triangulated and calibrated with data collected through participant observation, expert interviews, informal and in-depth interviews (not included in these sample numbers), as well as from secondary sources, census data, and survey results from large random samples (when existent). Relatively small sample sizes and a qualitative methodology allow for a closer inspection of the cases (Small, 2009) and for the observation of processes and mechanisms in different contexts leading to fruitful comparisons (Tilly and Tarrow, 2007).

Comparative Field Sites and the Derivative Salience of Immigrant Associations

Despite the French reluctance to recognize communitarian organizations (Bowen, 2007), when I arrived in France and I said that I wanted to interview immigrants, many people recommended that I contact immigrant associations: "How else would you find immigrants to interview?" They felt this would be the only way to find and interview immigrants. I decided against this approach since, while I am familiar with many Mexican associations in New York, I know that the average Mexican immigrant worker is not an active member of any of them. I suspected that in France the percentage would be even lower. Desiring to avoid sampling on the dependent variable, I talked to typical immigrants, whether or not they were politically organized or belonged to a hometown association or other transnational organization (see Table 2).

I conducted fieldwork for seven years in New York with Mexican immigrants and transnational organizations of all types including undocumented migrants, legal residents, American citizens, later-generation Mexican Americans, international students, and professionals. As a direct observer, I became familiar with the leaders and agendas of many migrant organizations, and I regularly attended their events. Yet I focused purposely on those immigrants who were not part of any of these organizations, since they constituted a numerical majority of immigrants and often their concerns and attitudes were very different from those expressed in public by those who are identified as community leaders. Political views and participation vary widely across class and generation. Drawing from in-depth interviews in California and Kansas, Jiménez (2010) writes that, "Later-generation Mexican Americans are not likely to spearhead a demonstration or a social movement advocating for immigrant rights. If we look at Mexican Americans' engagement only in the most visible forms of 'ethnic action'— protest politics, organizational involvement, and participation in an ethnic enclave—we miss the important ways that they create unity with and division from Mexican immigrants in daily life" (2010, p. 248). This is not unique to the United States.

When I arrived in Paris in 2007 to conduct fieldwork for a year, some local researchers advised me to contact immigrant associations in order to get in touch with this "hard to reach population." This answer is indicative of a larger social phenomenon across field sites: oftentimes (though not always) a newcomer may approach an organization for lack of personal familiarity with a certain ethnic group or a perceived social distance that may make unscripted or informal interactions with members of this group in public places a rare occurrence. It is in these contexts where immigrant *porte-paroles*, or spokespeople, gain more salience and can act as important cultural brokers. Not surprisingly, in Paris, immigrants experience strong spatial, symbolic, and social boundaries (Castañeda, forthcoming; Lamont, 2000; Lamont and Molnar, 2002), thus explaining the temptation to rely on local associations. Unfortunately there are few national or city-wide organizations representing migrants, and migrant needs vary across class and ethnic lines. The group-specific associations are often seen as illegitimate by the government and the dominant class since they go against French republican ideology (Bowen, 2007).

While doing fieldwork in Barcelona, I had no difficulty interacting and talking to immigrants in public places. Inside community centers one could hardly differentiate the immigrant component and the official governmental policies and funding sources that supported these initiatives of intercultural dialogue and active integration. The link between governmental funding in Barcelona is much more transparent than in New York and less paternalistic and nationalistic than in Paris. Writing in reference to Barcelona, Morales and Jorba (2010) state:

> Other than specific actions that must be undertaken for assuring the adequate initial settlement of newcomers to the city, migrants' integration is viewed as a 'natural' process that will emerge from migrants' equal access to all social welfare and services provided by the city, which are based on the same principles and requirements [as] for pre-existing residents (p. 272).

The goal is to have immigrants on the same playing field as locals; accordingly, immigrants tend to feel at home in and have rights in Barcelona. The Catalan state likes to connect with the immigrant communities through individuals and cultural collectives. There are important organizations in Barcelona which speak, for example, in favor of and in the name of Muslims whenever their community is attacked or addressed. Media consult them and cite their views. The print media take these leaders seriously and offer them a space in the Iberian public sphere, especially when it concerns issues touching on Islam in Spain. One of these often cited spokespeople is Mohammed Halhoul of the *Consejo Islámico Cultural de Catalunya* or Cultural Islamic Council of Catalonia.[5] The Catalonian organization is similar to, but probably a more organic and "real" organization than, the *Conseil Français du Culte Musulman* (CFCM) or the French Council of Muslim Religion, an official body created by the French government in 2003 to create a "French secular Islam." The CFCM is seen by average Muslim immigrants from

North Africa as not representing them (Strieff, 2006). This was true in my sample, even though most people were non-strict Muslims who were rather secular in the public sphere and who were very acculturated to French mores and values.

When I actually asked immigrants and their families if they were part of an association (club, HTA, or cultural organization) most respondents answered in the negative. The Moroccan sample had the highest participation rate, with most of the membership belonging to trade associations of vendors rather than political organizations. Class also plays a role in participation in political, social, and cultural organizations. Thus the sample of Mexican professionals abroad had the largest number of respondents participating in civil society associations.

Table 2. Participation in Civil Society Associations (in percentages)

	Paris	Barcelona	New York	Algeria	Morocco	Mx Pro
Yes	9	6	23	22	56	58
No	88	91	69	73	44	42
n a	3	3	8	5	0	0
Total	100	100	100	100	100	100

Given the generally small participation of working class immigrants (and natives) in civil associations it would have been problematic to have interviewed only members of associations. Furthermore, if, when studying overall immigrant political participation, I had only concentrated on politicized and organized immigrants, I would have been "selecting on the dependent variable" (Portes, Guarnizo, and Landolt, 1999). Yet it would be wrong to fully dismiss immigrant organizations as secondary since they reflect much of the institutional environment into which immigrants arrive. When such organizations manage to survive they can be socially productive and *performative* when calling for the right to the city of everyone regardless of their place of birth. Thus, the interesting sociological paradox: while most immigrants are NOT members of ethnic, civil, or social organizations, the existence, health, resources, and respect that these organizations have in a city can be taken as an indicator of the rights and freedoms that immigrants are allowed to have despite nationality, religion, or legal status.

Immigrant Organizations, Associations Ethniques, Colectivos Migrantes

Not all lobbies and ethnic associations are treated the same way by host governments. Local, national, and international politics affect the way the host state deals with particular groups. In the United States, Cuban or Jewish organizations carry different political weight than, for example, Salvadorian or Guatemalan organizations (Menjívar, 2006). The French state is suspicious of Algerian associations given the historical role of anti-colonial associations in Paris, most notoriously the Algerian nationalist group *Etoile Nord Africaine* founded by Messali Hadj in Paris in 1926, which acted as the forerunner of Algerian independentist groups like the Algerian National Liberation Front (Rosenberg, 2006). The further criminalization of Islam in the eyes of the West after the Iranian revolution (Deltombe, 2005), combined with the strong secular and even anti-religious *habitus* of many French politicians (Kuru, 2008), takes away much legitimacy from Muslim associations that are independent of the French state. To control and co-opt movements, the French government has tried in recent years to create a version of Islam that is more compatible with French traditions (Strieff, 2006). These efforts have been top-down and rather unsuccessful in connecting with the average French Muslim citizen. Contradictorily, the French government and society have been very supportive of Kabyle and Berber cultural and political organizations, which they see as distinct from the Arab ones. The Berbers, or *Imazighen*, as they prefer to be called, were the main inhabitants of North Africa before the Arab invasion of the seventh century. Cultural and political differences still exist between these groups, especially in Algeria. Unlike Arab or Muslim associations, Kabyle groups have been quite active in the Parisian region since they started migrating there at the beginning of the twentieth century. The French state has seen Kabyles as being closer to Europeans and Christianity and as a population through which to democratize North Africa (Mahé, 2006).

The Imazighen participate more in organizations. The integration of many of them into well-paying jobs in their host society allows them more time and resources to organize. They make claims to have their language and culture recognized, but not as much *vis-à-vis* their host societies as they do in relation to what they see as a historical and continuous "Arab" cultural colonization, exacerbated by a bloody confrontation with Algerian forces in the Black Spring of 2001 (Mahé, 2006).[6]

With the exception of the Kabyles, most first generation immigrants from the Maghreb are not organized socially, politically, or even religiously. While they may feel part of the *umma*, or global Muslim community, they do not go regularly to a Mosque, and most of them prefer to confine their religious activities to the private space of the household and around traditional familial practices, such as fasting during Ramadan. One informant told me that it is only possible to follow the tradition of Ramadan when done within a community, since someone—commonly a wife, sister, or mother—is needed to prepare the rich food that will be eaten by working and/or observing men in order to recover their strength after the sun sets. Thus most first generation working immigrants who are single or came alone rarely follow Ramadan. This further alienates them from each other; in their countries of origin, following this collective tradition had the effect of making the community visible.

Given the French republican normative and legal system that discourages the formation of associations or clubs around common nationality or religion,[7] Muslim Maghrebis lack a uniform political voice. There is dire misrepresentation of minorities within government and even in the slots for electoral posts (Geisser and Soum, 2008). Some token figures have been appointed by President Sarkozy, but French minorities do not feel represented by them at all (personal interview with Eros Sana, May 28, 2009). In the same sense the French government has established an official body in the Paris Mosque and a Muslim Council, but these are official organs that have very little contact with immigrants. The same is said about the well funded and visible organization "SOS Racisme," which many criticize as an arm of the Socialist Party that lacks any contacts on the ground and is especially disconnected from youth of Maghrebi origin (L'Information Citoyenne, 2006).

In Barcelona, immigrants who fail to learn Catalonia's language and history are sometimes seen as a cultural and political threat to the aspirations of many for fuller autonomy from Spain. Catalan nationalists sometimes see immigrants who embrace the Spanish language, but not Catalan, as a way in which their claim to be a distinct nation gets diluted. Thus efforts are made to teach Catalan language, culture, and history to the newcomers as a way to keep Catalonia alive. Despite local nationalism and certain xenophobic comments by locals, the Moroccan immigrants interviewed feel at home in Barcelona and make efforts to learn Spanish and Catalan. They have created new lives in Barcelona that often surpass the struggles they faced in their place of birth. As a Mexican interviewee in the US said, "Your country is where you succeed." This also represents the view of many Moroccans in Barcelona.

"Community"

To the question, "Do you feel part of a *community*?" respondents in the countries of arrival answered as shown in Table 3.

Table 3. Feelings of Belonging to a Community (in percentages)

	New York	Barcelona	Paris
Yes	59	64	18
No	32	9	79
n a	9	27	3
Total	100	100	100

In my sample, levels of participation often reflect cultural and institutional differences and not just participation in associations. One way to get at this is to further qualify a quantitative comparison by looking at the different and contextual meanings of the words "community," "*communauté*," and "*comunidad*" in New York, Paris, and Barcelona metropolitan areas respectively. Given the long history of the French nation-making project (E. J. Weber, 1976), in France "community" is a dirty word and "*communautariste*" is a put-down (Bowen, 2007; Wacquant, 2008). Not surprisingly immigrants in France report the lowest levels of communitarianism while the US has relatively high levels. Alexis de Tocqueville would not be surprised with these well-established differences in associational life (Tocqueville, 1969). In New York many respondents identified with a community, whether a neighborhood, their national or ethnic group, or the Latino or Hispanic pan-ethnicity. "New Yorker" and "American" were also salient identities. The percentage is even higher for Moroccans in Spain. While many reported feeling part of the *umma*, a transnational Muslim community, many also reported feeling part of a Spanish, Catalan, or cosmopolitan community. Clearly what the immigrants understood by the question depends on the context of reception and on their pre- and post-migration conceptions of community. For example, by not reporting participation in ethnic associations, French residents of immigrant origin are actively showing their normative incorporation into France's dominant culture. This accommodation is at strong odds with the frequently familistic and collectivistic North African *habitus*. This rejection of Muslim or North African associations further reduces the social capital of immigrants in France, thus hindering, for example, the incorporation and political participation of unemployed citizens of foreign origin.

The meaning of community differs widely in these three cities. As Patricia Hill Collins (2010) notes, the term "community" can be used politically under various guises. The idea of community often assumes homogeneity but "the city is where difference lives" (Mitchell, 2003, p. 18), so a real urban community should necessarily be heterogeneous. Yet for some it means a minority community; for others it means an older demographic and conservative politics; for others it has religious connotations. Thus, it is the case that "community" entails the definitional exclusion of others who are not part of it (e.g., immigrants).[8] Thus immigrants are expected to assimilate or show that they are an important part of spatial multiethnic communities. They may have to self-organize to show what Tilly calls their WUNC—worth, unity, numbers, and commitment—as a categorical group in order to be taken seriously by local politicians and to be given a say in policy making (Jones-Correa, 1998; Tilly, 2004).

Do ethnic organizations and coalitions actually change contemporary modes of urban authority? While immigrant associations are celebrated as part of the cultural richness of New York, the real political power of most of them is merely symbolic. There is a strong inertia benefitting the political *status quo* that favors well-established older immigrant groups: Jews, Irish, and Italians (Jones-Correa, 1998). Elites from the dominant group often do not welcome candidates from a new immigrant group until the demographic reality forces them to do so (Dávila, 2004). Thus inter-ethnic alliances at the institutional-political level are few beyond those on Election Day.

At the social movement level there are a few temporal exemptions. The Immigrants' Rights Coalition, the committee organizing the May 1st marches, and associations like Make the Road have tried to create—with some success—pan-Latino alliances, coalitions with some African American community leaders around social policies, and mobilizations with Asian and Arab Americans around immigrant rights. Human rights groups, labor unions, and Catholic and Protestant organizations have also been instrumental in mobilizing for immigrant rights and creating broader coalitions in these three cities.

The Barcelonan government often promotes its network of voluntary associations and partnerships with the city as a successful model to integrate immigrants. Although imperfect, the system has indeed been successful. However, perceived cultural differences and government policies that treat immigrant groups in a differential manner—implicitly favoring Latin American immigration (Rius Sant, 2007)—often divide collectives of Latinos and North Africans. And while there are Latin American coalitions, partnerships, and pan-ethnic parades like *La Fiesta de la Hispanidad* on October 12 (Columbus Day), the bulk of the associations are divided by national origin, and then by particular region, profession, etc. (Morales and Jorba, 2010).

The tendency in Paris is for associations to form around geographical areas (Maghreb, Sub-Saharan Africa, Latin America, North America, etc.), but the national differences and politics make these coalitions unstable and thus often unsuccessful in lobbying as a block. In the 1980s the *beur* movement had some provisional successes in bringing positive attention to the children of North African immigrants (Barsali, Freland, and Vincent, 2003). Currently some of the most interesting, and potentially most influential, groups are: *Les Indigènes de la République*, characterized by their smart manifesto against colonialism and the disenfranchisement of immigrants from the former colonies; *Siècle 21*, a group of successful professionals of color extolling the virtues of diversity and calling for affirmative-action-type programs in elite schools, top government posts, and big companies for educated minorities; and *Le Conseil Représentatif des Associations Noires de France* (CRAN), which is an association that asks for the political representation of French Blacks following both an American civil rights movement type of discourse and a French republican integrationist one. They often compare themselves to the NAACP, yet its President often talks against "communitarism" (Lozes, 2011)! Many see CRAN as a platform by which its leaders gain attention, are co-opted, and gain government positions. This was what happened with the leaders coming from the *beur* movement, *SOS Racisme* (Malik, 1990), and others. So while a couple of spokespeople get jobs in the system, their supposed constituencies see no real empowerment.

Discrimination, Exclusion, and Contentious Politics

While racial profiling happens in the streets and subways in New York City, especially since the rise of the "law and order" ideology (Wacquant, 2008; 2010),[9] Maghrebis in France report the highest degree of police harassment.[10] When I asked Maghrebis in Paris if they have had any problems with the police or the judicial system in general, the majority of them answered in the negative. But when I asked if they had been stopped and searched by the police for no apparent reason, the majority responded in the affirmative. Many of them even justified this by saying that they were used to these searches or that they thought the searches were normal. This is an example of how widespread and normalized the practice is, and it translates into an underreporting of police abuse in France. The surveys provide many other indicators of widespread discrimination, racism, and police harassment against "Arabs" in France. A study published in 2009 indicates that at the Châtelet train and subway station in Paris, blacks were 11.5 times more likely than whites to be stopped; and Arabs were 14.8 more times more likely to be stopped simply for wearing clothing associated with youth culture (Goris, Jobard, and Lévy, 2009).

Below, in Table 4, are answers to the question "Have you ever been unjustly stopped by the police?" from my surveys samples.

Table 4. *Racial Profiling* *(in percentages)*

	New York	Barcelona	Paris
Yes	13	33	48
No	77	58	49
n a	10	9	3
Total	100	100	100

The streets and subway stations in Barcelona (and especially Madrid) have seen a rise in racial profiling in recent years; Maghrebis and Latinos may be stopped and asked for documentation just because of their phenotype. This is done with the intention to deport the undocumented. The media and the larger and most vocal immigrant organizations have criticized this profiling. While the purpose of these laws is to target only the undocumented, racial profiling has the effect of making whole categorically defined groups feel like they do not belong to a city.

A touchy event amongst the Mexican professional community living in Spain has been the case of engineering doctoral student Alejandro Ordaz Moreno. He was the victim of mistaken identity in Seville in 2008. While coming home from a bar on a weekend night, two policemen dressed as civilians tried to arrest him; he thought they were criminals trying to kidnap him. He defended himself by retaliating and allegedly took a weapon from one of the agents who finally subdued him and charged him with attacking the officers. The professional Mexican community in Spain, including the diplomatic delegation,[11] interpreted the event as a result of the racialization of Mexicans and was very active in advocating for the student. Such an assault on persons of their educational and class standing added to the dissatisfaction of some Mexicans working in Spain, especially since they had expected to encounter racial and cultural similarities.

Table 5. Participation in Contentious Politics (in percentages)

	New York	Barcelona	Paris
Yes	20	9	28
No	71	91	68
n a	9	0	4
Total	100	100	100

In New York the participation in public protests (Table 5) refers to the marches of May 1, 2006, and marches in subsequent years in favor of immigrant rights. The most active individuals also have marched in favor of or against the war in Afghanistan and other issues important for New York activists. The French immigrant second generation gained much attention after the riots in 2005. These riots reflect their lack of political representation in government and the lack of avenues for political voice. The reported engagement of Parisian Maghrebis in contentious politics is relatively high in relation to their counterparts in Barcelona or New York, but it is still relatively low given the high level of political contention typical in France (Bréchon and Tchernia, 2009). Furthermore, much of their reported participation in contentious politics entails transnational participation in pro-democracy and minority rights movements in Morocco and Algeria, as well as in marches in France against the wars in Iraq, Afghanistan, and the situation in Palestine. Context matters, and participation in sanctioned protests is higher because of labor issues. Yet, it is not the unemployed and disenfranchised North Africans who participate in protest in Paris but the most integrated ones.

When French youth riot and attack public buildings and private property (e.g., as occurred in 2005), it should not be seen as innovative or outside of French cultural frames and repertoires of contention. Actually, they are borrowing performances from the historical repertoires of contentious politics performed by people in France (Tilly, 2008; Traugott, 1993). French history is full of small riots and rebellions against local figures of symbolic and real authority as well as against private property and members of the local aristocracy. While in the US the media commonly underline the cultural, symbolic, ideological, and political transgressions of the 1960s, the French recall and underline the riots, the occupation of the streets and universities, the construction of street barricades made with paving stones, and the resulting violent state repression, cultural incomprehension, and symbolic repression that accompanied and followed 1968.

In Barcelona, immigrants are fast to participate in anti-racist and anti-xenophobic marches along with the young people of Spanish descent who also play a leading role. New immigrants show their incorporation by fully participating in the public celebrations of sport and the local cultural celebrations (I can personally attest to their participation at the victory of Spain in the EuroCup in June 2008, at the victory of the *Real Madrid* Football Club in the same year, and in the celebration of the bicentennial of the events of 1808). In sum, immigrants also show their integration by adapting to the relevant contentious repertoires of a locality. Thus the contentious actions of the Maghrebi origin youth show their adoption of French current and historical forms of contentious political participation and collective action (Traugott, 1993). So while Maghrebis have some voice through contentious politics on certain topics (labor, benefits, the environment), they have fewer institutional avenues inside the political system to have their demands addressed than Latinos.

Latinos have not been free from attacks in the public sphere or in the streets; but, the barriers they have faced—like California's Proposition 187 passed in 1994,[12] the anti-immigrant law HR 4437[13] proposed by Republican congressman James Sensenbrenner, and Arizona's recent enactment of SB 1070[14]—have actually galvanized the Latino community and brought it together in reaction to these repressive laws targeting immigrants and their allies. The institutionalization of lobbying, letter writing, marching, and other contentious performances in the American mainstream political system have resulted in the lessening of the effects of these laws or their eventual outright defeat, often by being ruled unconstitutional in the federal judicial system.

Each legal attack against Latino immigrants results in larger calls for legalization of the undocumented and the naturalization of legal permanent residents (green card holders). Over time, the result is a larger number of Latino citizens and therefore a larger Latino voting bloc. Furthermore, new citizens can petition to legally reunify with family members left behind. This, along with natural growth and continued immigration, has resulted in Latinos becoming the largest minority in the US. While not all vote (or do so for the same party), there are enough commonalities in outlooks and interest, often cutting across class lines and national origin, to constitute them as a voting bloc, which increases their influence and political voice, if only moderately. This stands in stark contrast to the case of Muslims in France. Latino citizens have expressed their political voice by voting in the last federal elections, giving needed votes to Democratic candidates. Since Latinos participate mostly through accepted institutional channels they may be seen as docile or even "a-political" since their actions in many ways cannot be distinguished from those of African Americans, Mormons, Evangelicals, the National Rifle Association (NRA), or other advocacy groups.

The US is a federal system with diverse laws, state-society negotiations, and service and tax incentives that vary by state and locality; yet, its public sphere is largely national, so whatever happens in a state or county can affect the national imagination. A set of policies may have a demonstration effect that influences citizens and politicians in other states. The context of a whole country opens up so many more avenues and possibilities than a city can. This is more the case for the US and Spain than it is for France. The US, for example, can range from having "sanctuary cities" like New York and San Francisco, to efforts in Los Angeles to deflect migration (Light, 2006), to the extreme of Sheriff Joe Arpaio of Maricopa County in Arizona, whose theatrics include parading apprehended undocumented immigrants in orange suits and handcuffs through downtown areas and holding them in open-air prisons.

Paths and Contexts of Immigrant Political Participation and Contention

While Latinos' life chances are still behind those of whites (Massey, 2007), spaces for Latino figures to access important public roles have opened due to policy, the widespread practice of respect, the tolerance of difference, and avenues for meritocratic advancement (e.g., Bill Richardson, Alberto Gonzáles, Antonio Villaraigosa, Sonia Sotomayor). There are many Latino politicians in New York, and indeed Latinos hold public office in many places throughout the US. Mexican and other Latino leaders with national and international profiles serve as models of achievement to immigrant leaders in New York and inspire hopes for their own future inclusion. A good example of Latino political institutionalization is the National Association of Latino Elected and Appointed Officials (NALEO), which, according to its own website, "is committed to promoting the advancement and policymaking success of Latino elected and appointed officials." According to NALEO (2007), there were 3,743 Latino elected officials in 1996 and

5,129 in 2007, with 24 Latinos in the US House of Representatives in 2008 and 3 in the Senate. After Ken Salazar became Secretary of the Interior and Mel Martinez (R-FL) retired, Robert Menendez (D-NJ) became the only Latino Senator in 2009. Even if under-represented in relation to their population share, Latinos and other ethnic and racial minorities have representatives at all levels of government. This is less the case in Spain given the short period in which immigration has occurred. Yet there are cases of prominent Latino and Muslim politicians and leaders there. France lacks elected representatives of color except those coming from overseas colonies (Geisser and Soum, 2008). Thus the number of people of color in the French Senate decreased in the twentieth century after the independence of many of its colonies (Shepard, 2006).

An important difference between New York, Paris, and Barcelona is the profile that immigrant and minority organizations, business, and civic associations have in each city. New York City has a long tradition of ethnic mutual-aid societies. Some of them were founded by Jewish immigrants at the end of the nineteenth century to help these immigrants integrate into the city and to cover their basic needs. (The Jewish Board of Family and Children Services, for instance, has offices in all New York City boroughs. It is the largest social service agency in the city, and today it serves a majority non-Jewish population.) New York also has a long tradition of ethnic newspapers, radio, and television, which diffuse important information in the native tongue of the newcomers about the communities of origin as well as information about how to make the most out of the host city. Ethnic media may also act as a way to build social capital among immigrant groups by advertising events and the activities of immigrant and community organizations.

New York's relative openness to immigrants can be explained by demographics, history, and official memory. Around 40 percent of the population of New York is foreign-born, so immigrants and their children are not necessarily a numerical minority. New York has been an important entry point for new immigrants for well over a century. Part of the official history of the city and the country paints Ellis Island as a key point in the history of welcoming immigrants to the United States, even though this positive celebration dates only to the past few decades (Gabaccia, 2010; Zolberg, 2006).

For centuries Paris has also been a popular destination for immigrants. One in five French have foreign-born parents. Yet France's history of immigration is something that is not officially celebrated or generally recognized (Noiriel, 2006 [1988]). Paris has few private institutions that have specifically catered to immigrant needs. Because of the pressure to leave behind previous cultural traditions and the need to integrate immigrants to their new homeland as individuals, belonging to ethnic or nation-of origin mutual aid societies is generally discouraged.

In Paris, social capital among working class immigrants is much lower than in New York and Barcelona. French law aims at not making distinctions between types of citizens. Thus it is deemed unconstitutional to provide funds for subsets or ethnic categories of French citizens. Therefore, the type of funding that New York or Barcelona city governments now routinely give to private and public organizations that cater to immigrants is illegal in France. Sometimes Paris and its surrounding suburbs do violate this constraint by supporting immigrant and minority organizations at the local level through funds for cultural activities and festivals that, while represented as having a universal cultural value, have mainly a first- and second-generation immigrant constituency in mind (Doytcheva, 2007).

Much has been made in the last decades of the rise of "associations" in France, which are formed by and for immigrants. Yet there is a stigma when talking about them and an implicit condemnation of their aims and methods. There are important exceptions such as *SOS Racisme* (L'Information Citoyenne, 2006) and *Ni Putes Ni Soumises* (Neither Whores nor Submissive) (Amara and Zappi, 2006), organizations that have been fully co-opted by political parties and governments for electoral reasons and for public relations campaigns (Malik, 1990). These organizations have resources, media, national presence, and connections with celebrities and politicians; they use French republican and nationalistic statements in their antiracists campaigns. Immigrants and their children, however, rarely feel represented by them.

Today, Barcelona better resembles New York; ethnic organizations are able to get their own funds or to apply competitively for partial funding of their own proposed civil and cultural programs that aim both to showcase immigrant communities' food, music, dance, literature, and plastic arts to the Catalan community and to integrate immigrant communities into Catalan and Spanish cultures. Like New York, Barcelona has parades and holidays to celebrate the contributions of general and particular immigrant groups. In contrast, no high-profile member of the Sarkozy-Fillon government was present to inaugurate the new immigration museum in Paris, which is situated in a building that used to house a museum displaying French colonies (Blandin, 2007). So in the case of Paris, it is both the hostile environment of the receiving city and the lack of cultural associations that cause immigrants to feel as though they do not have a right to the city.

Urban Citizenship: Actual Claims-making and Belonging

The standard sociological story of the formation of cities in Medieval Europe describes them as the migrant destinations of craftsmen, liberal professionals, and traveling merchants—as well as free souls, fugitive slaves, soldiers, serfs, criminals, and dispossessed peasants—where residents could live outside the control of feudal lords, kings, and religious authorities. The German phrase *Stadtluft macht frei nach Jahr und Tag* ("city air makes you free after a year and a day") originates from the legal principle in the network of Hanseatic cities, where if a person lived in the city for more than a year and one day without a lord or employer making claim on him, then that person would be free of his previous bonds (Sennett, 1994, p. 151). *Burger* or *citizen* was the word used to designate the residents of a city, those who, with their dwellings and daily economic activity, established *de facto* local residence without the permission of any external authority (M. Weber, 1958).

After the American and French revolutions and the rise and global spread of the nation-state model (Wimmer and Feinstein, 2010), cities became parts of larger national units. Urban residents had to increasingly plead before a taxing national government for permission to be legal residents, and foreign-born residents had to request to be *naturalized* as citizens of the state in question (Ngai, 2004; Weil, 2008). This arrangement between the state and its citizens has become normalized. Thus, international migrants, who are often by definition non-citizens, have to deal with consequences in many arenas—abstract political theory, imagined homogenous communities, public opinion, police and other state agents—in order to exercise their right to inhabit the city as equals. By living their daily lives in the city and interacting with family, employers, education and government bureaucrats, and service providers, immigrants and their offspring are *de facto* citizens but the reification of the nation-state often denies them this reality *de jure*.

There have been some recent changes to this linear relation between citizen and state. Cities in the European Union must accept other European citizens, and some cities even accept some "extra-communitarian" inhabitants as legal residents as soon as they register with the local police station (e.g., English or Germans in Spain). Global cities increasingly put their capital accumulation and growth needs before the interests of the nation-state within which they are geographically contained (Sassen, 2001). Cities also have the power to grant practical citizenship (e.g., New York, Barcelona), or not (e.g., Phoenix, Paris). The extent of immigrant sanctuary cities is exaggerated by both proponents and critics, yet the idea holds water comparatively and could potentially be fully realized, as it has been historically. These truly democratic policies of inclusion of all residents could be enacted top-down by enlightened technocrats or be demanded bottom-up by grassroots self-organizing, mobilization, and immigrant organizations. The right to the city should require first, the legal permission to be in a city; second, the right to enjoy public spaces and services; and third, the right of all residents to shape and change their city by their collective actions (Harvey, 2008; Lefebvre, 1968; Mitchell, 2003). This may sound utopian, but it could be possible. One way to partially realize it could be through immigrant organizations, civil groups, and NGOs.

Discussions about immigration in academia and the public sphere tend to be of two types. In the first, immigrants, especially undocumented ones, are constructed as *illegal*, antithetical to the nation-state, or a threat to national security and cultural integrity; they are framed as foreign bodies to a national society and eccentricities to the nation-state. They are people that one wishes would go back to their "natural" homes (Sayad, 2004; Weil, 2008). In the second type of discussion, immigrants are often seen as helpless victims trapped between an economic demand for their cheap labor and a political system that denies their rights. While the origins of these polar views are understandable sociologically, they hide the complexities of immigrants' everyday lives.

The label "illegal" cloaks important forms of *de facto* or everyday citizenship. Besides keeping transnational links with their communities of origin through remittances and modern channels of communication (Smith and Guarnizo, 1998; M. P. Smith, 2003), after some time in their new places of residence, immigrants become embedded in local jobs, commuting routes, kin and friendship networks, and local institutions, in addition to their transnational commitments. They are active consumers who patronize local restaurants and businesses and pay for rent, groceries, transportation, and utilities. Where possible they may participate in immigrant enclaves and start their own businesses. Thus immigrants often participate in formal or informal chambers of commerce where they get into contact with local politicians and bureaucrats and by which they exercise some political power. For example, candidates running for public office in New York, and in the cities, states, and countries of origin, often meet with immigrant business groups and community organizations to look for their support, even though some of the members and constituents of these groups cannot vote (Jones-Correa, 1998). This is also increasingly the case in Barcelona, where many politicians including presidential candidates look to gain the support of new immigrants, even when sometimes their public rhetoric is opposed to illegal immigration. The Parisian case is the opposite, despite the fact that most people of foreign origin can vote. Politicians are reluctant to address immigrants and their children as a group since this would be negatively portrayed by the media and their opponents, and it would go against the nationalistic agenda.

Political theory and legalistic approaches overemphasize legal national citizenship. Yet, an analytical view shows that citizenship may appear *de facto* even when lacking *de jure*. This does not mean that legal citizenship is unimportant, nor does it deny that those without formal citizenship are potentially more prone to abuses and deportation. Immigrants may act as *de facto* citizens by participating in the labor market, bringing up families, paying taxes, participating in religious communities, volunteering, doing civil or social work, working for government agencies, acting as labor representatives or community organizers, forming community and neighborhood associations, and speaking at public events and in the media using their native language and that of their new country. Immigrant rights movements and organizations have an explicit political agenda, and while they rarely see all their claims addressed, they still act as political interest groups and can affect policy making; they act as *de facto* citizen groups even when many of their members may be undocumented or legal residents without the right to vote. The point here is that the concept of political activity includes much more than voting.

Who can participate in political and communal activities also varies across time and space. In New York, community residents and parents of school children do not need to be citizens or legal residents to vote in school board elections or to serve on community boards (Board of Elections, 2011; Jones-Correa, 1998). There have also been calls by local organizations and politicians to introduce resolutions to allow non-citizens to vote for mayoral and local elections. These resolutions have not passed city council because they would upset the *status quo*, but they could pass in the future if there were an open resident referendum on the issue. Similarly, Jordi Hereu, the Mayor of Barcelona, has called for Moroccan immigrants to be allowed to vote in municipal elections (if the Moroccan government reciprocates). "In the citizenship-building process, as well as all the social aspects, it is also necessary to work on political rights, so everyone can express themselves in the municipal elections," said the mayor during an official visit to Morocco (Ajuntament de Barcelona, 2009). Paris, in contrast, requires citizenship or residency papers even for private sector transactions such as renting an apartment or signing a cell phone contract.

In New York, landlords prefer Mexican renters because they pay the rent on time, and due to their undocumented status, they neither cause trouble nor demand too much. Furthermore, they often show a "do-it-yourself" attitude when it comes to apartment repairs and dealing with emergencies (Fuentes, 2007; Thompson, 2007). Through their formal and informal economic activity and their own labor to fix up housing in bad condition, immigrant groups have revitalized whole neighborhoods that were in economic decline, many of which have been subsequently gentrified by urban planners and the middle classes. This has been the case in El Raval and downtown Barcelona (Qu and Spaans, 2009; Serra del Pozo, 2006), neighborhoods throughout New York like the Lower East Side (Zukin, 2010), and Eastern Paris (Pinçon and Pinçon-Charlot, 2004; 2009). Immigrants move to dangerous and decaying neighborhoods because of their affordability. By exercising their right to the city, they change these neighborhoods. Immigrants are often precursors to gentrification by making neighborhoods safer. By opening restaurants and stores they also make these areas more appealing to middle class people looking for affordable places to move. The paradox is that as a result of improving the living conditions and cultural and economic offerings of urban areas, immigrants are often displaced involuntarily because of increasing prices and pressures brought about by gentrification. So while immigrants greatly shape the city and make areas more livable, the ultimate benefits are often enjoyed by others who have a legal right to the city, access to highly paid jobs, and some leisure time to consume the new and increasingly expensive and exclusive services.

Conclusion

Dense associational fields can be seen as indicators of the degree of immigrants' "right to the city." While not all immigrants are part of immigrant associations because of fear or a lack of time, interest, or resources, the health and high-profile of immigrant rights organizations can act as a proxy for the level of tolerance that cities have towards immigrants. The existence of certified and tolerated immigrant and pro-immigrant human rights organizations creates discursive fields and forums to propose a right to the city for minorities and immigrants—despite issues of national citizenship—and thus for everyone. Inclusive institutional discourses reflect the *de facto* urban citizenship that immigrants have in the cities where they live, work, and conduct family and economic activities, and through which they thus contribute to and constitute an integral part of their communities. National governments should recognize what is a *fait accompli* and provide avenues for legal citizenship that further help to incorporate immigrants into the communities of which they are already part.

Different state-society relationships, citizenship ideological models, and civil society and institutional arrangements have differential effects for the larger minority groups in these three cities (Castañeda, 2010). Each city has something to learn from the other—both things to improve as well as things to celebrate. The final table (Table 6), summarizes five key comparisons made in this chapter.

Table 6. Relative Positions of Cities across Key Dimensions

	New York	Paris	Barcelona
Citizenship Ideology	Multicultural	*Républicain*	Multicultural
How Civil Society Can Organize	Ethnicity	Class	Cultural practices
Public Funding for Ethnic Orgs.	Medium	Medium-Low	High
Density of Organizational Field	High	Low	Medium
Urban Citizenship	High	Low	High

The overall status of Latinos in the United States is aided by avenues of political voice and organization that benefit from the legacy of the civil rights movement and multicultural ideology. Even without having the largest voice of all groups, Latinos have a political voice that is heard in the streets, politicians' offices, and in the public sphere. Given its different history and ideology, France discourages communitarian discourses and thus robs disenfranchised, un-integrated, non-fundamentalist migrants not only of political voice but also of collective action and social capital. While many unemployed Muslim immigrants and citizens are disenfranchised from the French mainstream and from one another, Moroccans in Barcelona have social clubs, friendship networks within and across categorical groups, and a moderate political voice as city residents.

Unemployment and stigmatization are the major obstacles to a right to the city facing the offspring of immigrants in the Parisian metropolitan area (Castañeda, forthcoming). In New York, the challenges are the lack of papers and poverty wages. In Barcelona, they are local intolerance and stereotypes, which are often softened after social interactions in the public and private spheres. Practical everyday citizenship, including employment, cultural rights, freedom of religion, and avenues for political expression—as well as legal citizenship—are necessary in order to fully enjoy a right to the city and the country where new residents live.

Civil society and local socialization patterns foster processes of belonging and exclusion that are translated into different forms of contentious politics, exclusion, and everyday citizenship. Different configurations of social boundaries create parallel pathways of simultaneous exclusion and inclusion. These findings remind us how important everyday interactions, expectations, a sense of belonging, and *de facto* citizenship are, even when they may seem independent from policy goals and state-sanctioned markers of citizenship. The best possible scenario for immigrants is when legal citizenship and its associated welfare benefits and political rights are accompanied by *de facto* everyday citizenship, structural integration, and respect for cultural difference. None of these cities provides all of these conditions, but doing so would be beneficial for immigrants and their offspring. Providing these conditions would also benefit the receiving state, since immigrants would be allowed to contribute fully to their new societies.

Notes

1. Social integration of immigrants in this context does not mean forced cultural assimilation or cultural homogeneity, nor does it imply a normative ideal like that implicit in the Chicago School (see McQuarrie and Marwell, 2009). On the contrary, it follows William Bernard's procedural description of integration where "natives" and "newcomers" integrate with each other; "That is to say that each element has been changed by association with the other, without complete loss of its own cultural identity, and with a change in the resultant cultural amalgam…this concept of integration rests upon a belief in the importance of cultural differentiation within a framework of social unity. It recognizes the right of groups and individuals to be different so long as the differences do not lead to domination or disunity" (William S. Bernard, quoted in Gordon, 1964, p. 68).

2. This movement is parallel to the weakening of working class community organizations and political alliances and the general political disenfranchisement of peripheral urban areas in France often called the *banlieues* (see Castañeda, forthcoming).

3. This neo-liberal model clusters individuals by social class and/or race; and by excluding the poor and stigmatized groups from certain exclusive areas it decreases a universal right to the city. This was the model mastered by Von Haussmann in Paris and Robert Moses and his Triborough Bridge and Tunnel Authority in New York (Harvey, 2008). This model was also applied to Barcelona leading to the Olympic Games of 1992 (Qu and Spaans, 2009).

4. In the same way that the US Census does not ask about religion, the French Census does not have questions on race or ethnicity. It is considered illegal to use state resources to create statistical information that treats citizens as something other than French. While the US Census has questions about race and ethnicity, the categories change each decade and they are not self-explanatory or understood in the same way by respondents (Passel and Taylor, 2009). Furthermore the US Census clearly undercounts the number of poor minorities and undocumented workers that prefer not to or cannot give information to the state due to their unstable situation, frequent change of residence, and/or crowded and informal housing arrangements.

5. For a list of Muslim organizations in Spain see, for example,
   http://www.webislam.com/?sec=directorio&tipo=Organizaci%F3nes.

6. I have also observed the same while participating in cultural events organized by the Kabyle community in New York, including the celebration of the contentious events of the Berber Spring.

7. Despite the strong discourse against funding communitarian activities, some funds are allocated at the local level around cultural issues, or programs around social class, age, or disadvantaged status (see Doytcheva, 2007).

8. As in any closed social group newcomers have to pass a time of probation, where they may be asked to prove their worth and willingness to belong; e.g., new members rushing a fraternity in order to construct fictitious kinship relationships, in the same way that the nation-state imagines the common *patrie* or motherland.

9. This policy program was revamped after 9/11 to the point where the securitarian discourse has become commonplace and widespread.

10. Yet minorities in France have a lower imprisonment rate per capita than minorities in the US (Wacquant, 2010).

11. In a press release the Mexican Ministry of Foreign Affairs states that despite failing to comply with his parole conditions, it will continue to defend Alejandro Ordaz Moreno. See: http://portal3.sre.gob.mx/english/index.php?option=com_content&task=view&id=233&Itemid=9 running from parole his.

12. Proposition 187 alleged that Californians suffered "economic hardship caused by the presence of illegal aliens" and called for the denial of public benefits such as health care, education, and welfare to illegal aliens. The citizen proposition was passed on November 8, 1994 and was supported by almost 59 percent of the California voters with a 60 percent voter turnout. It was signed into law by Governor Pete Wilson (R). Following lawsuits filed in by the Mexican-American Legal Defense/Education Fund (MALDEF), the League of Latin American Citizens (LULAC), the American Civil Liberties Union (ACLU), and others, Proposition 187 was ultimately declared unconstitutional by US District Court Judge Mariana Pfaelzer in November 1997. In 1999 Governor Gray Davis (D), an earlier supporter of the proposition, decided not to appeal this ruling, killing the proposition but yet inspiring federal immigration bills like the Illegal Immigration Reform and Immigrant Responsibility Act of 1996 signed into law by President Bill Clinton.

13. HR 4437: The Border Protection, Antiterrorism, and Illegal Immigration Control Act of 2005 was introduced by James Sensenbrenner (R-WI) on December 6, 2005 and passed by the House of Representatives on December 16, 2005, but the Senate did not vote on it. The bill asked for more funds for border control, larger jurisdiction of the Department of Homeland Security, and fingerprinting of non-citizens entering and leaving the country (all these aspects were later incorporated and enacted in other bills). HR 4437 was very controversial since Title II Sections 201 and 203 sought to make being in an undocumented status an "aggravated felony" criminal offense, instead of a civil one. Furthermore, ambiguous language could have made any person, agency or institution helping undocumented people who had been previously deported also guilty of criminal behavior. This enraged the Catholic Church, social service agencies, employers, and regular people who often come in contact with the undocumented and helped foster the large immigrants rights marches of 2006.

14. This law allows local police to ask "people who look foreign" for their identification papers with no other reason. This was normally considered discrimination or a form of racial profiling and is illegal in other US cities. Yet this is the law of the land in Paris.

References

Ajuntament de Barcelona. (2009). "Hereu Supports Moroccan Voting in Local Elections." Retrieved May 20, 2011, from http://w3.bcn.es/V01/Serveis/Noticies/V01NoticiesLlistatNoticiesCtl/0,2138,1653_35144087_3_102 0205134,00.html?accio=detall&home=HomeBCN&nomtipusMCM=Noticia.

Amara, F., and S. Zappi. (2006). *Breaking the Silence: French Women's Voices from the Ghetto.* Berkeley: University of California Press.

Barsali, N., F.-X. Freland, and A.-M. Vincent. (2003). *Générations Beurs: Français à Part Entière.* Paris: Autrement.

Blandin, N. (2007, Oct). "Ouverture polémique de la Cité Nationale de l'Histoire de l'Immigration." *La République des Lettres*.

Board of Elections. (2011). "Voters' Guide to New York City Elections." Retrieved Feb 7, 2011, from http://vote.nyc.ny.us/votersguide.html.

Bowen, J. R. (2007). *Why the French Don't Like Headscarves: Islam, the State, and Public Space*. Princeton: Princeton University Press.

Bréchon, P., and J.-F. Tchernia (Eds.). (2009). *La France à Travers ses Valeurs*. Paris: Armand Colin.

Castañeda, E. (2010). *The Political Voice of Migrants in a Comparative Perspective* (Doctoral dissertation). Columbia University, New York, NY.

_____. (Forthcoming). "The Creation of Places of Stigma: The Parisian Banlieue." In R. Hutchison and B. Haynes (Eds.), *The Ghetto Reader: An Edited Collection of Contemporary Scholarship*. Perseus.

Collins, P. H. (2010). "The New Politics of Community." *American Sociological Review*, 75(1), 7-30.

Dávila, A. M. (2004). *Barrio Dreams: Puerto Ricans, Latinos, and the Neoliberal City*. Berkeley, CA: University of California Press.

Deltombe, T. (2005). *L'Islam Imaginaire: La Construction Médiatique de l'Islamophobie en France, 1975-2005*. Paris: Découverte.

DiMaggio, P. J., and W. W. Powell. (1983). "The Iron Cage Revisited: Institutional Isomorphism and Collective Rationality in Organizational Fields." *American Sociological Review*, 48(2), 147-60.

Doytcheva, M. (2007). *Une Discrimination Positive à la Française: Ethnicité et Territoire dans les Politiques de la Ville*. Paris: La Découverte.

Fassin, D., and E. Fassin (Eds.). (2006). *De la Question Sociale à la Question Raciale?: Représenter la Société Française*. Paris: La Découverte.

Fuentes, N. (2007). "The Immigrant Experiences of Dominican and Mexican Women in the 1990s: Crossing Boundaries or Temporary Work Spaces?" In C. Brettell (Ed.), *Crossing Borders and Constructing Boundaries: Immigration Race and Ethnicity* (pp. 94-119). New York, NY: Lexington Books Press.

Gabaccia, D. (2010). "Nations of Immigrants: Do Words Matter?" *The Pluralist*, 5(3), 5-31.

Geisser, V., and E. Y. Soum. (2008). *Discriminer pour Mieux Régner: Enquête sur la Diversité dans les Partis Politiques*. Ivry-sur-Seine: Éditions de l'Atelier.

Gordon, M. M. (1964). *Assimilation in American Life: The Role of Race, Religion, and National Origins*. New York: Oxford University Press.

Goris, I., F. Jobard, and R. Lévy. (2009). *Profiling Minorities: A Study of Stop-and-Search Practices in Paris*. New York, NY: Open Society Institute.

Harvey, D. (2008). "The Right to the City." *New Left Review*, 53(Sep-Oct), 23-40.

Jiménez, T. R. (2010). *Replenished Ethnicity: Mexican Americans, Immigration, and Identity*. Berkeley, CA: University of California Press.

Jones-Correa, M. (1998). *Between Two Nations: The Political Predicament of Latinos in New York City*. Ithaca, NY: Cornell University Press.

Kuru, A. T. (2008). "Secularism, State Policies, and Muslims in Europe: Analyzing French Exceptionalism." *Comparative Politics*, 41(1), 1-19.

L'Information Citoyenne. (2006). *Qu'est-ce que SOS Racisme?* Paris: L'Archipel.

Lamont, M. (2000). *The Dignity of Working Men: Morality and the Boundaries of Race, Class, and Immigration*. New York, NY/Cambridge, MA: Russell Sage Foundation/Harvard University Press.

Lamont, M., and V. Molnar. (2002). "The Study of Boundaries in the Social Sciences." *Annual Review of Sociology*, 28, 167-195.

Lefebvre, H. (1968). *Le Droit a la Ville*. Paris: Anthropos.

Light, I. H. (2006). *Deflecting Immigration: Networks, Markets, and Regulation in Los Angeles.* New York: Russell Sage Foundation.

Longhofer, W., and E. Schofer. (2010). "National and Global Origins of Environmental Association." *American Sociological Review*, 75(4), 505–33.

Lozes, P. (2011). "Noir tout Simplement Blog." *Le Nouvel Observateur.com.*

Mahé, A. (2006). *Histoire de la Grande Kabylie: XIXe-XXe siècles: Anthropologie Historique du Lien Social dans les Communautés Villageoises* (2. éd. corrigée ed.). Saint-Denis: Bouchène.

Malik, S. (1990). *L'Histoire Secrète de SOS-Racisme.* Paris: Albin Michel.

Marwell, N. P. (2004). "Ethnic and Postethnic Politics in New York City: The Dominican Second Generation." In P. Kasinitz, J. H. Mollenkopf, and M. C. Waters (Eds.), *Becoming New Yorkers: Ethnographies of the New Second Generation* (pp. 227-56). New York: Russell Sage.

————. (2007). *Bargaining for Brooklyn: Community Organizations in the Entrepreneurial City.* Chicago, IL: University of Chicago Press.

Massey, D. S. (2007). *Categorically Unequal: The American Stratification System.* New York, NY: Russell Sage Foundation.

McAdam, D., S. Tarrow, and C. Tilly. (2001). *Dynamics of Contention.* Cambridge, UK: Cambridge University Press.

McQuarrie, M., and N. P. Marwell. (2009). "The Missing Organizational Dimension in Urban Sociology." *City & Community*, 8(3), 247-268.

Menjívar, C. (2006). "Liminal Legality: Salvadoran and Guatemalan Immigrants' Lives in the United States." *American Journal of Sociology*, 111(4), 999-1037.

Mitchell, D. (2003). *The Right to the City: Social Justice and the Fight for Public Space.* New York: Guilford Press.

Morales, L., and L. Jorba. (2010). "Transnational Links and Practices of Migrants' Organisations in Spain." In R. Baubock and T. Faist (Eds.), *Diaspora and Transnationalism: Concepts, Theories and Methods* (pp. 267 ff.). Amsterdam, Netherlands: Amsterdam University Press.

NALEO. (2007). *A Profile of Latino Elected Officials in the United States and their Progress since 1996*: NALEO Educational Fund.

Ngai, M. M. (2004). *Impossible Subjects: Illegal Aliens and the Making of Modern America.* Princeton, NJ: Princeton University Press.

Noiriel, G. (2006 [1988]). *Le Creuset Français: Histoire de l'immigration, XIXe-XXe Siècles.* Paris: Seuil.

Pinçon, M., and M. Pinçon-Charlot. (2004). *Sociologie de Paris.* Paris: Découverte.

————. (2009). *Paris: Quinze Promenades Sociologiques.* Paris: Payot.

Portes, A., L. E. Guarnizo, and P. Landolt. (1999). "The Study of Transnationalism: Pitfalls and Promise of an Emergent Research Field." *Ethnic and Racial Studies*, 22(2), 217-37.

Powell, W. W., and DiMaggio, P. J. (1991). *The New Institutionalism in Organizational Analysis.* Chicago: University of Chicago Press.

Qu, L., and M. Spaans. (2009). "The Mega-Event as a Strategy in Spatial Planning: Starting from the Olympic City of Barcelona." Paper presented at the 4th Conference of the International Forum on Urbanism (The New Urban Question: Urbanism beyond Neo-Liberalism). Amsterdam.

Rius Sant, X. (2007). *El Libro de la Inmigración en España.* Córdoba, España: Almuzara.

Rosenberg, C. D. (2006). *Policing Paris: The Origins of Modern Immigration Control between the Wars.* Ithaca, NY: Cornell University Press.

Sassen, S. (2001). *The Global City: New York, London, Tokyo* (2nd ed.). Princeton, NJ: Princeton University Press.

Sayad, A. (2004). *The Suffering of the Immigrant.* Cambridge, UK: Polity Press.

Sennett, R. (1994). *Flesh and Stone: The Body and the City in Western Civilization*. New York: W.W. Norton & Co.

Serra del Pozo, P. (2006). *El Comercio Étnico en el Distrito de Ciutat Vella de Barcelona*. Barcelona: Fundación "la Caixa."

Shepard, T. (2006). *The Invention of Decolonization: The Algerian War and the Remaking of France*. Ithaca, NY: Cornell University Press.

Silberman, R., R. Alba, and I. Fournier. (2007). "Segmented Assimilation in France? Discrimination in the Labour Market against the Second Generation." *Ethnic and Racial Studies*, 30(1), 1-27.

Small, M. L. (2009). "'How Many Cases Do I Need?': On Science and the Logic of Case Selection in Field-based Research." *Ethnography*, 10(1), 5-38.

Smith, M. P. (2003). "Transnationalism and Citizenship." In B. Yeoh, M. W. Charney, and C. K. Tong (Eds.), *Approaching Transnationalisms: Studies on Transnational Societies, Multicultural Contacts, and Imaginings of Home* (pp. 15-38). Boston, MA: Kluwer.

Smith, M. P., and L. E. Guarnizo. (1998). *Transnationalism from Below*. New Brunswick, NJ: Transaction Publishers.

Smith, R. C. (2006). *Mexican New York: Transnational Lives of New Immigrants*. Berkeley, CA: University of California Press.

Strieff, D. (2006, Jun 6). "Will Islam à la française Take Hold? Paris' Grand Mosque is at Center of Effort to Build a Moderate French Islam." *MSNBC.com*. Retrieved Jun 16, 2011, from http://www.msnbc.msn.com/id/12812201/ns/world_news-islam_in_europe/t/will-islam-la-franaise-take-hold/.

Thompson, G. (2007). *There's No José Here: Following the Hidden Lives of Mexican Immigrants*. New York: Nation Books.

Tilly, C. (1984). *Big Structures, Large Processes, Huge Comparisons*. New York: Russell Sage Foundation. Retrieved Jun 16, 2011, from http://deepblue.lib.umich.edu/bitstream/2027.42/51064/1/295.pdf.

_____. (2004). *Social Movements, 1768-2004*. Boulder: Paradigm Publishers.

_____.(2008). *Contentious Performances*. Cambridge: Cambridge University Press.

Tilly, C., and S. Tarrow. (2007). *Contentious Politics*. Boulder, CO: Paradigm Publishers.

Tocqueville, A. d. (1969). *Democracy in America*. In J. P. Mayer (Ed. and Trans.). Garden City, NY: Doubleday.

Traugott, M. (1993). "Barricades as Repertoire: Continuities and Discontinuities in the History of French Contention." *Social Science History*, 17(2), 309-23

Wacquant, L. (2008). *Urban Outcasts: A Comparative Sociology of Advanced Marginality*. Cambridge, MA: Polity.

_____. (2010). "Class, Race & Hyperincarceration in Revanchist America." *Daedalus*, 139(3), 74-90.

Weber, E. J. (1976). *Peasants into Frenchmen: the Modernization of Rural France, 1870-1914*. Stanford, CA: Stanford University Press.

Weber, M. (1958). *The City*. Glencoe, IL: Free Press.

Weil, P. (2008). *How to Be French: Nationality in the Making Since 1789*. Durham, NC: Duke University Press.

Wimmer, A., and Y. Feinstein. (2010). "The Rise of the Nation-State across the World, 1816 to 2001." *American Sociological Review*, 75(5), 764-90.

Zolberg, A. R. (2006). *A Nation by Design: Immigration Policy in the Fashioning of America*. New York/Cambridge, MA: Russell Sage Foundation/Harvard University Press.

Zukin, S. (2010). *Naked City: The Death and Life of Authentic Urban Places*. New York: Oxford University Press.

5

Rights *through* the City:
The Urban Basis of Immigrant Rights Struggles in
Amsterdam and Paris

Walter Nicholls and Floris Vermeulen

How are cities strategic spaces through which immigrants struggle for general rights? We assert that immigrant struggles in cities are not necessarily about a "right to the city." Instead, battles over urban issues are often proxy battles for broader rights in the national society. As these battles are fought through urban policy areas like zoning, housing, and transit, immigrant activists must develop new alliances with organizations in possession of specialized resources and knowledge. Location in sizable cities with high organizational diversity provides immigrant activists with an opportune environment to identify and develop relations with specialized organizations in various policy areas. As campaigns come and go within the same city, relational bridges between diverse organizations broaden, creating a web of weak-tie connections between diverse actors within the activist environment. This can facilitate the flow of information between these activists while providing each with a reservoir of allies to call upon for successive campaigns. Activists embedded in those few cities that have developed rich and overlapping networks can draw upon the social, material, and cultural resources from these environments to engage in battles over threatening national legislation or policies. Thus, rather than stress the right *to* the city, we emphasize the right *through* the city: urban policies are proxy battles for larger rights struggles, and these struggles over time *can* (but do not necessarily) nurture complex and resource-rich activist networks that can be deployed for broader rights campaigns.

We explore these arguments through a comparison of immigrant rights struggles in Amsterdam and Paris. In both cases, urban policy was used to restrict the broader rights of immigrants, which transformed these cities into central arenas of contentious immigrant struggles. Whereas immigrants in Amsterdam fought for religious rights through urban planning and zoning, immigrants in Paris fought for their right to live with their families through housing. In both cases, immigrant activists struggled through the urban policy arena to attain general rights. Through these struggles, activists created new connections to organizations in possession of specialized knowledge and resources in these policy areas. These cases largely confirm our central proposition: cities are central spaces through which struggles for broader rights are fought, and through these 'urban' struggles immigrant activists build connections with a diverse range of supportive organizations and individuals.

However, while these cities have functioned as cradles of immigrant contentiousness, differences between them also show that not all contentious activities evolve in the same direction. In the Paris case, complex activist networks were cultivated through several campaigns

79

and these strong relations allowed activists in the city to go on and fight a national battle against restrictive legislation in the 1990s. By contrast, in the Amsterdam case, activist relations were disrupted at the end of the campaign because of conflicts between key organizations. The fragmentation of ties left the immigrant activists in Amsterdam isolated, undermining their abilities to call upon allies for campaigns unfolding at urban and national scales. Based on observations from our cases, we conclude that many cities are crucial spaces through which immigrant rights are fought, but not all these cities foster the kinds of relations that make them into driving hubs of national immigrant rights struggles.

The chapter develops these arguments in several sections. The first section outlines the major points of our theoretical argument. The second and third sections analyze the Amsterdam and Paris cases respectively. The final and concluding section of the chapter draws out similarities between our cases and attempts to explain some of the differences between them. We finish by arguing that cities should not be viewed as a domain of politics apart from the national but rather as one front (with its own unique qualities) in a broad and complex geopolitical field.

Rights through the City: The Importance of Cities for Immigrant Rights Movements

The concept of the "right to the city" is rooted in Henri Lefebvre's theoretical explorations of cities in a capitalist world (Harvey, 2003; Gottdiener and Feagin, 1987; Isin, 2000; Lefebvre, 1996; Soja, 2000). The concept provides important insights into how cities shape contentious mobilizations and give rise to new understandings of citizenship. Lefebvre argued that the commodification of urban space transformed the functions and uses of urban space. Urban space was not only a commodity that could be bought and sold like any other but it also provided capitalists with an outlet to switch investments from productive sectors in times of crisis. The importance of urban space for the capitalist system opened the floodgates to large investors, resulting in the commodification of urban space and the dominance of market logic. The commodification process subordinated alternative uses of urban space to market forces, ultimately alienating people from the means of producing and appropriating their lived space. This, for Lefebvre and others, was the principal grievance precipitating contentious struggles in the modern capitalist city (see Castells, 1977; 1983; Fainstein and Hirst, 1995). As diverse people faced these forces of displacement and alienation, they would form alliances between themselves, resist systemic market forces, and create an alternative vision of the city based on the de-commodification of urban space. He believed that such struggles would make it possible for all urban residents to have an equal right to engage in decisions and practices concerning the production of their common urban space. Thus, the 'right to the city' was a theory that identified the processes that caused *urban* mobilizations and the formation of alternative political communities based on distinctly anti-capitalist values.

The interpretations of the "right to the city" have varied markedly from these theoretical foundations, with some sticking closely to Lefebvre's radical project and others incorporating it into more reformist and liberal visions of the urban world (Mayer, forthcoming). In spite of these very different interpretations, they all assume that *urban processes* are a cause of distinctive grievances. Aggrieved activists develop frames and discourses that reflect their urban roots, and these activists target institutions and policy arenas that are directly charged with urban issues. In this sense, the city is conceived as a spatial unit that gives rise to a very distinct *type* of social movement: it is an *urban* movement which seeks to assert the rights of marginalized people to stay, live, and appropriate the city (Castells, 1983; Isin, 2000; Mitchell, 2003; Pickvance, 2003;

Soja, 2010). For example, Mitchell's treatment of the "right to the city" is firmly grounded on such assumptions. He highlights how neoliberal urbanization denied certain people access to public spaces in the city, which precipitated struggles to regain access and develop alternative imaginings for how cities should operate (Mitchell, 2003). Mayer's most recent work has shown that the "right to the city" has become the battle cry of a transnational alliance of urban activists, with cross-border networks serving to circulate information and reinforce a common identify among activists in countless localities (2009, forthcoming). Though Mayer's insightful work shows how the "right to the city" travels across space and scales, the city continues to be conceived as a unique site that gives rise to distinct types of grievances, targets, and identities.

We argue that the "right to the city" too narrowly defines the arena of activists' struggles. While many urban social movements maintain their singular focus on enhancing rights *to* the city, activists who mobilize in cities may view the urban arena as one front in a broader struggle to gain basic labor, sexual, minority, and immigrant rights (Nicholls, 2008; 2009). For example, in the case of the Gay Rights movement in the United States, the city (San Francisco in particular) played a strategic role in nourishing powerful activist ties and serving as a political arena to initiate innovative gay rights reforms. The aim was not to gain rights to this one city and stop the struggle at the city gates but to build on the relational and political advances made in this city to sustain the broader goal of gay rights in the country (Armstrong, 2006). This was not necessarily an *urban* social movement, but the *urban* did serve as the strategic space through which broader rights claims could be made. Thus, rather than simply focus on 'rights to the city,' we should conceptualize cities as important arenas *through* which diverse activists make their claims for general rights in complex citizenship regimes.

We make four basic assertions for how cities become strategic spaces through which broad immigrant rights movements are fought. First, the general rights of immigrants are often regulated and restricted *through* urban policy processes. Liberal states are bound by international and constitutional norms to provide immigrants with a basic set of rights, including the right to practice their religion, live with families, receive basic social supports, and so on (Joppke, 1999). While national governments are bound to protect the *abstract* rights of immigrant and minority residents, they exercise a wide degree of latitude over how rights are *substantively* distributed and regulated in their countries. It is in this context that the urban policy arena plays a uniquely important role. While liberal states may meet their formal obligations to respect the rights of immigrants, they also carry out restrictions on immigrant rights through the urban policy arena. Shifting the execution of immigrant policies to the urban arena transfers the responsibility of passing illiberal measures to local governments and justifies illiberal restrictions on 'technical' grounds (i.e., zoning violations, housing restrictions, etc.). For example, national courts may guarantee religious freedoms for all, but local officials can employ local zoning ordinances to impose severe restrictions on how and where actual mosques are built (Bowen, 2006; Maussen, 2009). As the general rights of immigrants are enabled, regulated, or restricted *through* the city, the city becomes a space where grievances concerning rights are concretized and made real to immigrants. Thus, restrictions on actual rights through urban policy turn the 'urban' arena into the political frontline of immigrant rights struggles. Second, as the urban becomes an important space for generating immigrants' grievances, it is also a distinctive environment that facilitates the emergence of complex alliances between diverse organizations. Large cities contain rich and heterogeneous social movement environments, constituted by diverse activists and organizations with specialized resources and knowledge in different policy areas (see Nicholls, 2008; Vermeulen, 2005; 2006). Moreover, immigrant grievances that arise in response to restrictive urban policies encourage the formation of alliances between the diverse organizations in the city. When policies concerning the rights of immigrants are shifted into the urban arena, grievances can arise in different policy areas, including housing, zoning, transit, and economic development, among others. Aggrieved immigrants facing restrictions on their rights in one policy area (e.g., transit) will often lack the sufficient skills and resources in this area to mount a successful campaign. This will require them to establish connections with organizations in possession of those specialized skills. Moreover, proximity between these diverse actors reduces the transaction costs between them, permitting them the time to experiment with new multi-actor coalitions and learn how to trust and work with one another. For example, contacts that first emerged in one-off, small-scale campaigns for the rights of various groups, such as street vendors, renters, day laborers, or religious minorities, can give rise to a web of weak-tie relations between various activist organizations. These networks provide the connected activists with information about their complex political field and a reservoir of potential allies to draw upon for successive campaigns. These ties are by no means free of personal, ideological, and power conflicts, but when the benefits of cooperation are seen to outweigh the costs, participants are likely to stay connected in spite of the various misgivings they may have about their allies. Thus, as central states shift immigration policies to the urban arena, immigrant grievances arising in a range of policy areas constantly spur complex networking processes in the city. The city in this instance is conceived as a 'relational incubator' that helps cultivate networks between the diverse supporters of immigrant rights (Nicholls, 2008).

Third, while most large cities are sites of contentious political activities, only a handful of these cities can evolve into powerful hubs and drivers of national social movements. New connections created through urban-based campaigns can evolve into strong and rich ties, which can then be drawn on in successive local and national mobilizations. However, ties that may emerge in one campaign may be cut at the end of it, with the various organizations going back to a state of relative isolation. To explain these contrasting networking trajectories, we suggest that organizations participating in local coalitions are often dependent on affiliations with broader organizations and institutions for resources, support, and legitimacy.

Some may receive subsidies from the local municipal council; others may be section affiliates of large national and transnational organizations; and still others may have important connections to national political parties. The broader dependencies of local coalition partners play an important role in influencing their relations with one another. While local organizations may respect their coalition partners and agree on a common strategy, parent organizations may believe that these partnerships and their strategies depart from broader goals and norms. Moreover, the *perceived* disjuncture between local maneuverings and broader organizational goals may be exacerbated when non-local patrons have not had the opportunity to engage in long deliberations with the diverse local coalition partners. These intimate and relationally intensive deliberations enable local partners to recognize the mutually beneficial possibilities of collective action. In this sense, the social or ideological *distance* of non-local patrons to local coalition work can be exacerbated by their geographic distance, with non-local organizations not being privy to the tacit and nuanced understandings that arise from intimate and grounded negotiations. This can result in superficial interpretations of local agreements, distrust for allies, and a misunderstanding of how local adaptations can contribute to achieving the broader goals of the parent organization. This is often the case when national labor unions or transnational religious organizations interpret the innovative practices of local affiliates as deviating from broader organizational norms and goals (Milkman, 2005). In other instances, however, the strategies and struggles of 'local' coalition partners may coincide well with the goals and norms of broader organizational patrons. Under such conditions, patrons may permit or even encourage local activists to continue their cooperation in these multi-actor coalitions. Thus, whether or not rich relations develop across local activist communities depends partly on the degree to which local actions coincide with or depart from the goals and norms of broader supporters.

Fourth, rights coalitions and mobilizations often begin and coalesce in cities, but they do not necessarily stay there. Issues concerning immigrant rights may shift back to the national level when new laws and regulations are introduced by the central state. When relations between urban activists are well structured and relatively cohesive, they can shift their targets from local restrictions on rights to broader national issues (Leitner, *et al.*, 2008; Nicholls, 2009; Sikkink, 2005; Tarrow and McAdam, 2005). This type of 'scale shift' is made possible because actors within urban coalitions may lobby their national organizations, allies, or supporters to back national campaigns. In such instances, national organizations can employ their infrastructure and networks to connect local coalitions of immigrant rights activists throughout a country. They can also help to set up information networks, sponsor meetings, and participate in organizing national protests. Once these networks are in place, activists in different urban coalitions contribute their own resources to the broader struggle while the national network coordinates how these resources are strategically circulated and deployed. Thus, when policies concerning the rights of immigrants shift to the national scale, participants in local activist networks can scale up and deploy their locally acquired social movement resources for these broader campaigns. In such instances, these powerful cities become the drivers of national social movements.

This section has maintained that cities are important political spaces through which immigrant activists struggle for broader rights within receiving societies. Cities are political sites through which general rights are restricted, making them into frontline arenas for catalyzing rights mobilizations. Urban struggles for rights, such as access to housing, building permits, parks, and improved transit, must therefore be considered proxy battles for general rights within receiving societies. Through these constant urban struggles, immigrant activists are compelled to draw on support and develop alliances with diverse organizations in their local activist environment. Lastly, if institutional forces permit the maturation of these horizontal activist ties, they can later be deployed to fuel and steer national immigrant rights campaigns. It is in this sense that the city becomes the strategic terrain through which broader rights to the country (not just the city) are made.

Rights through the City: The Amsterdam Case

Regulating Religious Rights through Urban Planning

Muslim immigrants have set up a range of religious institutions in the Netherlands over the last decades. The development of these religious institutions is primarily the result of interactions between different actors, with local and national Muslim organizations negotiating with a broad range of actors to establish an institutional foothold in the receiving context. Muslim immigrants set up relations of collaboration and conflict with a range of actors in order to claim certain basic religious rights (Maussen, 2009, pp. 16-7). The acquisition of places of worship plays an important role in the emancipation of these groups. The symbolic significance of places of worship cannot be overestimated. Places of worship, especially when they have been built for this purpose, materialize religious presence. At the same time, the building of new religious buildings provides local authorities the opportunity to exert control over religious demands (Sunier, 2009). In the Netherlands local authorities have tried to control these demands mostly by downplaying religious meanings, avoiding any ideological discussion, and regulating the building of mosques into urban planning (Lindo, 1999; Maussen, 2007; Rath, *et al.*, 2001; Sunier, 1996). This was possible because most mosques were built in poorer rundown immigrant neighborhoods, which had become the focus of attention of Dutch urban planners in the early eighties. Urban planners identified the primary problems of immigrant neighborhoods as poor housing, concentrated poverty, the chronic lack of space, and the perceived overconcentration of immigrants who lived isolated from the Dutch mainstream. Often, the construction of large visible houses of worship did not fit into their original plans, as the next example demonstrates.

The Beginning of the Conflict: Plans for an Orthodox Mosque in Amsterdam

The conflict over the Wester Mosque started as a typical local conflict over the building of a mosque. A group of Muslim immigrants, affiliated with the orthodox Turkish Islamic transnational movement, Milli Görüs, demanded the right to have their own place of worship in their neighborhood. The group had just purchased a vacant factory building in the middle of the neighborhood for the eventual construction of a large new mosque. At first, they were denied permission by the local authorities who said that the mosque was not included in the new zoning plan of the city district and that the factory was to be used for other purposes. Having been prohibited from using the building during the month of Ramadan, several hundred men marched to the district town hall in February 1994 and protested by kneeling in front of the building for a collective prayer. Six months later an even larger group of Turkish men, women, and children marched from their neighborhood to the city center to protest against a new decision to allow the organization to use only a small part of the factory for religious activities. In the following years the conflict between the Turkish immigrants and the local authorities escalated further; in one instance the use of police force to evict worshippers from the factory-turned-mosque was only barely avoided (Lindo, 1999). Now, more than 16 years later, the factory has been demolished, but the prestigious mosque that is supposed to replace the old factory has still not been built. It probably never will be.

One of the main reasons for this is the nature of the orthodox group that wants to build the mosque and the perceived mismatch between their values and those of mainstream Dutch society. The general Milli Görüs movement has been one of the most important oppositional forces to the state-led Turkish Islam from the 1970s to the 1990s. It is considered a conservative movement strongly linked to the dominant religious Islamic party in Turkey, the Refah Party, which for the last two decades has been in conflict with the Turkish authorities over the future direction of Turkish Islam. As Turks migrated to Western Europe as guest workers in the 1960s and 1970s, they brought the Milli Görüs ideologies with them. These can be summarized as a strict following of the Islamic norms and rules: no alcohol, clear separation of gender roles, rejection of other religious beliefs, and support of the Islamic judicial system. European authorities have reacted differently to the transnational Milli Görüs Movement. In Germany, where Milli Görüs established their European headquarters, authorities have always been very critical toward the movement since they considered it to be fundamentalist and anti-democratic. In some instances organizations affiliated with the movement were banned (Østergaard-Nielsen, 2003). In the Netherlands, especially in Amsterdam, it seemed that Milli Görüs had developed somewhat independently from the political and religious influences proceeding from either Turkey or Germany. However, while the leadership in Amsterdam became more open for dialog with the authorities and expressed 'modern' opinions on social and religious matters, the constituency in the city seemed to remain far more traditional and conservative in their opinions (Vermeulen, 2006).

Leadership of the local Milli Görüs movement in Amsterdam has not always been open and liberal. In the beginning of the conflict, Milli Görüs was just mainly interested in building their own prominent mosque, which represented their orthodox religious beliefs. Local authorities resisted the building of this "Turkish orthodox bastion," as they called it, because they feared that it would influence the neighborhood negatively (Lindo, 1999). They were concerned that it would reinforce conservative and ethnic Turkish identities among the Turkish immigrants in the neighborhood. This would, according to local officials, lead to more segregation and an inward looking immigrant community, which would hamper social and cultural integration. The claim of the Milli Görüs movement to have their own place of worship was perceived by authorities as a claim to have an orthodox sectarian worldview and to make it publicly visible.

As mentioned before, local authorities used the neighborhood urban restructuring plan to successfully block the building of the mosque. After many court cases on different technical issues (which were tried and appealed as high as the Dutch Supreme Court), it became clear to the local Milli Görüs leadership that they would not win. The mosque would not be built in the middle of the neighborhood, and in addition to that, Milli Görüs would lose the entire factory as well. This insight led to a new strategy among the local Milli Görüs leadership. They tried to convince local authorities that the mosque would not become a Turkish bastion; on the contrary, they argued that it would become a symbol for the successful and peaceful integration of Islam in the Netherlands. In order to do this they needed to build coalitions with powerful actors outside their own community.

The Relational Advantages of the City: Building Alliances across Religious Differences

One of the board members of the Milli Görüs had established contacts with an influential local Dutch NGO, the Amsterdam Center for Foreigners[1] (ACB by its Dutch initials), an organization founded in the early 1970s to support immigrants settling in Amsterdam. Through this contact, the board member also came into contact with one of the largest housing corporations in the city, *Het Oosten*. The housing corporation owned many buildings in the neighborhood in which the mosque was supposed to be built and had a large number of Turkish tenants. They were interested in the plans of Milli Görüs since many of their tenants were affiliated with this transnational movement. The Milli Görüs board member, together with the contact person of the ACB, was eventually able to convince the housing corporation that Milli Görüs—contrary to the perception of those who would view the mosque as a Turkish bastion— would follow a path toward establishing a first, exemplary, Dutch Islamic mosque. The idea was to create a new mosque, named Wester Mosque after the famous Wester Church in the center of Amsterdam, in close collaboration with the housing corporation. The property owned by Milli Görüs around the factory would be used by the housing corporation to build luxurious apartments. The mosque would be built in the same architectural style of the luxurious apartments and the rest of the neighborhood, reflecting the aesthetic form of the internationally renowned Amsterdamse School. The entire complex would consist of a central mosque, conference halls, sporting and shopping facilities, and the housing complex.

The housing corporation contacted the local authorities, who were very apprehensive about entering into any type of collaboration with Milli Görüs given the history of conflict. However, the new coalition between Milli Görüs and the housing corporation and the ambitious new plans led the local authorities to reconsider. At first, negotiations between Milli Görüs, the Housing Corporation, and local authorities were held in secret. The parties worked on the new designs for more than two years before they publically announced their willingness to collaborate. Most people were impressed by the ambitious and expensive plans for this massive complex, which was held up as a symbol for the integration of Muslims in Dutch society. The new alliance and the plans themselves were an illustration of this integration: an Islamic organization working closely together with a respected housing corporation to make a Dutch mosque in which everyone would be welcome and all distinctively Turkish signs would be silenced. A French Jewish architect was even hired to design the mosque in a typical Dutch Amsterdam style.

The alliance of the Milli Görüs organizations with the housing corporation did not only provide access to the decision-making process, but it also provided Milli Görüs with essential information and knowledge on how to reframe the mosque project and how to integrate it into an overall urban vision for the neighborhood. In addition to that, the alliance provided symbolic capital that increased the legitimacy for their claim to be visibly present in the public sphere. In the negotiations between Milli Görüs, the housing corporation, and the local authorities, the Milli Görüs organization received external expertise and knowledge in city planning matters while also gaining cultural capital from their influential partners. These acquired resources made it easier for local Milli Görüs leadership to present the plans for the new mosque as something that would be a contribution to the neighborhood, the city, and even the entire country. This would not just be another Turkish mosque in an Amsterdam neighborhood; it would be a Dutch mosque in a neighborhood in which people of different backgrounds and religious beliefs could be properly integrated. The housing corporation would now also speak on behalf of Milli Görüs when explaining and presenting the new plans. Again, this increased the credibility and reliability of the Milli Görüs organization significantly, as many people were not convinced in the beginning whether the appearance and purpose of the mosque would indeed be different from the original plans.

The alliance remained mostly local, with only local actors involved, except for the transnational Milli Görüs movement; the alliance did not shift to the national level. However, it did gain national appeal. National actors were looking as well for more liberal forms of Islam that could be integrated more easily into Dutch society. The character of the Dutch public debate on Islam had become more negative after 9/11. Increasingly, national politicians from all parties (from both the left and the right) were questioning the possibility of a peaceful coexistence of Islam with mainstream liberal Dutch norms and values. The more orthodox Islamic movements were perceived to be especially irreconcilable with a Western worldview. Within this national debate there was a great demand for a version of Islam that would encompass more liberal ideas. For proponents of this line, the Wester Mosque seemed to reflect a prime example of a more liberal and Dutch version of Islam. This prompted more national actors to publicly support the attempt to build this mosque. Another important factor enhancing the national resonance of this local struggle was the emergence of a new president of Milli Görüs in Amsterdam, Haci Karacaer, who is the son of a Kurdish guest worker. He happened to be an appealing liberal and progressive spokesperson who, within a few years, was able to develop a strong and influential position in the Amsterdam political system. He almost managed to get on the electoral list of the Amsterdam Labor Party for the elections of the City Council of Amsterdam in 2002. Five years earlier, it would have been inconceivable that a local president of the orthodox Milli Görüs organization would be considered as a candidate for the left-wing, secular Labor Party. This example illustrates how local alliances and the different framing of their missions had shifted the opportunities for this group.

Within just a few years, the moderate and progressive leadership of Milli Görüs was able to change the public perception of their movement completely. The entire city district council supported and approved the new plans, and only a few neighborhood residents showed signs of protest. This protest was able to slow down the process, but it proved to be rather ineffective against a powerful coalition made up of a large religious organization, a rich housing corporation, and the city district's authorities. After the final court case on the height of the minaret in 2005, which was won by Milli Görüs and the housing corporation, the building of the mosque could begin. The original problems of the city district with the size of the mosque were not problems anymore, and the zoning plans for the neighborhood were adjusted. Whereas in the beginning the zoning plan was used by officials as a tool for blocking the building plans of Milli Görüs, now it was used to block the protests of native neighborhood residents.

The festivities for laying the first stone were illustrative of how the plans for the mosque had changed, how extensive the new powerful alliance had become, and how the entire project had received national attention and support. The cornerstone was placed by the national minister for Justice of the Christian Democratic Party, who spoke about the beauty of the project and how it would be a symbol for the integration of Islam in Dutch society. After him, different religious leaders—Jewish, Protestant, Catholic, and Muslim—provided their blessings for the new mosque. The whole neighborhood seemed to be there; people of all different national backgrounds were celebrating the beginning of the construction of a mosque that would be an asset not only to the neighborhood but to the entire city. No one from the transnational Milli Görüs movement was present. Nevertheless, Milli Görüs was still an important actor; they served as the official owners of the factory property and as major contributors to the project. Indeed, the new project plans were much more expensive than the original plans. The city council would even provide substantial additional subsidies for the mosque construction, even though it was very difficult to finance a religious building under Dutch church-state relations. This illustrates again how eager the local authorities were to integrate the orthodox, inward-looking Turkish Milli Görüs community into Dutch society and how powerful the new alliance had become.

Network Fragmentation: Status Quo in the Neighborhood

In spite of the abilities of Milli Görüs to develop a robust coalition of supporters for the mosque project, it remained unclear how its strategy to gain acceptance in Amsterdam would be received by the movement's conservative leadership in Germany and Turkey. In fact, the transnational Milli Görüs leadership abruptly decided to disrupt the local project. The transnational leadership felt that the local liberal leadership had gone too far in designing a mosque devoid of Turkish references. Also, they viewed the liberal religious views of the Amsterdam group as highly problematic. Finally, it was an insult to them that a Christian Minister of Justice was asked to start the construction process, whereas they themselves seem to have had no official function in the mosque even despite their ownership of the ground. In April 2006 the German leadership of Milli Görüs replaced the liberal board of the Amsterdam Milli Görüs with a more compliant one. The housing corporation and the local authorities in Amsterdam tried to ensure continuity with previous agreements by introducing additional contracts and agreements. However, the new conservative board of the mosque resisted these efforts and pulled out of their alliances with their local partners. Contacts between the housing corporation and Milli Görüs dissolved, and soon after the city district pulled out of the collaboration. The powerful local coalition that had successfully overcome local resistance, ushered into being a new mosque project, and presented the Netherlands with a model of religious integration had now come to an abrupt end.

At present, the mosque has not yet been constructed and probably never will be. Court cases have started again over technical issues, building permits, and other legal matters. Recently, members of the Milli Görüs organization again occupied the city district hall to protest the fact that they still do not have an adequate mosque. In this contested field of citizenship, the conflict was not just about the character of the neighborhood and the position of newcomers in it, but it was also about the nature of Dutch society and its perceived incompatibility with conservative and orthodox religious worldviews. Local authorities explicitly mentioned that they did not want a "Turkish bastion" in the neighborhood and referred to the fact that the Dutch way of living would be threatened by these conservative Muslim ideologies. The urban became the space from which Turkish immigrants could generate claims for visibility and equality in Dutch society without changing their beliefs and opinions. However, Amsterdam authorities also used urban institutions as a way to deal with and to regulate, primarily using urban zoning ordinances to deny these immigrants and their Milli Görüs organization a prominent position in the neighborhood. The conflict was not about the position of immigrants in general or Islamic immigrants and Turkish immigrants in particular; it was about conservative orthodox Muslim immigrants and their position in Dutch society.

Rights through the City: The Paris Case

Paris: Regulating Family Rights through Housing

In France during the years following World War II, housing became a key policy area for regulating and shaping the rights accorded to immigrants. The Social Action Fund for Immigrant Workers and their Families[2] (FAS by its French initials) was created in 1958 to regulate the settlement process of immigrants. The FAS was charged with providing a range of welfare services, but the majority of its resources were dedicated to fund housing for immigrants (Heins, 1991). A semi-public housing agency, the National Society for the Construction of Housing for Workers[3] (SONACOTRA by its French initials), assumed responsibility for producing, distributing, and managing immigrant housing while FAS provided the financing. The SONACOTRA provided housing only to males because this would restrict the possibility of family migrants and ensure the temporary nature of migration. Housing was not only used to produce a desirable population of migrants (i.e., temporary, male, non-reproductive), but it was also used as a technique to discipline and civilize this population (Hmed, 2006). Hostel managers were recruited from among non-commissioned officers and veterans from France's colonial wars for the purposes of disciplining and civilizing the migrant residents (Hmed, 2006; 2007).

The use of housing to manage migrant populations took on additional importance in the 1970s. The national government responded to the economic crisis by introducing severe restrictions on labor and family migrants in 1973. In spite of the government's efforts, the Constitutional Council pronounced that the ministerial decree restricting the right to family migration violated international law and demanded that the government reverse course (Wihtol de Wenden, 1994). Although the government was forced to formally recognize the right of family reunification, it also introduced a number of restrictive criteria for obtaining family visas. The head of the family in France had to present, among other things, a certificate of 'decent housing' with the visa application for his family. Another ministerial decree in 1977 required mayors to certify the housing conditions of immigrant applicants. This decree introduced an additional hurdle for immigrants while providing mayors with a tool to block migrants from settling in their jurisdictions. Facing severe housing shortages in the public and private sector, many immigrant families were denied their right to live together in France, compelling them to enter the country without their visas and settle in dilapidated hotels or abandoned buildings in the city. Having settled in these accommodations, the families could not acquire the certificate of decent housing needed to regularize their immigration status. "For immigrants, housing takes on a dimension that it simply does not have for French families. It affects the right to live as a family and to obtaining papers for the family which are in order" (Péchu, 1999, p. 734).

Urban housing policy was therefore a critical instrument for regulating the rights accorded to immigrants in the country. While agreeing to formally grant immigrants the right to live with their family, the government was able to retain its power to limit these rights by introducing onerous housing requirements on visa applicants. This act of dissimulation was of great strategic importance because it allowed the state to abide by legal and normative obligations while also allowing it to exercise control over how 'real' rights were distributed within the national territory. In doing this, the mayor (charged with distributing public housing and housing certificates to immigrants) was transformed into one of the most important gatekeepers in the country. When grievances arose amongst immigrants, the mayor's authority over housing made him an important target for these campaigns.

The Relational Advantages of the City: Building Alliances across Ideological Differences

During the 1980s and 1990s, immigrant mobilizations unfolded throughout Paris, and housing was a central arena of contention (Ireland, 1994; Péchu, 2001; 2004; Wihtol de Wenden, 1994). As noted above, immigrant families continued to come to the country (without residency visas) and settled in dilapidated Parisian hotels or abandoned apartment buildings. Several fires prompted the city to launch a campaign to evict immigrant residents from these establishments. Families in one building resisted these measures and called on the mayor to provide them with public housing and a certificate of decent housing (Péchu, 2004). Housing was viewed by these families as a means to regularize their status. The city, in this instance, became the principal arena through which these families would need to struggle in order to obtain their rights to settle together in the country.

This initial struggle drew the support of Housing First[4] (ULA), a well-established housing rights association in the city. While the immigrant families were prepared to fight an extensive struggle with the city, ULA possessed the resources, specialized knowledge, and connections necessary for a successful campaign. ULA activists settled in the occupied building with the immigrant families and worked closely with them to devise a general strategy for their struggle. These intimate conditions placed very different activists into constant contact with one another, building up stronger ties between them while also building their knowledge of how to mobilize together around these issues (Péchu, 2004, p. 305). In addition to strengthening ties between these actors, ULA employed its own networks to mobilize additional support for their campaign (i.e., media support and support from prominent associations). The association gained the support of a number of strategic groups, including the country's most prominent housing association, Emmaus, the immigrant rights association Movement against Racism and Friendship between People[5] (MRAP), and the trade union branch of the Office for Public Housing. Each of these supportive organizations contributed different sets of specialized resources and expertise to the campaign.

In 1990, ten immigrants in the occupied building initiated a hunger strike. The leaders of ULA used the hunger strike to enlist more political, associational, and media support for the struggle. At this stage, MRAP played an important brokering role by connecting these immigrant families to some of the most prominent immigrant rights and anti-racist associations in the country, including FASTI, LDH, GISTI,[6] and *SOS Racisme*. These associations provided legal expertise in the area of immigration rights, and they also provided the campaign with more material resources and better political connections. This networking strategy succeeded in pressuring the government to concede and provide families of the building with housing and a certificate of decent housing. In 1993, the leaders of ULA launched another campaign to support an occupation by immigrants of an apartment building on the *rue de Dragon*. The accumulated experience of these activists permitted them to quickly turn this new campaign into a national media event and to frame this action as a struggle against social exclusion. As a part of this strategy, the organizers of the campaign created a new association, Rights First,[7] which was charged with leading the general struggle against social exclusion (with Paris leading the charge, of course). As this campaign became a focal point of media attention, the rights and anti-racist associations, unions, and parties threw their support behind these efforts.

In sum, housing was a proxy battle for a larger struggle to obtain residency rights for immigrant families. Because of this, the battle for immigrant rights largely unfolded through the city, with the city being both the target of the struggle (obtaining decent housing for immigrants) and the strategic space for nourishing powerful relational exchanges between activists. The urban nature of the immigrant grievances (i.e., access to housing) required immigrant activists to develop ties with diverse Parisian organizations that possessed more specialized resources. Housing associations, unions, and immigrant rights associations formed the backbone of a coalition to secure housing for these families. Spatial proximity allowed these actors to meet repeatedly through these various struggles, with these repeated interactions permitting the different actors to learn how to carry out a housing campaign on behalf of undocumented immigrants. Thus, the *urban* character of this struggle provided an opportunity for nurturing a complex and enabling relational web.

Paris: The City as a Platform of National Social Movements

In 1993 the Minister of Interior introduced a series of restrictive reforms that restricted the number of visas available to immigrants, limited the criteria to qualify for a 'family reunion' visa, imposed random identity checks on foreigners, and implemented measures to accelerate deportations (Berezin, 2009; Hayward and Wright, 2002). The Pasqua laws closed down the path to regularization for many immigrants while amplifying the risk of immanent deportation. These measures increased the barriers to regularization far beyond the restrictions on housing. These changes would precipitate a shift in the struggle from the urban (housing policy and the mayor) to the national (legislation and the government) political arena.

In 1994, undocumented immigrants throughout the Paris region formed informal collectives (*collectif de sans papiers*[8]) to demand the regularization of their status from the department prefect (the official charged with processing immigration applications). Although they had sought out the support of rights and anti-racist associations, these associations remained locked in the housing campaign at the *rue de Dragon*. Their inability to gain broader support from other activists undermined their capacities to exert pressure on the Paris prefect. Facing this impasse, Foreign Parents of French Children[9] embraced a direct action approach by occupying a public building and initiating a hunger strike during the presidential elections. Moreover, rather than target the prefect with their demands, the *collectif* shifted its target to the national government. Their aim was to use the presidential campaign to raise the national profile of their struggle and to pressure the government to compel the prefect to regularize their status. The tactics (i.e., hunger strike) and the timing (i.e., presidential election) drew the attention of the media and Paris's most prominent rights and anti-racist associations into the campaign. While many of these associations had been mobilizing in support of the squatters at the *rue de Dragon*, the end of that campaign and the growing media attention on the *collectif* resulted in a rather quick shift of support to this new front in the immigrant rights struggle. The same associations that had been providing support to immigrant squatters seeking housing from the mayor now found themselves providing similar support to immigrant hunger strikers demanding their rights from the national government.

The Paris associations provided Foreign Parents of French Children with crucial supports that enabled the *collectif* to continue its struggle. In addition to providing the *collectif* with access to basic resources (e.g., an office, telephone, photocopy machines, fax), the associations (GISTI and LDH in particular) provided extensive legal support to help them identify major inconsistencies in the Pasqua laws. Moreover, the prominence of the associations and the cultural capital of their leaders immediately enhanced the legitimacy of the *sans papiers* struggle. The associations possessed important insights into the nuances of national cultural politics and were able to craft representations of immigrants that resonated with national norms. They drew from the discursive tradition of *misérabalisme* to create a compelling moral narrative of the striking parents (Passeron and Grignon, 1989). These were hard-working, family-loving migrants who had been made 'illegal' and 'clandestine' by an arbitrary and unjust state. The human rights and anti-racist associations also had extensive contacts with national print, radio, and television media, which enabled them to disseminate this representation throughout the country.

Many of the rights and anti-racist groups involved in the campaign were national organizations with branch sections located throughout the country. They encouraged local sections to launch their own campaigns to support immigrant rights in their respective cities. The infrastructure of the national associations was not used to micromanage local sections but to encourage their engagement in local mobilizations and the dissemination of information and discourses across the country. This information included legal analysis conducted by expert lawyers from LDH and GISTI in Paris and analyses concerning the dynamics of mobilization and the shifting positions of the government. The specialized information was used by activists in provincial sections to develop their own mobilizations in support of the *sans papiers*. Moreover, the national headquarters of the associations provided their sections with the discourses for framing their local struggles and claims. In words taken from FASTI's minutes: "You can, if you wish, employ the texts emanating from the *intellectuals* and *writers* that affirm, 'The procedures of expulsion are unjust and render hardworking families into clandestine criminals....' You can even take up the pen to write something along these lines." By employing infrastructure and networks of national associations to extend the movement beyond the walls of Paris, there emerged homologous coalitions across the country, each employing structures, frames, and strategies similar to that of their parent organizations in Paris.

Although these successive campaigns in Paris strengthened relations between important immigrant rights advocates, these relations were by no means trouble free. On the contrary, different political affiliations, ideologies, and strategic preferences presented constant tensions and challenges throughout this period. The political context (a right wing government from 1993-1995) provided the associations with a common adversary to mobilize against. However, once the government changed to the Socialist Party in 1997, the dynamics of these relations changed significantly. While all the associations continued to pressure the new Socialist government to modify or rescind the Pasqua laws, there was disagreement over how far they should criticize the government. Associations strongly affiliated with the Socialist Party (LDH and FAST in particular) argued that the movement should pressure the government through protests but should not alienate their most influential allies in the government. Others in this coalition believed that the coalition needed to retain its autonomy from the government and continue placing maximum pressure on the government through disruptive protests. While all parties agreed to stay unified at least until the Left government made several important concessions, the coalition split when the more autonomous associations objected to the limited character of the government concessions. Their desire to continue the struggle until the Pasqua laws were totally rescinded did not gain the support of the more moderate associations. The more moderate associations accepted the government concessions and withdrew from efforts geared toward a total revocation of the Pasqua laws. Thus, important political and strategic divisions existed between the main partners in this coalition, but the organizations were able to override the divisions as long as they operated in a political environment with a common adversary. Once the Socialist Party came to power, the political environment became more complicated. So too did the organizational relations, which contributed to the movement's fragmentation after 1997.

The relative success of extending the rights of immigrants in France was partially the result of the strong relational exchanges forged in the Parisian activist community. The relations between immigrants and their supportive advocates were largely nourished through a series of urban-oriented struggles. Working through these various campaigns, they also learned how to mobilize and work together as a unit; this cluster of activists was thus provided a certain degree of collective expertise in the area of immigrant rights mobilizations. While the 'urban' played a strategic role in both catalyzing and nurturing these relations, these place-based relations were by no means confined to the city. The momentum of the housing campaign at the *rue de Dragon* certainly motivated the rights associations to keep focused on the urban policy arena, but the emergence of another struggle targeting national legislation and national officials resulted in a rather prompt shift to the national scale. Thus, political and associational ties forged through the city eventually enabled actors to engage forcefully in a national level campaign for immigrant rights.

Struggling for Rights in Amsterdam and Paris: Concluding Remarks

This chapter has examined how the city became a strategic space for making broader citizenship claims in receiving countries. By gaining the rights to build mosques and access to public housing, immigrants were asserting their broader rights within their new countries. We maintain that the localization of immigration policy in the city transformed urban policy areas, (such as zoning, planning, and housing) into key fronts in the struggles for broader immigrant rights. Both cases reveal that aggrieved immigrants developed alliances with supporters in possession of specialized resources. In both instances, these supporters provided scarce knowledge and expertise in the different policy areas and they also served as brokers who connected immigrants to other strategic actors in the urban milieu (i.e., parties in Amsterdam and human rights associations in Paris). The spatial proximity between these various actors permitted them to work closely with one another over extended periods of time. Their enhanced capacities to work and politic together enabled these coalitions to make rather powerful rights claims in their respective cities. In both cases, the city was a strategic space through which immigrant grievances were first catalyzed and which facilitated the formation of innovative multi-actor coalitions.

In spite of these important similarities, we have also identified several striking differences between the cases. Most importantly, relations within the urban-based coalition broke down in Amsterdam but they evolved into the central hub of a national immigrant rights movement in France. We explain these different trajectories by highlighting the types of dependencies local activists have on broader organizational and institutions supporters. In Amsterdam, the local section of Milli Görüs had embraced the local liberal discourses of the city in order to achieve its goal of creating a mosque. This strategy enabled members of the local movement to develop ties with the local political elite and make important inroads in a restrictive cultural environment. However, the more conservative parent transnational movement objected to the maneuverings of Amsterdam leaders, resulting in their replacement with a more conservative leadership team. In Paris, the main actors in the coalitions also had different and conflicting ideologies and positions. However, supporters in the larger Socialist Party saw the activities of their allied associations as conforming to their own political goals. In this instance, the broader political context favored and supported the urban coalitions. Thus, immigrants struggled through both cities to achieve their broader rights; however, institutional contexts favored their consolidation and growth in Paris while blocking and derailing them in Amsterdam.

We conclude by arguing that using the "right to the city" framework to conceptualize the urban basis of immigrant rights struggles is limiting. The city is a terrain for broader rights struggles, which serve to catalyze and foster powerful immigrant rights coalitions. Cities are the spaces that enable stigmatized immigrants to concentrate their collective resources and deploy them in broader political struggles. Moreover, the rights coalitions that arise through the city can also become hubs of important national mobilizations. Just as the coalition in Paris became a hub of the national immigrant rights movement in France, cities like Los Angeles and London have become the driving hubs of movements in their respective countries. The perspective taken here, however, breaks with urban social movement and "right to the city" positions. Rather than see urban movements as a distinctive *type* of social movement, we argue that cities play distinctive *functions* in broad based social movements seeking to expand the rights of people. In the case of the immigrant rights movement, we argued that these are generative sites for these movements because they are the first sites for spurring grievances and for fostering multi-actor networks.

By identifying how broader social movements unfold through cities, urban sociologists can begin making a contribution to the more general social movement literature. This literature has largely dismissed the city as either a backdrop of social movements or a site of particularistic struggles (e.g., NIMBYism, "reactive utopias," etc.). The arguments developed here and elsewhere (see Nicholls, 2008; 2009) outline a conceptual framework that identifies the processes and mechanisms that make the 'urban' a particularly unique space for movements that unfold at a variety of spatial scales. The 'urban' ceases to be a backdrop or container of contentious political activities and instead becomes a strategic site for activating and incubating complex activist networks. Moreover, this particular perspective also lays the conceptual ground for analyzing the spatial contours of broad social movement networks. As activist relations flourish in certain cities (e.g., Paris, Los Angeles, San Francisco), key social movement resources—including money, knowledge, cultural capital, and legal skills—become geographically concentrated there. The geographically uneven character of these movements introduces powerful cleavages and rivalries between more and less powerful cities in dispersed social movement networks. Geographically-driven rivalries and conflicts affect the interaction between activists within the network. Thus, the arguments developed in this paper provide the tools for explaining how cities matter for broader social movements, and they also provide insights into the geographical underpinnings of national and transnational social movements. We believe that conceptual schema like 'rights to the city' and 'urban social movements' block scholars of urban contention from seeing beyond the city walls and examining how relations forged through cities enable activists to play strategic roles in broad anti-systemic movements.

Notes

1. *Amsterdam Centrum voor Buitenlanders.*
2. *Fonds d'action sociale pour les travailleurs immigrés et leur familles.*
3. *Société nationale de construction de logements pour les travailleurs.*
4. *Un Logement d'Abord.*
5. *Mouvement contre le racisme et pour l'amitié entre les peuples.*
6. Respectively: *Fédération des associations de solidarité avec les travailleurs immigrés*, *Ligue des Droits de l'Homme*, and *Groupe d'examen des programmes sur les étrangers en France.*
7. *Droits Devant.*
8. Translation: Collective of the Undocumented.
9. *Parents Etrangers d'Enfants Français.*

References

Armstrong, E. (2002). *Forging Gay Identities: Organizing Sexuality in San Francisco, 1950-1994.* Chicago: University of Chicago Press.

Berezin, M. (2009). *Illiberal Politics in Neoliberal Times: Culture, Security and Populism in the New Europe.* Cambridge: Cambridge University Press.

Bowen, J. (2006). *Why the French Don't Like Headscarves: Islam, the State, and Public Space.* Princeton: Princeton University Press.

Buijs, F. (1998). *Een moskee in de wijk: De vestiging van de Kocatepe moskee in Rotterdam-Zuid.* Amsterdam: Het Spinhuis.

Castells, M. (1983). *The City and the Grass-roots: A Cross-cultural Theory of Urban Social Movements.* London: Edward Arnold.

_____. (1977 [1972]). *The Urban Question: A Marxist Approach.* A. Sheridan (Trans.). London: Edward Arnold.

Fainstein, S., and C. Hirst. (1995). "Urban Social Movements." In D. Judge, G. Stoker, and H. Wolman (Eds.), *Theories of Urban Politics* (pp. 181-204). London: Sage.

Gottdiener, M., and J. Feagin. (1988). "The Paradigm Shift in Urban Sociology." *Urban Affairs Review*, 24(2), 163-87.

Harvey, D. (2003). "The Right to the City." *International Journal of Urban Regional Research*, 27 (4), 939-41.

Hayward, J., and V. Wright. (2002). *Governing from the Center: Core Executive Coordination in France.* Oxford: Oxford University Press.

Hmed, C. (2006). *Loger les étrangers 'isolés' en France. Socio-histoire d'une institution d'État: la Sonacotra (1956-2006)* (Doctoral dissertation). Université de Paris-I, Paris.

_____. (2007). "Contester une institution dans le cas d'une mobilisation improbable: la «grève des loyers» dans les foyers Sonacotra dans les années 1970." *Sociétés contemporaines*, 65(1), 55-81.

Ireland, P. (1994). *The Policy Challenge of Ethnic Diversity: Immigrant Politics in France and Switzerland*. Cambridge: Harvard University Press.

Isin, E. (2000). *Democracy, Citizenship and the Global City*. New York: Routledge.

Joppke, C. (1999). *Immigration and the Nation-State: The United States, Germany, and Great Britain*. New York: Oxford University Press.

Lefebvre, H. (1996). "The Right to the City." In E. Kofman and E. Lebas (Eds. and Trans.), *Writings on Cities* (pp. 147-59). Malden, MA/Oxford: Blackwell.

Leitner, H., E. Sheppard, and K. Sziarto. (2008). "The Spatialities of Contentious Politics." *Transactions of the Institute of British Geographers*, 33(2), 157–72.

Lindo, F. (1999). *Heilige wijsheid in Amsterdam: Ayasofia stadsdeel De Baarsjes en de strijd om het Riva terrein*. Amsterdam: Het Spinhuis.

Maussen, M. (2007). "Islamic Presence and Mosque Establishment in France: Colonialism, Arrangements for Guest Workers and Citizenship." *Journal of Ethnic and Migration Studies*, 33(6), 981-1002.

_____. (2009). *Constructing Mosques: The Governance of Islam in France and the Netherlands* (Doctoral thesis). Amsterdam School for Social Science Research (ASSR), Amsterdam.

Mayer, M. (2009). "'The 'Right to the City' in the Context of Shifting Mottos of Urban Social Movements." *CITY*, 13(2-3), 362-74.

_____. (Forthcoming). "Multiscalar Mobilization for the Just City: New Spatial Politics of Urban Movements." In W. Nicholls, J. Beaumont, and B. Miller (Eds.), *Spaces of Contention: Places, Scales, and Networks of Social Justice Movements*. London: Ashgate.

Milkman, R. (2005). *L.A. Story: Immigrant Workers and the Future of the U.S. Labor Movement*. Berkeley: University of California Press.

Mitchell, D. (2003). *The Right to the City: Social Justice and the Fight for Public Space*. New York: Guilford Press.

_____. (2009). "Place, Relations, Networks: The Geographical Foundations of Social Movements." *Transactions of the Institute of British Geographers*, 34(1), 78-93.

Nicholls, W. (2008). "The Urban Question Revisited: The Importance of Cities for Social Movements." *International Journal of Urban and Regional Research*, 32(4), 841-59.

Østergaard-Nielsen, E. (2003). *Transnational Politics: Turks and Kurds in Germany*. London: Routledge.

Passeron, J. C., and C. Grignon. (1989). *Le Savant et le Populaire, Misérabilisme et Populisme en Sociologie et en Littérature*. Paris: Seuil-Gallimard.

Péchu, C. (1999). "Black African Immigrants in France and Claims for Housing." *Journal of Ethnic and Migration Studies*, 25(4), 727-44.

_____. (2001). "Générations Militantes a Droit au Logement." *Revue français de science politique*, 51(1), 73-103.

_____. (2004). *Du Comité des Mal Logés au Droit au Logement, Sociologie d'une Mobilisation* (Doctoral thesis). Institute d'Etudes Politiques de Paris, Paris.

Pickvance, C. (2003). "From Urban Social Movements to Urban Movements: A Review and Introduction to a Symposium on Urban Movements." *International Journal of Urban and Regional Research*, 27(1), 102-9.

Rath, J., R. Penninx, K. Groenendijk, and A. Meijer. (2001). *Western Europe and Islam*. Leiden: Brill Publishers.

Sikkink, K. (2005). "Patterns of Dynamic Multilevel Governance and the Insider-outsider Coalition." In D. della Porta and S. Tarrow (Eds.), *Transnational Protest and Global Activism* (pp. 151-74). Boulder, CO: Rowman & Littlefield.

Siméant, J. (1998). *La Cause des Sans-Papiers*. Paris: Presses SciencesPo.

Soja, E. (2000). *Postmetropolis: Critical Studies of Cities and Regions*. Oxford: Blackwell.

_____. (2010). *Seeking Spatial Justice*. Minneapolis: University of Minnesota Press.

Sunier, T. (2009). "Houses of Worship and the Policies of Space in Amsterdam." In L. Nell and J. Rath (Eds.), *Ethnic Amsterdam: Immigrants and Urban Change in the Twentieth Century* (pp. 159-76). Amsterdam: Amsterdam University Press.

Tarrow, S., and D. McAdam. (2005). "Scale Shift in Transnational Contention." In D. della Porta and S. Tarrow (Eds.), *Transnational Protest and Global Activism* (pp. 121-50). Boulder, CO: Rowman & Littlefield.

Vermeulen, F. (2005). "Organisational Patterns: Surinamese and Turkish Associations in Amsterdam, 1960-1990." *Journal of Ethnic and Migration Studies*, 31(5), 951-73.

_____. (2006). *The Immigrant Organising Process: Turkish Organisations in Amsterdam and Berlin and Surinamese Organisations in Amsterdam, 1960-2000*. Amsterdam: Amsterdam University Press.

Wihtol de Wenden, C. (1994). "Immigrants as Political Actors in France." *Western European Politics*, 17(2), 91-110.

PART III

ORGANIZING THE RIGHT TO THE CITY: ORGANIZATIONS, CITIZENSHIP, AND THE INSTITUTIONALIZATION OF BELONGING

6

Dancing with the State:
Migrant Workers, NGOs, and the
Remaking of Urban Citizenship in China

Xuefei Ren

The large-scale, high-speed urbanization in China over the past three decades has produced a vast number of dispossessed. As the majority of the country's population will be living in cities in the next decade, Chinese cities have become strategic sites for the disenfranchised to make claims for their "right to the city" (Lefebvre, 1996). These marginalized groups include, for example, landless farmers, displaced homeowners, laid-off state-sector workers, and the 150 million migrant workers who have become the majority of China's new working class. Although it is problematic to list specific disadvantaged groups in discussions of the right to the city—because such an approach inevitably excludes those who do not get listed (Mayer, 2009)—any study of remaking urban citizenship in China would be incomplete without an in-depth analysis of the rights conditions of migrant workers. The plight of migrant workers in Chinese cities reveals the core issues that underlie the current legal, but illegitimate, urban citizenship regime premised on the urban-rural hierarchy.

This chapter examines the remaking of urban citizenship in contemporary China through the lens of migrant workers' rights movements led by NGOs. I will first discuss the theoretical debate on urban citizenship and the right to the city and then examine what the "right to the city" entails in the Chinese context. Specifically, I identify three central issues for expanding urban citizenship rights in China—the discrepancy between formal laws and substantive rights, the urban-rural hierarchy as reinforced by the *hukou* system, and the repression of civil and political rights in the conceptualization of Chinese citizenship. Next, I will discuss migrant workers' rights conditions in Chinese cities: by the year 2010, their number had grown to between 150 and 200 million, and they have become by far the largest marginalized group suffering from the current exploitive urban citizenship regime. From an urban organizational perspective, i.e., focusing on meso-level social organizations in urban settings (McQuarrie and Marwell, 2009), I examine the role of NGOs in expanding migrants' rights to the city and discuss both the limitations and the potential of migrant NGOs in remaking urban citizenship in China.

The Right to the City and Urban Citizenship

The discussion on urban citizenship and the "right to the city" can be situated in the larger debate on the evolution of citizenship. Marshall (1977) examines the expansion of citizenship rights from civil, to political, to social rights—in that order—from the eighteenth to the twentieth century in England. He views modern capitalism as a self-contradictory scheme in which the economic system tends to produce inequalities while the political system is to a greater extent based on egalitarian principles of citizenship. In a review of Marshall's work, Turner (1986) defines citizenship as social participation and conceives of it as a series of expanding circles of rights pushed for by social movements, class struggles, and migrants. Turner (1986) argues that capitalism gives birth to a set of institutions and conditions that favor the expansion of citizenship rights. Instead of viewing the expansion of social rights as mere reformism—a cooptation strategy to pacify the working class and stabilize capitalism—both Marshall and Turner argue that social rights gained by the working class—through hard struggles, warfare, and migration—are real rather than illusory, and these newly gained rights form the basis of the modern welfare state.

If modern capitalism gives rise to a set of conditions for expanding citizenship rights, then it is capitalist cities, where large amounts of capital and large numbers of the dispossessed coexist, that have become strategic sites for social struggles to expand citizenship rights and, more specifically, urban citizenship rights (Isin, 2000; Sassen, 2006). Holston (2001) articulates that cities have become strategic arenas for the development of new forms of citizenship, simply because cities make capitalism an everyday, lived experience for residents and thus provide not only the context but also the substance for new forms of citizenship. The right to the city, according to Lefebvre, should not be defined as a simple "visiting right or as a return to traditional cities," but should be "formulated as a transformed and renewed right to *urban life*" (Lefebvre, 1996, p. 158, author's emphasis). *Urban life* here implies the larger process of capitalist urbanization that often dominates the countryside; and the demand for the right to urban life, in the context of the social movements in 1968, is a wake-up call that challenges the unjust, system-wide, exploitive urbanization process that has produced much inequality and discontent in both cities and the countryside. Based on a close reading of Lefebvre, Marcuse (2009) further specifies that the right to the city debate must specify three issues—*whose rights*, *what rights*, and *what city*.

As to the question of *whose rights*, Lefebvre (1996) posits that the right to the city concerns firstly the interests of those who inhabit the city as well as the interests of the whole society. Lefebvre makes a distinction between the working classes who inhabit the city but do not have full rights to urban life, and the economic elites who do not inhabit the city but enjoy exclusive rights to it. Similar to Lefebvre, Holston (2008) defines urban citizenship rights claims as being based on residency, as addressing urban experiences such as housing, infrastructure, and labor conditions, and as legitimating practices on the basis of residents' contributions to the city. In other words, the city is the primary political community for mobilization (Holston, 2008). Marcuse (2009) further adds that the right to the city concerns not only the deprived but also the discontented—those who are alienated and oppressed along lines of race, gender, lifestyle, and ideology. Marcuse (2009) formulates the right to the city as "an exigent demand by those deprived of basic material and existing legal rights," and as "an aspiration for the future by those discontented with life as they see it around them, perceived as limiting their own potentials for growth and creativity" (p. 190). He argues that both the deprived and the discontented will lead the fight for the right to the city.

As to the question of *what rights*, Lefebvre mentions the rights to training, education, work, culture, rest, health, and housing—all essential for the reproduction of labor power. Marcuse (2009) distinguishes rights in legalistic terms from rights in a moral sense, and he argues that the right to the city does not have to be limited to those legal rights that can be enforced by law, but should also incorporate moral claims for a better, more just system. In both legal and moral terms, the rights concerned here are not individual rights, protecting individual access to urban resources, but collective rights (Marcuse, 2009). David Harvey further elaborates this latter point and argues that the right to the city should be a collective rather than an individualistic right because "the transformation inevitably depends upon the exercise of a collective power to reshape the processes of urbanization" (Harvey, 2008, p. 23). For Harvey, the right to the city means the right to have control over the production and deployment of surplus and also over the globalized and capitalist urban process. The two are increasingly intertwined because the urban process opens up new circuits for producing and absorbing surplus. To gain the right to the city, therefore, is to gain democratic control over the nexus between urbanization and surplus production, and this entails a collective, rather than individual, struggle by the dispossessed (Harvey, 2008).

Lastly, as to the question of *what city*, Lefebvre, Marcuse, and Harvey all point toward a future city, or an "urban society"—in Lefebvre's formulation—where the hierarchical distinction between cities and countryside disappears, where the command over surplus production and the urban process is fully democratized, and where system-wide exploitation and repression are eliminated. Lefebvre sees the deprived working class as the main agent that can realize this ideal, while for Marcuse, coalition building between the deprived and discontented members of the intelligentsia can push the fight for the right to the city to a new level. Marcuse writes, "only in the experience of getting there, in the democratic decisions that accompany the process, can a better future be formed" (2009, p. 194).

The Right to the Chinese City

The right to the city debate in the Western context of urban social movements is helpful for specifying what the right to the city entails in contemporary China. In the latter environment, the answer to the question of *whose rights* should include those who inhabit the Chinese city—long-term urban residents, foreign expatriates, and rural migrant workers. The answer to the question of *what rights* should encompass civil, political, and social rights, and also the rights for control over urbanization and surplus production. Lastly, as to *what city*—it should be a future Chinese city that is no longer controlled by the small group of financial elites, transnational corporations, the party-state, and the media. Below, I identify three central issues for the expansion of urban citizenship rights in China.

First, there are large gaps between formal rights and substantive rights, or between laws and implementation. This is reflected in the current social movements in China; many of these demand that the government deliver what it has promised in the law but do not necessarily challenge the legitimacy of the law *per se*. For example, O'Brien and Li (2004) examine how rural peasants in China actively defend their rights guaranteed by law, or "rights they believed could be derived from the regime's policies, laws, principles, and legitimating ideology," and they use the term "rightful resistance" to describe this type of legal activism (p. xii). The rightful resisters in the countryside do not intend to challenge the legitimacy of the law or government policies, nor do they aim for wider civil rights of free association. Rather, they focus on the large gap between what is promised in the law and what is delivered in reality, and they often invoke central government regulations to fight land seizure and corruption. In a similar fashion, legal activism also characterizes labor protests by migrant workers. Lee (2007) observes that compared to the state-sector workers in the north, who tend to take their protests to the streets and engage in direct confrontations with the authorities, migrant workers in the south often resort to legal activism. Migrant workers have never been part of the socialist welfare system, and therefore, when labor disputes arise, they tend to resort to laws and formal labor contracts as their weapons. Their claims-making is largely focused on the gap between formal rights and substantive rights.

The second core issue underlying the current unequal citizenship regime is the urban-rural hierarchy, which relegates rural residents to second-class citizenship in relation to urban residents; it is institutionalized in the *hukou* (household registration), a system that dates back to the 1950s. *Hukou* was the predominant institutional mechanism for unequally distributing socio-economic rights (i.e., jobs, housing, food, social security) in the urban and rural sectors under socialism. Although the system has been relaxed in the post-reform era, the lack of rights for migrant workers in cities still can be primarily traced to this system. There are further fragmentations of citizenship rights within the urban and rural sectors along the lines of gender, class, and ethnicity, but the rural-urban hierarchy enforced by the *hukou* system lies at the core of the current unequal citizenship regime. The expansion of urban citizenship rights will have to eliminate this legal, but unjustifiable, urban-rural divide.

Third, the meaning of citizenship in China is mostly confined to socioeconomic rights, and the struggle for a just citizenship regime will have to involve new claims-making for political and civil rights. The development of citizenship rights does not necessarily follow a linear trajectory, as depicted by Marshall (1977), and the course might be interrupted and undermined by other factors. In China, in the post-1949 era through today, political and civil rights have been largely repressed. This unique characteristic of Chinese citizenship rights casts a shadow on contemporary social movements, as most movements focus on improving socioeconomic rights and make no demands for political and civil rights.[1]

Overall, the project of building a just urban citizenship regime and achieving the right to the Chinese city will have to address the gap between formal rights and substantive rights, eliminate the urban-rural hierarchy, and fully develop political and civil rights in addition to social rights.

Migrant NGOs in China: Remaking Urban Citizenship

As the largest marginalized group, migrant workers have received wide attention for their precarious working and living conditions in cities. According to various estimates, the number of migrant workers in China grew to between 150 million and 200 million by 2006, rivaling the volume of international migrants worldwide (Wang, 2006; Fan, 2008). The geographic distribution of migrant workers in China corresponds closely with the uneven patterns of regional development—with the wealthier eastern coastal provinces as the largest recipient areas for migrants and the poorer southwestern provinces as the largest sending areas. The higher income levels and availability of job opportunities in large coastal cities are the primary drivers of rural-to-urban migration.

What lies at the foundation of the current migrant labor regime is the *hukou* system installed in the 1950s, which divides the national population into two segments—urban and rural—and distributes rights and benefits to urban and rural residents unequally. During the socialist decades, residents with urban *hukou* were entitled to state-subsidized food, housing, education, and secure employment. At the same time, those with rural *hukou* status were deprived of such social rights and rendered second-class citizens in their own country, and their mobility was strictly controlled (Fan, 2008; Solinger, 1999). Rural migrants in many other developing countries face similar disadvantages in cities, but the *hukou* system makes China stand out, as the system legalizes institutional discrimination against migrant workers and deprives rural peasants of the socioeconomic rights enjoyed by urbanites. Under socialism, the allocation of resources for the reproduction of labor was tied to *hukou*, and it was nearly impossible for peasants to survive in the city, as they had no access to food, housing, work, and education. With the market reform, the *hukou* system has been substantially relaxed as the state has needed to channel surplus rural labor to fill the factories in the new industrial zones in the south and to provide the promised cheap labor for foreign and joint-venture enterprises. Although the restriction on peasants' residential mobility was lifted and migrant workers can now legally reside in cities—by obtaining temporary residency permits and a range of other documents—their rural *hukou* status is unchanged. Their status continues to make them the most vulnerable and exploited group in the city, with local governments and employers treating them as outsiders and underclass citizens. For more than half a century, the Chinese state has been using *hukou* to fulfill its development goals, first by squeezing the peasantry to subsidize urban industrialization during the socialist era and then by channeling the surplus rural labor into the lowest-paid urban sectors, such as construction and low-skill manufacturing, in the reform era. The market reform and the unprecedented scale of rural-to-urban migration have brought opportunities to expand citizenship rights for rural residents (i.e., those living in the countryside) and migrant workers (i.e., those working in cities); however, the *hukou* system prevents a linear path toward the full development of citizenship (Solinger, 1999).

There have been policy experiments in extending urban *hukou* status to rural residents and migrant workers, such as encouraging permanent settlement by rural residents in small and medium-sized cities (State Council, 2006), and a few cities, like Shanghai, have allocated a small quota of urban *hukou* annually to "model migrant workers."[2] However, these fragmented policy efforts do not alter the larger picture: the vast majority of migrant workers are deprived of the same citizenship rights enjoyed by their urban counterparts, even though they live and work in the same cities. There have also been policy debates about abolishing the *hukou* system altogether, but as many point out, what is at stake here has less to do with whether migrant workers can obtain urban *hukou* and more to do with the actual rights they can acquire in cities (Fan, 2008). Due to the highly decentralized fiscal structure in China, local governments need to cover most social security costs of their residents. Therefore, many municipalities have passed their own policies that exclude migrant workers from accessing social insurance schemes. Some migrant workers eventually obtain urban *hukou* in the city where they reside only to find out that they are still barred from social welfare services that are exclusively reserved for long-term urban residents. Under such an exploitative labor regime, labor rights abuses such as long working hours, below-minimum wages, and discriminatory hiring practices are widespread in migrant workers' experiences.

The state is unwilling and unable to address labor rights abuses and to attend to the welfare needs of migrant workers. This gap has been increasingly filled by non-government organizations (NGOs). In 2002-2003, the central government called for the protection of the legal rights of migrant workers. This change in the state stance toward migrants has since opened up opportunities for migrant NGOs. Most migrant NGOs work in three areas—providing legal aid for migrant workers in labor disputes; delivering services such as education for migrant children, vocational training, and medical aid; and building solidarity and facilitating social networking among migrant workers by organizing cultural events. Many migrant NGOs receive funding from overseas foundations, individual foreign donors, and foreign embassies in China.

Over the past few years, they have quickly become the leading advocacy groups working on behalf of migrants to improve their labor conditions in cities.

There are three major types of migrant NGOs in terms of organizational origins (Froissart, 2006; Hsu, 2007). The first type is known as GONGOs (Government Organized NGOs), which are sponsored by the government and work as extensions of the state. Beijing Dagongmei Zhijia—an NGO working for migrant women and affiliated with the All China Women's Federation—is one example. Second, there are migrant NGOs founded by urban residents that are not directly affiliated with any state organization. Examples of this type include Facilitator, a migrant NGO based in Beijing and Nanjing, and Friends of Migrant Workers, a legal clinic based at Sun Yat-Sen University in Guangzhou. Third are the NGOs founded by migrant workers themselves. These include, for example, Little Bird Hotline (in Beijing, Shenyang, and Shenzhen), Zaixingdong (in Beijing and Suzhou), Gongyou Zhijia (in Beijing), and the Institute of Contemporary Observation (in Shenzhen). Due to the heavy requirements set up by the state for NGO registration, such as endorsement from a state organization, most NGOs are registered as enterprises with the Bureau of Industry and Commerce instead of as NGOs with the Ministry of Civil Affairs.

Beijing and Shenzhen have by far the largest concentrations of migrant NGOs. The NGOs in Beijing are diverse and have extensive international connections. Their activities go beyond providing legal aid to delivering services and organizing cultural activities, to facilitating socialization among migrants, and to helping migrants better integrate into urban life. Located in the heartland of Guangdong province—the factory zone in southern China—the Shenzhen-based NGOs mostly focus on labor disputes and do work such as offering legal aid to migrant workers and helping them with labor arbitration. Many of the labor NGOs in Shenzhen have close ties with activist groups across the border in Hong Kong and with international organizations.[3] Ironically but unsurprisingly, the most progressive labor NGOs—those trying to organize workers and eventually change the system—are found in Shenzhen, the first Special Economic Zone in the country. The Institute of Contemporary Observation (ICO) is one of the earliest labor NGOs in Shenzhen, founded in 2001. According to statistics compiled by ICO, from 2001 to 2005, the organization carried out training programs for worker-employer relationship management in 15 factories, set up internal complaint mechanisms in more than 500 factories, conducted corporate social responsibility audits in 150 factories, provided legal aid to over 10,000 migrant workers, and offered vocational training to 1,500 workers. The workers who have benefited from ICO's various programs exceed 200,000.[4]

The space of operations for migrant NGOs in China is largely constrained by the state, and this has to some extent undermined their ability to challenge the system. First, as Gallagher (2004) points out, China's civic associations are tightly monitored by the state through mechanisms such as legal and administrative guidelines, restricted financial autonomy, double posting of officials, and the penetration of the party-state's ideology. All of these mechanisms apply in the case of migrant NGOs. For instance, the requirement of sponsorship by a state-sector work-unit makes it difficult for many migrant NGOs without government connections to register. Also, there have been increasing restrictions on receiving funding from overseas sources. For GONGOs, the double posting of officials is a widespread practice. The independent NGOs without government affiliations have to constantly court local governments in order to continue their activities. Over time, some of these NGOs have become transmission belts of the party-state, helping to foster the official ideology and to exert social control over migrant workers (Froissart, 2006).

The second major limitation of migrant NGOs is their strong orientation toward service delivery. The services delivered by migrant NGOs, such as legal aid, medical care, and children's education, have unquestionably improved the working and living conditions of migrant workers in the city. Local governments encourage and support such NGO activities but crack down on NGOs whenever they engage in labor organizing, make political claims, or try to build coalitions among themselves.[5] Beja (2006) argues that the NGOs in China after the 1990s did not play the same combative role as the ones that emerged in Eastern Europe and China in the 1980s. Many NGOs are humanitarian associations that seek to lobby the government to implement policies to solve specific problems. Beja (2006) notes that, instead of framing these problems (such as housing, migrant children's education, and labor rights abuses) in political terms so that they can be debated in public, NGOs tend to present these as technical problems and make policy recommendations for technical solutions.

The last major limitation of migrant NGOs is their tendency to perceive and represent migrant workers' problems as individual problems rather than as collective problems; consequently, their solutions are also individualized (Lee and Shen, 2009). As Friedman and Lee (2010) note, labor NGOs have been active participants in the state project of "rule by law," and by providing legal assistance and encouraging workers to sue their employers, the NGOs are individualizing the systemic problems of labor conflicts. This tendency has to do with the funding sources of migrant NGOs: since many foreign donors and foundations are more likely to fund programs that promote the rule of law rather than programs for labor mobilization and organizing, the NGOs tend to adopt a legalistic approach to labor rights disputes.

In a case study on legal aid services, Gallagher (2007) describes the paradox and dilemmas generated by this individualistic and legalistic approach of migrant NGOs. She notes that the legal aid services provided by labor NGOs help to heighten the legal consciousness of migrant workers by making them more aware of their legally guaranteed rights. Overall, participation in legal aid programs is an empowering experience for migrant workers. However, their chance of succeeding in court systems is fairly limited because China's court system is already over-burdened by the skyrocketing number of lawsuits; moreover, the system is not truly independent: many local courts work as *de facto* branches of the party-state.

Some of the limitations identified above are not unique to Chinese NGOs, and similar orientations can also be seen in urban social movements in the West, such as the shift in strategy from protest to program and service delivery and from challenging the status quo to claims-making for inclusion in the current system (Mayer, 2009). What makes the Chinese NGO sector unique is the very deliberate intervention of the state in shaping NGO activities—through both direct administrative restrictions and indirect measures that encourage migrant NGOs to adopt an individualistic, legalistic, and service-oriented approach. It is tempting to jump to the conclusion that, due to these limitations, migrant NGOs are incapable of truly challenging the current labor regime and reformulating urban citizenship. It is overly simplistic, however, to construct a dichotomy of state-versus-society and frame the question in terms of whether civil society can overthrow the authoritarian Chinese state or whether the state will trump civil society and maintain the status quo. Instead of viewing the state and civic associations as engaged in a zero-sum game, we need to examine how the state and the civil society have mutually transformed one another. In the case of migrant NGOs, despite the severe constraints under which they operate, it is necessary to recognize their transformative potential. I briefly identify a number of such possibilities below.

First, the service delivery undertaken by migrant NGOs *is* challenging the current urban citizenship regime by expanding social rights to migrant workers because the meaning of citizenship in China is largely defined in terms of social rights. The rural-urban inequality mostly concerns social rights. Since there is little difference in political and civil rights across the rural-urban divide, such rights are fairly limited on both sides under current one-party rule. Second, despite the limitation of the legalistic approach of NGOs, the various legal aid programs have greatly empowered migrant workers, heightened their rights awareness, and fostered their collective identity. In addition to the expanded services enjoyed by migrants, the heightened rights awareness provided by these programs is another major step toward reformulating urban citizenship and making the progression from social rights to political and civil rights. Furthermore, having these pockets of non-profit, democratic organizations in a non-democratic, non-electoral regime produces new sources of pressure and instability within the system. For example, the legal aid services provided by NGOs have generated a sense of "informed disenchantment" (Gallagher, 2007). The future expansion of the right to the city is dependent upon such bottom-up pressure, instability, and disenchantment.

Conclusions

As cities have become sites for profit-making and capital accumulation, the "right to the city," as both a research agenda and a political slogan, is garnering increasing attention in the field of global urban studies (Brenner, Marcuse, and Mayer, 2009). Cities in the global South in particular, with their drastic socioeconomic inequality, lack of democratic institutions, and vast dispossessed populations, harbor real revolutionary possibilities for realizing the political ideal of the right to the city (Ren, 2008; 2011, Weinstein and Ren, 2009). The right to the city should not only concern the struggle between labor and capital, as Harvey (2008) suggests, but should accommodate the interests of all those who inhabit the city (e.g., children, women, the elderly), and the whole urban society (Lefebvre, 1996). In this chapter, I have specified what the right to the city entails in the Chinese context by identifying the major areas of disjuncture that must be overcome in order to achieve a more egalitarian regime of urban citizenship. These include the large gap between formal rights and substantive rights, the urban-rural hierarchy, and the repression of civil and political rights in the conceptualization of Chinese citizenship.

In the case of migrant workers, I have shown that the migrant rights movements led by NGOs, in spite of their limitations and constraints, embody real possibilities for changing the current legal, but unjustifiable, urban citizenship regime, which is premised on the urban-rural hierarchy. The migrant workers' demand for their rights to the city challenges the very core of the current citizenship regime in China—the *hukou* system. By law, rural migrant workers in cities are second-class citizens without the same access to social welfare services enjoyed by their urban counterparts. The state is unwilling to attend to the social welfare needs of the migrants but has opened up spaces of operation for migrant NGOs. Relying on mostly international sources of funding, migrant NGOs provide social welfare and legal services to migrants, and by doing so, they are changing the current citizenship regime that distributes socioeconomic rights unequally across the urban-rural divide. Their legalistic and individualistic approach—a result of both the state policies constraining NGO activities and the orientations of international donors—is undeniably limited. However, these pockets of non-profit, democratically-oriented organizations in a non-democratic regime are transforming the state from within by heightening rights awareness among migrant workers and by generating instability and pressure in the current system.

The development of citizenship rights is not a linear process, as witnessed in modern Chinese history; substantial contractions of citizenship rights occurred in the socialist decades and after the Tiananmen student movement of 1989. The expansion of citizenship rights must be fought for by means of painstaking negotiations with the state, popular struggles, and class conflicts, all of which can be witnessed in the social movements unfolding in Chinese cities today. The rights movements led by migrant NGOs have led to gradual but substantial expansions of migrant workers' rights, and they are part of the larger movement of remaking urban citizenship in China.

Notes

1. See Goldman and Perry (2002) for a detailed discussion on the changing meaning of citizenship in China over the twentieth century.
2. "Shanghai Opens the *Hukou* Door, 43 Migrant Workers Might Become Shanghai Residents," Jan 8, 2010. Retrieved Feb 7, 2011, from http://unn.people.com.cn/GB/14794/21778/10732813.html.
3. See Chen (2006) on the growing presence of international NGOs in China and the collaboration between Chinese and international NGOs.
4. Retrieved Feb 6, 2011, from http://www.ico-china.org.
5. Interview with Kan Wang of China Institute of Labor Relations, Jul 2010, Beijing.

References

Beja, J.-P. (2006). "The Changing Aspects of Civil Society in China." *Social Research*, 73(1), 53-74.

Brenner, N., P. Marcuse, and M. Mayer. (2009). "Cities for People, Not for Profit." *CITY*, 13(2-3), 176-84.

Chen, J. (2006). "The NGO Community in China: Expanding Linkages with Transnational Civil Society and Their Democratic Implications." *China Perspectives*, 68(Nov-Dec), 29-40.

Fan, C. (2008). *China on the Move*. London: Routledge.

Friedman, E. (2009). "External Pressure and Local Mobilization: Transnational Activism and the Emergence of the Chinese Labor Movement." *Mobilization: An International Journal*, 14(2), 199-218.

Friedman, E., and C. K. Lee. (2010). "Remaking the World of Chinese Labour: A 30-year Retrospective." *British Journal of Industrial Relations*, 48(3), 507-533.

Froissart, C. (2006). "Escaping from Under the Party's Thumb: A Few Examples of Migrant Workers' Strivings for Autonomy." *Social Research*, 73(1), 197-218.

Gallagher, M. (2004). "The Limits of Civil Society in a Late Leninist State." In M. Alagappa (Ed.), *Civil Society and Political Change in Asia: Expanding and Contracting Democratic Space* (pp. 419-52). Stanford: Stanford University Press.

_____. (2007). "Hope for Protection and Hopeless Choices: Labor Legal Aid in the PRC." In E. Perry and M. Goldman (Eds.), *Grassroots Political Reform in Contemporary China* (pp. 196-227). Cambridge: Harvard University Press.

Goldman, M., and E. Perry (Eds.). (2002). *Changing Meanings of Citizenship in Modern China*. Cambridge: Harvard University Press.

Harvey, D. (2008). The Right to the City. *New Left Review*, 53(Sep-Oct), 23-40.

Holston, J. (2001). "Urban Citizenship and Globalization." In A. Scott (Ed.), *Global City-regions: Trends, Theory, Policy* (pp. 325-48). Oxford: Oxford University Press.

_____. (2008). *Insurgent Citizenship: Disjunctions of Democracy and Modernity in Brazil*. Princeton: Princeton University Press.

Hsu, J. Y. (2007). "Defining Boundaries of the Relationship: Beijing Migrant Civil Society Organisations and the Government." *Graduate Journal of Asia-Pacific Studies*, 5(2), 16-33.

Isin, E. F. (Ed.). (2000). *Democracy, Citizenship and the Global City*. London: Routledge.

Lee, C. K. (2007). *Against the Law: Labor Protests in China's Rustbelt and Sunbelt*. Berkeley/Los Angeles: University of California Press.

Lee, C. K., and Y. Shen. (2009). "China: The Paradox and Possibility of a Public Sociology of Labor." *Work and Occupations*, 36(2), 110-25.

Lefebvre, H. (1996). *Writings on Cities*. E. Kofman and E. Lebas (Eds. and Trans.). Malden, MA/Oxford: Blackwell Publishers.

Marcuse, P. (2009). "From Critical Urban Theory to the Right to the City." *CITY*, 13(203), 185-97.

Marshall, T. H. (1977). *Class, Citizenship and Social Development*. Chicago: University of Chicago Press.

Mayer, M. (2009). "The 'Right to the City' in the Context of Shifting Mottos of Urban Social Movements." *CITY*, 13(2-3), 362-74.

McQuarrie, M., and N. P. Marwell. (2009). "The Missing Organizational Dimension in Urban Sociology." *City and Community*, 8(3), 247-68.

O'Brien, K. J., and L. Li. (2006). *Rightful Resistance in Rural China*. New York: Cambridge University Press.

Ren, X. (2008). "Forward to the Past: Historical Preservation in Globalizing Shanghai." *City and Community*, 7(1), 23-43.

_____. (2011). *Building Globalization: Transnational Architecture Production in Urban China*. Chicago: University of Chicago Press.

Sassen, S. (2006). *Territory, Authority, Rights: From Medieval to Global Assemblages*. Princeton: Princeton University Press.

Solinger, D. J. (1999). *Contesting Citizenship in Urban China: Peasant Migrants, the State, and the Logic of the Market*. Berkeley/Los Angeles: University of California Press.

State Council. (2006). The Eleventh Five-year Plan.

Turner, B. (1986). *Citizenship and Capitalism: The Debate over Reformism*. Winchester, MA: Allen & Unwin Ltd.

Wang, C. (2006). "The Changing Situation of Migrant Labor." *Social Research*, 73(1), 185-96.

Weinstein, L., and X. Ren. (2009). "The Changing Right to the City: Urban Renewal and Housing Rights in Globalizing Shanghai and Mumbai." *City and Community*, 8(4), 407-32.

7

Making the Case for Organizational Presence: Civic Inclusion, Access to Resources, and Formal Community Organizations

Irene Bloemraad and Shannon Gleeson

When asked about ethnic groups in his city in 2006, a San Jose city councilor had trouble mentioning more than a few organizations. When pressed further, he acknowledged,

> We have the Italian groups, we have the Mexican group, the Mexican heritage group.... We have various chambers of commerce...a Hispanic chamber, we have the African American chamber...the Italian, and so forth.

Ethnic organizations, for this local politician, were vaguely known, largely confined to business groups, and mostly located on the political periphery.[1] The politician's lack of knowledge is striking, especially given the extensive literature on past and present immigrant incorporation into the civic landscape of places such as New York, Boston, and Chicago.

This chapter is about civic invisibility and the importance of immigrant-origin community organizations. While New York, Boston, and Chicago are iconic immigrant metropolises, immigrants account for a greater proportion of the population in San Jose than in these traditional immigrant gateways. Almost two of every five people living in San Jose are foreign-born, with about 60 percent from Asia and a third from Mexico and Latin America.[2] At over 350,000 people, immigrants in San Jose are almost as numerous as the entire population of Oakland, the third largest city in the San Francisco Bay Area, and they hail from around the world. Civic invisibility is not due to a lack of immigrant presence.

These immigrants and their supporters have not been silent inhabitants of the city. At least one hundred thousand people, mostly Mexican, marched through San Jose's streets on May 1, 2006, opposing HR 4437, a federal bill that would have made undocumented status a felony (Vital, 2010). The following year, members of the Vietnamese community engaged in a series of demonstrations and counter-demonstrations over the most appropriate name for a business district that is home to many Vietnamese American stores (Molina, 2007). Such actions can be considered a realization of the "right to the city" ideal (Purcell, 2003; Smith and Guarnizo, 2009): immigrant and low-income residents of color took to the streets to call for better living conditions and to articulate their vision of the city.

Yet protestors' actions have not transformed immigrants into equal and invited participants in local politics. As the city councilor's reaction suggests, despite their mass mobilization, immigrants and ethnic minorities remain largely invisible to the decision-makers who oversee the city's day-to-day civic and political life. The juxtaposition between mass protest politics and immigrants' relative invisibility in ordinary politics shows, we believe, that protest is not sufficient for acquiring voice and influence. Sometimes officials are conscious of their foreign-born constituents, but they rarely register at the top of local agendas.

In this chapter we argue that civic and political visibility depends on having an organizational presence in city life. Groups that are better organized around an interest or cause, or around a shared background or common barriers to inclusion, have better odds of being seen, heard, and acknowledged.

Furthermore, not all organizations have equal access. Formal nonprofit organizations, whether working to help someone rent a hall for an event or to advocate for bilingual public services, tend to be better at opening up civic and political spaces to immigrants. Bureaucratization and formalization can present challenges to those who favor grassroots participation, but formal organizations play an important role in bringing immigrants into local decision-making. It is critical to document and understand the degree of formal organizing within immigrant communities and to evaluate the consequences of organizational inequality.

In what follows, we first review various models of urban political inclusion with a focus on immigrant incorporation. We then introduce our research site, San Jose, California. We examine the city's organizational landscape and demonstrate that immigrant empowerment is severely hindered by the limited number of formal immigrant organizations in San Jose—many fewer than what we would expect given the city's demography. We explore some of the unfavorable consequences of civic inequality by considering resource allocation, protest politics, and immigrants' civic and political presence in the eyes of local officials.[3] We end the chapter by outlining some policy suggestions to reduce such inequality.

Theorizing Urban Citizenship and Political Inclusion

American scholarship on the political inclusion of urban minorities has long vacillated between a focus on electoral politics and an emphasis on social movement activism. Seminal work by Robert Dahl (1961) describes urban political parties' strategy of ticket balancing by running one or two "ethnic" politicians to secure the "ethnic vote" in New Haven, Connecticut. With a different purpose, but with similar attention to electoral politics, Ira Katznelson (1982) outlines the conceptual and participatory divide between New Yorkers' workplace activism around class and their ethnic orientation to local politics. Having been rooted in the experience of European-origin immigrants and their descendants in the Northeast and Midwest, the attention to electoral contests has a distinguished lineage in studies of urban politics.

This paradigm, however, became a target for criticism for failing to deal adequately with the second class citizenship and political disenfranchisement of low-income city residents and racial minorities. The civil rights movement of the 1960s and the urban protests that followed generated scholarship on social movement activism as the primary means for political outsiders to challenge elite insiders (e.g., McAdam, 1982; Piven and Cloward, 1977). Scholars differed in their evaluation of whether the formal political system could improve the lives of those excluded from power, but they agreed that civil disobedience, civil society mobilization, and contentious street-based action offered a surer path to political power than voting and electoral representation.

The debate over an electoral path to inclusion in urban politics continues to the present, although it has evolved as immigration to the United States has changed. Browning, Marshall, and Tabb (1984) challenged the adequacy of protest politics to explain the political empowerment of African Americans and Latinos in San Francisco, concluding that electoral coalitions were better for advancing minority interests. Other scholars have followed suit, acknowledging that although contemporary political parties do not incorporate immigrants and ethnic minorities as fully as in earlier periods, urban politics remains a battleground for votes and winning coalitions (Jones-Correa, 1998; Mollenkopf and Sonenshein, 2009; Rogers, 2009).

Yet other observers deem the electoral lens to be inadequate (de Graauw, 2008a; Minnite, 2009; Ramakrishnan and Bloemraad, 2008a). Today, many immigrants do not hold US citizenship and are formally barred from voting. Cultural and linguistic divides make accessing information about electoral campaigns difficult. The diversity of today's immigrants renders the creation and mobilization of a politically-oriented collective identity—as has been achieved by African Americans—problematic. Some also contend that the transnational orientations of some contemporary immigrants mesh imperfectly with local political activism, although the bulk of available evidence appears to suggest the opposite: civic and political engagement in the sending community breeds engagement in the country of settlement (Black, 1987; Smith, 2007).

In the search for alternatives, Mark Purcell (2003) lays out an anti-capitalist "right to the city" model that highlights the declining centrality of the nation-state. As Smith and Guarnizo (2009) suggest, the right to the city model suffers from an overly simplified view of group power relations, but it provides room for migrant agency. Other scholars have advanced the notion of "cultural citizenship," drawing attention to how immigrants articulate social and political membership through their everyday practices (Coll, 2005; Flores and Benmayor, 1997; Rosaldo, 1994). These alternative membership approaches move beyond standard electoral or contentious politics models.

Before abandoning electoral or contentious politics, however, we believe scholars should bridge the divide between the two by focusing on the organizations that link individuals to the political system. These organizations can include political parties, but more frequently they involve a host of civil society organizations that can communicate information down to immigrants and up to decision makers. These community organizations can also serve as sites for the development of collective identities, formulate and articulate the interests of immigrant communities, act as advocates on immigrant issues before city government (both elected officials and salaried staff), and provide a convenient way for local media to broadcast the perspectives of the immigrant community (de Graauw, 2008a; Ramakrishnan and Bloemraad, 2008a). While these diverse roles also mean that organizations can co-opt or mislead, we argue that immigrants run a serious risk of civic invisibility without a rich organizational infrastructure.

The focus on organizations does not inherently privilege one political strategy or another: electoral politics and contentious mobilization are both important, as are strategies of legal claims-making, bureaucratic incorporation, and local identity construction. Indeed, community-based organizations can, and do, engage in all these different political activities. Here our focus is on the role of organizations in furthering urban inclusion generally. Our approach builds on a growing literature recognizing the importance of community and nonprofit organizations in immigrants' political integration (Bloemraad, 2006b; Chung, 2007; de Graauw, 2008a; Gleeson, 2010; Marwell, 2007; Ramakrishnan and Bloemraad, 2008b; Sampson, et al., 2005; Vermeulen and Berger, 2008; Wong, 2006). This analytical lens also falls in line with recent calls for greater attention to organizations in urban sociology (McQuarrie and Marwell, 2009). Put simply, formal organizations matter; thus, evidence of organizational inequality and under-representation carries disquieting implications for immigrants' ability to achieve voice and influence in the places they live.

San Jose: 21st Century Immigrant Gateway

Founded in 1777, San Jose is one of the oldest cities in California. The city was incorporated in 1850 and was home to the first and second sessions of the California state legislature in 1850 and 1851. In subsequent decades, the city grew steadily as it became the service and processing center for the region's agricultural economy. From a population of about 18,000 in 1890, the city more than doubled in size to almost 40,000 in 1920. Immigrants, many of them from Mexico and Portugal, were a significant part of this growth. Between 1900 and 1920, over 20 percent of the city's residents were foreign-born (Gibson and Lennon, 1999).

San Jose, however, does not have a continuous experience of international migration and newcomer settlement like its northern neighbor, San Francisco. Exclusionary immigration laws that barred Asian and most European migration effectively ended immigration to San Jose in the 1920s; Mexican immigration also declined. When new migration did occur, especially in the decades following World War II, it consisted of US veterans and their families as well as other Americans seeking cheap housing and economic opportunities in California. These domestic, mostly native-born, migrants fueled significant economic growth, especially through industrial and real estate development. International migrants, however, were not a significant part of this story. By 1970, only 8 percent of the city's inhabitants were born outside the United States (Gibson and Lennon, 1999).

This has all changed in the last four decades. San Jose has been transformed into the Bay Area's largest urban center and the high tech capital of Silicon Valley. Today about 900,000 city residents live sprawled across 175 square miles of land. In 2006, 39 percent of these residents were foreign-born, 58 percent from Asia and 34 percent from Latin America. Immigrants' imprint on the city's landscape is clear in neighborhoods such as the largely working-class Eastside. This area is home to many Vietnamese and Mexican residents and includes the city's new "Saigon Business District" (Molina, 2007) and the well-known Mexican cultural hub at King and Story roads. About a fifth of the city's immigrants had lived in the United States less than 6 years in 2006. Whereas some US cities such as San Francisco and New York have been continuous migrant destinations, the recent and explosive increase in San Jose's immigrant population distinguishes the city as a 21st century immigrant gateway (Singer, 2003; Singer, *et al.*, 2008). Consequently, San Jose faces new structures and must develop new ways for dealing with its foreign-born population.

As outlined in Table 1, San Jose's immigrants are diverse in their needs and resources. San Jose's dual labor market epitomizes that of a global city (even though, strictly speaking, San Jose does not conform to Sassen's (1991; 1999) definition). One finds a wealth of professional jobs demanding high human capital, especially (but not exclusively) in the computer and biotech industries. Fully 34 percent of the foreign-born living in San Jose held a college or more advanced educational degree in 2006. Demand for high-skilled labor is accompanied by a strong demand for low or semi-skilled workers. During San Jose's tech-boom of the late 1990s, this included many electronic assembly workers. Today, the low-wage immigrant workforce is critical to many post-industrial sectors, such as construction, cleaning, restaurants, and other services. Twenty-seven percent of San Jose's immigrants have not completed high school, a much higher proportion than the 10 percent of US-born residents with a similarly modest level of education.[4] This "paradox of poverty in the midst of the affluence" has become a central feature of Silicon Valley's landscape (Zlolniski, 2006, pp. 3-4). Additionally, the diversity of immigrants' backgrounds—including factors such as their cultural origins, religions, languages, and migration statuses—further complicates San Jose's socio-economic stratification; thus, a milieu of complex integration needs is generated for both newcomers and established immigrant populations.

Table 1. *Demographic Profile of San Jose, American Community Survey, 2005-2007 Estimates*

	Number	Percent
Total population	**898,901**	**100.0%**
Non-Hispanic White (only)	285,249	31.7%
Non-Hispanic Asian (only)	274,338	30.5%
Non-Hispanic Black (only)	27,761	3.1%
Hispanic or Latino (of any race)	281,651	31.3%
Native-born	548,092	61.0%
Foreign-born	350,809	39.0%
Entered the US in 2000 or later	74,054	21.1%
Naturalized US citizen (% of foreign-born population)	177,498	50.6%
Not a US citizen (% of total city population)	173,311	19.3%
Individuals who speak English less than "very well" (of pop. 5 yrs old+)	222,585	26.8%
Ethnic ancestry and national origins (foreign and native-born)*		
Mexican	246,410	27.4%
Vietnamese	89,371	9.9%
Chinese	64,773	7.2%
German	62,652	7.0%
Filipino	50,603	5.6%
Irish	47,955	5.3%
English	44,851	5.0%
Italian	41,045	4.6%
Asian Indian	32,709	3.6%
Portuguese	14,977	1.7%
Education and poverty		
Less than a high school degree (of pop. 25 yrs old+)		
Native-born (% of all native-born)	25,863	9.0%
Foreign-born (% of all foreign-born)	82,764	27.1%
Bachelor's degree or higher (of pop. 25 yrs old+)		
Native-born (% of all native-born)	103,911	36.2%
Foreign-born (% of all foreign-born)	106,109	34.7%
Individuals living in poverty		
Native-born (% of all native-born)	50,704	9.3%
Foreign-born (% of all foreign-born)	36,375	10.3%

* Figures are taken from sub-categories of Census tallies for "Hispanic or Latino" (for Mexican), "Race" (for Vietnamese, Chinese, Filipino, Asian Indian), and "Ancestry" (for German, Irish, English, and Portuguese).

San Jose Politics and Immigration

San Jose is a peculiar microcosm of liberal California politics. It combines progressive viewpoints on social issues with the laissez-faire gusto that has powered Silicon Valley. Given the importance of real estate and industrial development for San Jose's post-World War II expansion and the city's dependence on high-tech companies today, pro-business and pro-growth interests have long played a critical role in San Jose politics. This can be seen in the prominence of groups like the Silicon Valley Leadership Group and the many chambers of commerce. In recent years, San Jose residents have also elected mayors who explicitly promote job growth and take on the entrenched interests of unions. For instance, in his 2006 bid for office, the current mayor, Chuck Reed, promised to check the power of unions over city politics (Mayor Watch, 2006; Office of the Mayor Chuck Reed, 2009); his platform garnered campaign endorsements from the Santa Clara County Deputy Sheriffs' Association but not from any major Democratic organizations.

Nevertheless, like much of the San Francisco Bay Area, partisan politics are largely absent in this liberal, northern California city. Seventy percent of registered voters in Santa Clara County cast a ballot for Barack Obama in the 2008 presidential election (Santa Clara County Registrar of Voters, 2009); only 20 percent of registered voters considered themselves "conservative" in 2009 (Jackson, 2009); and, with one exception, the entire San Jose City Council in 2009 consisted of registered Democrats, including Mayor Chuck Reed.[5] Electoral wrangling in San Jose centers on a candidate's relative position on the Democratic spectrum rather than polarized right-left conflicts.

As a result, San Jose is a largely pro-labor and pro-immigrant city. The Justice for Janitors campaign was launched from San Jose in the early 1990s. This movement to ensure fair wages for poorly paid service workers—many of whom are immigrants—garnered strong support from local elected officials and eventually led to agreements with several major tech companies and their subcontractors (Preston, 2004; Zlolniski, 2006). In 1998, the city council approved one of the most generous living wage ordinances in the country (Reynolds and Kern, 2003); an expansion of this ordinance was approved in 2008 (South Bay Labor Council, 2008).

On immigration, most elected city officials stand in solidarity with undocumented residents. This is evidenced by Resolution No. 73677, which the San Jose city council unanimously adopted in March 2007 after Immigration and Customs Enforcement conducted raids in neighboring cities in 2006 (National Immigration Law Center, 2008). The resolution reaffirmed the San Jose Police Department's policy of non-engagement with immigration enforcement officers. More recently, the city council publicly condemned SB 1070, an Arizona law passed in 2010 that allows state and local enforcement of federal immigration law and that makes unlawful presence or aiding undocumented immigrants a misdemeanor (Rodriguez, 2010; Woolfok, 2010). The city has also taken a number of steps to build a stronger day-to-day relationship with its immigrant residents and organizations, perhaps most notably through the San Jose's Strong Neighborhood Initiative, which was established in 2002 (City of San Jose, 2010). In contrast to the experiences of immigrants in other localities that are characterized by anti-immigrant reactions (e.g., Bump, 2005; Odem, 2008), immigrants in San Jose generally find that officials and businesses appreciate their economic and cultural contributions.

Nevertheless, San Jose's bureaucratic structure and programming reveal an urban center that has not yet established a mature infrastructure for dealing with its immigrant population. San

Jose—again unlike San Francisco—lacks any city agency that is specifically dedicated to immigrant affairs (National League of Cities, 2009). Instead, like most cities in the South Bay, San Jose relies largely on Santa Clara County to fund English as a Second Language and citizenship courses, to address hate-crime prevention, and to foster immigrant leadership (Castellanos, 2009). Relations between the San Jose Police Department and the city's immigrant population are not uniformly positive. For example, when his liberal counterparts in San Francisco and Oakland embraced the label of "sanctuary city," San Jose mayor Chuck Reed initially proclaimed that his city would follow federal and state laws since "we don't need to be a sanctuary city as other cities have done" (Normand, 2007). His comments prompted a wave of criticism, but they also hinted at the relatively weak electoral power of immigrants. As of 2006, only about half of all San Jose's foreign-born residents had acquired citizenship through naturalization, making the other half legally unable to pressure elected officials through the ballot box. Though the electoral power of immigrants appears to be growing (discussed further below), we stress that in a context where half of the immigrant population is barred from voting, immigrant organizations become vital to civic voice and political influence.

Assessing Immigrant Civil Society in San Jose

Scholarly and public interest in social capital and civic engagement has shined a spotlight on the importance of community-based organizations and voluntary associations for everything from democratic vitality to the good health of group members (Putnam, 2000). It is thus troubling that a small but growing body of evidence shows substantial under-representation of immigrants and racial minorities among US non-profit and voluntary organizations, both nationally (Bell, et al., 2006; Hung, 2007; Ostrower, 2007) and in California (De Vita, et al., 2009; Ramakrishnan and Bloemraad, 2008b). If mainstream organizations were including immigrants in their membership and services, this imbalance would be less problematic. However, as our research and other studies have found, mainstream groups often actively or passively keep immigrants out (Aptekar, 2008; Jones-Correa, 2005; Ramakrishnan and Viramontes, 2006). With fewer immigrant organizations to advocate, mobilize, and provide services, existing inequalities between foreign-born and native-born residents, or between particular foreign-born groups, will be exacerbated.

Following standard practice in assessing civil society, we enumerate the number of formal nonprofit organizations in San Jose that primarily target or represent immigrant communities in order to gain a sense of the character of immigrant civil society. To do this, we assembled a database of all formally registered 501(c)3 non-profit organizations (excluding private foundations) from the National Center for Charitable Statistics (NCCS). We then classified these 1,987 organizations as either "immigrant-origin" or "non-immigrant" organizations, basing our designation on identifiers and indicators found in the organization's name, group mission statements, other documents, and in-depth interviews.[6] In a fashion similar to Cortés (1998), we considered an organization to be of immigrant-origin if it focused on the problems or aspirations of a group with similar national origins, notwithstanding whether members, clients, or leaders were first, second, or third generation.[7]

Of the 1,987 formally registered nonprofits in San Jose, we identified 412 immigrant-origin organizations, which constitute just 20.7 percent of all nonprofit organizations in the city. This underrepresentation of immigrant-origin organizations is astonishing given that the foreign-born make up 39 percent of the population and that less than a third (32 percent) of city residents identify as non-Hispanic white on census surveys. Consequently, our research reveals significant inequality in the civil society landscape of San Jose.

Formal organizations represent, however, only the tip of the iceberg when assessing the vitality of civil society. Small and informal organizations are commonly overlooked by these methods (Smith, 1997; Toepler, 2003). Official sources typically produce a gross undercount (Grønbjerg, 2002), with registered 501c(3) organizations comprising only a portion of all voluntary associations (Colwell, 1997). Accordingly, we also identified publicly present community-based organizations in San Jose that are not found in these official data.[8] To find these organizations, we followed a method similar to Grønbjerg's (2002, p. 1757) "informant/community based approach" and relied on references from 62 interviews with leaders of community groups, public officials, and government staff that were conducted between June 2004 and December 2006. We also identified and enumerated organizations by means of ethnic newspapers, resource directories, and web searches.[9]

For focus and clarity, we limited our analysis to four immigrant communities: Mexican, Vietnamese, Indian, and Portuguese. Persons who self-identify with these backgrounds comprise 43 percent of San Jose's residents. We chose these groups due to their distinct migration histories, their different modes of entry into the country, and the significant variation in their socio-economic profile. Mexican and Portuguese immigrants have been settling in the area for over a hundred years. Mexican migration continues to be significant, and today a quarter of San Jose's residents report some Mexican ancestry. While contemporary migration from Portugal is minimal, the legacy of both flows is still apparent. Some Mexican and Portuguese organizations have been around for decades and have generated ties with local bureaucracies and political structures. In contrast, Indian and Vietnamese migration only began on a large scale in the 1970s. Today, people of Vietnamese descent constitute a tenth of the city's population, and the number of those born in India is even more modest. Indian and Vietnamese immigrants had to establish organizations *de nouveau*, rather than build on previous efforts.

These four immigrant communities also differ in their modes of entry into the country and their legal status. All four groups have significant proportions of people who arrived legally in the United States via family sponsorship, which is the primary means by which most immigrants acquire permanent residency in the US. In addition, a large number of Vietnamese migrated as refugees fleeing the communist regime or under special visas related to US involvement in Southeast Asia. Refugee status provides migrants with public assistance and more settlement help than that offered to other migrants. This includes help with setting up mutual assistance organizations, which facilitates nonprofit organizing (Bloemraad, 2005; Hein, 1993). In contrast, over half of all Mexican immigrants in the US are estimated to lack legal residency documents (Passel, 2006); fear of public scrutiny likely presents a significant barrier to civic engagement for this group. In comparison, the Portuguese, comprising an older and more established group, have higher rates of legal permanent status and naturalization (60 percent of Portuguese immigrants are naturalized), while Indians represent the largest number of legal, temporary workers in the US (Department of Homeland Security, 2007). Indian immigrants, in particular, arrive in the US with high levels of education. This fact serves as an advantage for civic and political engagement, but due to the temporary nature of some visas—such as the six-year H1-B high skilled work visas—some Indian migrants face uncertain time horizons in the US. This examination of a range of historical trajectories, contemporary resources, and migrant experiences helps us to capture a wide diversity of immigrant experiences.

From our database of officially registered organizations, we then identified 173 formal nonprofit organizations that had a substantial relationship with the Mexican, Vietnamese, Indian, or Portuguese communities. These 173 organizations represent just 8.7 percent of all registered nonprofit groups in the city (out of 1,987 total), a number which is much lower than these communities' 43 percent share of the city's total resident population. Based on our interviews and field research, we subsequently identified an additional 87 publicly present organizations that are not in the official database and 3 ethnic-specific chambers of commerce.[10] Of all the organizations identified, through both formal and informal means, only 67 percent appeared in the official database. Even when adding the uncounted organizations to those that are formally registered, we see nowhere near the number of community organizations we might expect, especially given the significant presence of Mexican- and Vietnamese-origin residents and, to a lesser extent, residents of Portuguese and Indian origin.[11]

We draw three important lessons from this examination of nonprofit organizations in San Jose. First, immigrant origin communities are severely under-represented in the universe of formal 501(c)3 organizations in the city. As we discuss further below, this results in serious, negative consequences for everything from immigrants' ability to acquire public resources to immigrants' civic and political presence in the eyes of local decision-makers. Second, reliance on official databases of voluntary organizations—a standard practice in many studies of the nonprofit sector—underestimates the vitality of immigrant civil society. Such underestimates could reinforce perceptions of political apathy or silence (Huntington, 2004) or lead observers to misjudge the mobilization potential of immigrant communities, as occurred most dramatically in the 2006 immigrant rights protests (Voss and Bloemraad, 2011). Finally, civic inequality varies dramatically across immigrant communities, with Mexican-origin communities having a considerable disadvantage. Twenty-seven percent of San Jose residents report some Mexican background, but *only three percent* (60 out of 1,987) of formally registered nonprofits serve or represent this community. Adding in non-registered publicly present organizations increases the number of Mexican organizations, but the total of 87 organizations still represents only a minute fraction of what we might expect given the demography of San Jose.

The Consequences of Organizational Inequality

What are the implications of organizational inequality in San Jose? For those who adhere to a radical grassroots perspective on political inclusion, the absence of formal organizations might not matter much, or it could be seen as a benefit. In the words of one of our informants, a local community activist,

> You know how we have to comply with the state rules [for nonprofit status], and they give you this little book about how you're supposed to organize the group? I say...don't they do this precisely so that you don't organize? As I see it, it's all with the purpose of keeping us from organizing people.[12]

This activist feels that the requirement to create a formal board of directors and the funding regulations that come with being a formal organization detract from the group's central mission. Commenting on his colleagues in the advocacy world, he believes that "most organizations spend all their time looking for funding to do things." Lacking an office, he works from home and carries a laptop to meetings; most of the group's initiatives are financed from his personal earnings and with the help of his family. He questions whose perspective other organizations represent. In an immigration reform gathering in Washington, DC, he told a leader of a major immigrant rights group:

> You are here in this tall building...but we, the workers, the ones who produce and bring you this food you have on the table...we are the ones who labor, and never have you come and asked us what we want.

This activist believes that formalization of collective energies could lead to organizational sclerosis, the domination of many by a small group of elites, co-optation, bureaucratization, and other processes antithetical to a radical participatory view of social action (Incite!, 2007; Silliman, 1999; Staggenborg, 1988).

While this perspective is understandable, we believe that dismissing the importance of formal organizations is a serious mistake. Organizational inequality, as reflected in the absence of formal organizations, not only reflects underlying inequalities in resources, social situation, and political power among different groups in society, but it can also aggravate those differences. Put another way, organizations have an independent and consequential effect on immigrants' civic and political inclusion in urban centers. We consider three instances of how organizational inequality matters.

Access to Public Resources

Cities provide important resources to their residents through services, access to space and buildings, and disbursement of funding for programs or initiatives that the city does not provide directly. Communities with more publicly present organizations are better able to access these services and resources.

These dynamics are most evident in city contracting and public grant-making to nonprofit organizations. Often 501(c)3 status is necessary to receive certain kinds of funding (Bell, *et al.*, 2006). Inequality in organizational capacity can thus lead to funding inequality for immigrant-centered services, which are sorely needed but often inadequately resourced. A needs assessment conducted in 2000 by Santa Clara County found that, compared with US-born residents, immigrants had between 2 and 4 times greater the service needs, yet they received only half as many services as the native-born (Santa Clara County Office of Human Relations, 2004).

An analysis of San Jose's disbursement of federal Community Development Block Grants found similar inequalities (de Graauw, *et al.*, 2010). In 2005-06, the US Department of Housing and Urban Development dispersed $11,476,479 to San Jose in CDBG funds. Added to carry-over funds from prior years, the city made $13,150,009 in expenditures to city agencies, non-profit organizations, and other grantees. The amount allocated to community-based organizations was about $4.1 million, which was disbursed to 38 groups.[13] Among the 38 organizations, only 7 groups (18 percent of grantees) were primarily oriented to immigrants. These immigrant-serving organizations received 23 percent of the total grant monies allocated to community-based organizations ($957,307 out of $4,082,095).

It is worth noting that the proportion of organizations funded, and the amount of money given to these organizations, is roughly similar to the proportion of immigrant-origin organizations among all registered non-profits in San Jose (21 percent). This suggests that the source of the funding inequality for the city's immigrants—who make up almost 39 percent of residents—lies less in the process of allocation to formal nonprofits and more in the relative lack of such immigrant-oriented nonprofits in the city. As we noted above, major segments of immigrant civil society are not registered as nonprofit organizations, and less formalized groups, of course, are ineligible for this type of city support.

Access to other city resources is also affected by organizational capacity. Cities can provide local groups with access to sports fields, meeting space, and venues for cultural productions often at no cost or with a modest fee. Such public goods greatly facilitate residents' ability to create a thriving civil society, which includes volunteers who run baseball leagues (or, in Silicon Valley, cricket and soccer leagues) as well as those who teach children the dances and songs of their parents' homeland. Access through organizational capacity, for example, is an underlying factor in the frustration expressed by a young, second-generation Latina who heads up an Aztec dance troupe:

> The city Parks and Recreation Department provided space [for rehearsal] and for years it was $50 for every three months. But a couple of years ago, it was really stressful because you have to be a nonprofit [501(c)(3)] organization, and we don't have that. We haven't—we just haven't done it. Half of it's because I don't know how the heck to do it....

Organizational inequalities consequently make it harder for immigrants to access municipal spaces and carry out the type of grassroots, community activities that many scholars of social capital and urban citizenship prize.

Since the members of immigrant community organizations often have modest resources, private donations can rarely serve to provide access to public resources. One staff person at a social service agency that works with small grassroots organizations to help them gain formal nonprofit status explained that many of the groups are located in low-income areas of the city that are affected by urban blight and where the majority of members tend to be undocumented. The social service agency provides technical assistance and funding to the grassroots groups for "capacity building." According to the staff member, funding often goes towards things as basic as 501(c)3 application fees.[14]

Foundations and corporations can be a major source of private sponsorship, but as a recent study of nonprofit organizations in Silicon Valley reported, ethnic organizations often lack the appropriate knowledge to put together successful grant applications (LaFrance Associates, 2006). A number of our respondents, especially in the Mexican community, recounted obstacles in accessing private grants. Organizations often need to establish legitimacy with private funders first. Among the organizations we interviewed, one grassroots immigrant rights group received early financial support and office space from a larger, established social service agency in San Jose. The established group's support and reputation, a representative explained, was critical in eventually winning backing from prominent San Jose foundations. In other cases, the existence of a dominant group crowds out funding opportunities. This was felt by one arts organization, which considers itself the only community-based Latino arts group in San Jose (its service audience is 70 percent Latino). A member of the group explained that when the organization seeks foundation funding, it often lives in the shadow of a larger Mexican performance venue that is better known to non-Latinos: "Sometimes it's hard for people to understand what we do." This problem was echoed in the study of Silicon Valley nonprofits: ethnic organizations that had asked for corporate donations recounted that businesses often "denied their organization funding because it was not considered a major institution, or because the corporation had already given to a Latino organization" (LaFrance Associates, 2006, p. 29). Private funders, perhaps much like public officials, still tend to see immigrants or minorities as a special interest warranting token support rather than as an integral part of the city.

Collective Action and Organizational Capacity

Building organizational capacity is critical to mass protest mobilization. Social movement scholars have long recognized the importance of social movement organizations, from the churches of the civil rights movement (McAdam, 1982; Morris, 1984) to local Sierra Club chapters in the environmental movement (Andrews, *et al.*, 2010). In their review of the scholarly literature on advocacy and the political process, Andrews and Edwards (2004) conclude that organizations set agendas, provide access to decision-making arenas, help pass policies, monitor and shape policy implementation, and shift the long-term priorities and resources of political institutions.

Although often depicted as a spontaneous grassroots eruption of protest, organizations clearly facilitated the unprecedented mobilization in the spring of 2006 against HR 4437, the federal bill that would have made undocumented status a felony. In San Jose, marchers represented a diversity of immigrant communities, but the majority appeared to be first and second generation people of Mexican origin. Police estimate that on May 1, one hundred thousand people took to the street in San Jose; ethnic media reported levels closer to 330,000 (Vital, 2010). By any account, this march was the largest demonstration that San Jose has ever experienced, and it was one of the biggest in the United States (Bada, *et al.*, 2006; Wang and Winn, 2006).

Vital's (2010, p. 32) retrospective of the San Jose march acknowledges that 71 organizations contributed to the mass mobilization, including immigrant rights organizations, unions, and faith-based groups. One labor leader we interviewed discussed the contribution of these organizations, which included the Central Labor Council, the Catholic Diocese of San Jose, a coalition of interfaith leaders, and even, in an unofficial capacity, the Santa Clara County Office of Human Relations.

> In many ways, the march was a spontaneous movement, *but* I also think that it [happened] *because* of the capacity of the coalition that met to shape the march.... We shouldn't underestimate our capacity to organize an orderly march with good press coverage.

This organizational capacity included both explicit and implicit promotion of turnout, logistical planning, and even direct funding for the effort.[15]

The importance of organizational capacity is clear when we consider how organizations not usually at the forefront of civil disobedience and collective action played a major role in the 2006 mobilizations. In the words of one key activist, "For the first time we saw a very large participation by clergy people. They were able to produce a large number of marchers through the churches." This was true despite the common perception that churches stay out of politics. For example, the director of a prominent faith-based senior center that serves mostly Vietnamese and Chinese elders—an organization which usually remains removed from political issues—recounted,

> I offered [the day off] to the whole staff or anybody who wanted to march. [...] So we didn't take exactly a political stand but when families are separated due to immigration issues we're against that because we think families need to be together.

Or, as a priest for a Catholic parish located in a largely Latino immigrant neighborhood explained,

[We had] two Lent services about social justice [and]...have been involved in promoting marches for drivers' licenses for undocumented people, and the marches for a more comprehensive immigration reform.

As Heredia (2008) argues, churches and other faith-based groups can draw on a potent mix of ritual and religious language to legitimize and encourage participation.

Spanish-language media also played a critical role, although such organizations are not usually considered part of the voluntary "third sector" since they are technically for-profit businesses (Bloemraad and Trost, 2008; Ramirez, 2011). One Latino organizer explained,

I'm someone who has been doing this for a long time, and I sincerely doubt that we would have garnered so many people if it had not been for the voluntary participation of the [Spanish] radio stations. [...] [T]he English-language press almost never covers these types of events, [not] until after a million people take to the streets.

The media provided information to the public and urged residents to participate. Other groups were also pivotal behind the scenes, including student organizations at local universities and some non-Latino and even non-immigrant organizations. Thus, the view of the 2006 protests as spontaneous collective action underestimates the organizational backbone behind the marches (Voss and Bloemraad, 2011).

We acknowledge that organizational capacity does not necessarily have to come from formal organizations. As we document above, the organizational universe of publicly present Mexican groups in San Jose is extremely modest. The activist quoted above, who opposes the formalization of organizations, laid some of the groundwork for the marches through earlier activities around the issue of driver licenses for undocumented migrants. He spoke of his frustration with the minimal resources and conservative strategies of local organizations:

I started to hold [rallies] only because the organizations I knew, and the unions, didn't want to do them weekly [as I did]. I asked them, 'Why?' And they would say, 'Because it's a lot of work, we have to get a permit, and it's costly to organize. It's better to do them every 6 months.' ...[And I would tell them] 'People are suffering every second, and we need to work faster to get things done.' And they didn't want to.... And I never got a permit, because I didn't need one. I asked, and they told me that it wasn't necessary if I was just going to walk on the sidewalk. They [the organizations] had never held marches along the sidewalk. But, for me, this is more effective, to have a one hour march, where people can see you and witness what happened.

This activist's organizing strategies generated substantial conflict with other groups' leaders, but his efforts garnered broad-based support from residents. Thus, San Jose's massive demonstration shows that despite the existence of very few formal 501(c)3 organizations, the Mexican origin community came together for an impressive display of solidarity and political engagement due, in part, to the mobilization of groups outside the formal nonprofit universe.

Yet the collapse of large-scale protests since May 2006 hints that a modest organizational landscape makes it hard to *sustain* a concerted social movement for immigrant rights, as studies of other social movements have also found (Andrews, 2001; Staggenborg, 1988). The priority of churches is to tend to the spiritual needs of their members, and ethnic media need to prioritize profit to stay alive. These organizations' missions are not primarily about collective action and political change. Similarly, grassroots organizing can energize and mobilize many, but it is hard to sustain a movement on the back of one extremely dedicated volunteer. Sustained collective action requires substantial organizational capacity.

Though immigrant-origin groups probably take the interests of the immigrant community more to heart than other groups, the coalition organizations do not need to be exclusively Mexican or Latino.[16] In 2006, alliances between Latino and immigrant rights organizations, on the one hand, and unions and faith-based groups, on the other, provided important support for the marches in San Jose. However, labor organizations, which are very important players in local San Jose politics, have made strategic decisions to focus their activism on broad policy issues, such as health insurance, rather than the technical or bureaucratic needs of immigrant workers, especially those who are undocumented (Gleeson, 2008a). Unions also face legitimacy issues with immigrant communities. As one labor council leader explained,

> The [union] leadership is still relatively white and relatively male, and its membership is not....
> So that's a tension within the labor movement [that] we've been dealing with...an issue of
> having credibility with our membership....

This is not to say that immigrants do not figure prominently into the concerns of labor leaders, but rather that immigration is not seen as *the* central focus. In the words of the labor leader,

> All the recent activism around [immigration] hasn't changed our work. [...] From our
> perspective, we want to go places where the need is the most. And we think that the future of
> that movement is with the poor, communities of color, and immigrants.

Despite San Jose's historic labor-friendly climate and the demographic opportunity immigrants offer to labor organizers, unions are positioned to be, at best, alliance partners rather than constant members of the vanguard for immigrant rights. The rapid collapse of sustained collective action following the marches of 2006 probably lies, at least in part, in the very small number of formal non-profit organizations run by and for Mexican or Latino immigrants.

Civic and Political (In)Visibility among City Officials

A final measure of the importance of a mature and developed organizational landscape lies in the civic and political invisibility of immigrant organizations in the eyes of San Jose city officials. According to Ramakrishnan and Bloemraad (2008a), civic and political presence—a function of visibility, alliances, and legitimacy—are indicators of "the degree to which immigrants are recognized as full partners in their communities" (p. 21). Visible organizations tend to be connected to other civic groups or with elected and appointed officials and are recognized by the general population, mainstream media, and government officials.

To assess political presence, we draw on our interviews with elected and non-elected officials in San Jose.[17] Using a semi-structured interview format, we asked our respondents to list all the organizations they knew which are active within a specific issue area, such as in the arts, healthcare, or business development. Among the issue areas we asked about were "immigrant or refugee" concerns, citizenship and voting, and "ethnic and cultural" groups. We use these answers to measure the organizational presence of immigrants and immigrant-origin minorities among San Jose city officials. While we do not assess the degree to which visibility translates into real political influence, we echo Ramakrishnan and Bloemraad's (2008a) proposition that political presence is a likely precursor to actual weight in local decision-making.

Overall, officials who did not have an immigrant background themselves listed few immigrant or ethnic organizations in their enumeration of groups active in San Jose. For example, the US-born elected official quoted at the beginning of this chapter listed an impressive 67 different groups active on a wide variety of issues in San Jose and the surrounding area. Of these, only 5 were an ethnic or immigrant-oriented organization: the Hispanic Chamber of Commerce, La Raza Roundtable, Mexican American Community Services Agency (MACSA), the Mexican Heritage Plaza, and the Portuguese Historical Museum. The councilor also offered a vague identification of 3 other organizations or groups of organizations, mentioning: "that Hispanic group" that worked on naturalization and immigrant voting; "immigrant groups" in general when asked about advocacy; and "the Italian American group" in relation to naturalization/voting and ethnic/cultural organizations. At best, 12 percent of organizations listed by the city councilor served immigrant-origin communities, less than the proportion of ethnic and immigrant organizations we counted among formally registered nonprofits (21 percent), and less than the proportion of the San Jose population that is of immigrant background (39 percent).[18] Furthermore, this official, like others, tended to name ethnic organizations largely in response to our questions about which groups were active with ethnic, cultural, or refugee issues, but rarely in relation to other policy fields. This suggests a division in officials' minds between "mainstream" policy areas, in which ethnic organizations play a limited role, and "minority" policy areas, to which such groups are relegated.

In a similar manner, the three non-elected city officials who were not first or second generation immigrants mentioned few immigrant-origin organizations. Neither the official on the city's Parks and Recreation Commission nor the official on the Senior Commission named a single immigrant organization. An official at the Housing Advisory Commission mentioned five immigrant-oriented organizations out of 32 (16 percent).

Our findings do suggest that the election of officials with an immigrant background might increase immigrant organizations' visibility and political presence. A city councilor with an immigrant background mentioned many more ethnic organizations than the US-born councilor discussed above. Due to constraints on the councilor's time, our interview was shorter, eliciting a list of 25 separate groups. Twelve of these, or 48 percent, were national-origin specific or pan-ethnic organizations, ranging from a Sikh temple and a multi-ethnic service and advocacy organization, SIREN (Services, Immigrant Rights and Education Network), to various Vietnamese organizations and the International Rescue Committee, which is dedicated to refugee resettlement. Surprisingly, there was limited overlap in the specific ethnic or immigrant organizations listed by the two elected officials.

We also interviewed two immigrant-origin school board trustees elected to two different boards in San Jose. One mentioned 9 immigrant-oriented organizations out of 36 (25 percent), while another listed 30 such organizations out of 41 (73 percent). In comparison, the one non-elected official with an immigrant background who we interviewed, a staff member of the San Jose's Strong Neighborhood Initiative, mentioned only two ethnic or immigrant organizations out of 26 (8 percent).

With our limited number of cases, it is hard to draw strong conclusions, but our data suggest that electing someone of immigrant origins can increase the political presence of immigrant organizations.[19] There might, however, be limits to using immigrant-origin elected representatives as a channel to increase the visibility of immigrant civil society. For example, of the 9 ethnic groups mentioned by a Mexican-origin school board member, 6 were Mexican organizations, which may be due to the official's background and relationship with that community. When asked about other community organizations in the highly diverse school district the official represents, the board member referred us to a staff member who keeps track of relevant stakeholders. The official could not immediately name additional organizations representing other immigrant communities.

The data also hint that elected officials might be more aware of immigrant organizations than non-elected officials. Perhaps San Jose's elected officials are forced, by the political competition for votes, to pay more attention to such organizations than non-elected officials. If this finding holds, it is noteworthy since almost half of all immigrants living in San Jose did not hold US citizenship in 2007 and thus could not vote. The modest level of ethno-racial segregation in the city mitigates immigrants' relative lack of formal political voice in the city. San Jose has been classified as one of the five most integrated cities in the United States, with ethno-racial minorities spread throughout the city (Robinson and Grant-Thomas, 2004). No elected representative, therefore, has the luxury of ignoring immigrant voters and their allies. The electoral strength of immigrants has become more prominent in recent years: San Jose residents elected their first Vietnamese American councilmember, Madison Nguyen, in 2005, and their first Indian American councilmember, Ash Kalra, in 2008.

Nevertheless, the lack of formal citizenship among many immigrants, especially balanced against immigrants' demographic significance and need for services, worries many scholars and public commentators. Indeed, some researchers focus increasingly on bureaucratic incorporation, which highlights the relationships that non-elected public officials can forge with immigrant communities to help them access services and resources (de Graauw, 2008b; Jones-Correa, 2005; Marrow, 2009). Our research, however, might serve to temper some of the optimism around bureaucratic incorporation as a pathway to urban civic inclusion. All four non-elected officials with whom we spoke mentioned relatively few immigrant organizations, regardless of personal background. Our findings instead suggest that electoral politics might remain important in increasing the profile of immigrant civil society. This speaks to our general contention that there are likely important complementarities between electoral politics and contested political action; an understanding of increased urban political inclusion should not exclude either.[20]

Beyond Elite Brokers

Absent a rich infrastructure of publicly-present immigrant organizations, how do city officials learn about the needs of immigrant residents? In some cases, they do not learn about them. The lack (or perceived lack) of a rich organizational structure removes important communication channels linking the voices of individual residents to the ears of urban government.

In other cases, decision-makers take a "liaison" view of the city's relationship with immigrant communities, calling on other individuals and institutional actors to serve as conduits of information and services (de Graauw, *et al.*, 2010). For example, the city councilor who opened this chapter highlighted the liaison work done by the Mexican consulate around immigrant day-labor issues:

> We work very closely with the consulate here to rectify [issues]. [One] issue is jobs and sometimes people can't find jobs.... They're not here legally sometimes and they'll go stand alone...or somebody's at a large construction site and waiting to be picked up for a day job.... So the community complained about that and we try to work out some way to say, 'Here's an

appropriate place for you, in this property.' ...[W]e work directly with organizations, not necessarily a small group, but the consulate...

Relations between local government and immigrants are also often compartmentalized and relegated to specific boards or commissions focused on minority affairs or human relations. In our interviews, officials often mentioned the San Jose Human Relations Commission and the Santa Clara Office of Human Relations when we asked about addressing immigrant tensions in San Jose. In other cases, decision-makers assume that immigrant-origin elected officials will serve as liaisons between government and immigrant communities. It was striking, for example, that almost all city officials with whom we spoke had a hard time naming any of the many Vietnamese organizations in San Jose—a city which is home to one of the largest Vietnamese communities in the US. Instead, they would reference the recently elected Vietnamese American councilmember, Madison Nguyen, as the key person with knowledge about the community.

This liaison approach is, at best, a stop-gap measure. It is better than nothing, but not sufficient to ensure full membership and political inclusion in civil society. What is even more problematic is that a liaison approach can serve as an excuse to put little effort into getting to know a city's immigrant residents. Relying on consulates to mediate relations between cities and immigrant communities underscores the view that immigrants are foreigners; immigrants are seen as the citizens of other countries rather than as full residents and local citizens of San Jose. Relying on the handful of immigrant-origin elected officials is also problematic, since any one person will have trouble representing a diverse community. This has certainly been the case for Madison Nguyen, San Jose's lone Vietnamese American city councilor, and the target of political attacks from a segment of San Jose's large Vietnamese community (Molina, 2008a; 2008b; Staff, 2009). Furthermore, as we noted with the example of the Mexican-origin school board member, relying on an immigrant-origin official might promote a relationship with only one specific community, thus excluding the full diversity of immigrants in a district. Creating space for a vibrant civil society would be more likely to reflect and express the diversity found in immigrant communities.

Finally, special immigrant or minority commissions can play a valuable role in furthering immigrant-friendly policies and ensuring implementation of those policies (de Graauw, 2008b). However, in the case of San Jose, few such structures exist. Santa Clara County has a more developed bureaucratic infrastructure geared to immigrant concerns, and it has done important work in this regard. The existence of these institutions and programs has, however, arguably allowed San Jose politicians to offload this work to the county, which is problematic given significant reductions in county funding and staffing. As of 2010, the Immigrant Relations and Integration Services for Santa Clara County had only one full-time staff member in the midst of a (likely worsening) fiscal crisis. Furthermore, as with all such liaison strategies, off-loading "immigrant" issues to other levels of government or special boards reinforces the failure of city decision-makers to recognize that immigrants and their children constitute a *majority* of city residents in places like San Jose and that immigrant communities are integral, rather than marginal, to city life. Hence, while a sustained focus on immigrant-specific issues is needed, the concerns of these communities must also be brought into the fold of everyday politics. One of the crucial mechanisms for doing so is organizational capacity.

Concluding Thoughts

Organizations play an important role in the political and civic life of cities. However, many of the organizations active in San Jose, including the vast majority of formal nonprofit groups, do not focus directly on representing or serving immigrant communities. We document significant inequality between the number of mainstream and immigrant organizations—given the city's demographics there are only half as many immigrant-origin nonprofits as we would expect—and we show significant differences in organizational capacity across immigrant communities. Here, the Mexican-origin community stands out as being at a particular disadvantage, despite its long history in San Jose and the significant proportion of city residents who are of Mexican origin. Space limitations prevent a thorough discussion of the factors driving such differences, but two stand out. First, the modest socio-economic resources of the community, which are not offset by public or private assistance aimed at fostering organizational development, limits the organizational capacity of the community. Second, the prevalence of undocumented status within the Mexican-born community stifles civic engagement and further reinforces the inequalities created by economic conditions and illegality. Thus, civic and political inequalities are not only a product of other inequalities; they are producers of an independent effect that reinforces disenfranchisement and powerlessness. More broadly, we contend that the lack of an extensive organizational structure among *all* immigrant communities harms the immigrant groups living in the city by limiting their access to city resources, hindering their ability to sustain collective protest, and preventing them from being recognized and included in political decision-making.

Our findings also suggest several ways to reduce inequalities. These include dedicating additional city resources to assisting low-resource immigrant communities in obtaining formal 501(c)3 status and making more funding and in-kind resources—such as technical assistance, leadership training, and facility use—available to groups beyond formally registered nonprofits. In this regard, it is striking that the Vietnamese-origin community, which also includes many low-income individuals of modest educational backgrounds, counts slightly more formally registered nonprofits than the Mexican-origin community. This is due in large part to Vietnamese immigrants' more secure legal status (almost none are undocumented) and the fact that they are predominately a refugee population that has benefitted more from public settlement assistance—which includes help with developing an organizational infrastructure—than other immigrants in the United States (Bloemraad, 2006a; Hein, 1997).

Cities such as San Jose also need to invest resources to mitigate the dwindling number of county programs dedicated to immigrant communities. Not only would this help fill growing service gaps, but it would create urban infrastructures that help establish and sustain long-term municipal relationships with immigrant communities. The successes of smaller, informal immigrant organizations suggests that collaboration and mentorship with larger established organizations—whether immigrant-specific or not—can provide important opportunities for leadership development and capacity building while also introducing new opportunities for much needed funding.

Lastly, public officials, elected and appointed, need to be educated about the fact that San Jose has become a 21st century immigrant gateway. The number and variety of foreign-born residents equals—and in some cases surpasses—the demographic diversity in cities of continuous migration like Chicago, New York, and San Francisco. Municipal leaders need to change their mindset from one that perceives immigrants as a special interest and minority issue to one that sees them as an integral part of the city's economic, social, cultural, and political life.

Such initiatives should also proceed with the understanding that immigrant communities are diverse and dynamic, like any other group, and that immigrants cannot be easily or accurately represented by a few minority elected officials, foreign consulates, or even a number of well-established immigrant groups from earlier waves of immigration. A vibrant civil society demands deep and broad engagement by all of a city's residents.

Notes

1. Personal interview, Jul 17, 2006.

2. The American Community Survey estimates that in 2006, 39 percent of San Jose's residents were foreign-born. The comparable figures for New York, Boston, and Chicago were 36, 27 and 21 percent, respectively.

3. We focus on documenting and evaluating the consequences of organizational inequality to make the case that protest politics are not sufficient for immigrant incorporation. Space constraints prevent an analysis of why immigrants are poorly represented in the formal nonprofit sector. As Gleeson, Bloemraad, and Ramakrishnan (2006) find, this is in part due to socio-economic and linguistic barriers, and for some, it is further exacerbated by undocumented status.

4. Statistics are calculated by the authors using three-year averages (2005-2007) from the American Community Survey. For one portrait of some of the area's high-skilled international migrants, see Saxenian (2007). See Dohan (2003) and Zlolniski (2006) on the low-skilled migrants who live and work in Silicon Valley.

5. San Jose city council consists of ten council members, each elected to represent a particular district of San Jose, and a mayor elected by all voters. The city runs on a council-manager system of government; the mayor nominates a city manager, who must be approved by city council.

6. Thus, "non-immigrant" organizations include those whose mission is not directed at any given national-origin or ethno-racial group (e.g., an Elks Lodge, a mainstream Parent-Teacher Association), while an "immigrant-origin" organization largely serves a particular group, such as the Santa Clara County Vietnamese Parent-Teacher Association.

7. Other studies, such as Hung (2007) and De Vita, Roeger, and Niedzwiecki (2009), identify minority and immigrant nonprofits by examining directors and board members, while Cordero-Guzmán's (2005) study of immigrant social service providers focuses on the origins of clients. To cast as broad a net as possible, we did not limit our categorization by leadership, membership, or clientele thresholds; we focused instead on overall mission and activities. For more on the methodology, see Gleeson and Bloemraad (2010).

8. By "publicly present" we mean all organizations known by local officials, ethnic or mainstream media, or key nonprofit sector leaders and volunteers as relevant to a particular migrant community. These organizations render their community visible to mainstream society, for example, through their advocacy efforts or their cultural activities. Our search, consequently, is biased towards groups that have moved beyond an incipient stage of development and have the potential to build bridges between the immigrant community and mainstream society.

9. These data are from the Immigrant Civic Engagement Project. For more on this project and additional findings, see Ramakrishnan and Bloemraad (2008).

10. Chambers of Commerce hold 501(c)6 status and thus do not appear in our official database of 501(c)3 organizations. Because informants consistently mentioned these groups as publicly present organizations, we include them in our discussion but not in the undercount statistics reported below.

11. Broken down by national origin, 62 percent of all publicly present Portuguese organizations (8 formally registered out of 13 publicly present) appeared in the NCCS data; these numbers can be compared with 64 percent of Vietnamese organizations (68 out of 107), 69 percent of Mexican organizations (60 out of 87), and 70 percent of Indian organizations (37 out of 53).

12. Translated from Spanish: *Tú ya sabes que hay que cumplir con las reglas del estado, que te dan un librito, que así debes de organizarte. Digo: No, es que ellos lo hacen así precisamente para que no te organices, porque todo eso es con el fin, lo que yo veo, de que no organices bien a la gente, tienes un tope, esto no puedes hacer.*

13. The remainder went to municipal government departments and publicly run programs.

14. Not all immigrant organizations face such challenges. For example, the leader of one political advocacy organization explained, "It's not like [we're] a state or federally recognized organization. We don't have a tax I.D. code. We're not a seed corporation. We're not a limited liability corporation. The best way I can describe it is we just happen to be a very well organized group of friends, who happen to have dinner together, and we happen to have expert people." The group relies on the expertise of its members, who are mostly young Asian professionals, to organize themselves through social media. They operate entirely on member donations and matching corporate donations. Other immigrant groups are not as well-resourced.

15. Data in this section include interviews conducted from October 2005 to August 2007 for Gleeson (2008b), as well as participant observation at a symposium, "Reflections on the Marches of 2006," held in San Jose on April 25, 2009.

16. We do not mean to romanticize ethnic solidarity and acknowledge that exploitation can occur between co-ethnics (Sanders and Nee, 1987). There is also significant variation in the priorities held within immigrant communities and across generations (Gleeson, 2007; Gleeson *et al.*, 2006). However, immigrant-origin organizations that emerge from immigrant communities identify priorities that are often missing from the agendas of mainstream groups (Ramakrishnan and Bloemraad, 2008b).

17. Our interviews span the period between June 2004 and December 2006. However, our organizational reputation data are limited to interviews conducted between August 2005 and December 2006.

18. The councilor also mentioned a few organizations run by and primarily focused on African Americans. These groups are not included in our tallies of immigrant-oriented organizations; only a very small percentage of blacks in San Jose are of immigrant origin.

19. Whether US-born or of immigrant-origin, the two city councilors we interviewed both represent districts that are home to large immigrant communities. Consequently, simple electoral calculations cannot account for the difference in reported immigrant organizations between councilors with immigrant backgrounds and those without.

20. For a similar argument centered on the Mississippi civil rights movement and black electoral success see Andrews (1997).

References

Andrews, K. T. (1997). "The Impacts of Social Movements on the Political Process: The Civil Rights Movement and Black Electoral Politics in Mississippi." *American Sociological Review*, 62(5), 800-19.

————. (2001). "Social Movements and Policy Implementation: The Mississippi Civil Rights Movement and the War on Poverty, 1965 to 1971." *American Sociological Review*, 66(1), 71-95.

Andrews, K. T., and B. Edwards. (2004). "Advocacy Organizations in the U.S. Political Process." *Annual Review of Sociology*, 30, 479-506.

Andrews, K. T., M. Ganz, M. Baggetta, H. Han, and C. Lim. (2010). "Leadership, Membership and Voice: Civic Associations That Work." *American Journal of Sociology*, 115(4), 1191-242.

Aptekar, S. (2008). "Highly Skilled but Unwelcome in Politics: Asian Indians and Chinese in a New Jersey Suburb." In S. K. Ramakrishnan and I. Bloemraad (Eds.), *Civic Hopes and Political Realities:*

Immigrants, Community Organizations, and Political Engagement (pp. 222-43). New York: Russell Sage Foundation Press.

Bada, X., J. Fox, and A. Selee (Eds.). (2006). *Invisible No More: Mexican Migrant Civic Participation in the United States*. Washington, DC: Mexico Institute and the Woodrow Wilson International Center for Scholars.

Bell, J., R. Moyers, and T. Wolfred. (2006). *Daring to Lead 2006: A National Study of Nonprofit Leadership*. Compass Point Nonprofit Services. Retrieved May 12, 2011, from http://www.compasspoint.org/assets/194_daringtolead06final.pdf.

Black, J. H. (1987). "The Practice of Politics in Two Settings: Political Transferability Among Recent Immigrants to Canada." *Canadian Journal of Political Science*, 20(4), 731-53.

Bloemraad, I. (2005). "The Limits of de Tocqueville: How Government Facilitates Organizational Capacity in Newcomer Communities." *Journal of Ethnic and Migration* Studies, 31(5), 865-87.

_____. (2006a). "Becoming a Citizen in the United States and Canada: Structured Mobilization and Immigrant Political Incorporation." *Social Forces*, 85, 667-95.

_____. (2006b). *Becoming a Citizen: Incorporating Immigrants and Refugees in the United States and Canada*. Berkeley: University of California Press.

Bloemraad, I., and C. Trost. (2008). "It's a Family Affair: Intergenerational Mobilization in the Spring 2006 Protests." *American Behavioral Scientist*, 52(4), 507-32.

Browning, R. P., D. R. Marshall, and D. H. Tabb. (1984). *Protest Is Not Enough: The Struggle of Blacks and Hispanics for Equality in Urban Politics*. Berkeley: University of California Press.

Bump, M. (2005). "From Temporary Picking to Permanent Plucking: Hispanic Newcomers, Integration, and Change in the Shenandoah Valley." In E. Gozdziak and S. F. Martin (Eds.), *Beyond the Gateway: Immigrants in a Changing America* (pp. 137-75). Lanham, CT: Lexington Books.

Castellanos, T. (2009, Jun 26). "Santa Clara County Model of Immigrant Integration: Overview of SCC County Programs." Presentation given at the Latino Immigrant Civic Engagement Trends Conference. Washington, DC: Mexico Institute and the Woodrow Wilson International Center for Scholars. Retrieved May 12, 2011, from http://www.wilsoncenter.org/events/docs/SCC.Wash.D.C.Pres.2009.final.version.pdf.

Chung, A. Y. (2007). *Legacies of Struggle: Conflict and Cooperation in Korean American Politics*. Palo Alto: Stanford University Press.

City of San Jose—Department of Planning, Building and Code Enforcement. (2010). "City of San Jose Census 2000." Retrieved May 12, 2011, from http://www.sanjoseca.gov/planning/Census/dstprofiles.asp.

Coll, K. (2005). "'Yo No Estoy Perdida': Immigrant Women (Re)locating Citizenship. In B. Epps, K. Valens, B. J. González (Eds.), *Passing Lines: Sexuality and Immigration* (pp. 389-410). Cambridge, MA: Harvard University Press.

Colwell, M. A. C. (1997). "The Potential for Bias When Research on Voluntary Associations is Limited to 501(c)3 Organizations." *Nonprofit Sector Research Fund Working Paper Series*. Washington, DC: The Aspen Institute.

Cordero-Guzmán, H. (2005). "Community-Based Organisations and Migration in New York City." *Journal of Ethnic and Migration Studies*, 31(5), 889-909.

Cortés, M. (1998). "Counting Latino Nonprofits: A New Strategy for Finding Data." *Nonprofit and Voluntary Sector Quarterly*, 27(4), 437-58.

Dahl, R. A. (1961). *Who Governs? Democracy and Power in an American City*. New Haven: Yale University Press.

de Graauw, E. (2008a). *Nonprofit Organizations and the Contemporary Politics of Immigrant Incorporation in San Francisco* (Doctoral dissertation). Retrieved from ProQuest Dissertations and Theses Database (AAT 3353241).

_____. (2008b). "Nonprofit Organizations: Agents of Immigrant Political Incorporation in Urban America." In S. K. Ramakrishnan and I. Bloemraad (Eds.), *Civic Hopes and Political Realities: Community Organizations and Political Engagement among Immigrants in the United States and Abroad* (pp. 323-50). New York: Russell Sage Foundation Press.

de Graauw, E., S. Gleeson, and I. Bloemraad. (2010). "Immigrant Suburbs and Central Cities: Understanding Differences in Municipal Support for Immigrant Organizations." (Unpublished manuscript).

De Vita, C. J., K. L. Roeger, and M. Niedzwiecki. (2009, Nov 9). *Measuring Racial-Ethnic Diversity in California's Nonprofit Sector*. Washington, DC: The Urban Institute. Retrieved May 12, 2011, from http://www.urban.org/uploadedpdf/411977_CA_Diversity.pdf.

Department of Homeland Security. (2007). *2007 Yearbook of Immigration Statistics*. Retrieved May 12, 2011, from http://www.dhs.gov/xlibrary/assets/statistics/yearbook/2007/ois_2007_yearbook.pdf.

Dohan, D. (2003). *The Price of Poverty: Money, Work, and Culture in the Mexican-American Barrio*. Berkeley: University of California Press.

Flores, W. V., and R. Benmayor. (1997). *Latino Cultural Citizenship: Claiming Identity, Space, and Rights*. Boston: Beacon Press.

Gibson, C. J., and E. Lennon. (1999). *Historical Census Statistics on the Foreign-Born Population of the United States: 1850-1990. Population Division Working Paper*, 29. Washington, DC: United States Bureau of the Census.

Gleeson, S. (2007, Sep 1). "Civic Inequality: Civic and Political Presence among Immigrants in the Silicon Valley." Paper presented at the American Political Science Association Annual Meeting. Chicago.

_____. (2008a). "Organizing for Latino Immigrant Labor Rights in Two U.S. Cities: The Case of San Jose and Houston." In S. K. Ramakrishnan and I. Bloemraad (Eds.), *Civic Hopes and Political Realities: Immigrants, Community Organizations, and Political Engagement* (pp. 107-33). New York: Russell Sage Foundation Press.

_____. (2008b). *The Intersection of Legal Status and Stratification—The Paradox of Immigration Law and Labor Protections in the United States* (Doctoral dissertation). Retrieved from ProQuest Dissertations and Theses Database (AAT 3331626).

_____. (2010). "From Rights to Claims: The Role of Civil Society in Making Rights Real for Vulnerable Workers." *Law and Society Review*, 43(3), 669-700.

Gleeson, S., and I. Bloemraad. (2010). "Where Are All the Immigrant Organizations? Reassessing the Scope of Civil Society for Immigrant Communities." *Working Paper Series*. Berkeley, CA: Institute for Research on Labor and Employment. Retrieved May 12, 2011 from http://escholarship.org/uc/item/840950m0.

Gleeson, S., I. Bloemraad, and K. Ramakrishnan. (2006, Aug 14). "Latino Civic Organizing in Comparative Perspective: How Individual, Community, and Contextual Determinants Shape Civic and Political Participation." Paper presented at the American Sociological Association Annual Meeting. Montreal, Quebec, Canada.

Grønbjerg, K. A. (2002). "Evaluating Nonprofit Databases." *American Behavioral Scientist*, 45(11), 1741-77.

Hein, J. (1993). "Refugees, Immigrants, and the State." *Annual Review of Sociology*, 19(1), 43-59.

_____. (1997). "Ethnic Organizations and the Welfare State: The Impact of Social Welfare Programs on the Formation of Indochinese Refugee Associations." *Sociological Forum*, 12(2), 279-95.

Heredia, L. L. (2008). *Faith in Action: The Catholic Church and the Immigrant Rights Movement, 1980-2007* (Doctoral dissertation). Retrieved from ProQuest Dissertations and Theses Database (AAT 3312381).

Hung, C.-H. R. (2007). "Immigrant Nonprofit Organizations in U.S. Metropolitan Areas." *Nonprofit and Voluntary Sector Quarterly*, 36(4), 707-29.

Huntington, S. (2004). *Who Are We: The Challenges to America's National Identity*. New York: Simon and Schuster.

Incite! Women of Color Against Violence. (2007). *The Revolution Will Not Be Funded*. Brooklyn, NY: South End Press.

Jackson, M. (2009). *Spring 2009 SPRI Omnibus Survey Report*. San Jose State University, Survey Policy Research Institute. Retrieved May 12, 2011, from http://www.sjsu.edu/spri/Documents/Spring%202009%20Omnibus%20Survey%20Report.pdf.

Jones-Correa, M. (1998). *Between Two Nations: The Political Predicament of Latinos in New York City*. Ithaca, NY: Cornell University Press.

———. (2005). "Bringing Outsiders In: Questions of Immigrant Incorporation." In C. Wolbrecht and R. Hero (Eds.), *The Politics of Democratic Inclusion* (pp. 75-101). Philadelphia, PA: Temple University Press.

Katznelson, I. (1982). *City Trenches: Urban Politics and the Patterning of Class in the United States*. Chicago: University of Chicago Press.

LaFrance Associates. (2006). *The 2005 Santa Clara County Nonprofit Benchmark Study*. Santa Clara, CA: Community Foundation Silicon Valley and CompassPoint Nonprofit Services. Retrieved May 12, 2011, from http://www.siliconvalleycf.org/docs/1276CFSVreportF2.pdf.

Marrow, H. (2009). "Immigrant Bureaucratic Incorporation: The Dual Roles of Government Policies and Professional Missions." *American Sociological Review*, 74(5), 756-76.

Marwell, N. P. (2007). *Bargaining for Brooklyn: Community Organizations in the Entrepreneurial City*. Chicago: University of Chicago Press.

Mayor Watch. (2006, Aug 1). "Is Chuck Reed a Closeted Republican?" Retrieved May 12, 2011, from http://mayorwatch.blogspot.com/2006/08/is-chuck-reed-closeted-republican.html.

McAdam, D. (1982). *Political Process and the Development of Black Insurgency, 1930-1970*. Chicago: University of Chicago Press.

McQuarrie, M., and N. P. Marwell. (2009). "The Missing Organizational Dimension in Urban Sociology." *City & Community*, 8(3), 247-68.

Minnite, L. C. (2009). "Lost in Translation? A Critical Reappraisal of the Concept of Immigrant Political Incorporation." In J. L. Hochschild and J. H. Mollenkopf (Eds.), *Bringing Outsiders In: Transatlantic Perspectives on Immigrant Political Incorporation* (pp. 48-60). Ithaca, NY: Cornell University Press.

Molina, J. (2007, Dec 10). "2,000 Push for 'Little Saigon'." *The Mercury News*. San Jose, CA.

———. (2008a, Apr 23). "Activists Begin Attempt to Recall San Jose Councilwoman Madison Nguyen." *The Mercury News*. San Jose, CA.

———. (2008b, Oct 1). "Madison Nguyen Recall Backers Start Massive Letter Campaign." *The Mercury News*. San Jose, CA

Mollenkopf, J. H., and R. Sonenshein. (2009). "The New Urban Politics of Integration: A View from the Gateway Cities." In J. L. Hochschild and J. H. Mollenkopf (Eds.), *Bringing Outsiders In: Transatlantic Perspectives on Immigrant Political Incorporation* (pp. 74-92). Ithaca, NY: Cornell University Press.

Morris, A. D. (1984). *The Origins of the Civil Rights Movement: Black Communities Organizing for Change*. New York: Free Press.

National League of Cities. (2009). "Mayoral Immigrant & Latino Affairs Offices: A City Practice Brief." *City Practices Briefs*, Spring 2009. Washington, DC: *Author*. Retrieved May 12, 2011, from http://nlc.org/File%20Library/Find%20City%20Solutions/Research%20Innovation/Immigrant%20Integration/mayoral-immigrant-latino-affairs-offices-apr09.pdf.

National Immigration Law Center (NILC). (2008). "Laws, Resolutions and Policies Instituted Across the U.S. Limiting Enforcement of Immigration Laws by State and Local Authorities." Los Angeles: *Author*. Retrieved May 12, 2011, from http://www.nilc.org/immlawpolicy/LocalLaw/locallaw-limiting-tbl-2008-12-03.pdf.

Normand, V. (2007). "Selling Sanctuary." *MetroActive*. San Jose, CA. Retrieved May 12, 2011, from http://www.metroactive.com/metro/06.27.07/sanctuary-city-0726.html.

Odem, M. E. (2008). "Unsettled in the Suburbs: Latino Immigration and Ethnic Diversity in Metro Atlanta." In A. Singer, S. W. Hardwick, and C. Brettell (Eds.), *Twenty-First Century Gateways: Immigrant Incorporation in Suburban America* (pp. 105-36). Washington, DC: Brookings Institution Press.

Office of the Mayor Chuck Reed. (2009). "Mayor Reed's Green Vision for San José." Retrieved May 12, 2011, from http://www.sanjoseca.gov/mayor/goals/environment/GreenVision/GreenVision.asp.

Ostrower, F. (2007, Jun 25). *Nonprofit Governance in the United States: Findings on Performance and Accountability from the First National Representative Study*. Washington, DC: Urban Institute.

Piven, F. F., and R. Cloward. (1977). *Poor People's Movements*. New York: Pantheon.

Preston, R. (2004). "'Justice for Janitors' Not 'Compensation for Custodians': The Political Context and Organizing in San Jose and Sacramento." In R. Milkman and K. Voss (Eds.), *Rebuilding Labor: Organizing and Organizers in the New Union Movement* (pp. 133-49). Ithaca: Cornell University Press.

Purcell, M. (2003). "Citizenship and the Right to the Global City." *International Journal of Urban and Regional Research*, 27, 564-90.

Putnam, R. D. (2000). *Bowling Alone: The Collapse and Revival of American Community*. New York: Simon and Schuster.

Ramakrishnan, S. K., and I. Bloemraad. (2008a). "Introduction: Civic and Political Inequalities." In S. K. Ramakrishnan and I. Bloemraad (Eds.), *Civic Hopes and Political Realities: Immigrants, Community Organizations, and Political Engagement* (pp. 1-44). New York: Russell Sage Foundation Press.

_____. (2008b). "Making Organizations Count: Immigrant Civic Engagement in California Cities." In S. K. Ramakrishnan and I. Bloemraad (Eds.), *Civic Hopes and Political Realities: Immigrants, Community Organizations, and Political Engagement* (pp. 45-76). New York: Russell Sage Foundation Press.

Ramakrishnan, S. K., and C. Viramontes. (2006). *Civic Inequalities: Immigrant Volunteerism and Community Organizations in California*. San Francisco, CA: Public Policy Institute of California.

Ramirez, R. (2011). "Political Mobilization en Español: Spanish Language Radio and the Activation of Political Identities." In K. Voss and I. Bloemraad (Eds.), *Rallying for Immigrant Rights*. Berkeley: University of California Press.

Reynolds, D., and J. Kern. (2003). *Living Wage Campaigns: An Activist's Guide to Building the Movement for Economic Justice*. Detroit and Boston: Wayne State University Labor Studies Center with the ACORN Living Wage Resource Center. http://www.laborstudies.wayne.edu/research/guide2002.pdf

Robinson, L., and A. Grant-Thomas. (2004). *Race, Place, and Home: A Civil Rights and Metropolitan Opportunity Agenda*. Cambridge, MA: The Civil Rights Project at Harvard University. http://www.civilrightsproject.ucla.edu/research/metro/Race_Place_Home.pdf

Rodriguez, J. (2010, Jun 8). "San Jose to Boycott Arizona, Sort Of." *Mercury News*. San Jose.

Rogers, R. (2009). "Political Institutions and Rainbow Coalitions: Immigrant-Minority Relations in New York and Hartford." In J. L. Hochschild and J. H. Mollenkopf (Eds.), *Bringing Outsiders In: Transatlantic Perspectives on Immigrant Political Incorporation* (pp. 93-110). Ithaca, NY: Cornell University Press.

Rosaldo, R. (1994). "Cultural Citizenship in San José, California." *PoLAR: Political and Legal Anthropology Review*, 17(2), 57-63.

Sampson, R. J., D. McAdam, H. MacIndoe, and S. Weffer-Elizondo. (2005). "Civil Society Reconsidered: The Durable Nature and Community Structure of Collective Civic Action." *American Journal of Sociology*, 111(3), 673-714.

Sanders, J. M., and V. Nee. (1987). "Limits of Ethnic Solidarity in the Enclave Economy." *American Sociological Review*, 52(6), 745-73.

Santa Clara County Office of Human Relations—Immigrant Relations and Integration Services (SCCOHR-IRIS). (2004). "Bridging Borders In Silicon Valley: Summit On Immigrant Needs And Contributions." Retrieved May 12, 2011, from http://www.immigrantinfo.org/borders/index.html.

Santa Clara County Registrar of Voters. (2009). *November 4, 2008 Presidential Election Official Final Results*. Retrieved May 12, 2011, from http://www.sccgov.org/elections/results/nov2008/.

Sassen, S. (1991). *The Global City: New York, London, Tokyo*. Princeton, NJ: Princeton University Press.

———. (1999). *Globalization and Its Discontents*. New York: New Press.

Saxenian, A. (2007). *The New Argonauts: Regional Advantage in a Global Economy*. Cambridge: Harvard University Press.

Silliman, J. (1999). "Expanding Civil Society: Shrinking Political Spaces—The Case of Women's Nongovernmental Organizations." *Social Politics*, 6(1), 23-53.

Singer, A. (2003). "The Rise of New Immigrant Gateways." Washington, DC: Center on Urban and Metropolitan Policy, the Brookings Institution. Retrieved May 12, 2011, from http://www.brookings.edu/urban/pubs/20040301_gateways.pdf

Singer, A., S. W. Hardwick, and C. Brettell. (2008). *Twenty-First Century Gateways: Immigrant Incorporation in Suburban America*. Washington, DC: Brookings Institution Press.

Smith, D. H. (1997). "The Rest of the Nonprofit Sector: Grassroots Associations as the Dark Matter Ignored in Prevailing 'Flat Earth' Maps of the Sector." *Nonprofit and Voluntary Sector Quarterly*, 26(2), 114-31.

Smith, M. P. (2007). "The Two Faces of Transnational Citizenship." *Ethnic and Racial Studies*, 30(6), 1096-116.

Smith, M. P., and L. E. Guarnizo. (2009). "Global Mobility, Shifting Borders and Urban Citizenship." *Tijdschrift voor Economische en Sociale Geografie*, 100(5), 610-22.

South Bay Labor Council (SBLC). (2008, Oct 29). *San Jose Council Approves Higher Standards At Airport*. Retrieved May 12, 2011, from http://www.atwork.org/?San_Jose_Council_Approves_Higher_Standards_At.

Staff. (2009, Mar 4). "Nguyen Survives San Jose Recall Vote." *Silicon Valley/San Jose Business Journal*. Retrieved May 12, 2011, from http://sanjose.bizjournals.com/sanjose/stories/2009/03/02/daily71.html.

Staggenborg, S. (1988). "The Consequences of Professionalization and Formalization in the Pro-Choice Movement." *American Sociological Review*, 53(4), 585-605.

Toepler, S. (2003). "Grassroots Associations Versus Larger Nonprofits: New Evidence from a Community Case Study in Arts and Culture." *Nonprofit and Voluntary Sector Quarterly*, 32(2), 236-51.

Vermeulen, F., and M. Berger. (2008). "Civic Networks and Political Behavior: Turks in Amsterdam and Berlin." In S. K. Ramakrishnan and I. Bloemraad (Eds.), *Civic Hopes and Political Realities: Immigrants, Community Organizations, and Political Engagement* (pp. 107-33). New York: Russell Sage Foundation Press.

Vital, R. (2010). "Coming Out and Making History: Latino Immigrant Civic Participation in San Jose." Translated by L. Lopez. *Reports on Latino Immigrant Civic Engagement*, 7. Washington, DC:

Woodrow Wilson International Center for Scholars. Retrieved May 12, 2011, from http://www.wilsoncenter.org/news/docs/MEX_090307_SanJose.rpt_ENG_0507L.pdf.

Voss, K., and I. Bloemraad (Eds.). (2011). *Rallying for Immigrant Rights*. Berkeley: University of California Press.

Wang, T., and R. C. Winn. (2006). "Groundswell Meets Groundwork: Recommendations for Building on Immigrant Mobilizations." Four Freedoms Fund and Grantmakers Concerned With Immigrants and Refugees. Retrieved May 12, 2011, from http://www.publicinterestprojects.org/wp-content/uploads/downloads/2010/06/Groundswell-Meets-Groundwork.pdf.

Wong, J. S. (2006). *Democracy's Promise: Immigrants & American Civic Institutions*. Ann Arbor: University of Michigan Press.

Woolfok, J. (2010, May 7). "San Jose Mayor, Council Members Tee Off on Arizona Immigration Law." *Mercury News*. San Jose.

Zlolniski, C. (2006). *Janitors, Street Vendors, and Activists: The Lives of Mexican Immigrants in Silicon Valley*. Berkeley: University of California Press.

8

The Inclusive City: Public-Private Partnerships and Immigrant Rights in San Francisco

Els de Graauw

In the spring of 2006, immigrants and their supporters took to the streets in over 160 cities nationwide to urge Congress to defeat HR 4437, legislation that would criminalize undocumented immigrants and those who aid them (Bloemraad, Voss, and Lee, forthcoming). Community-based immigrant organizations, which saw HR 4437 as a direct attack on their mission to assist immigrants, helped mobilize the unprecedented turnout that made the 2006 demonstrations for immigrant rights the largest protests the country has ever seen (Cordero-Guzmán, *et al.*, 2008; Pallares and Flores-González, 2010). Congress' failure to enact immigration reform in 2005-07 brought about an explosion in state and local immigration policies that aimed to fill the federal policy void (Newton, 2010; Ramakrishnan and Wong, 2010). Many sub-national policies have similarly targeted undocumented immigrants, restricting either their settlement or the services and benefits available to them. The most draconian, including the Illegal Immigration Relief Act adopted in Hazleton, Pennsylvania, in 2006 and Arizona's SB 1070 of 2010, also sparked rallies in various cities.[1] In all these instances, immigrant organizations used protests to put pressure on government to promote, rather than discourage, the social, economic, and political inclusion of immigrants, including those without legal status.

It is not surprising that recent immigrant mobilizations were staged in urban areas. American cities, and the civic organizations located in them, have long been at the heart of processes of immigrant integration, and they continue to be salient sites for the practices of citizenship today (de Graauw, 2008a; de Graauw, Gleeson, and Bloemraad, 2010; Wong, 2006). Protests are among the most contentious strategies that immigrant organizations can use to transform local government institutions, but they have sought to realize immigrants' "right to the city" (Dikeç and Gilbert, 2002; Lefebvre, 1996; Purcell, 2003) by other means as well. City-based immigrant organizations, for example, provide critical social services to newcomers (Cordero-Guzmán, 2005; Marwell, 2004), help immigrants fight labor law violations (Gleeson, 2009), express identities through cultural, religious, and other activities (Kasinitz, 1992; Smith, 2006), advocate for public policies that benefit immigrants (de Graauw, 2008a), and mobilize immigrants' participation in the political process (Bloemraad, 2006; Wong, 2006). These essentially are all different strategies that immigrant organizations employ in efforts to secure equal rights, in both a material and participatory sense, for immigrants in the cities where they live and work.

In this chapter, I argue that immigrants' "right to the city" is difficult to realize when there is no institutionalized recognition of their unique needs and interests. Protests might help, but immigrant organizations also need to work collaboratively with local government officials if they want to secure both material and participatory equality for immigrants. Using the case of San Francisco, I show that immigrant organizations and local government officials have become mutually constitutive around issues that are advantageous to marginalized immigrants. Immigrant organizations use city funding to provide social services to immigrants and they use both confrontational and collaborative tactics to advocate with local government officials to enact policies that advance immigrants' interests. They also serve as training grounds for public officials, and various elected and appointed ethnic city leaders trace the roots of their professional careers to local immigrant organizations. I argue that without public-private partnerships between city government and immigrant organizations, immigrants in San Francisco would not enjoy the degree of socio-economic and political inclusion we can observe today.

In what follows, I provide an overview of the role immigrant organizations had in improving the everyday conditions of marginalized immigrants in American cities in the past and how they continue to do so today despite added challenges. I next introduce the research site, San Francisco, and highlight how the city's continuous history of immigration has yielded a rich infrastructure of immigrant organizations and created a capacity for public-private partnerships to advance immigrant integration. I then explore three aspects of the public-private partnerships between city government and immigrant organizations that have reduced the material and participatory inequalities of marginalized immigrants. The chapter concludes with a discussion of the emergence of urban citizenship (Baubӧck, 2003; Smith and Guarnizo, 2009) in San Francisco.

Immigrant Organizations and the Right to the City

Immigrant-serving organizations have a long history in helping to improve the conditions of marginalized immigrants in American cities. At the turn of the 20th century, immigrant settlement houses and ethnic mutual aid societies in various gateway cities aided the integration of European immigrants who lacked access to political parties and labor unions due to gender, language, ethnicity, citizenship, or occupation (Beito, 2000; Sterne, 2001; Wong, 2006). They provided these immigrants with needed services, including English-language instruction, job referrals, health care, and unemployment and funeral benefits. They also taught immigrants leadership skills, mobilized their civic and political participation, and lobbied local government for policies that were responsive to immigrants' needs. For example, Chicago's Hull House and New York's Henry Street Settlement—two of the best known settlement houses—successfully pressured city officials to improve living conditions in poor immigrant neighborhoods and to provide public bathhouses, neighborhood parks, better sanitation, and night classes in public schools (Davis, 1994; Trolander, 1987). Also, mutual aid societies such as the Order Sons of Italy and the Ancient Order of Hibernians fought ethnic and religious discrimination against Italian and Irish immigrants, respectively, in cities like Boston, New York, and Philadelphia (Soyer, 2006; Sterne, 2001).

As a result of renewed mass immigration since 1965, American cities today are home to large numbers of Asian, Latino, and Caribbean immigrants who face some of the same integration challenges that made immigrant organizations so important to earlier newcomers from Europe. The work of immigrant organizations to improve the wellbeing of immigrant communities therefore remains critical today, particularly given welfare state privatization, government devolution, the absence of a national integration policy, and the elusive goal of federal immigration reform (Bloemraad, 2006; Cordero-Guzmán, 2005; de Graauw, 2008a; Marwell, 2004). There are additional reasons, however, why contemporary immigrant organizations feature prominently in the struggle for immigrants' material and participatory equality. Compared to yesteryear's urban political machines, local political parties today are less able and less willing to mobilize immigrants into the political process (Jones-Correa, 1998; Rogers, 2006; Wong, 2006). Also, contemporary labor unions remain divided on a number of immigrant issues, and they can be insensitive to the diversity within immigrant communities (Gleeson, 2009; La Luz and Finn, 1998). In other words, today's immigrant organizations fill a gap left by other institutional engines of immigrant integration.

Contemporary immigrant organizations, however, face two challenges as they pressure local government officials to strengthen immigrant rights. First, today's immigrant organizations often depend on government funding for their survival (Bloemraad, 2005; Cordero-Guzmán, 2005; de Graauw, 2008a; Tseng, 2005). Although there is no hard data to prove that government funding suppresses organizational advocacy (Chaves, Stephens, and Galaskiewicz, 2003), some immigrant organizations might nonetheless hesitate to advocate with local government officials for fear of biting the hand that feeds them. Second, immigrant organizations formally registered as 501(c)(3) not-for-profit organizations are subject to federal restrictions on the amount and types of political work they can do. First enacted in 1934, these restrictions did not exist when immigrant organizations helped integrate the great wave of European immigrants at the turn of the 20th century. Today, formally registered immigrant organizations are barred from partisan politics and they can engage in only a limited amount of lobbying directed at legislators at any level of government (Berry with Arons, 2003). So, while contemporary immigrant organizations are more prominent institutional actors in the process of immigrant integration, they need to be more mindful than their earlier historical counterparts, as well as other institutions such as labor unions, have needed to be in how they go about their advocacy.

These challenges do not mean it is impossible for immigrant organizations to advance immigrant integration through the political process. There are in fact many political activities that they can freely engage in, including advocacy with officials in the executive and judicial branches of government, advocacy that is nonpartisan or educational in nature, and advocacy for or against ballot measures. Also, these challenges are less consequential when local government and immigrant organizations see the need for each other. City officials are responsible for devising and implementing policies that lay the foundation for a productive local economy and a healthy and safe community for all. This makes it impractical for cities with large foreign-born populations to ignore the needs and conditions of immigrants because doing so could jeopardize the wellbeing of all city residents. City officials, though, find it difficult to learn about the rapidly changing needs of immigrants firsthand, given language barriers, immigrants' mistrust and fear of government, and immigrants' low rates of electoral participation (Ramakrishnan and Lewis, 2005). Immigrant organizations, in contrast, do not have sufficient power and resources by themselves to transform local government institutions, but they have an unrivalled expertise on local immigrant communities that they can share and leverage with government officials (de Graauw, 2008a). Collaborations between local government and immigrant organizations thus can be mutually beneficial, and public-private partnerships can provide opportunities to advance immigrant integration and institutionalize immigrants' "right to the city."

Left Coast Gateway: Immigrants and Immigrant Organizations in San Francisco

San Francisco is a continuous gateway city, or a city that consistently has attracted large numbers of immigrants over the past 100 years (Singer, Hardwick, and Brettell, 2008). In 1900, 50 years after the city's incorporation, 34 percent of San Francisco's 343,000 residents were foreign-born (Gibson and Lennon, 1999). When the US foreign-born population bottomed out at 5 percent in 1970, immigrants never made up less than 18 percent of San Francisco's population. In 2007, 36 percent of San Francisco residents were born abroad, 21 percent of whom had immigrated to the United States since 2000.[2] The largest proportion of the city's immigrants, 62 percent, came from Asia, while 20 and 14 percent, respectively, were born in Latin America and Europe. San Francisco's immigrant groups have recognizable turfs, much like immigrant neighborhoods in the continuous gateway cities of New York and Chicago (Pamuk, 2004). Chinese immigrants continue to find a home in Chinatown and increasingly in the Sunset district in the West and Visitation Valley in the southern part of the city. Many Filipinos settle in the South of Market area near downtown, while Vietnamese immigrants live in the Civic Center area by city hall. The heart of the city's Hispanic community lies in the Mission district.

Starting in the 1960s, San Francisco shifted to a post-industrial economy specializing in advanced corporate services in management, law, finance, and communications (DeLeon, 1992). The rapid internationalization of economic activity during the 1980s further transformed San Francisco into a regional center in the global economy with marked occupational and income polarization. As is characteristic of other global cities (Sassen, 2001), San Francisco today has a dual labor market with job growth concentrated at the top (high-skill professional and managerial jobs) and bottom (low-skill service jobs, such as janitors, security guards, food servers, and garment workers). As a consequence, San Francisco has attracted immigrants with a range of socio-economic backgrounds. In 2007, 34 percent of the city's foreign-born held a bachelor's or higher educational degree, while 30 percent had not completed high school. Similarly, 36 percent worked in high-paying professional or managerial occupations in 2007, while 27 percent held low-wage jobs in the city's service sector and hospitality industry. Furthermore, 59 percent of the city's foreign-born spoke English less than "very well" in 2007, and 39 percent were not US citizens and thus could not vote. All in all, San Francisco's immigrants today are a diverse lot but include many individuals whose weak demographic profiles put them in a socially, economically, and politically marginalized position.

Given its long history of immigration, San Francisco has a rich infrastructure of immigrant organizations. In 2004, San Francisco was home to 314 immigrant organizations, which I define as 501(c)(3) not-for-profit organizations that serve or advocate on behalf of a particular immigrant origin group, promote their cultural heritage, or engage with issues related to immigrants' country of origin.[3] Similarly to Bloemraad and Gleeson in this volume, I initially used cues in the organization's name and mission statement to identify immigrant organizations among the 5,034 San Francisco-based nonprofits that had formally registered with the federal government as 501(c)(3) organizations by the end of 2004. I then used web searches, in-depth interviews with over 50 immigrant organizations, a survey of 100 immigrant organizations, and newspaper articles to enumerate more fully the universe of immigrant organizations in San Francisco. My approach to counting immigrant organizations draws on techniques used by Cortés (1998), Cordero-Guzmán (2005), and Hung (2007) but emphasizes organizations' client characteristics rather than their names or staff characteristics.

As testament to the city's status as a continuous gateway, 32 percent of the 314 immigrant organizations active in San Francisco in 2004 had acquired nonprofit status before 1980. These older immigrant organizations are important because they have served as incubators for new organizations as the immigrant population has changed. The International Institute of San Francisco, for example, was founded in 1918 to help settle early immigrants from Europe. In response to the arrival of large numbers of Asian immigrants to San Francisco after 1965, the Institute helped found the Chinese Newcomers Service Center in 1969, the Filipino Newcomer Service Center in 1972, and the South East Asian Community Center in 1976. Older and newer organizations learn from each other, in cooperative and sometimes competitive ways, and staff and volunteers rotate among immigrant organizations. It was not uncommon for me to learn that staff members I interviewed at the beginning of my fieldwork in San Francisco, in 2005 or 2006, were working for other immigrant organizations in the city in 2008 or 2009. This kind of staff rotation facilitates information sharing among immigrant organizations and has made it easier for immigrant organizations to build collaborative networks. Because there have been successive generations of immigrant organizations, contemporary immigrant organizations in San Francisco can boast of an expertise on a wide range of immigrant issues.

Given that San Francisco has a well-developed immigrant nonprofit sector, the staff of immigrant organizations also have easy access to an array of valuable support services. CompassPoint, for example, is an organization that provides skill-building workshops to nonprofits and courses on how to conduct advocacy, and Partnership for Immigrant Leadership and Action provides technical assistance specifically to nonprofits that serve low-income immigrant communities in the city. At times, formally registered immigrant organizations act as fiscal sponsors that provide informal organizations with office space and technical assistance such as on how they can obtain their own 501(c)(3) status, which is often a requirement for receiving government funding. *Mujeres Unidas y Activas* (United and Active Women), for example, was founded in 1989 by two immigrant women who wanted to empower other Latina immigrant women to be their own advocates. With the support of the Northern California Coalition for Immigrant Rights, *Mujeres* grew to a membership of 200 and a staff of four by 1996, and it received its 501(c)(3) status in 2005. Today, *Mujeres* is widely regarded as an effective immigrant organization and receives funding from the Mayor's Office and the San Francisco Department on the Status of Women to support its activities. An easily accessible infrastructure of support organizations means that contemporary immigrant organizations in San Francisco have been able to acquire the knowledge and capacity necessary to engage local government on immigrant integration issues.

As a result of having worked in immigrant communities for years, immigrant organizations today also articulate the conviction that their advocacy with local officials is necessary if immigrants are to attain economic and participatory equality. A staff member of Chinese for Affirmative Action, a Chinatown-based organization that serves low-income Asian immigrants, explained that despite San Francisco's reputation as a progressive haven, "nothing moves in this city unless there is some sort of community impetus." A staff member with *La Raza Centro Legal* (The Legal Center of La Raza), an organization in the Mission district that serves low-income Hispanic immigrants, added that "immigrant rights become viable, they become real only when immigrants and their community organizations fight for them." San Francisco's long exposure to immigration means that immigrant organizations have acquired not only a keen understanding of immigrant issues but also the confidence to advocate with local officials to demand immigrants' "right to the city."

City officials also know that immigrant organizations can be vocal and pushy advocates for immigrant rights, and some are more appreciative of this than others. The City Administrator, for example, commented that immigrant groups

> play a key role in identifying problems for us to solve. I think it's absolutely insane for anybody to think that they don't identify a problem for government to solve. They have to, that's their role, I think, and that should be an accepted role. [...] They should be there, because essentially they represent people who have yet to gain access to government.

Yet, an elected city legislator wryly noted that, "A lot of these various organizations come to us...and expect us to be able to deliver. And we hear things like, 'Well, we ignore the federal laws on medicinal marijuana. We ignore state laws on gay marriage. Why can't we also ignore federal laws on immigration?' That can be a little trying." San Francisco officials today generally are appreciative of immigrants and understanding of their needs, but it requires constant advocacy by immigrant organizations to get them to act on their inclusive political philosophies.

Public-Private Partnerships and Immigrant Rights

To show that immigrant organizations and local government in San Francisco have become mutually constitutive around issues pertaining to marginalized immigrants, I consider three instances where they have worked together in ways that have helped to institutionalize these immigrants' "right to the city." I first turn to the use of public-private partnerships to bring critical social services to hard-to-reach immigrants in the city. Next, I consider how public-private partnerships have advanced the representation of immigrants' substantive policy interests. Finally, I discuss the role of immigrant organizations in strengthening immigrants' demographic representation by fostering ethnic city leaders who have taken immigrants' interests to heart while serving in public office.

Access to Public Services

As occurs elsewhere in the United States, many immigrants in San Francisco experience material hardship as they adjust to life in American society. Lack of English proficiency is an important obstacle to immigrants' integration into the American labor market (as well as their civic and political participation) and puts them at an earnings disadvantage with native-born workers (Park, 1999). Labor market challenges and lack of economic mobility tend to be more severe and longer lasting for immigrants with little formal education, the undocumented, and immigrants of color (Gleeson, 2009; Hersch, 2008; Rivera-Batiz, 1999). Public services focused on language acquisition, job training, and socio-economic security can lower the hurdles to immigrant integration and help minimize the economic gap between immigrants and similarly situated US-born workers. Increasingly, it is nonprofits like the immigrant organizations I discuss in this chapter that provide such government-funded services to immigrant communities.

The practice of government contracting with nonprofit organizations goes back several decades. To implement the Great Society programs of the 1960s, the federal government paid nonprofits to provide services to extinguish poverty and foster community development in poor urban areas where many immigrants resided. The privatization of the American welfare state since the late 1970s further fueled the growth of the nonprofit sector by making nonprofits the key vehicles for the provision of social services to the poor and other disadvantaged groups, including immigrants (Grønbjerg, 1993; Salamon, 1999; Smith and Lipsky, 1993). Finally, the devolution of government policy in the 1980s shifted decisions regarding public service programs from the federal government down to lower levels of government and consequently gave cities more power in regulating contracts with nonprofit vendors (Marwell, 2004). In San Francisco, the effects of privatization and devolution of public services in recent decades are clear: whereas nonprofit organizations controlled a third of public funded services in the city in 1980 (Hirsch, 2005), they provided half of the city's public services in 2006, according to the City Administrator.[4]

The provision of public services has long been a joint public-private enterprise in San Francisco and local officials understand that they would not be able to deliver public services to the city's immigrants without the help of immigrant organizations. The City Administrator, for example, noted that, "Our efforts at reaching out to immigrants and refugees in this city, I think, would be a lot less effective without the various immigrant groups that we fund. We simply wouldn't be able to reach into some pockets of the immigrant community. These organizations—and they'll also tell you that—they have a better ability to connect and deliver the kinds of services that immigrants need." Similarly, a high-level official in the city's Department of Human Services commented that, "One of the key reasons we contract with community-based groups is that they have the language capacity...they know the community, they have the languages available on their staff to serve our immigrant clients." Because immigrant organizations are located in the neighborhoods where immigrants live and because they serve immigrants in linguistically and culturally competent ways, they are considered better able than government agencies to cater to the needs of immigrants.

Immigrant organizations also offer a safer place for immigrants to seek the services they need. Although San Francisco has the image of being friendly towards immigrants,[5] many immigrants still avoid contact with public officials because they had bad experiences with government in their native countries, experience language barriers, or fear being apprehended because they are undocumented. A program officer at the Zellerbach Family Foundation, who previously worked for a number of immigrant organizations in San Francisco, described immigrant organizations as "a home away from home" for immigrants and as institutions that have developed a longstanding reputation and trust with immigrant communities. Contracting out services to immigrant organizations also helps the city to lower the overall cost of care to needy populations. A staff member with Asian Perinatal Advocates, a Chinatown-based organization that contracts with the Department of Human Services (DHS) to provide family support services to Asian immigrants, reflected that, "It is difficult for DHS to provide our services in a way that is effective and efficient...the salary of city workers is a lot higher than our salary, so it is cheaper for DHS to give funding to the community to provide these types of services than to try to do things in-house."

For immigrant organizations, contracting with local government provides opportunities to direct city resources towards improving the wellbeing and self-sufficiency of immigrant residents in the city. Contracting data from the San Francisco Office of the Controller provide evidence of the success immigrant organizations have had in competing for city funding to provide services to marginalized immigrants. In fiscal year 2005-06, 108 of 314 immigrant organizations received one or more contracts with city agencies. Immigrant organizations received at total of $89,513,599 in contracts, or 23 percent of the $394 million the city paid out to all its nonprofit vendors that year. The amount has gone up, and in fiscal year 2009-10, the city awarded $134,979,421 in service contracts to 106 immigrant organizations, equaling 28 percent of the $478 million given to nonprofit vendors. While these contract percentages are less than immigrants' share of the city population (36 percent in 2007), immigrant organizations nonetheless have controlled a significant amount of the city's discretionary budget distributed to nonprofits.

San Francisco also allocates and administers a number of state and federal grants from which immigrant organizations and immigrant communities have benefitted. A good example is the Community Development Block Grant (CDBG), which is a program of the US Department of Housing and Urban Development (HUD) to fund community development activities, including direct services that benefit low- and moderate-income persons, affordable housing, and infrastructure improvements. In fiscal year 2005-06, city officials allocated $12,924,218 in CDBG funding to 157 nonprofit organizations in the city. Among the grantees were 46 immigrant organizations that received $4,976,257 in CDBG funds, or 39 percent of the total. San Francisco allocates CDBG funding through a competitive process, which has become more competitive in recent years as a result of cuts in HUD entitlement grants. The fact that immigrant organizations have been able to win a percentage of CDBG grants that exceeds immigrants' share of the city population testifies to the strength of public-private partnerships to advance immigrants' socio-economic inclusion in San Francisco.

Policy Representation

In recent years, immigrant organizations also have worked with city officials to enact and implement policies that are of substantive interest to marginalized immigrants. For city officials, the benefit of working with immigrant organizations is that they have an expertise on immigrant issues that is difficult for city officials to develop given limited staff resources and immigrants' fear and mistrust of government. The eleven city legislators, for example, represent districts with over 70,000 residents, but they have only two staffers each to support them in their many legislative endeavors. Also, officials responsible for implementing city policies are under constant pressure to do so in more effective and less costly ways, yet they have a hard time getting up-to-date assessments of the rapidly changing needs in immigrant communities. Without immigrant organizations as allies in the public policy process, both legislative and administrative officials in San Francisco would struggle to learn about the needs and interests of a large portion of the city's residents. In describing immigrant organizations, one elected official commented that they play a

> critical role in representing a part of the population that at times is so invisible and that many of us...including some of the people I work with here in city hall, don't really come across all that often. I mean, it's sad to say, but we live in the same city, but often move in separate worlds. ...[T]he immigrant rights groups sort of function like a bridge between these two worlds.

Immigrant organizations, in turn, want to work with city officials because it presents them with opportunities to effect policy change on immigrants' behalf. While most are founded for a purpose other than advocacy, immigrant organizations today often combine the provision of social services with policy activism (de Graauw, 2008a). They are motivated to do so because they realize that service provision and public policy advocacy are two interrelated activities that they need to pursue in unison in order to fulfill their mission to serve the needs and interests of the immigrant population. In explaining why her organization engaged in public policy advocacy, a staff member with *La Raza Centro Legal* noted that, "Our mission is to promote a just and equal society and the way we do that is through the provision of direct legal services and a community empowerment-style of advocacy. And the reason we do it this way is that we recognize that services alone don't challenge the causes of the injustice or inequality; you need advocacy for that as well." Immigrant organizations provide direct social services in efforts to remedy the symptoms of a limited public service system, while they see local political advocacy as a way to fight the root causes of the injustices that immigrants experience in American society today.

The sense of partnership and willingness to engage each other in the policymaking process are recent phenomena and follow decades of struggle between immigrant organizations and city hall. Poor immigrant communities, for example, have long battled San Francisco officials and developers over decisions affecting the use of the city's small land area (47 square miles in total). Between the 1950s and 1980s, city officials approved various large-scale development projects that expanded the downtown business sector and helped attract new capital to San Francisco, but they also displaced thousands of residents. This raised the ire of community activists who demanded that the land instead be used to build more affordable public housing for the city's poor (DeLeon, 1992; 2003). The struggle to save the International Hotel, which offered low-cost housing to mostly Filipino seniors in what once was San Francisco's thriving Manilatown, epitomizes this clash over immigrants' right to city space. For nine years starting in 1968, residents and immigrant organizations such as the Manilatown Information Center, the International Hotel Tenants Association, and the Asian Community Center staged demonstrations and filed lawsuits to prevent the Hotel's demolition. They were unsuccessful: residents were evicted in 1977 and the building was destroyed two years later (Habal, 2007).[6] Similar anti-displacement and anti-gentrification campaigns are ongoing in the heavily Hispanic Mission district, involving immigrant organizations such as the Central American Resource Center (CARECEN), Mission Economic Development Agency (MEDA), and *Causa Justa* (Just Cause). Immigrant organizations may not always have gotten their way with city officials, but their long history of advocacy around land use issues has helped normalize their participation in the policymaking process today.

The 1990s—when legislators with progressive agendas started to dominate the San Francisco Board of Supervisors—inaugurated a period of increased public policy collaboration between immigrant organizations and city officials. One outcome of that is the Equal Access to Services Ordinance, a 2001 San Francisco ordinance that mandates city departments to offer government information and public services in a number of foreign languages, including Chinese and Spanish.[7] A coalition of ten immigrant organizations headed by Chinese for Affirmative Action proposed the policy to city legislators in 1999 after having received numerous complaints from immigrants who were unable to access city services due to their inability to speak English. Immigrant organizations worked in partnership with then Supervisor Mark Leno to win support for the policy among a majority of city legislators. Together, they calmed concerns that legislators had about the cost of translating government documents into Chinese and Spanish and about the hiring of bilingual staff eligible to receive additional pay, as the policy would require. They also collaborated to stop one legislator's attempt to strip the bill of its bilingual staff requirement. Finally, Leno used research conducted by immigrant organizations on best language access practices elsewhere in the country to convince his colleagues on the Board that the policy's implementation was doable in San Francisco. In reflecting on his partnership with immigrant organizations, Leno said, "Oftentimes, we come up with our own ideas for legislation or people bring us ideas, but [immigrant organizations] not only brought the idea, they brought the entire package and they have followed through on the issue ever since."

Since the policy's enactment in 2001, immigrant organizations have switched their advocacy to city departments and worked with them to get the Equal Access to Services Ordinance implemented. Commenting on the necessity of this kind of administrative advocacy, a staff member with Chinese for Affirmative Action noted that, "The ordinance looked great on paper, but it was an entirely different thing to get it institutionalized into the daily practices of the departments that needed to comply. It required constant, and I mean *constant*, advocacy pressure from folks like us." Administrative officials understood that many immigrants face language barriers to accessing local government; yet, they were reluctant or unwilling to make language access a departmental priority. Immigrant organizations had to educate administrators on the importance of language access and provided them with technical assistance to facilitate the implementation process. For example, they helped department heads determine which staff positions in their agencies required bilingual personnel, what forms and notices needed to be translated, and how to draw up annual compliance plans. Immigrant organizations also served on the Cultural Competency Task Force to provide Mayor Gavin Newsom with recommendations on how to improve translations of the city's websites. All in all, the collaboration between immigrant organizations and city legislators and city administrators has helped to make San Francisco government more accessible for limited English proficient immigrants.

There are other instances where immigrant organizations and city officials have collaborated in enacting and implementing policies that benefit immigrants. In 2007, for example, immigrant organizations worked with then Supervisor Tom Ammiano to pass the Municipal ID Ordinance, which allows San Francisco to issue its own identification cards and aims to help undocumented immigrants integrate into local civic life (de Graauw, 2009). Also, in 2003, San Francisco voters approved the Minimum Wage Ordinance, which raised the wage for all employees in the city (including those who are undocumented) above the federal and state minimum wages. Since then, immigrant organizations have helped city administrators enforce the ordinance against non-compliant employers who fail to pay the mandated minimum wage to immigrant workers, who often are the victims of wage theft and other labor law violations (de Graauw, 2008b). Finally, in the initiative process, city officials often have given their support to ballot measures championed by immigrant organizations. In 2004, then Supervisor Matt Gonzalez supported the narrowly defeated ballot measure that would have allowed noncitizens with children in San Francisco public schools to vote in school board elections (Hayduk, 2006). Supervisor David Chiu, the chief supporter of a similar measure on the city's ballot for the November 2010 elections, also is working with immigrant organizations to make local voting rights for noncitizens a reality. It is fair to conclude, therefore, that without these collaborations between immigrant organizations and city officials, immigrants in San Francisco would not enjoy the degree of policy representation we can observe today.

Ethnic City Leaders

Immigrant organizations have helped to institutionalize the socio-economic and political inclusion of immigrants in San Francisco not only through public service provision and public policy advocacy but also by acting as training grounds for ethnic city leaders. Since the late 1990s, there have been several non-Anglo officials in elected and appointed positions who have used their seats in city government to improve immigrant wellbeing and whose public service careers have roots in San Francisco's immigrant nonprofit sector. Their backgrounds in community organizing and immigrant rights advocacy have been formative for their work as public officials and help explain why they continue to be sympathetic towards the causes that immigrant organizations pursue. Once in public office, these ethnic city leaders make it easier for immigrant organizations to access the governmental process, and they serve as influential supporters for immigrant integration initiatives inside city hall. All in all, these ethnic city leaders have helped to further normalize the practice where city officials engage in partnerships with immigrant organizations to address immigrant integration issues.

A good example of a community advocate who crossed over into San Francisco government is Mabel Teng. Originally an immigrant from Hong Kong, Teng worked for the Chinese Progressive Association, which provides services to and advocacy on behalf of low-income Chinese immigrants in San Francisco. She later became program manager and then executive director at the Career Resources Development Center, an immigrant organization in San Francisco's Tenderloin district that provides employment services to predominantly Asian immigrants. This position offered Teng a springboard into elected posts, and in 1990 she was elected to the San Francisco Community College Board, where she fought to improve conditions for minorities in the city's community colleges (Wei, 1993). In 1994, she became the first Asian-American woman to serve on the San Francisco Board of Supervisors, where she created the Immigrant Rights Commission in 1997. To this day, the Immigrant Rights Commission functions as a consultative body with the duty to provide advice and make policy recommendations to the Board of Supervisors and the mayor on issues affecting the city's immigrants. Teng also was the first city legislator to support the idea of an Equal Access to Services Ordinance in 1999.

There are many other telling examples of nonprofit advocates-turned-city officials. Phil Ting, a Chinese-American, served as executive director of the Asian Law Caucus, an immigrant organization that provides legal services to low-income Asians and Pacific Islanders in San Francisco. He was appointed, and later elected in 2005, to the position of Assessor-Recorder. Once in government, Ting headed the mayor's Cultural Competency Task Force in 2005 and recommended the creation of the Office of Language Services to improve the implementation of the city's language access policy. Ed Lee, also a Chinese-American, was an attorney with the Asian Law Caucus for ten years before entering public service in 1989. He has held various appointive positions in San Francisco government and became City Administrator in 2005. Lee oversees the Immigrant Rights Commission and the city's Office of Civic Engagement and Immigrant Affairs. Renee Saucedo, a Latina and attorney at *La Raza Centro Legal*, served on the Immigrant Rights Commission and the Mayor's Taskforce on Welfare Reform and then made an unsuccessful run for the Board of Supervisors in 2004. Sheila Chung Hagen, a former director of the Bay Area Immigrant Rights Coalition who is of mixed Argentinean-Korean descent, was appointed as Immigrant Rights Administrator in 2007 to enforce the city's Sanctuary Ordinance and Municipal ID Ordinance. In 2008, she became legislative aide to Supervisor David Campos, who represents an area that includes the heavily Hispanic Mission district. Finally, Eric Mar, an Asian-American, was the past director of the Northern California Coalition for Immigrant Rights and a long-time activist with the Chinese Progressive Association. He served on the San Francisco Board of Education for eight years and was elected to the Board of Supervisors in 2008.

These individuals' career trajectories suggest that immigrant organizations can act as training grounds for ethnic politicians to become city leaders. As is true of civic organizations more generally (Verba, Schlozman, and Brady, 1995), immigrant organizations served as civic incubators and provided these individuals with opportunities to develop leadership potential and skills, such as budgeting, personnel practices, and bargaining, that carry over into a career in local politics. Nonprofit advocacy and community organizing, furthermore, earned these individuals the name recognition, public visibility, and street credentials necessary to win elective and appointive office. Nonprofit-government interactions also allowed them to learn about the mechanics of local government and the different ways in which local politics can advance social change. Finally, years of service in the nonprofit sector enabled them to amass resources, such as manpower and connections with community leaders and government officials, which they later could draw on for help in gaining and sustaining their positions in local government. This underscores in yet another way the extent to which immigrant organizations and government have become intertwined in San Francisco. Also, it highlights that immigrant organizations are of twofold importance: not only do they advocate for immigrant-friendly policies and practices from outside government today, but they also train leaders who can advance immigrant rights from inside city hall tomorrow.

Urban Citizenship and the Cage of Federalism

In San Francisco, public-private partnerships between city government and immigrant organizations have reduced the material and participatory inequalities of marginalized immigrants. Immigrant organizations have used funding from city agencies to deliver public services to hard-to-reach immigrants, thereby improving immigrants' socio-economic status. They also have worked with both legislative and administrative city officials to enact and implement local policies to advance immigrants' substantive representation. Finally, immigrant organizations have activated immigrants' demographic representation by fostering ethnic city leaders with co-ethnic backgrounds who have taken immigrants' interests to heart while serving in public office. What is noteworthy about these public-private efforts to institutionalize immigrants' "right to the city" is that they have been inclusive of *all* immigrants residing in the city. As a result, many of the rights and benefits that immigrants enjoy in San Francisco today are available to them regardless of citizenship and documentation status. We can take this as evidence of the emergence of urban citizenship (Bauböck, 2003; Smith and Guarnizo, 2009), or the idea that membership in a society is based upon residence in the city (*jus domicili*) rather than national birthright (*jus soli*) or ancestry (*jus sanguinis*).

On more than one occasion, I heard the staff of immigrant organizations and city officials invoke cosmopolitan (Carens, 1989) and post-national (Soysal, 1994) ideals of membership in explaining why they thought that all immigrants should be recognized as equal members of San Francisco. This was most obvious in discussions of the Municipal ID Ordinance, which allows San Francisco to issue identification cards to undocumented immigrants living in the city. For example, a staff member with *Alianza Latinoamericana por los Derechos de los Inmigrantes* (Latin American Alliance for Immigrant Rights), the immigrant organization that proposed the policy to city legislators in 2007, commented that, "It's a basic human right that someone has an identity that they can prove. Nobody should have to walk around without papers and be excluded from the community because they're undocumented." A staff member with Chinese for Affirmative Action similarly explained that, "Our advocacy around the city ID card is informed by our belief that because immigrants live and work here, that that creates grounds for claims-making." Then Supervisor Tom Ammiano, who was the policy's lead sponsor on the San Francisco Board of Supervisors, also commented that, "We're a city full of immigrants, who were forced here for no other reason than out of necessity and hardship. [...] The least the city can do is provide the human dignity of an identity, and the municipal ID card is a gesture towards that." The proponents of the Municipal ID Ordinance, in other words, all viewed the city as the space where cosmopolitan and post-national ideals for an expanded circle of membership, which includes undocumented immigrants, could take root.

The emergence of urban citizenship in San Francisco, on the one hand, is a welcome development. It provides the city's most marginalized immigrants with certain rights and benefits no longer available to them from the state and national governments. Especially since the federal welfare and immigration reforms of 1996 and the terrorist attacks of 2001, legal immigrants have experienced a rollback of their rights and benefits, and undocumented immigrants, being considered a threat to national security, receive still fewer rights. As a result, formal citizenship in the United States has become an increasingly privileged status. Lawful immigration status, furthermore, has become a rather tenuous designation, and undocumented status has become synonymous with labor market exploitation, fear of government, and life in the shadows of society. If we measure the strength of the American democracy by the political representation and government protections it affords to the least privileged segments of society, we have reason to criticize the turn against immigrants in many states and by the national government. San Francisco reminds us that there is an alternative, more grounded way in which membership rights and benefits can be allocated to immigrants who already live and work in cities around the country. As this chapter has shown, immigrant organizations have been instrumental in making San Francisco the inclusive city it is today.

We cannot, however, discuss the emergence of urban citizenship in San Francisco without considering US federalism and acknowledging San Francisco's continued subservience to the national government (as well as the state of California). The rights and benefits immigrants enjoy in San Francisco today are place-bound and therefore limited. City ID cards, for example, can only be used for intra-city affairs, and they do not confer legal status, give permission to drive, or increase cardholders' eligibility for public services. Only immigrants who work in San Francisco are entitled to receive the city's minimum wage. And San Francisco cannot translate into Spanish and Chinese government documents originally published in English by the state of California or the national government. Because there is no uniform or coordinated national immigrant integration policy, the equal treatment immigrants find in San Francisco generally stops at the city's borders. Also, only the national government can legalize the status of undocumented immigrants and offer them the opportunity to become formal citizens of the United States. Without comprehensive immigration reform, San Francisco's policies offering sanctuary and ID cards to undocumented immigrants cannot live up to their full potential. San Francisco, in other words, shows us the promises of an inclusive local community, but many of the city's immigrant-friendly policies are caged in by anti-immigrant national laws aimed at excluding immigrants from US society. San Francisco also teaches us that it is unlikely for the national government to enact inclusive immigration or immigrant integration policies without the sustained involvement of immigrant organizations in the process.

Notes

1. In September 2010, the US Court of Appeals for the Third Circuit ruled—in a unanimous decision—that Hazleton's act was unconstitutional. In July 2010, a federal judge granted a preliminary injunction that blocked the most controversial parts of Arizona's SB 1070 from going into effect.

2. All population statistics are from the three-year averages (2006-08) of the Census Bureau's American Community Survey.

3. I excluded churches and foundations, which also have the 501(c)(3) not-for-profit status, from my count of immigrant organizations. As a result, I capture primarily secular organizations that provide services to and/or advocate on behalf of immigrant communities in San Francisco.

4. In-person interview: Aug 15, 2006.

5. San Francisco has offered sanctuary to undocumented immigrants since 1989. Also, in response to federal immigration raids in the Bay Area in 2007, San Francisco spent $83,000 in 2008 on a multi-lingual public awareness campaign to inform undocumented immigrants that they can safely access city services (Vega, 2008).

6. Despite the building's demolition in 1979, the International Hotel movement was not entirely defeated. Due to persistent community activism, the parking garage slated for the site was never built and a new International Hotel—a 14-story housing development for low-income seniors—opened in San Francisco's Chinatown in 2005 (Habal, 2007).

7. For a more detailed analysis of how the Equal Access to Services Ordinance came about, see de Graauw (2008a; 2008b).

References

Bauböck, R. (2003). "Reinventing Urban Citizenship." *Citizenship Studies*, 7(2), 139-60.

Beito, D. T. (2000). *From Mutual Aid to the Welfare State: Fraternal Societies and Social Services, 1890-1967*. Chapel Hill: University of North Carolina Press.

Berry, J. M. (with D. F. Arons). (2003). *A Voice for Nonprofits*. Washington, DC: Brookings Institution Press.

Bloemraad, I. (2005). "The Limits of de Tocqueville: How Government Facilitates Organizational Capacity in Newcomer Communities." *Journal of Ethnic and Migration Studies*, 31(5), 865-87.

_____. (2006). *Becoming a Citizen: Incorporating Immigrants and Refugees in the United States and Canada*. Berkeley: University of California Press.

Bloemraad, I., K. Voss, and T. Lee. (Forthcoming). "The Immigration Rallies of 2006: What Were They, How Do We Understand Them, Where Do We Go?" In K. Voss and I. Bloemraad, *Rallying for Immigrant Rights* (Eds.). Berkeley: University of California Press.

Carens, J. H. (1989). "Membership and Morality: Admission to Citizenship in Liberal Democratic States." W. R. Brubaker (Ed.), *Immigration and the Politics of Citizenship in Europe and North America* (pp. 31-49). University Press of America.

Chaves, M., L. Stephens, and J. Galaskiewicz. (2004). "Does Government Funding Suppress Nonprofits' Political Activity?" *American Sociological Review*, 69(2), 292-316.

Cordero-Guzmán, H. R. (2005). "Community Based Organizations and Migration in New York City." *Journal of Ethnic and Migration Studies*, 31(5), 889-909.

Cordero-Guzmán, H. R., N. Martin, V. Quiroz-Becerra, and N. Theodore. (2008). "Voting with Their Feet: Nonprofit Organizations and Immigrant Mobilization." *American Behavioral Scientist*, 52(4), 598-617.

Cortés, M. (1998). "Counting Latino Nonprofits: A New Strategy for Finding Data." *Nonprofit and Voluntary Sector Quarterly*, 27(4), 437-58.

Davis, A. F. (1994). *Spearheads for Reform: The Social Settlements and the Progressive Movement, 1890-1914* (3rd ed.). New Brunswick: Rutgers University Press.

DeLeon, R. E. (1992). *Left Coast City: Progressive Politics in San Francisco, 1975-1991*. Lawrence, KS: University Press of Kansas.

_____. (2003). "San Francisco: The Politics of Race, Land Use, and Ideology." R. P. Browning, D. R. Marshall, and D. H. Tabb (Eds.), *Racial Politics in American Cities* (3rd ed., pp. 167-98). White Plains, NY: Longman Publishers.

Dikeç, M., and L. Gilbert. (2002). "Right to the City: Homage or a New Societal Ethics?" *Capitalism Nature Socialism*, 13(2), 58-74.

Gibson, C. J., and E. Lennon. (1999). "Historical Census Statistics on the Foreign-Born Population of the United States: 1850-1990." *Population Division Working Paper*, 29. Washington, DC: United States Bureau of the Census.

de Graauw, E. (2008a). "Nonprofit Organizations: Agents of Immigrant Political Incorporation in Urban America." In S. K. Ramakrishnan and I. Bloemraad (Eds.), *Civic Hopes and Political Realities: Community Organizations and Political Engagement among Immigrants in the United States and Abroad* (pp. 323-50). New York: Russell Sage Foundation Press.

_____. (2008b). *Nonprofit Organizations and the Contemporary Politics of Immigrant Incorporation in San Francisco* (Doctoral dissertation). Retrieved from ProQuest Dissertations and Theses Database (AAT 3353241).

_____. (2009, Oct). "Documenting the Undocumented: Nonprofit Organizations and Intergovernmental Tensions over Municipal ID Cards in San Francisco." Paper presented at The Undocumented Hispanic Migration: On the Margins of a Dream Conference. Connecticut College, New London, CT.

de Graauw, E., S. Gleeson, and I. Bloemraad. (2010). "Funding Immigrant Organizations: Central City Differences and Suburban Free-riding." Unpublished manuscript.

Gleeson, S. (2009). "From Rights to Claims: The Role of Civil Society in Making Rights Real for Vulnerable Workers." *Law and Society Review*, 43(3), 669-700.

Grønbjerg, K. A. (1993). *Understanding Nonprofit Funding: Managing Revenues in Social Services and Community Development Organizations*. San Francisco: Jossey-Bass.

Habal, E. (2007). *San Francisco's International Hotel: Mobilizing the Filipino American Community in the Anti-Eviction Movement*. Philadelphia: Temple University Press.

Hayduk, R. (2006). *Democracy for All: Restoring Immigrant Voting Rights in the United States*. New York: Routledge.

Hersch, J. (2008). "Skin Color, Immigrant Wages, and Discrimination." In R. E. Hall (Ed.), *Racism in the 21st Century: An Empirical Analysis of Skin Color* (pp. 77-90). New York: Springer Press.

Hirsch, M. (2005). "The Nonprofit Gold Rush." *San Francisco Bay Guardian*, 39(23), 16-8.

Hung, C.-K. R. (2007). "Immigrant Nonprofit Organizations in U.S. Metropolitan Areas." *Nonprofit and Voluntary Sector Quarterly*, 36(4), 707-29.

Jones-Correa, M. (1998). *Between Two Nations: The Political Predicament of Latinos in New York City*. Ithaca: Cornell University Press.

Kasinitz, P. (1992). *Caribbean New York: Black Immigrants and the Politics of Race*. Ithaca: Cornell University Press.

Lefebvre, H. (1996). *Writings on Cities*. E. Kofman and E. Lebas (Eds. and Trans.). Malden, MA/Oxford: Blackwell Publishers.

Marwell, N. P. (2004). "Privatizing the Welfare State: Nonprofit Community-Based Organizations as Political Actors." *American Sociological Review*, 69(2), 265-91.

Newton, L. (2010). "Immigration Federalism: Patterns of Integration and Resistance among the States: 2005-2008." Paper presented at The Annual Meeting of the Law and Society Association, May 27-30. Chicago.

Pallares, A., and N. Flores-González. (2010). *¡Marcha! Latino Chicago and the Immigrant Rights Movement*. Chicago: University of Illinois Press.

Pamuk, A. (2004). "Geography of Immigrant Clusters in Global Cities: A Case Study of San Francisco." *International Journal of Urban and Regional Research*, 28(2), 287-307.

Park, J. H. (1999). "The Earnings of Immigrants in the United States: The Effect of English-Speaking Ability." *Journal of Economics and Sociology*, 58(1), 43-56.

Purcell, M. (2003). "Citizenship and the Right to the Global City: Reimagining the Capitalist World Order." *International Journal of Urban and Regional Research*, 27(3), 564-90.

Ramakrishnan, S. K., and T. Wong. (2010). "Partisanship, Not Spanish: Explaining Municipal Ordinances Affecting Undocumented Immigrants." In M. W. Varsanyi (Ed.), *Taking Local Control: Immigration Policy Activism in U.S. Cities and States* (pp. 73-93). Stanford: Stanford University Press.

Ramakrishnan, S. K., and P. G. Lewis. (2005). *Immigrants and Local Governance: The View from City Hall*. San Francisco: Public Policy Institute of California.

Rivera-Batiz, F. L. (1999). "Undocumented Workers in the Labor Market: An Analysis of the Earnings of Legal and Illegal Mexican Immigrants in the United States." *Journal of Population Economics*, 12(1), 91-116.

Rogers, R. R. (2006). *Afro-Caribbean Immigrants and the Politics of Incorporation: Ethnicity, Exception, or Exit*. New York: Cambridge University Press.

Salamon, L. M. (1999). *America's Nonprofit Sector: A Primer* (2nd ed.). New York: Foundation Center.

Sassen, S. (2001). *The Global City: New York, Tokyo, London* (2nd ed.). Princeton: Princeton University Press.

Singer, A., S. W. Hardwick, and C. Brettell. (2008). *Twenty-First Century Gateways: Immigrant Incorporation in Suburban America*. Washington, DC: Brookings Institution Press.

Smith, M. P., and L. E Guarnizo. (2009). "Global Mobility, Shifting Borders and Urban Citizenship." *Tijdschrift voor Economische en Sociale Geografie*, 100(5), 610-22.

Smith, R. C. (2006). *Mexican New York: Transnational Lives of New Immigrants*. Berkeley: University of California Press.

Smith, S. R., and M. Lipsky. (1993). *Nonprofits for Hire: The Welfare State in the Age of Contracting*. Cambridge: Harvard University Press.

Soyer, D. (2006). "Mutual Aid Societies and Fraternal Orders." In R. Ueda (Ed.), *A Companion to American Immigration* (pp. 528-46). Malden, MA: Blackwell Publishers.

Soysal, Y. N. (1994). *Limits of Citizenship: Migrants and Postnational Membership in Europe*. Princeton: Princeton University Press.

Sterne, E. S. (2001). "Beyond the Boss: Immigration and American Political Culture from 1880 to 1940." In G. Gerstle and J. Mollenkopf (Eds.), *E Pluribus Unum? Contemporary and Historical Perspectives on Immigrant Political Incorporation* (pp. 33-66). New York: Russell Sage Foundation Press.

Trolander, J. A. (1987). *Professionalism and Social Change: From the Settlement House Movement to Neighborhood Centers, 1886 to the Present*. New York: Columbia University Press.

Tseng, W. (2005). "Government Dependence of Chinese and Vietnamese Organizations and Fiscal Politics of Immigrant Services." *Journal of Health and Social Policy*, 20(4), 51-74.

Vega, C. M. (2008, Apr 3). "City Making Clear Illegals Can Obtain Services Here." *San Francisco Chronicle*, B-1.

Verba, S., K. L. Schlozman, and H. Brady. (1995). *Voice and Equality: Civic Voluntarism in American Politics*. Cambridge: Harvard University Press.

Wei, W. (1993). *The Asian American Movement*. Philadelphia: Temple University Press.

Wong, J. S. (2006). *Democracy's Promise: Immigrants and American Civic Institutions*. Ann Arbor: University of Michigan Press.

9

Tipping the Scale: State Rescaling and the Strange Odyssey of Chicago's Mexican Hometown Associations*

William Sites and Rebecca Vonderlack-Navarro

First generation Mexican immigrant hometown associations (HTAs) in Chicago expanded dramatically during the 1990s and early 2000s. While enjoying strong support from the Mexican government, these clubs grew into federated organizations and remained, for a time, strongly tied to their country of origin, where they were becoming significant political actors and development partners. More recently, however, after their larger confederation (CONFEMEX) played a leading role in Chicago's 2006 marches for immigrant rights, HTA federation leaders became deeply involved in US domestic politics, particularly interest-group and voter-mobilization activity at the state and local level, even as tensions within their organizations came to the fore. Why have HTA organizations evolved from inter-local civic associations focused on Mexican hometowns to organizations focused primarily on US-based interest-group activity in Chicago?

There are a number of ways to address this question. Recent approaches to US migrant politics vary considerably, with certain studies emphasizing its continuity with longstanding patterns of immigrant incorporation (Hochschild and Mollenkopf, 2009a) and others pointing to simultaneous migrant activism in Mexico and the United States as a new form of transnational citizenship (Levitt and Glick Schiller, 2004; Smith, 2007). Employing a bi-national historical framework, this paper attempts to understand the political trajectory of Chicago HTAs in relation to an evolving series of state projects on both sides of the border. We argue that various state actors in Mexico and the United States played powerful roles in reshaping the HTA political agenda, in part by *rescaling* that agenda and, along with it, the structure of HTA organizations themselves. Drawing on theoretical insights into the scalar processes implicated in state-led economic and political restructurings, we examine the *scale shifts* that accompanied HTA activity across three distinct historical moments of development: first, the gradual shift in scalar engagement from local to national Mexican politics that took place during the decade prior to 2001; second, a proliferation of scalar involvements (including national and local entanglements in both the United States and Mexico) that emerged during the period 2001-2005; and third, a "tipping" of scale that occurred post-2005, when US state and local politics became a newly privileged field of HTA organizational engagement. By emphasizing the scalar components of various cross-cutting state projects, we attempt to show how scale-shift dynamics not only help to explain the peculiar, multi-step evolution of the CONFEMEX political agenda but also shed significant light on the shifting fortunes of the confederation itself. If contemporary migrant politics in Chicago have recently come to revolve, as we will suggest, within the orbit of US state and local politics, then this is no small matter; state-led re-scalings on both sides of the border have tended, perhaps surprisingly, to facilitate localist forms of US political incorporation.[1]

A Long and Winding Road for HTAs? Migrant Politics, States, and Scales

Mexican hometown associations in US cities began as efforts to sustain cross-border ties between migrants and their places of origin, and they are still most often understood, like HTAs in other parts of the world, in relation to their development activities back home (Boruchoff, 2007; Goldring, 2002; Orozco and Lapointe, 2004; Portes, Escobar, and Radford, 2007; Smith, 2006; see also Caglar, 2006). If so, how should we understand the apparent shift in activity by Chicago's HTAs from Mexico to the United States?

One way to view this shift in focus would be to see it simply as a vindication of traditional theories of immigrant political incorporation. After all, both classic and recent approaches in this field emphasize that, historically, immigrant groups in the United States tend to experience social assimilation and political incorporation more quickly than in many other developed countries, primarily because of the relatively open character of its polity (Gertle and Mollenkopf, 2001; Hochschild and Mollenkopf, 2009b; Mollenkopf and Sonenshein, 2009). Yet it is not at all clear that Chicago's HTA members, despite their recent engagements with state and local politics in Illinois, have forsaken their political ties to Mexico. Indeed, involvement in US-centered politics seems to continue alongside many of the traditional activities of these associations: the hometown festivals, the fundraising efforts, and the development projects back home. Furthermore, the *process* whereby CONFEMEX became involved in Illinois state and local politics has been much less straightforward than the "pull" factors emphasized in conventional notions of immigrant incorporation might suggest. The Mexican government, for example, has actively encouraged Chicago's HTAs to move more deeply into US domestic affairs; the recently anti-immigrant tenor of US national political debates, moreover, may have played a role in spurring the clubs to focus on local politics. Thus it is not clear that the host-society-centered and relatively linear conceptions of political incorporation—whereby immigrants gradually, or not so gradually, evolve from home-tied to host-tied forms of political participation—adequately capture the recent dynamics of Chicago's HTA activity.

For this reason, there may be enduring merit in the more "transnational" conceptions of migrant identities that emerged so prominently during the past several decades. In these conceptions, hometown associations are seen as significant agents in the creation of ongoing ties between migrants and their countries of origin—ties that persist irrespective of, or in addition to, the host-country involvements that engage them (Goldring, 2002; R. C. Smith, 1998; 2006; Smith and Bakker, 2008). Michael Peter Smith (2007), for example, has recently investigated what he views as the "two faces" of transnational citizenship experienced by Mexican migrants residing in the United States. Through exploring the varied political engagements of California-based migrant activists (ranging from grassroots politics and civil rights advocacy in California to government office-holding in Mexico), Smith suggests that the bi-national or "multiplex" identities of many cross-border activists indicate the emergence of a new kind of transnational citizenship. What is attractive about Smith's conception of migrant politics is not only its rejection of linear or evolutionistic notions of host-country incorporation but, more broadly, its attention to the possibility for growing political opportunities for migrant participation at various scales on both sides of the border. Indeed, Smith sees the varied forms of political engagement that he examines as resulting as much from migrant agencies and contingent circumstances as from any determinative sociopolitical or institutional mechanisms.

Yet the political agenda of Chicago's hometown associations has undergone a discernible, but by no means simple, evolution. Its development is a patterned trajectory in which, over the course of the past two decades, US-centered work has taken up an increasingly preponderant (though by no means exclusive) share of HTA activities. Furthermore, there are signs that this trajectory has been profoundly shaped by a powerful, if ever shifting, field of institutional forces—political opportunity structures and state actors—on both sides of the US-Mexico border. The early development and capacities of Chicago HTAs, for example, were strongly directed by the Mexican government, and government actors from south of the border have continued to influence the activities of CONFEMEX as they focus on state and local politics in Illinois. Meanwhile, US governmental actors have also played an influential role, as national politicians and local power-brokers alike have repeatedly pushed and pulled Chicago HTA leaders into multiple currents of domestic immigrant politics. It is difficult, in fact, to understand the evolving activities of CONFEMEX over the course of recent decades without attending to the effects of various state actors in Mexico and the United States on the strategic actions taken by HTAs and their leaders. We need to take seriously, then, the possibility that the combined impacts of a diverse array of governmental and political processes in both Mexico and the United States tend to channel contemporary migrant groups in a particular direction, such as toward urban-based arenas of US-centric political engagement. If so, then the task of explaining this evolution may require examining a broader array of political actors and institutional fields—and employing a longer-term historical focus—than has been common within the literature on migrant political activism.

The interpretive challenge is compounded by the sometimes cross-cutting nature of state projects. In other words, at key moments certain government actors have encouraged CONFEMEX to move in one direction while others have pushed the confederation toward a somewhat different path. Although these colliding state pressures relate in part to the dissimilar interests of the US and Mexican governments, they also relate to the divergent agendas of national, as against state and local. government officials in both countries. Recognizing the distinctive interests of public-sector actors at different levels of government points to the relevance of *scale* for understanding state and migrant projects alike.

Recent work by human geographers re-theorizes the concept of scale in ways that emphasize its constructed and relational qualities. Rather than being seen as ontological givens or preconfigured scaffolds, scales—such as neighborhood, urban, regional, national, and transnational—are now understood as socially created. Since it is produced through an array of material and discursive processes, scale may also shape, in turn, the social practices that constitute it (McMaster and Sheppard, 2004). Scholars of political economy, in particular, have emphasized the production of scale in relation to the strategies of capitalist firms, political institutions, and social movement actors (Leitner, 2004; Swyngedouw, 2004). At key historical moments, these strategies result in hierarchical relations in which social, economic, and political activities organized at certain scales tend to predominate over others (Collinge, 1999). Brenner (2004) and other scholars have employed the terms "scaling" and "rescaling" in order to emphasize the dynamic processes whereby scales and their interrelation become formative at pivotal moments of historical development. Following periods of crisis and innovation, these processes of rescaling lead to new and provisionally enduring hierarchical relations between territorial units.

Geographers have focused in particular on scalar processes in late-twentieth century capitalist societies. Over the past three decades, the once taken-for-granted centrality of *nationally* scaled forms of economic and political organization has in many contexts yielded to a "relativization" or multiplication of scale in which supranational, regional, and local scales of activity have grown in importance (Brenner, 2004, p. 97; Jessop and Sum, 2006, p. 281). For states, these scale shifts have figured in significant restructurings of intergovernmental relations through which the institutional capacities of different levels of government and their roles in policymaking have been redefined. For non-state political actors such as interest groups, non-governmental organizations, and social movements, the scalar reconfiguration of political-institutional fields has similarly presented new opportunities and challenges, with implications for both strategic operation and organizational structure (J. Smith, 2007). As we will see later in this chapter, processes of privatization, deregulation, and transnational interdependency, which have been articulated in part through scale shifts, have increased the need for state actors to forge alliances with non-state actors—including migrants—in order to pursue governmental projects and to secure political legitimacy. The result has been a more complex, fluid, and multidirectional field as different state and non-state actors work in concert (or in opposition) to pursue resources and create political leverage at new scales (Nicholls, 2007).

Social scientists have used the terms "scale jumping" (Leitner, *et al.*, 2008; M. P. Smith, 2001) or "scale shift" (Tarrow, 2005) to conceptualize how political elites, civic groups, and movement organizations seek to gain strategic advantage by repositioning their activities at different geographical scales. In the United States, for instance, a partial decentralization of immigration policy has encouraged activists (both pro- and anti-immigrant) to shift their struggles to state legislatures and local city councils (Leitner, *et al.*, 2008; Zolberg, 2006, pp. 445-7). Yet these efforts at rescaling are not invariably zero-sum political investments; new supranational policies can facilitate certain kinds of local policy (Brenner, 2004), and social movements can use openings at one scale to create opportunities for themselves at others (Sikkink, 2005). In Mexico, for example, a decentralization of national policies with respect to emigration spurred certain state level governmental actors to launch their own efforts to reincorporate US-based Mexican migrants—efforts that would come to benefit, as we will see, national-level officials as well.

Civil society or social movement groups have sometimes adopted new organizational structures in order to "scale up" or "scale down" their activities. Scholars have noted that different organizational forms tend to entail different strategic advantages, and these trade-offs may have implications for subsequent movement trajectories. Thus, a number of transnational movement organizations have developed federated structures in which national, regional, and/or local branches combine in a nested scalar hierarchy (Miller, 2004; J. Smith, 1997). Compared with horizontal networks (a typical coalition structure), federated structures tend to facilitate quick reactions to major events and policy decisions, and their enhanced mobilizing capacities assist organizational response to multi-scalar challenges or opportunities. By the same token, the leaders of federated organizations may move more quickly than movement supporters, risking strain in the federation's ties to its grassroots base (Chapman, 2001).

Issues of scale, then, may prove relevant for understanding the political-economic contexts in which contemporary migrant groups are operating as well as the organizational advantages and tensions these groups encounter. The following sections of this paper attempt to trace the political evolution of Chicago HTAs in relation to the shifting state projects on both sides of the border. Mobilizing the insights of the preceding discussion, we examine HTA activism as a process of scale shift across three distinct historical moments of organizational development. By emphasizing the scalar characteristics of various cross-cutting state projects, we attempt to explain the peculiar, multi-step evolution of the CONFEMEX political agenda not simply as a product of migrant agency—and also not merely as the consequence of ineluctable mechanisms of US political incorporation—but instead as a trajectory patterned in part by the politically differentiated implications of particular scale-shift dynamics.

Scaling Up: Mexico's Neoliberal Transformation and HTA Growth Through Early 2001

Mexican hometown associations in Chicago and the broader Midwest grew enormously over the course of the 1990s. They began the decade as a loosely connected set of inter-local civic associations focused, appropriately enough, on hometowns back in Mexico. New migrant arrivals, along with mounting support by Mexican government officials, led to an increase in the size of HTAs and significantly remade their structure. Spurred by state-level politicians back home, the associations combined into state-level federations largely based in Chicago, and soon national officials in Mexico saw opportunities of their own in increasing the south-of-the-border political capacities of HTAs. By the end of the decade, Chicago's state-level federations had become major players in Mexican national politics, to the extent that they were beginning to insist on a new level of autonomy in order to define their own political agenda.

Hometown associations in Chicago, as elsewhere, first developed to maintain cultural links to the homeland and to provide informal support for migrants in an often-unfriendly land. As early as the 1960s, Mexican immigrant hometown clubs (*clubes de oriundos*) celebrated hometown traditions and worked to cultivate friendships with fellow migrants. Their early activities were similar to the Mexican mutual aid societies (*mutualistas*), which date back in the United States to the nineteenth century, but unlike their predecessors the hometown associations did not enjoy particularly close ties with the Mexican consulate (Cano and Délano, 2007). Another important difference was that, as the clubs grew and developed over the coming decades, their relationships with local governments back home—as well as their community influence there—grew stronger. Only gradually, as expanded migration to the United States was accompanied by an increasing economic role for remittances in many hometowns, did Mexican political notables begin to see HTAs as a major source of political and financial support.

The development of Chicago's HTAs took shape within a far-reaching restructuring in the political economies of Mexico and the United States. From the 1970s onward, international competition and corporate deregulation brought about a dramatic reorganization of US labor markets. Rapid growth in low-wage service jobs combined with the downgrading of the manufacturing sector within the new urban economy (Bluestone and Harrison, 2000; Sassen, 1998). As trade liberalization spurred economic integration with Mexico, unevenly restrictive immigration laws facilitated low-wage employment opportunities for growing populations of documented and (increasingly) undocumented migrant workers in large US cities (Massey, *et al.*, 2002). By the 1990s Mexican workers in Chicago, employed mostly in service and manual labor jobs, comprised a major cohort within the lower strata of the metropolitan labor market (Paral, 2006). Politically, these Mexican migrants, like those in other US cities, faced a somewhat contradictory set of pressures. Immigration policies in the United States after 1986 had brought increasingly coercive sanctions and border controls as well as regularization to some undocumented workers; the result was a growing number of Mexican-origin permanent settlers who were differentiated by political status (undocumented "illegals," documented immigrants, and naturalized citizens) and by disparate levels of economic wellbeing (Durand, *et al.*, 1999). On the one hand, these migrants became convenient political scapegoats during economic downturns or moments of public-sector fiscal stress. On the other hand, status regularization was increasingly supported by business organizations, and Latino communities were beginning to be selectively targeted as voting blocs by party political strategists.

Meanwhile, Mexico's own neoliberal transformation rested in part on labor export and return remittance flows as mechanisms of national income generation and political stability. Encouraged by post-1970s global governance priorities, macroeconomic policies in Mexico began to emphasize open trade, export-sector production, and the privatization of state enterprises (Aboites, *et al.*, 2002; Dussel Peters, 2000). Redirection of state support from domestic manufactures to *maquiladora* industries produced highly differentiated regional impacts within Mexico, and particular states experienced growing levels of unemployment and underemployment. As uneven development intensified and as land tenure and agricultural subsidies were restructured by the state, certain areas of the country saw sharp increases in rural outmigration (Assies, 2008; Delgado-Wise and Covarrubias, 2008). These economic developments were also accompanied by a major political transformation of the Mexican state. As political liberalization and electoral competition weakened the *Partido Revolucionario Institucional* (PRI), which had dominated politics and the state for over half a century, the Mexican government sought to reestablish its legitimacy in part by developing stronger state-society linkages both outside (e.g., with multinational capital and migrant groups) and inside the country (Cameron and Wise, 2004; Valdes Ugalde, 1996).

Emigrants became increasingly important to Mexico's politicians over the final two decades of the twentieth century. Whereas earlier historical periods had seen efforts by the Mexican government to constrain emigration, policymakers after the 1970s came to view "the permanent emigration of 10 percent of the population as desirable" (Fitzgerald, 2006, p. 280) because of the economic rewards of remittance flows as well as hopes for the growing influence of an ethnic lobby within the United States. As the Mexican national government decentralized a significant portion of its emigration policy apparatus, certain states created aggressive provincial-level policies aimed at reincorporating US-based emigrants based on their provincial origin. Key to many of these policies were the remittance-matching programs, whereby state governments would add their own subsidies to the remittance funds donated by migrant clubs for hometown infrastructure and development projects. Soon enough, the federal government, recognizing the potential economic rewards as well as the political costs of letting state-government officials dominate the field, would also respond with its own programs.

Central to Mexico's neoliberal governmental projects, then, was a growing level of political attention to its burgeoning migrant population in the United States. Party competition played a major role in initial steps to reconnect Chicago's migrants to the homeland. Presidential candidate Cuauhtémoc Cardenas visited the city in 1988, and this trip was soon followed by political stopovers by other major politicians. When incumbent President Carlos Salinas de Gortari traveled to Chicago to drum up support for NAFTA among Chicago business leaders, he also took the occasion to promote new consular programs intended to shore up the allegiance of the diaspora (Gzesh, 2007). One of these was its Program for Mexican Communities Abroad (*Programa de Comunidades Mexicanas en el Exterior*), which supported cultural events, assisted migrant organizations, and coordinated the growing stream of visits to the US by national-level Mexican officials and state governors. Encouraged by the consulate, HTAs in Chicago undertook initiatives that soon evolved into the 3-for-1 (*tres por uno*) program, under which each level of

Mexican government—national, state, and municipal—matched every dollar that a club provided for development (Gomez and Aguilar, 2005; Gomez, *et al.*, 2004). As the number of HTAs in the Chicago-centered Midwest burgeoned from 35 to 170 between 1995 and 2000 (Chicago Mexican Consulate, 2009), the HTAs were increasingly courted as interest-group blocs by politicians back home. Meanwhile, after the Mexican Congress passed a dual nationality law in 1997, expectations ran high among US-based migrants that the ability to cast real votes in national elections might be achieved before long.

In this political context, building up Chicago's HTAs became an important way for Mexican government officials to keep tabs on the emigrant community. By the second half of the 1990s, associations were rapidly coalescing into federated structures that united HTAs according to their Mexican states of origin. The seven state-level federations (Guerrero, Zacatecas, Jalisco, Guanajuato, Michoacán, Durango, and San Luis Potosí) already established in Chicago were characterized by increasingly formalized leadership structures; most featured democratically elected boards of directors and were led by established officers (Gomez and Aguilar, 2005; Gomez, *et al.*, 2004). Although federated structures were pushed initially by state-level officials in Mexico, consular officials discovered that grouping the HTAs by federation made it easier to stay informed about what community actors were doing. Larger organizational entities and coordinated leaderships also furnished institutional levers for national officials in Mexico to guide the HTA agenda. Under this arrangement the Mexican government saw federation leaders as intermediaries who could maintain dialogue with emigrant communities and facilitate implementation of its programs (Dante Gomez, coordinator of the Institute for Mexicans Abroad [IME by its Spanish initials], personal interview, Jun 8, 2008).

Chicago HTAs grew in political influence as they scaled up over the course of the 1990s. Despite the fact that increasing numbers of Mexican migrants to the city were undocumented, HTA members' participation throughout the Chicago-centered Midwest (including the states of Illinois, Wisconsin, and northern Indiana) provided them with a new sense of importance. As one federation leader from Michoacán explained, the HTAs now served multiple functions for the new arrivals who joined them:

> [Migrants] participate because it is a form, a mechanism of mental hygiene in order to escape the oppression and the lack of participation in this [US] society…. When you go to the real world…everyone tries to ignore you. They try to ignore your rights and you are a second-class citizen. [Yet from] the moment the *diputados* [Mexican officials] come and they listen to you and respect you, you [begin to] have a certain amount of respect for what you represent as a collective mind (former Michoacán federation president, personal interview, May 15, 2008).

Migrants' prior experiences with political elites in Mexico had tended, of course, to involve routine disregard and marginalization. Now, in Chicago, these same political notables from south of the border were addressing migrants as valued contributors to the nation. This new treatment tended to legitimate migrants as national political subjects, which in turn imparted a new sense of purpose and agency upon the migrant community and its organizations.

Over the second half of the 1990s, Chicago's HTA federations became increasingly active in redefining their relationship to the Mexican government. No longer content to operate merely as the grateful recipients of official attention, the federations began to negotiate more assertively with Mexican elites over development projects and even over the terms of their reincorporation into the homeland. Federation and HTA leaders became active advocates for dual nationality rights (granted in 1997), and henceforth they devoted significant energies toward translating the symbolic voting participation now enjoyed by US-based Mexican migrants into real votes and political power (Fitzgerald, 2006). The drive of Chicago's HTAs for political independence reached a new level in 1999 when migrant leaders joined together in opposition to proposals by the Mexican government to impose a dramatic increase (from only $15 to $400 or more) on mandated deposits for cars crossing over the border from the United States. This "car tax protest" brought together federation activists into an *ad hoc* coalition that called itself *Grupo David*—a name intended to capture the proud contentiousness with which they were now confronting a Goliath-like Mexican government (CONFEMEX, 2006). The ensuing success of the campaign— the Mexican government withdrew its proposal—suggested that the power dynamics between Chicago's HTAs and the "friendly" Mexican consulate had changed. As one federated leader noted, "We showed the consulate that we could change politics and that we didn't need them as intermediaries" (Durango federation leader, personal interview, May 6, 2008).

The decade of the 1990s, therefore, saw not only a process of enormous growth for Chicago's HTAs but also a profound shift in their scale and scope. They had begun the decade as a collection of inter-local clubs focused largely on home*town* activities. Ten years later HTA migrants saw themselves increasingly as important home-*country* political subjects, providing crucial contributions to the nation and making legitimate demands on their democratic government for the right to full political participation. If Mexico's restructuring state had spawned new government autonomies throughout the federal system, state actors at multiple levels had worked to build the organizational capacities of the HTAs, equipping their federations for newly ambitious tasks within a nationally scaled political agenda. In the process, HTAs had hardly turned their backs on their hometowns: indeed, new clubs in Chicago were still forming, and local development projects remained the core involvement for many migrant members. But scaling up had politically repositioned the HTAs, and their federations were now seen as significant players in the national polity south of the border.

Of course, for all their attention in Mexico, Chicago-based migrants continued to have a much more tenuous political status in the United States. Yet, by early September 2001, direct negotiations between Mexican President Vicente Fox and US President George W. Bush were edging toward a comprehensive immigration-reform proposal. It seemed reasonable to expect that soon enough Mexican migrants would enjoy a new level of political standing in the United States as well.

Scaling Out: Post-9/11 Threats and the Bi-national HTA Agenda, 2001-2005

The political landscape for US-based Mexican migrants changed sharply after September 2001. Following the terrorist attacks on the World Trade Center and the Pentagon, the Bush administration's determination to forge a new national-security agenda had major repercussions for migrant communities and for other state projects, in both the United States and Mexico. As the US "war on terrorism" reconfigured immigration debates around the issue of border security, national officials in Mexico recalibrated their approach to HTAs. They began pushing the migrant organizations to forge protective connections with various US-centered political actors. The resulting process for Chicago's hometown associations was a kind of scalar proliferation, leading to new HTA involvements at multiple levels of the US political system. By late 2005, Chicago HTAs had significantly "scaled out": even as the federated clubs retained their multi-leveled connections to Mexico, they were developing an array of local, state, and national linkages north of the border that paralleled their involvements south of the Rio Grande.

Immigration politics in the United States underwent a major realignment after 9/11. As national politicians embraced a security approach with implications for many areas of government policy, immigration "reform" was quickly redefined as fixing America's porous borders. New border security initiatives were passed by the US Congress in early 2002. Later that year, legislators refashioned border enforcement by creating new agencies—most notably Customs and Border Protection (CBP) and Immigration Customs and Enforcement (ICE)—and housing them within the newly formed Department of Homeland Security, which, henceforth, would spearhead the nation's immigration policy (Tichenor, 2009; Zolberg, 2006, pp. 445-7). Propelled by this new era of national "state-building," interdiction efforts along the border with Mexico grew sharply over the coming years, and ICE expanded the use of work-site raids, detention, criminal prosecution, and deportation against both undocumented and legal immigrants. There was also a significant effort to tighten intergovernmental enforcement mechanisms; the policies created new partnerships and extensive database-sharing to support internalized "border control" measures undertaken by state and local agencies. As growing numbers of Mexican migrants remained in the United States to avoid the dangers of exit and re-entry, the role of migrant organizations in cities such as Chicago became more complicated (Chacón, 2008; Fernández-Kelly and Massey, 2007; Meissner and Kerwin, 2009).

The national policy shift in the United States also reconfigured relations with its southern neighbor. As the Bush administration closed the door on any bi-nationally negotiated immigration reform, Mexico's lack of support for the US campaign against Iraq further ruptured diplomatic relations between the countries. Fox, now left without any direct leverage on Washington, turned his efforts toward safeguarding emigrants and their remittance flows within an increasingly hostile US environment. The Mexican consulate in Chicago played a key role in implementing several new programs to strengthen ties between migrant residents and the national homeland to protect these migrants from deportation.

Beginning in 2002, Fox restructured and expanded his government's diaspora programs with the formation of the Institute of Mexicans Abroad *(Instituto de los Mexicanos en el Exterior)*, or IME. The IME became the umbrella for an extensive overhaul of consular services throughout the United States. There were also more targeted efforts, including the revamping of the 3-for-1 remittance programs in US cities into a nationally organized program. To support the institute, the Mexican government also created a migrant advisory council that included HTA and federation leaders, US-focused Latino advocacy groups, immigrant leaders from Canada, and state-government officials in Mexico. Meanwhile, Fox continued to support the national-level campaign for migrants' absentee voting rights in Mexico (McCann, *et al.*, 2009; Smith and Bakker, 2008). In Chicago, the Mexican consulate initiated bi-monthly meetings between federation leaders and various consular officials, working hard to repair ill feelings from the car tax episode and to reassert influence (but in a less heavy-handed way) over the HTA organizations *(Partido de la Revolución Democrática* (PRD) activists, multiple personal interviews, Oct 19, 2008 and Feb 2, 2009).

More concretely, the consulate attempted to develop an identity card that could be widely used by migrants residing in Chicago who were without documentation. Launched in March 2002, the *matrícula* (short for *Matrícula Consular de Alta Seguridad*) caught on rapidly, and already by the end of 2003 there were an estimated 150,000 in use in Chicago. They were used most commonly for remittance transfers.[2] The consulate also brought together banks, federal regulators, secondary market companies, mortgage insurance providers, and Mexican federation leaders and other community organizations in an effective effort to facilitate acceptance of the card as a legitimate form of identification by major US economic institutions. But the card was intended to be more than an economic tool. For the Mexican government, it was hoped in the medium-term that the economic rewards of the *matrícula* might bring the powerful US banking industry onboard as an active political ally in the fight for regularization of migrant status in the United States. One of the longer-term goals of the *matrícula* was to satisfy time-of-residency requirements in the event that settled undocumented Mexicans were given an opportunity to apply for legal status in the US.

The Mexican consulate, however, was not the only force edging Chicago's hometown associations into the sphere of US domestic politics. Beginning in 2002, a local Chicago non-profit organization, called *Enlaces America*, began working with the HTA federations to develop new leaders for their organizations. Although it was intended to generate support for a bi-national approach to US immigration reform, this leadership-training program also created an opportunity for Chicago's HTAs to reexamine their organizational goals within a political space that was not shaped by Mexican consular officials. This program began to connect HTA leaders to their counterparts in US-focused immigrant rights groups while also raising the visibility of the federations in the city of Chicago. The initiative also led to a growing professionalization among the HTA leadership that, in 2003, culminated in the formation of the Confederation of Mexican Federations (*Confederación de Federaciones Mexicanas*), an umbrella organization initially comprising eight of the Chicago-based federations and 175 Midwestern HTAs. CONFEMEX, as it was called, was created to stand apart from the guiding hand of the Mexican government, and the confederation explicitly embraced a bi-national Mexico-US focus (CONFEMEX, 2006). Yet, this organizational scaling-up was also strongly supported by the Mexican government, and the enhanced unity and coordinating capacities brought about by the confederation were intended to facilitate a more ambitious, multi-scalar agenda.

One new arena of involvement was soon signaled by the CONFEMEX decision to participate directly in interest-group efforts to influence US immigration policy debates. In January 2004, President Bush, facing a contest for re-election later in the year, floated a new proposal for comprehensive immigration reform. Though this proposal was an effort to regenerate political support from business groups and Latino voters (Dlouhy, 2004), it also gained attention from immigrant groups. By the end of the year, CONFEMEX had joined with more than 85 migrant-led organizations from many US cities to form the National Alliance of Latino and Caribbean Communities (NALACC). While offering a bi-national approach to migration and legalization, the alliance advocated for both balanced development strategies in Latin America and comprehensive immigration reform in the US, all the while pressing for immigrant integration programs in various US state and local contexts (Chacón and Shannon, 2006). Although the latest Bush reform proposal faded quickly after his reelection in 2004, CONFEMEX leaders would henceforth work closely with NALACC to press this agenda in Washington, DC, and in Illinois.

CONFEMEX was also pulled into US politics by state-level actors in Illinois. Democratic Governor Rod Blagojevich first took a strong electoral interest in Chicago's Mexican immigrants after his 2002 victory was attributed to strong support by Latino constituency groups (Fornek, 2002; Neal, 2002). Yet, as Blagojevich looked ahead to his reelection campaign in 2006, advocacy groups made clear that a significant political gesture would be required to mobilize Latino voters and the expanding immigrant community (Rogal, 2004). In November 2005, the governor issued an executive order that created new state-level services to promote immigrant integration, including citizenship acquisition efforts and increased accessibility to healthcare, regardless of legal status. Blagojevich also named José Luis Gutiérrez, a CONFEMEX leader from the state of Michoacán, to become the director of his new Office of New Americans Policy and Advocacy (Illinois Government News Network, 2006). This political connection to state government would inspire, in turn, new interest group activity by federation leaders, which particularly focused on naturalization and electoral participation.

Between 2001 and 2005, then, CONFEMEX extended its activities into US political arenas at multiple scales. As the Bush administration's post-9/11 agenda encouraged Mexican officials to create initiatives to protect its Chicago-based migrants, the city's HTAs were developing new connections—through local financial institutions, national migrant-rights coalitions, and state-level interest groups—to a heterogeneous field of US-centered engagement. The Mexican government, of course, retained its role as chief supporter, but an advocacy group called Illinois Coalition for Immigrant and Refugee Rights (ICIRR) increasingly operated as a key "broker" (Nicholls, 2007) in this process, connecting CONFEMEX leaders to important allies throughout this domestic political field.

Establishment of the confederation's new connections, however, did not involve turning its back on the old ones. Chicago's HTAs continued to build their local and state ties back home. For example, when the Mexican Chamber of Deputies suddenly approved absentee-voting legislation in early 2005, CONFEMEX joined a campaign called Vote from Abroad (*El Voto en el Exterior*) and began energetic efforts to mobilize participation in the national elections scheduled for the following year (CONFEMEX meeting minutes, Nov 7, 2005 and Jan 9, 2006). Yet, the confederation had also become a multi-scalar US actor, and it remained to be seen how these many-leveled involvements, on both sides of the border, might play out over time.

Scaling Down: From Sensenbrenner to Chicago Politics, 2006–2009

On March 10, 2006, and then scarcely seven weeks later on May 1, hundreds of thousands of residents marched through downtown Chicago to press their claims for US immigrant rights (Ávila and Olivo, 2006a; 2006b; Olivo and Ávila, 2006). CONFEMEX played a central role in organizing and mobilizing these protests, thus becoming a new and important actor on the national stage of US immigration politics. Very quickly after the May 1st protest, however, CONFEMEX plunged much deeper into Illinois state and local politics. Encouraged by Mexican national officials and by powerful Democratic Party allies in Chicago and Springfield, federation leaders created formal partnerships with local advocacy groups, formed a political action committee, and took leadership positions within Illinois interest-group organizations and government agencies. By 2009, federation leaders had become major players on the state and local political scene, even as the marches dwindled and the national immigration agenda increasingly shut them out. In effect, CONFEMEX rescaled its agenda downward, and in the process the confederation was forced to navigate new tensions that accompanied this US-centered, localizing turn.

The Sensenbrenner bill, of course, was the initial catalyst for the organization's full-fledged jump into US immigrant politics. Passed by the US House of Representatives in December 2005, HR 4437 threatened to criminalize undocumented residents as well as citizens who might even attempt to assist such people (Wayne, 2005a; 2005b). As details of the bill and the full measure of its chilling implications filtered down, HTA leaders also began to recognize that legal restrictions in the upcoming Mexican national elections would severely limit the electoral participation of US-based emigrants. The golden opportunity of widespread participation in Mexican elections was diminished. As one CONFEMEX leader recalls:

> We were going with the vote of the Mexicans [in Mexico]. But when we became aware of the fiasco, of the lack of people with [Mexican] electoral credentials, there was great disenchantment, and all of that hope we had of being able to have major political weight in Mexico [disappeared]. So then it grabbed our attention: Mexico is very far from here, many kilometers. Here is where we are, here is where we are living, and they are at the point of passing a law that is going to make you a criminal—and you continue thinking about voting in Mexico's next elections? (Michoacán federation leader, personal interview, May 15, 2008).

By early 2006, CONFEMEX leaders were hosting an unprecedented combination of migrant and immigrant organizations at the Michoacán federation headquarters in Chicago in order to develop plans for a protest demonstration (CONFEMEX meeting minutes, Feb 15, 2006).

It was clear on March 10, as upwards of 100,000 people assembled in Chicago's Federal Plaza, that CONFEMEX's large membership and federated structure were major contributors to the success of the protest. Federation chiefs had been able to transmit directions downward through their HTA leaders, who in turn called on massive numbers of volunteers to do the logistical work of preparing the march and enlisting and mobilizing marchers. Many federations also used lists of contacts developed through their recent drives to register Mexican absentee voters (Shannon, 2007). As one Chicago activist later commented:

> Without the HTAs that thing [the marches] does not happen.... They have a spirit of volunteerism. They have organized events with actually *no* resources. So...they don't have as much of an established political perspective in the US.... [But] I mean, who's going to do all the work for stuff to happen that made that thing a reality? (ICIRR Board President, personal interview, Jan 9, 2009).

In spring 2006, then, as a result of the marches, CONFEMEX was recognized as a major new force in north-of-the-border immigrant politics.

In the wake of the March 10th protest, many Democratic Party politicians in Illinois eagerly endorsed the upcoming May 1st rally, and the confederation hoped to capitalize on the new level of political attention. Yet, even amid the post-May Day elation, CONFEMEX leaders complained among themselves that other Chicago organizations involved in planning the marches—with their seasoned, paid organizers and savvy media strategies—were routinely getting the lion's share of the publicity (Guerrero federation leader and CONFEMEX president, personal interview, May 2, 2008). Over the following months, a pronounced drive for professionalization emerged within the confederation, along with an even stronger focus on encouraging statewide citizenship applications and mobilizing the eligible voters among its base in order to increase the immigrant electoral turnout (CONFEMEX meeting minutes, Jul 11, 2006).

A key step in this direction was the confederation's newly formalized partnership with ICIRR, the immigrant and refugee rights advocacy coalition. Several top CONFEMEX leaders accepted leadership positions with the coalition, having been attracted in part by its well-financed and politically connected role in Illinois state politics. The ICIRR envisioned the migrant confederation, with its deep and strongly mobilized base, as an ideal successor to Chicago's Hispanic Democratic Organization (HDO). (The HDO, by funneling votes to top Democratic state and local officials in exchange for favors, had operated as a kind of Latino political machine until criminal indictments of several HDO leaders led to the organization's dissolution.) Beginning in the summer of 2006, a group of ICIRR and HTA federation leaders also began to discuss the formation of a political action committee. Called Mexicans for Political Progress, the committee would direct its energies toward providing financial and volunteer support for the election campaigns of Blagojevich and Congressman Luis Gutiérrez, along with other statewide and local aldermanic candidates. Over the next two years, CONFEMEX and ICIRR citizenship campaigns contributed to major surges in naturalization rates for Mexican immigrants, and the groups' voter registration drives sought to mobilize this growing electoral base (Olivo, 2008).

It was not simply Illinois politicians and advocates who encouraged the confederation's growing involvement in state and local electoral politics. Mexican national leaders were beginning to see CONFEMEX as their own well-positioned bridge to those same US state and local power-brokers. By 2007, Chicago consular officials were working to facilitate Blagojevich's immigrant integration initiatives and relying on CONFEMEX leaders to help set up mechanisms whereby new migrant arrivals to the consulate might be routinely connected to Illinois service programs. Early in the following year, during a visit to Chicago, Mexican President Felipe Calderón and CONFEMEX leaders met with Blagojevich and Mayor Richard M. Daley to set up new cross-border partnerships in the areas of educational exchange and workforce training (CONFEMEX meeting minutes, Mar 10, 2008).

Over the two years following the 2006 marches, then, CONFEMEX became a major player in state and local politics. One cost of this intensive organizational investment in localized interest-group activity, however, was a rapid move away from contentious mobilization, which meant, in turn, a reduced impact on US national-level politics as the mood in Washington became more anti-immigrant. Even as the numbers of ICE-led workplace raids and deportations grew, fierce divisions between CONFEMEX and other Chicago protest planners—who increasingly viewed one another as competitors for local resources—nearly scuttled a unified May 1, 2007 demonstration. By the following year's May Day march, most confederation officials were refusing to take a leadership role at all; they did not want to take time away from their naturalization and voter registration drives (CONFEMEX meeting minutes, Apr 14, 2008). At the same time, the 2008 economic downturn began to take its toll on Illinois' well-oiled Democratic political machine. While facing serious fiscal problems, Springfield legislators refused to fund much of the governor's immigrant-related budget, and even Blagojevich himself was forced to cut deeply into his own citizenship programs (Sacchetti, 2008). The softened economy also affected the Mexican government, which cut back on expenditures on emigrant programs. CONFEMEX leaders, feeling the squeeze, agitated for more of the Illinois state funding that flowed through ICIRR (CONFEMEX meeting minutes, Mar 10, 2008).

As economic and political conditions worsened, several federation leaders began to contend that CONFEMEX had become too integrated into state and local politics. The former president of the Zacatecas federation accused CONFEMEX leaders of opportunism: "The personal missions [of leaders] have come first" (personal interview, Jun 18, 2008). Internal rivalries within CONFEMEX mounted as the two largest federations (Guerrero and Michoacán) now vied for control. As corruption rumors surrounded Blagojevich, federation leaders also grew concerned about their political action committee's close ties to the governor. After they withdrew support later in the year, Mexicans for Political Progress closed down—only shortly before Blagojevich himself was arrested on criminal charges (which included obtaining campaign contributions in exchange for official actions and attempting to sell Illinois' vacant Senate seat) in December 2008; he was soon impeached by the Illinois Senate (Coen and Pearson, 2008; Long and Pearson, 2009).

By early 2009, contention between the Guerrero and Michoacán federations grew so intense that the latter withdrew from CONFEMEX. Support for the confederation within the base membership grew weaker. As many members complained that CONFEMEX had pulled the HTAs away from their traditional focus on the hometowns, others criticized the larger organization for failing to beat back the growing numbers of deportations (personal interviews: Hidalgo federation leaders, Jun 23, 2008; Durango co-founder and former CONFEMEX president, May 10, 2008; Michoacán federation leader, May 15, 2008; Oaxaca federation founder and president, Jul 17, 2008; Guerrero federation leader and CONFEMEX president, May 2, 2008). It had now become difficult—partly because of fear and partly because of disillusionment—to mobilize HTA members on behalf of any larger collective project. The confederation was floundering, with the way forward uncertain.

For CONFEMEX, then, the post-2006 period saw a dramatic shift in organizational activity, not only in terms of focus but also in terms of scale. The preceding moment had been one of gradual expansion and diversification; the capacity-building process of confederation had accompanied the development of a multi-tiered political agenda, which was pursued with growing confidence at different levels on both sides of the border. For a brief moment, the combined powers of all these involvements seemed to converge as CONFEMEX drew on its unique capacities to play a major role in the stirring mobilizations of spring 2006. Surprisingly, though, this sudden entry onto the US national political stage was soon succeeded by a rapidly deepening investment in the institutional arena of state and local politics. Various government officials and powerful allies encouraged CONFEMEX to dive into Illinois interest-group activism, and for a time the federation chiefs responded with enthusiasm. As the larger organization became embedded within the political worlds of Chicago and Springfield, however, its new activities—the lobbying, advocating, electioneering, and service-connecting—tended to tie the confederation to a tightly localized sphere, thus weakening its connections to other, still-important scales of operation. Rescaling downward had seemed to offer CONFEMEX unprecedented local leverage, charting out a new path within US politics that promised to lead to migrant rights and protections. However, as the 2006 moment receded and the confederation's new ties became political liabilities, CONFEMEX experienced this "tipping" of scale as a road with limited returns.

Conclusion

What is one to make of the trajectory of Chicago's hometown associations and their larger organizational entities? We have tried to understand the odyssey of these HTAs in relation to the shifting, scale-inflected projects of different state actors in Mexico and the United States. The clubs were "born" as migrant civil society organizations with trans-local ties to hometowns of origin. However, from early on, their unusual growth and development became linked to governmental actors on both sides of the border. Building on studies of the scalar processes implicated in economic and political restructurings, we have examined how state-related shifts in the two countries have configured new scales of opportunity for Chicago's hometown associations and generated capacities for new organizational responses. Over the course of several decades, the evolution of hometown associations and their federations took shape as a complex series of vertical repositionings—scaling up, scaling out, scaling down—with important implications for the arena of engagement and for the kinds of impacts these groups might have. Without reducing the CONFEMEX story *simply* to an account of organizational rescaling, we believe that scale-shift dynamics do offer genuine insights into the political course taken by Chicago's HTAs.

Traditional theories of immigrant incorporation may not perceive the need for such a complicated story; perhaps they may view the most recent position of CONFEMEX as a fairly typical point of destination. In this perspective, the political incorporation of US immigrants tends to proceed apace, as host-country institutional mechanisms within local political systems draw in migrant groups over time. Yet, home-country state actors were crucial for building up HTA structures in the first place, and it was precisely their capacities to do so—exhibited most dramatically in a nationally-scaled US protest movement—that made the federated HTAs so attractive to Illinois powerbrokers. Although CONFEMEX, in its current state, has ended up more or less where theories of incorporation might predict, these HTAs were unlikely to have gotten there at all without traversing a multi-scaled bi-national political field.

Finally, the question of precisely *where* Chicago HTAs have "ended up" may not yet be settled. If our historical account has ended up focusing on recent moves by CONFEMEX leaders into the thickets of US state and local politics, the disappointing returns from those ventures already have spurred a renewed appreciation for the homeland, particularly among the migrant base. In short, Chicago HTA members have not responded to recent processes of US incorporation by turning their backs on Mexico or their hometowns. Instead, these migrants appear to be reengaging with traditional HTA activities even as they look to their leaders—state and non-state, in Mexico and in the United States—to address their increasingly difficult political situation.

Their sentiments are likely to augur a complicated agenda. One federation leader summed up the back-to-basics mentality of his members as follows: "They want their dances, their 3-for-1 [development projects], and they do not want to talk about politics" (Durango federation co-founder and former president of CONFEMEX, personal interview, May 10, 2008). Nevertheless, another federation leader observed that the realities for undocumented migrants within the HTA member base remain urgent and acknowledged that pressure for a larger political agenda is unlikely to go away:

> They're still telling us, 'Keep going!' There's so much pressure on us [as federation leaders]...because you think, 'oh my God,' they look at us like we're going to do the [immigration] reform. To *help* them. And it's a lot, because for the one who gets deported, what explanation can I give them? (Hidalgo federation president and secretary, personal interview, Jun 23, 2008).

Notes

The authors would like to thank the Chicago Confederation of Mexican Federations (CONFEMEX) for making this research possible.

1. The research for this chapter is drawn from a multi-method case study focused on the political involvements of Chicago's Mexican hometown associations. This study has employed archival research, direct observation, and key-informant interviews to explore the emergence and development of CONFEMEX, Chicago's HTA confederation. Archival sources included Chicago Mexican consular publications and materials, HTA federation and CONFEMEX meeting minutes, newspaper archives, and protest flyers and pamphlets. Analysis of recent organizational

developments draws from direct observation within the leadership circles of CONFEMEX (2005-2007) as well as interviews with past and present HTA federation leaders, Mexican and US government officials, and local immigrant activists. Interviews with former and current HTA leaders encompassed ten federations (Aguascalientes, Chihuahua, Durango, Michoacán, Jalisco, Hidalgo, Zacatecas, Guanajuato, Guerrero, and Oaxaca); other interviewees were selected because of their significant involvement in Chicago HTA developments over the past 20 years.

2. Remittances from Illinois to Mexico were substantial, amounting to about $1.3 billion in 2003, while remittance transmission costs dropped significantly (Hernandez-Coss, 2005).

References

Aboites, J., L. Miotti, and C. Quenan. (2002). "Regulationist Approaches and Accumulation in Latin America." In R. Boyer and Y. Saillard (Eds.), C. Shread (Trans.), *Regulation Theory: The State of the Art* (pp. 280-8). New York: Routledge.

Assies, W. (2008). "Land Tenure and Tenure Regimes in Mexico: An Overview." *Journal of Agrarian Change*, 8(1), 33-63.

Ávila, O., and A. Olivo. (2006a, Mar 11). "A Show of Strength: Thousands March to Loop for Immigrants' Rights: Workers, Students Unite in Opposition to Toughening Law." *Chicago Tribune*. Retrieved Mar 11, 2006, from www.chicagotribune.com/news/nationworld/chi-0603110130mar11,1,6447756.story.

_____. (2006b, Mar 12). "Rally Stirs Both Sides; Across U.S., Immigration Supporters, Foes View Chicago Rally as Catalyst." *Chicago Tribune*, 1.

Bluestone, B., and B. Harrison. (2000). *Growing Prosperity: The Battle for Growth with Equity in the Twenty-First Century*. Boston: Houghton Mifflin.

Boruchoff, J. (2007). "Transnational Perspectives on Migrant Civic and Political Engagement." Background paper for Latin American Migrants: Civic and Political Participation in a Transnational Context. October 26-27, Chicago.

Brenner, N. (2004). *New State Spaces: Urban Governance and the Rescaling of Statehood*. New York: Oxford University Press.

Caglar, A. (2006). "Hometown Associations, the Rescaling of State Spatiality and Migrant Grassroots Transnationalism." *Global Networks*, 6(1), 1-22.

Cameron, M. A., and C. Wise. (2004). "The Political Impact of NAFTA on Mexico: Reflections on the Political Economy of Democratization." *Canadian Journal of Political Science*, 37, 2(Jun), 301-23.

Chacón, J. M. (2008). "The Security Myth: Punishing Immigrants in the Name of National Security." In A. Chebel d'Appollonia and S. Reich (Eds.), *Immigration, Integration, and Security: America and Europe in Comparative Perspective*. Pittsburgh: University of Pittsburgh Press.

Chacón, O., and A. Shannon. (2006). "Challenges and Opportunities for Transnational Community Building: Immigrant Organizations as Change Agents." Unpublished manuscript prepared for the Ford Foundation Initiative on Transnational Community Building.

Chapman, J. (2001). "What Makes International Campaigns Effective? Lessons from India and Ghana." In M. Edwards and J. Gaventa (Eds.), *Global Citizen Action* (pp. 259-74). Boulder, CO: Lynne Rienner.

Chicago Mexican Consulate. (2009). Consular Materials on Midwest Region HTA Growth.

Coen, J., and R. Pearson. (2008, Dec 9). "Blagojevich Arrested on Federal Charges." *Chicago Tribune*. Retrieved Jun 1, 2011, from http://archive.chicagobreakingnews.com/2008/12/source-feds-take-gov-blagojevich-into-custody.html.

Collinge, C. (1999). "Self-Organization of Society by Scale: A Spatial Reworking of Regulation Theory." *Environment and Planning D: Society and Space*, 17, 557-74.

CONFEMEX. (2006). "Estatutos: Anexo, Historia, Mística y Metodología de Trabajo." Unpublished internal document.

Delgado-Wise, R., and H. Marquez Covarrubias. (2008). "Capitalist Restructuring, Development and Labour Migration: The Mexico-U.S. Case." *Third World Quarterly*, 29(7), 1359-74.

Dlouhy, J. A. (2004). "Committed White House Push a Must for Immigration Plan." *CQ Weekly*, 95.

Durand, J., D. S. Massey, and E. A. Parrado. (1999). "The New Era of Mexican Migration in the United States." *Journal of American History*, 86(2), 518-36.

Dussel Peters, E. (2000). *Polarizing Mexico: The Impact of Liberalization Strategy.* Boulder, CO: Lynne Rienner.

Fernandez-Kelly, P., and D. S. Massey. (2007). "Borders for Whom? The Role of NAFTA in Mexico-U.S. Migration." *Annals of the American Academy of Political and Social Science*, 610(Mar), 98-118.

Fitzgerald, D. (2006). "Inside the Sending State: The Politics of Mexican Emigration Control." *International Migration Review*, 40(2), 259-93.

Fornek, S. (2002, Jan 8). "Blagojevich Aims at Hispanics; Gutierrez Appears in Spot for Governor Hopeful." *Chicago Sun-Times*, 8.

Gerstle, G., and J. Mollenkopf. (2001). "The Political Incorporation of Immigrants, Then and Now." In G. Gerstle and J. Mollenkopf (Eds.), *E Pluribus Unum? Contemporary and Historical Perspectives on Immigrant Political Incorporation* (pp. 1-30). New York: Russell Sage Foundation.

Goldring, L. (2002). "The Mexican State and Transmigrant Organizations: Negotiating the Boundaries of Membership and Participation." *Latin American Research Review*, 37(3), 55-99.

Gomez, D., and S. Aguilar. (2006). "Organizaciones Comunitarias Mexicanas en Chicago." *Mexicanos en el Exterior*, 1(14), 1-5.

Gomez, D., S. Aguilar, G. Arochi, S. Sarmiento, and G. Gonzalez. (2004). "Clubes de Oriundos." *Mexicanos en el Exterior*, 1(7), 1-6.

Gzesh, S. (2007). "Paper for the Wilson Center/Enlaces America Roundtable." Background paper for the Mexico Institute of the Woodrow Wilson International Center for Scholars and Enlaces America in collaboration with the National Alliance of Latin American and Caribbean Communities (NALACC). Retrieved Feb 7, 2011, from http://www.wilsoncenter.org/news/docs/Gzesh-revisedPaper%20for%20the%20Wlison%20Center.pdf.

Hernandez-Coss, R. (2005). "The U.S.-Mexico Remittance Corridor: Lessons on Shifting from Informal to Formal Transfer Systems." *Working Paper Series*, 47. Washington, DC: World Bank.

Hochschild, J. L., and J. H. Mollenkopf (Eds.). (2009a). *Bringing Outsiders In: Transatlantic Perspectives on Immigrant Political Incorporation.* Ithaca, NY: Cornell University Press.

———. (2009b). "Modeling Immigrant Political Incorporation." In J. L. Hochschild and J. H. Mollenkopf (Eds.), *Bringing Outsiders In: Transatlantic Perspectives on Immigrant Political Incorporation* (pp. 15-30). Ithaca, NY: Cornell University Press.

Illinois Government News Network. (2006, Apr 5). "Governor Blagojevich Appoints Director of the Office of New Americans Policy and Advocacy" [Press release]. Retrieved Jun 16, 2011, from http://www.illinois.gov/PressReleases/ShowPressRelease.cfm?SubjectID=65&RecNum=5599.

Jessop, B., and N.-L. Sum. (2006). *Beyond the Regulation Approach: Putting Capitalist Economies in Their Place.* Northampton, MA: Edward Elgar.

Leitner, H. (2004). "The Politics of Scale and Networks of Spatial Connectivity: Transnational Interurban Networks and the Rescaling of Political Governance in Europe." In E. Sheppard and R. B. McMaster (Eds.), *Scale and Geographic Inquiry: Nature, Society, and Method* (pp. 236-55). Malden, MA: Blackwell.

Leitner, H., E. Sheppard, and K. M. Sziarto. (2008). "The Spatialities of Contentious Politics." *Transactions of the Institute of British Geographers*, 33(2), 157-72.

Levitt, P., and N. Glick Schiller. (2004). "Transnational Perspectives on Migration: Conceptualizing Simultaneity." *International Migration Review*, 38(3), 1002-40.

Long, R., and R. Pearson. (2009, Jan 30). "Impeached: Illinois Gov. Rod Blagojevich Has Been Removed from Office." *Chicago Tribune*. Retrieved Jun 1, 2011, from http://www.chicagotribune.com/news/local/chi-blagojevich-impeachment-removal,0,5791846.story.

Massey, D. S., J. Durand, and N. J. Malone. (2002). *Beyond Smoke and Mirrors: Mexican Immigration in an Era of Economic Integration*. New York: Russell Sage Foundation.

McCann, J. A., W. A. Cornelius, and D. L. Leal. (2009). "Absentee Voting and Transnational Civic Engagement among Mexican Expatriates." In J. I. Domínguez, C. Lawson, and A. Moreno (Eds.), *Consolidating Mexico's Democracy* (pp. 89-106). Baltimore: Johns Hopkins University Press.

McMaster, R. B., and E. Sheppard. (2004). "Introduction: Scale and Geographic Inquiry." In E. Sheppard and R. B. McMaster (Eds.), *Scale and Geographic Inquiry: Nature, Society, and Method* (pp. 1-22). Malden, MA: Blackwell.

Meissner, D., and D. Kerwin. (2009, Feb). "DHS and Immigration: Taking Stock and Correcting Course." Migration Policy Institute. Retrieved May 24, 2011, from http://www.migrationpolicy.org/pubs/DHS_Feb09.pdf.

Miller, B. (2004). "Spaces of Mobilization: Transnational Social Movements." In C. Barnett and M. Low (Eds.), *Spaces of Democracy: Geographical Perspectives on Citizenship, Participation and Representation* (pp. 223-46). London: Sage.

Mollenkopf, J. H., and R. Sonenshein. (2009). "The New Urban Politics of Integration: A View from the Gateway Cities." In J. L. Hochschild and J. H. Mollenkopf (Eds.), *Bringing Outsiders In: Transatlantic Perspectives on Immigrant Political Incorporation* (pp. 74-92). Ithaca, NY: Cornell University Press.

Neal, S. (2002, Oct 28). "Gutierrez's Aid Boosts Blagojevich; Hispanic Voters May Have Big Impact on Governor's Contest." *Chicago Sun-Times*, 37.

Nicholls, W. J. (2007). "The Geographies of Social Movements." *Geography Compass*, 1(3), 607-22.

Olivo, A. (2008, Jul 11). "Citizenship for Mexican Immigrants Surged in '07." *Chicago Tribune*, 2.

Olivo, A., and O. Ávila. (2006, May 2). "United They March." *Chicago Tribune*, 1.

Orozco, M., and M. Lapointe. (2004). "Mexican Hometown Associations and Development Opportunities." *Journal of International Affairs*, 57(2), 31-49.

Paral, R. (2006). "Latinos of the New Chicago." In J. P. Koval, L. Bennett, M. I. J. Bennett, F. Demissie, R. Garner, and K. Kim (Eds.), *The New Chicago* (pp. 105-14). Philadelphia, PA: Temple University Press.

Portes, A., C. Escobar, and A. Walton Radford. (2007). "Immigrant Transnational Organizations and Development: A Comparative Study." *International Migration Review*, 41(1), 242-81.

Rogal, B. J. (2004, Jan 1). "Great Expectations: Latino Lawmakers and Advocates Are Gaining Influence in Springfield, and Warning the Governor Not to Take Them for Granted." *Chicago Reporter*. Retrieved Jan 7, 2009, from http://findarticles.com/p/articles/mi_m0JAS/is_1_33/ai_112794748/.

Sacchetti, M. (2008, Aug 13). "Welcomed, Wearily: Illinois Offered Aid to Immigrants, Budgets Intervened." *Boston Globe*, 1.

Sassen, S. (1998). *Globalization and Its Discontents: Essays on the New Mobility of People and Money*. New York: The New Press.

Shannon, A. (2007). "Mobilizing for Political Power: Immigrant Marches and Their Long-term Impacts." *Voices of Mexico*, 78, 28-32.

Sikkink, K. (2005). "Patterns of Dynamic Multilevel Governance and the Insider-outsider Coalition." In D. della Porta and S. Tarrow (Eds.), *Transnational Protest and Global Activism* (pp. 151-74). Boulder, CO: Rowman & Littlefield.

Smith, J. (1997). "Characteristics of the Modern Transnational Social Movement Sector." In J. Smith, C. Chatfield, and R. Pagnucco (Eds.), *Transnational Social Movements and Global Politics* (pp. 42-58). Syracuse, NY: Syracuse University Press.

————. (2007). "Transnational Processes and Movements." In D. A. Snow, S. A. Soule, and H. Kriesi (Eds.), *The Blackwell Companion to Social Movements* (pp. 311-35). Malden, MA: Blackwell.

Smith, M. P. (2001). *Transnational Urbanism*. Oxford, UK/Malden, MA: Blackwell.

————. (2007). "The Two Faces of Transnational Citizenship." *Ethnic and Racial Studies*, 30(6), 1096-116.

Smith, M. P., and M. Bakker. (2008). *Citizenship across Borders: The Political Transnationalism of El Migrante*. Ithaca, NY: Cornell University Press.

Smith, R. C. (1998). "Transnational Localities: Community, Technology and the Politics of Membership within the Context of Mexico and U.S. Migration." In M. P. Smith and L. E. Guarnizo (Eds.), *Transnationalism from Below* (pp. 196-238). New Brunswick/London: Transaction Publishers.

————. (2006). *Mexican New York: Transnational Lives of New Immigrants*. Berkeley: University of California Press.

Swyngedouw, E. (2004). "Scaled Geographies: Nature, Place, and the Politics of Scale." In E. Sheppard and R. B. McMaster (Eds.), *Scale and Geographic Inquiry: Nature, Society, and Method* (pp. 129-53). Malden, MA: Blackwell.

Tarrow, S. (2005). *The New Transnational Activism*. New York: Cambridge University Press.

Tichenor, D. J. (2009). "Navigating an American Minefield: The Politics of Illegal Immigration." *The Forum*, 7(3), 1-21.

Valdes Ugalde, F. (1996). "The Private Sector and Political Regime Change in Mexico." In G. Otero (Ed.), *Neoliberalism Revisited: Economic Restructuring and Mexico's Political Future* (pp. 127-48). Boulder, CO: Westview Press.

Wayne, A. (2005a, Dec 26). "Getting Tough on Illegal Immigration." *CQ Weekly*, 3332. Retrieved Aug 18, 2008, from http://library.cqpress.com/cqweekly/weeklyreport109-000001998134.

Wayne, A. (2005b, Jan 17). "Views of Senate GOP, Bush Threaten Tighter Immigration." *CQ Weekly*, 3396-7. Retrieved Aug 18, 2008, from http://library.cqpress.com/cqweekly/weeklyreport109-000002018227.

Zolberg, A. R. (2006). *A Nation by Design: Immigration Policy in the Fashioning of America*. New York: Russell Sage Foundation/Harvard University Press.

PART IV

POLITICAL PRACTICE AND URBAN CITIZENSHIP: ALTERNATIVE MODES OF POLITICAL EMPOWERMENT

10

Insistent Democracy:
Neoliberal Governance and Popular Movements in Seattle

Mark Purcell

There is now broad consensus among scholars that urban governance in the global North has been greatly transformed by the diverse processes of neoliberal globalization (e.g., Brenner and Theodore, 2002; Harvey, 2005; Peck and Tickell, 2002). The main feature of that shift has been an assault on the Keynesian compact, in which capital and labor agreed to a coherent policy regime administered by a strong national government. Neoliberal reforms have sought to break up that national-Keynesian regime, primarily through initiatives that both devolve authority from the national scale to smaller scales and shift authority from institutions of formal govern*ment* to informal arrangements of gover*nance* (Jessop, 2003). The intent of this devolution and informalization is to decrease the power of the national government to regulate capital and thereby increase the freedom of capital to operate.

Such is the main narrative in the literature on neoliberal governance. It gives the sense of a long and irresistible march toward the rule of the market. We learn how neoliberal globalization forecloses a politics of justice, how it installs economic competition and private property as common sense, and how it marginalizes alternative logics (e.g., Giroux, 2004; Harvey, 2005; Jessop, 2000; Keil, 2002; Larner, 2000). We read cases in which new governance arrangements close off participation, hollow out citizenship, and undermine democracy (e.g., Gill, 1996; International Network for Urban Research and Action [INURA], 2003; Miller, 2007; Mitchell, 2003; Purcell, 2008; Swyngedouw, 2005; Swyngedouw, *et al.*, 2002). At the same time, however, the more we learn about neoliberal governance the more we see it is also characterized by inconsistencies, contradictions, and uncertainties (Hajer, 2003). The upheaval involved in dismantling the Keynesian regime and inventing neoliberal alternatives has produced landscapes of urban governance that are increasingly complicated and shifting. New institutions and arrangements arise frequently and are layered over an older order that never completely disappears. The logic of the market is strong, but old logics endure and new ones are continually emerging.

It is in this complex environment that movements to remake urban citizenship and increase popular control over decision-making must operate. As new barriers to popular power are raised, others are lowered, and new opportunities emerge. Some of these new opportunities are generated by neoliberal reforms themselves. Others are generated by the insistent efforts of popular movements. Many movements have shown that they are not merely passive victims of neoliberal globalization, that they are able to understand what is going on and to react creatively and effectively to the changing governance environment. There is a growing body of work that examines the successes, failures, and future prospects of such movements (Bakker, 2007; Brown, 2004; DeFilippis, 2003; Leitner, *et al.*, 2007; Miller, 2007; Staeheli and Mitchell, 2008, especially chapter 5; Robbins and Luginbuhi, 2005). As this volume makes clear, many of these movements have explicitly taken up the idea of the right to the city, as well as associated concepts like the social use value of urban space, as a political fulcrum around which to organize their efforts (see also Fernandes, 2006; Heller and Perera, 2007; Leavitt, *et al.*, 2009; Purcell, 2008; Right to the City Alliance, 2007). But whatever agenda they articulate, urban populations are actively engaging the new governance environment by learning, adapting, and imaging alternatives to the neoliberal city.

This chapter offers a case study of one such movement in Seattle, the Duwamish River Cleanup Coalition (DRCC), which is working to increase popular control over a Superfund cleanup of the city's main river. The case emphasizes the complex, contradictory, and contingent nature of neoliberal governance. It shows how even though paths to popular power are being closed off, innumerable openings also exist that organized and capable movements can use to their advantage. But much depends on the presence of such movements. They must be able to draw together a broad coalition that can act effectively in concert to exploit existing opportunities and create new ones. The case of the DRCC also points to the potential of the right to the city as an idea that can help hold together such broad coalitions without reducing them to homogeneity. Such effective action is essential: it is precisely these insistent efforts by mobilized groups to democratize urban governance that can interrupt the march toward a neoliberal future. Such insistent democracy also, at the same time, involves a struggle to imagine and realize another city.

The Duwamish River Cleanup[1]

The Duwamish River is Seattle's main river. Together with the Green River it drains a large watershed south and east of downtown Seattle that begins in the Cascade Mountains and ends up in Elliott Bay, the body of water just west of downtown Seattle. The Duwamish runs entirely through urbanized areas, although the Green begins in the wilderness of the Cascades. The last several miles of the river are channelized, and the most downriver stretch of the Duwamish is the site of the largest concentration of industrial activity in the Puget Sound region. The bulk of that industrial activity, including such uses as cement production, food processing, aerospace manufacturing, paper and metals fabrication, and boat building and repair, is inside the Seattle city limits. That stretch is also the site of the Port of Seattle, one of the largest ports on the West Coast. As one might expect with a heavily industrialized river, the lower Duwamish is extremely polluted. Chemical pollutants from industry include high levels of hazardous materials in water, sediment, and soil near the river, including polychlorinated biphenyls (PCBs), polyaromatic hydrocarbons (PAHs), mercury and other metals, and phthalates. In addition, over 100 storm drains carry a variety of pollutants from pavement into the river. More periodic but more destructive are combined sewer overflows (CSOs), which dump untreated sewage into the river when rains have been heavy and sustained enough to overload the city's sewage system. As a result of that intense pollution, the United States Environmental Protection Agency listed the final five-mile stretch of the Duwamish as a federal Superfund site on September 13, 2001.

The Superfund designation sets in motion a complex mixture of federal, state, and local governance procedures that are shaped to a significant degree by the political, economic, and cultural specifics of the Seattle context. At the national-scale, Superfund regulation is based largely on a law called the Comprehensive Environmental Response, Compensation, and Liability Act (CERCLA). The original idea of Superfund was for the federal government to tax chemical and petroleum companies to build up a "super fund" that would pay for environmental cleanup in places where such companies had been primarily responsible for polluting. In addition, CERCLA is a 'polluter-pays' law: where specific parties responsible for the pollution can be identified, they are held liable (in part) for the cost of the cleanup. That extremely assertive federal law was passed in December of 1980, in the last weeks before Ronald Reagan became president. It was born, therefore, at what is commonly considered the dawn of neoliberalism's ascendancy in the United States. However, the Nixon administration had launched the beginnings of the neoliberal agenda earlier in the decade. Those initiatives actively undermined relatively more Keynesian federal programs. Under Nixon, for example, community development was increasingly devolved to local authorities, and the federal government withdrew significantly from both funding and oversight. In a sense Superfund, which created strong federal regulation and mitigation of the harm corporations do to the environment, can be seen as a parting shot from a dying Keynesian tradition. In the Nixon/Ford era, a wave of other laws were enacted that gave the federal government much greater authority to protect the environment from corporate malfeasance. The Environmental Protection Agency was created in 1970. It was followed by the Clean Air Act (1970), the Safe Drinking Water Act (1974), the Toxic Substances Control Act (1976), the Resource Conservation and Recovery Act (1976), and, under Carter, the Clean Water Act (1977) and CERCLA (1980). All of these are federal laws that provide for extensive national-state regulation of the environment. They are enforced at the national scale by the EPA. So CERCLA was also part of a surge in the 1970s of what might be called 'environmental Keynesianism' that ran counter to the fledgling neoliberalism.

As we might expect, however, in the full-blown, post-1980 era of neoliberalism such strong federal regulation of the environment has come under fire. The EPA in general and CERCLA in particular have been subject to significant neoliberalization. One major shift has been greater devolution of authority over cleanups (Adler, 1998; and see Schoenbrod, 1996). Partly as a result of the neoliberal philosophy that central government should not dictate solutions to people and places, local agencies (both governmental and not) at the state, county, and city scales have taken on increasing responsibility for the everyday management of cleanups, and the EPA increasingly plays a more removed oversight role, merely ensuring that the provisions of CERCLA (and other laws) are met. So in that sense, contemporary CERCLA governance increasingly resembles the more general neoliberal pattern of devolving and outsourcing governance. But as with all such governance shifts, the federal-local relationship is highly malleable and contested. While the trend has been toward devolution, for a given Superfund cleanup a whole constellation of different decision-making arrangements can be made. Within broad limits, each cleanup can be governed very differently from the next. Each can have a different mix of agencies at different scales, and the authority each holds with respect to the others can vary widely as well. While such 'flexibilization' of government is a common neoliberal strategy to undermine national-state regulation, it can easily have a double edge. As reorganization and uncertainty in the governing regime intensifies, it opens up political opportunities that social movements can exploit.

In Seattle, an extremely complex governance regime has emerged for the Duwamish Superfund site. The EPA and the Washington State Department of Ecology (usually just called "Ecology") have assumed joint oversight for the cleanup. The agency that is actually carrying out the cleanup, the entity that EPA and Ecology oversee, is called the Lower Duwamish Waterway Group (LDWG). LDWG is a public-private entity that was created, from scratch, just for the purpose of studying and conducting the cleanup. It is made up of four members: the Boeing Company, the City of Seattle, King County, and the Port of Seattle (see Figure 1). Their selection was not random: each is an identifiable contributor to the pollution in and around the Duwamish. Recall that CERCLA requires parties responsible for the pollution (called "potentially responsible parties" or PRPs)[2] to help pay for and sometimes conduct the cleanup. In the Duwamish case, Boeing is an identifiable polluter. King County and the City of Seattle are identifiable polluters as well since they are responsible for some of the combined sewer overflows on the river. The activities of the Port and their tenants also directly contribute to contamination. All four parties also own a great deal of property in the Superfund site, and so they have assumed liability through purchase as well.[3]

Figure 1. The Governance Structure of the Duwamish Cleanup

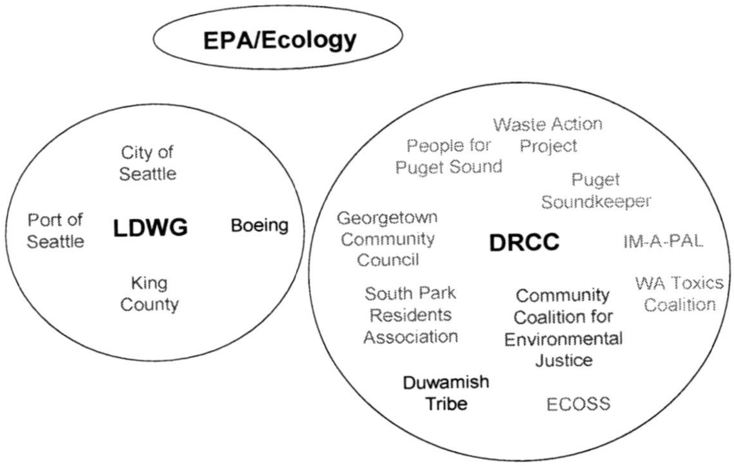

The story of LDWG's birth, like Superfund more generally, reveals an enduring and still-lively struggle between Keynesian and neoliberal agendas in contemporary environmental regulation. Typically, when a Superfund site is declared, the EPA will identify PRPs and ask them to investigate pollution levels and carry out a cleanup. In this case, there was little doubt that the County, City, Port and Boeing would be identified as PRPs if a Superfund site were declared. Seeing the writing on the wall, the four PRPs attempted to create an alternative governance structure that would conduct the cleanup outside of Superfund purview. They formed LDWG as a legal entity in order to enter into a binding agreement with EPA to do the cleanup, and that agreement would obviate the need to declare a Superfund site. In preempting Superfund law, the *ad hoc* agreement would allow LDWG members to negotiate specialized terms that were more favorable to them. That "creative approach," they claimed, would be "more efficient and cost-effective than a Superfund listing" and would achieve cleanup "in a shorter amount of time with less process" (Port of Seattle, 2000). They offered well-worn neoliberal arguments about the inefficiency of state regulation and the superiority of "creative" new governance approaches. In order for the *ad hoc* agreement to become official, however, it needed the consent of the EPA, the State Department of Ecology, each of the four members of LDWG, and the trustees, which are a category in CERCLA law designed to ensure protection of natural resources. In this case trustees included the National Oceanic and Atmospheric Administration, the US Fish and Wildlife Service, and two federally-recognized native tribes: the Muckleshoot and the Suquamish. Despite extensive effort, the parties could not finalize the agreement. It fell apart largely because Boeing was not willing to accept the demand of many trustees that the cleanup restore fish runs to a particular level (Torvik, 2000).

Once this *ad hoc* alternative failed, a federal Superfund site was declared in 2001. The declaration triggered all sorts of Federal laws and regulations. For example, it makes it possible to assign formal legal liability to PRPs. However, the Superfund designation should not be seen as a wholesale return to Keynesianism but as a step away from the more neoliberal option of an *ad hoc* agreement. Superfund governance, like so much neoliberal governance, is really something of a palimpsest. It is made up of more typically neoliberal elements (e.g., devolution and public-private partnerships) that have been laid on top of and woven into old Keynesian ones (e.g., federal imposition of legal liability on polluters). Sometimes the old Keynesian structures have been entirely erased, sometimes partly, and sometimes not at all. As Superfund governance has been increasingly neoliberalized, it has become fairly typical for the EPA to turn over most of the study and management of cleanup to PRPs. In urban areas, PRPs are often public agencies because they tend to own lots of urban land. So it is not unusual to have both public and private entities identified as PRPs. As a result, they often form some kind of public-private partnership to directly govern urban Superfund cleanups. That fact might be read as simply a manifestation of the wider neoliberalization of governance. Asking polluters to study the problem and carry out a cleanup seems like a clear case of the fox guarding the henhouse. However, the genesis of this structure lies in the Keynesian roots of CERCLA: the federal government requires polluters to pay to clean up the mess they made. Any time the actual polluter cannot be identified, money from the 'Superfund' must be used to pay for the cleanup, and the EPA wants to minimize such public funding as much as possible. So the structure intends for the national government to hold polluters financially accountable in a direct way. On the other hand, this accountability is mitigated for PRPs by the significant control they have over the cleanup process, and that control is an outcome of the ongoing neoliberalization of Superfund governance. While EPA/Ecology's oversight role means they have final approval over all cleanup decisions, there is much room for LDWG to shape the extent and the cost of the cleanup.

The governance literature has stressed that such outsourcing of control undermines the structures of liberal, representative democracy. This is true, to a degree. In the Duwamish case Boeing is formally unaccountable to the public, and the public agencies in LDWG are accountable only partly. That is, most decisions made in the name of the Port, City, or County are made not by elected officials but by professional staff (planners, ecologists, engineers, etc.).[4] But at the same time, those decisions do have some formal connection to liberal-democratic publics. The elected councils of the Port, City, and County all have veto power over staff decisions. Such power has already been used once in the cleanup, as we will see below in the case of Terminal 117. Moreover, a more typically Keynesian alternative, in which the EPA (and Ecology) outsourced less and retained greater control over decisions, would only be as democratic as EPA and Ecology themselves, both of which are at best limited in that respect.

This governance palimpsest is further complicated by yet another layer. Like many similar federal laws, CERCLA includes explicit provisions for what the EPA calls "community involvement" in the Superfund process (Office of Emergency and Remedial Response [OERR],

2005). These provisions are part of the legacy of Lyndon Johnson's "Great Society" initiatives of the 1960s, which were themselves a response to popular anger at the horrors of urban renewal in the 1950s. Great Society policies required that community members be allowed to participate in decisions that affect their community. CERCLA similarly requires that people affected by the Superfund cleanup be involved in cleanup decisions. The EPA sets out specific procedures to govern that involvement. Once a site is listed for cleanup, members of the public can form what is called a Community Advisory Group (CAG). A CAG serves as the officially recognized liaison between the community, the EPA, and the entity conducting the cleanup. In other words, once a CAG is formed, it becomes the official "community" in the eyes of the EPA. That structure can operate as a way to tame public involvement, making sure it conforms to predetermined parameters and does not spill over to become unmanageable resistance. My discussions with EPA officials support this notion. While they themselves might personally support robust public involvement, as representatives of the EPA they are cautious about pushing any envelopes in terms of participatory practices. They are not optimistic about how receptive the agency, broadly speaking, would be to vigorous public involvement. As a general rule, while Superfund law calls for public participation, the EPA wants to make sure that participation is contained and manageable (Holifield, 2004).

However, the participation requirements are not fine-grained enough to overly constrict CAGs if they are insistent, active, and imaginative. That legal indeterminacy opens up political opportunity. If CAGs claim access or rights or privileges, there is rarely an explicit *prohibition* in the existing law. A sympathetic cadre of officials can allow robust participation if they choose to or if they are convinced to do so by the CAG. In the more general climate of uncertainty associated with neoliberal governance, there is often no well-established precedent by which to judge a CAG's claim. As a result, there is quite a lot of flexibility for EPA staff to allow new forms of participation. In addition to that openness, the participation provisions in CERCLA (and in state law) make a range of very useful tools available to CAGs. One resource is Technical Assistance Grants (TAGs), which allow the CAG to hire their own technical experts. Such expertise is critical because the first step in a cleanup is a series of scientific studies of the pollution problem. The entity carrying out the study (LDWG in this case) samples the site to determine pollution levels for a range of pollutants; they conduct ecological, hydrological, geological, atmospheric, chemical, and other analyses to determine what impact the pollution is having, how much should be removed, and how that removal should be done. Then they must plan and conduct technical engineering tasks to carry out the cleanup. Average citizens lack most of those specialized types of knowledge, and so they need to hire experts to help them evaluate and respond to the lead entity's proposals in a way that cannot be brushed aside as uninformed or unrealistic. Citizens have to reach a certain threshold of scientific sophistication in order to participate in the conversation. Moreover, the science is highly malleable. Scientific arguments can be mobilized to support many different sampling procedures, data analysis methods, or removal techniques. In the DRCC's case, being able to hire *their own* expert, rather than experts loaned to them by the state, allows the CAG to use scientific expertise to support their claim for a much more comprehensive cleanup than LDWG or EPA scientists envision.

Equally critical for the CAG's success is its ability to maintain and manage itself. In the Duwamish case, the CAG has funding from the Washington State Public Participation Grant Program, through the Washington Department of Ecology, to hire a full-time, experienced coordinator.[5] As a result, in this case the job of running the CAG is professional, not volunteer-based. Participating meaningfully in a cleanup as complex as the Duwamish requires more than just an activist's spare time. It requires a talented and full-time professional. In the Duwamish case, the CAG has used their grant to hire a full-time organizer who coordinates a social movement that advocates for increased popular control over the cleanup. It is important to stress that each of the tools that EPA and Ecology make available can be used or not, and used effectively or not. Much depends on the will of an organized movement, one that intelligently takes advantage of (and even expands) the structural opportunities the EPA and other entities offer. Where such popular will and expertise is lacking, the structures, by themselves, do not produce robust popular involvement.

The River as "Habitat"

In the Duwamish case, the DRCC petitioned to be the CAG for the cleanup and was accepted by the EPA. The DRCC is a coalition of environmental, resident, tribal, environmental justice, and small-business groups (see Figure 1). The environmental activist element is the largest cluster and includes People for Puget Sound and the Puget Soundkeeper Alliance, which advocate for clean and ecologically healthy marine ecosystems in the Seattle area. They are made up primarily of middle- and upper-class white residents from all over the city. They are well-educated, have a long history of environmental advocacy, and are quite well connected with decision-makers at the local and state levels. Another environmental group, Washington Toxics Coalition, is a statewide organization working to reduce human exposure to toxic pollution. Waste Action Project is a public interest group that uses lawsuits primarily to ensure enforcement of environmental laws. And the IM-A-PAL Foundation is the creation of John Beal, a well-known activist who restored creeks and habitats in the Duwamish basin to greater ecological health.

The environmental groups are joined by two neighborhood-resident groups, the South Park Neighborhood Association and the Georgetown Community Council. South Park and Georgetown are the two residential neighborhoods most affected by the sites in the cleanup. Their residents are relatively low-income and non-white compared with the rest of the city. According to the 2000 US Census, the population of Seattle is 74 percent white; in South Park it is 34 percent white; and in Georgetown it is 56 percent white. South Park has a notable concentration of Hispanic residents: 37 percent (compared with 5.3 percent citywide). The median household income for the city is $49,469. In South Park it is $30,917, and in Georgetown it is $33,654. Not surprisingly, the two neighborhoods—being in close proximity to a range of industrial land uses and being relatively poor and non-white—are disproportionately burdened with environmental hazards like air pollution (e.g., cement and paint industries in South Park), water pollution (e.g., the river, as well as plumes of toxins in the groundwater under Georgetown), and soil contamination (e.g., PCBs in public rights of way and residential yards in South Park). Partly because of the glaring environmental justice issues in South Park and Georgetown, another member of the DRCC is the Community Coalition for Environmental Justice (CCEJ), which is itself a coalition of various activists across the city who campaign against environmental and economic injustice, gentrification, and racism. In the context of a city that is extraordinarily white compared to other major US metropolises, it is important to note that the CCEJ leadership is predominantly made up of people of color.

Another DRCC member is the Environmental Coalition of South Seattle, an association of small businesses in the Duwamish area that advocates for their interests, with a particular focus on helping them develop sustainable environmental practices. The last member of the DRCC is the Duwamish Tribe. The Duwamish are the people of Chief Si'ahl (Seattle) who inhabited the lower Duwamish watershed (as well as parts of the Cedar and Black watersheds) at the time of the first white expeditions to the area in 1851. They are not a federally recognized tribe, but rather a 501(c)3 non-profit corporation.[6] That distinction is important because Superfund law makes significant provisions for federally recognized tribes. Such tribes are considered "trustees" with decision-making power, as are the Muckleshoot and Suquamish in this cleanup. Because the Duwamish are not federally recognized, the EPA does not consider them trustees. Nevertheless, the Duwamish have extensive interests in the lower Duwamish and in the cleanup. The river and its wider system are part of their ancestral lands and traditional fishing grounds. They also have cultural and historical connections to the river. Many sites along the river are of great archeological importance to the tribe. Such cultural memory is critical for a group whose continued existence as a people is at stake. Moreover, that cultural memory is bound up tightly with the ecological health of the river. Before white conquest, the Duwamish lived in and relied on the Duwamish Valley. The industrialization of the Valley and the progressive destruction of the river's ecology are intimately connected to the assault on the tribe's way of life. In many ways, a claim to restore the river's ecological health is also a claim to redress the injustice of white conquest. For the Duwamish, their cultural, historical, economic, and environmental claims are intertwined. They see the cleanup as an opportunity for, in some sense, a reparation: a revitalization of the idea that the Duwamish River is not just an industrial waterway but a complex riverine ecosystem that should be preserved, restored, and valued for its own sake.

So the DRCC is a coalition of dissimilar groups. It brings together many different cross-cutting interests—environmental, cultural, residential, small-business, health, and justice—into a mobilized network. While the coalition includes more than just the inhabitants of the watershed, the members' shared agenda nevertheless is constructed around the importance of *inhabitance* in the watershed. This idea of inhabitance resonates strongly with most conceptualizations of Henri Lefebvre's idea of the right to the city (e.g., Mitchell, 2003; Purcell, 2002).

Despite their distinct differences, DRCC members share a commitment to the river and its watershed as habitat, as a complex place that is inhabited by humans and other species. Given the nature of their coalition, the DRCC is careful to very clearly include both humans and non-human species. While human health and wellbeing is crucial, it does not necessarily trump, or is it even separable from, the wellbeing of the river's ecological system. Such shared commitment among dissimilar groups can of course be difficult to sustain. Each group has a different relationship to the river and a different set of interests in the cleanup. Yet they also mobilize around a shared (though not identical) idea of the river as inhabited. For the neighborhood groups, the watershed as habitat means things like reducing the risk of cancer from PCBs or building a waterfront park on a cleaned-up site. For the ecological groups, it means constructing sand bars that aid salmon migration or bringing a denuded tributary back to ecological health. For the Duwamish Tribe, the watershed as habitat means restoring cultural sites as well as salmon runs, and, as we have seen, it also takes on a dimension of historical justice. The challenge is to hold this diversity together without reducing it to a single, homogenous identity or agenda. So far, despite the coalition's distinct diversity of interests, it has been able to achieve this difficult trick fairly well. It has been quite cohesive. It makes decisions by the agreement of all members, so that dissent by any one member can potentially prevent them from going forward. While they do have provisions for making decisions by majority vote if necessary, they have not yet failed to reach agreement on a decision.

The River as "Waterway"

The DRCC's relatively cohesive agenda of watershed inhabitance is important because it represents a way to imagine the river that stands in contrast, broadly speaking, to the agenda of the LDWG public-private partnership. To understand that contrast, it is instructive to note the different names of the groups. DRCC is the Duwamish *River* Cleanup Coalition; LDWG is the Lower Duwamish *Waterway* Group. The lower Duwamish was straightened and deepened years ago to accommodate the Port and industry, and the straightened stretch has long been referred to as a "waterway." A waterway is a transportation corridor that is functional for an industrial economy. A river is something else, something more explicitly ecological, complex, and unpredictable. A waterway is economic infrastructure; a river is inhabited. While the members of LDWG are also multiple and have different interests, an overarching commonality is that 1) they are funding the cleanup and so have an interest in minimizing its cost, and 2) they are major landowners in the area and so have an interest in the property values along the river. Those two goals sometimes conflict, of course, since more comprehensive cleanup is more costly but results in more saleable land. But the predominant concern from a property owner's perspective is the line between saleable and non-saleable. To make saleable a polluted property that cannot be legally sold on the market, one must reduce pollutants to below the legal maximum level. However, in a cleanup of this scale and scope there is much more one can do than merely reduce pollution to below legal maximums. While for the most part LDWG members (especially the public agencies) recognize and value the idea of doing better than just what is required by law, they are liable, nevertheless, for both the cost of cleanup and the interests of major property owners along the river. Great structural imperatives motivate them to value the riverbank as property, to minimize the cost of cleanup, and to see cleanup primarily as a process of property rehabilitation.

Those structural imperatives are reinforced by the fact that most of the holdings, for both Boeing and the public agencies, are portfolio investments. They are not used by the members of LDWG for their operations but are investments that are valued in terms of their exchange value. The main exception is the Port, whose holdings include the land on which port operations take place. But the Port has extensive portfolio holdings as well. So for LDWG an overriding motive is to carry out a cost-effective cleanup that brings pollution levels down to legal maximums. That is also the primary mandate for EPA and Ecology in their oversight role: to remove pollution to meet legal requirements. Such a cleanup would result in the property near the river, much of which is currently unsaleable brownfield, to return, rehabilitated, to the market. The motivation for anything beyond is largely an optional desire, and it is always disciplined by the need to minimize costs and ensure marketable property.

The Contested Politics of "Cleanup"

For the DRCC, by contrast, the wider goal is a much more comprehensive cleanup that makes the river system more fully inhabitable by humans and other species in the very long term. Such fuller inhabitance not only aims at a more extensive removal of pollution but also some measure of active ecological restoration. The DRCC does not advocate *complete* restoration, because a return to the meandering river of the 19th century would leave residents of South Park and Georgetown with a river that floods their neighborhoods every few years. Rather, the DRCC wants to keep alive the *idea* of that 19th century river, to remind us that a waterway is not the only thing the Duwamish has been or can be. They want a cleanup that enables the Duwamish to be as natural as possible and to be as fully inhabited as possible. While the idea of a revitalized riverine ecosystem may seem laughable in the face of the massive industrialization and pollution along the river, the DRCC member IM-A-PAL Foundation, in the person of activist John Beal, has proved it is possible. Beal has restored a once mostly lifeless small tributary of the Duwamish, Hamm Creek, to fairly robust ecological health (Sato, 1997). Beal's restoration testifies that the Duwamish is a river, not a waterway, and it is not dead yet.

In claiming inhabitance in this way, the DRCC is claiming a right for inhabitants to fully and completely use the watershed, a claim that directly challenges the property-rights claims of owners. This claim has much in common with contemporary struggles for the right to the city (Fernandes, 2006; Heller and Perera, 2007; Right to the City Alliance, 2007). To buttress that claim, the DRCC also makes an innovative case about ownership. They insist that the river is in fact *unowned*. That is, the river is not legally owned by anyone. It is not private property, nor is it public property in the sense that it is owned by a public agency. It is, rather, not owned at all. It is, therefore, legally, truly a commons, a public trust, a space that is the collective responsibility of all its inhabitants. To be more specific, the *banks* of the river are owned, either by private firms or public agencies. But the river itself is not. And Superfund's mandate is specifically focused on the river itself, not the banks. As a result, according to the claims of DRCC, the property rights of landowners should have little standing in decisions about the cleanup of the river. Instead, a regime of something more like collective stewardship should govern decisions about the cleanup. They argue that whatever decision-making structures actually govern the cleanup, decision-making authority in the cleanup *should* properly rest with the collective inhabitants of the wider watershed. Any other claims to authority, by this logic, are usurping the legitimate authority of inhabitants. LDWG has certain obligations because they are the PRPs, but according to the logic of an unowned river, they are not the legitimate decision-makers. Nor is the EPA or Ecology. Therefore, public participation in the cleanup should not be an addendum to the primary decision-making process. It is instead fundamental: inhabitants have a right to decide what happens to the river because they are its stewards.

Despite these innovative arguments, the actual governance structure of the Duwamish River cleanup is not so collective. LDWG, as we have seen, is the cleanup's lead entity. They carry out studies to evaluate pollution levels and contract specialty firms to plan and conduct the cleanups. The EPA and Ecology jointly oversee their work. For a Superfund cleanup like the Duwamish, CERCLA law sets out two main strategies for addressing pollution. The first is to declare "early action sites" (often also called 'hotspots') where there is a severe threat to public health or the environment and where immediate action must be taken. The second is a longer-term remediation of the river as a whole that seeks both to undo much of the harm pollution has caused in the ecosystem and to prevent further pollution. The latter, more comprehensive action can take years and can only be conducted in a Superfund site. In the Duwamish case, the Superfund cleanup involves both sorts of actions. Of course, the first actions have been early-action, hotspot cleanups. Five principal sites have been identified as hotspots: the Norfolk CSO, Duwamish-Diagonal Way, Terminal 117, Slip 4, and Boeing Plant 2 (USEPA and Washington State Department of Ecology, 2003) (I discuss terminal 117 in more detail below). The cleanup of the first two has been partly completed, although not without incident. The second two have a completed plan and await actual cleanup, and the last is beginning the planning phase.

Typically, not every member of LDWG participates actively in a hotspot cleanup. Rather the primary PRP takes the lead. For example, King County took the lead on the Duwamish-Diagonal Way site because its CSO was a direct polluter. The Port took the lead on Terminal 117 because it owned and had assumed liability on land polluted in the past. For Slip 4, the City and County have taken a joint lead, and for Boeing Plant 2, Boeing will lead. Each PRP leads a cleanup differently from the others. One dimension of that difference is that the public agencies have a different sense of mission than Boeing does. And even among the public agencies, each has a different combination of interests (e.g., the Port conducts much of its most basic operations in the waterway, the County is more concerned with the CSOs, the City has constituents in the area). Moreover, the staff of each PRP is different from the next. They hold different values and employ different practices (e.g., some are more experienced or more committed to public participation, salmon preservation, source control, etc.). Moreover, staff turns over quite frequently, so even within the same PRP, staff will behave differently over time. To make matters still more complicated, sometimes EPA takes oversight, sometimes Ecology does, and sometimes they act jointly. Because EPA is a federal agency and Ecology a state one, they apply partly different oversight requirements. Standards, staff, strategies, and community involvement can therefore vary significantly from hotspot to hotspot. That governance variability imposes burdens on DRCC, but it also creates opportunities. In order to understand more fully just how a group like the DRCC navigates this shifting governance terrain, the next section examines one hotspot, Terminal 117, in more detail. While one example cannot completely capture the political complexities of the Superfund site as a whole, it can provide one concrete snapshot of how the governance process works and how popular groups can take advantage of it.

Contesting Terminal 117: Use vs. Exchange Value

The site at Terminal 117, also known as the Malarkey Asphalt site (named after the principal polluter), is along the river in the South Park neighborhood. Very high levels of PCBs have been found on both the property itself and in the river next to it. Moreover, PCBs have been found in the front yards of nearby houses, as well as on the road leading out of the property. The site and its surroundings pose a clear threat to both human health and the area's ecology. Malarkey is now out of business; they stopped operating on the site in 1993. The property is currently owned by the Port, and so they are the lead agency from LDWG handling the cleanup. The Port began the process by hiring an engineering firm to study the pollution and draft a cleanup plan.

That plan then entered what in the Duwamish River cleanup is called the "enhanced process." In normal Superfund procedure, the lead entity conducts studies, drafts their plan, and submits it to the EPA, who then evaluates and approves it. Only then, after the EPA has approved the plan, does CAG provide its input. In the Duwamish case, however, the DRCC pressed early on for access to the *draft* studies and plans so that they could comment on them *before* the EPA/Ecology approves them. When the PRP submits their draft to EPA/Ecology, the DRCC gets a copy at the same time and they work with their expert (hired through the Technical Assistance Grant) to evaluate the draft and formulate critiques and alternatives. Based on both the DRCC's feedback and their own evaluation, EPA/Ecology then requires revisions from LDWG. A revised document is then submitted to EPA/Ecology for approval. This enhanced public input is not required by CERCLA law. But there is also no formal prohibition against it. This *ad hoc* arrangement is the result of the DRCC's initiative. They pushed for it, and no one in EPA/Ecology or LDWG objected. There is opportunity in Superfund governance, but it needs to be created by strategic action.

Early access to documents has greatly increased DRCC's ability to meaningfully participate in making decisions for the Duwamish cleanup. In addition to the substantive input they can have in revising the plans before they are approved, they also gain more ability to mobilize organized public feedback on the approved plan. Once the enhanced process takes place and EPA/Ecology approves LDWG's plan, EPA holds a public meeting to get feedback from citizens. Typically, both in Superfund and beyond, such public meetings are impoverished: the decision-makers show a slick, well-thought-out presentation of their plans and then ask the public to comment. An unorganized public made up of a variety of people interested in the issue for different reasons offers diverse responses. They take turns at the microphone offering a wide range of different comments, some lucid, some uninformed, and some incoherent. Each speaker gets only a couple of minutes and is often cut off before they finish. Usually such meetings are more pageants to perform (if poorly) the idea of democratic decision-making than they are meaningful opportunities to realize it. The Duwamish case is different. Not only has the DRCC already had substantive input into the approved plan through the enhanced process, but also their access to the plan allows them to organize a community deliberation on the draft plan in advance of the public meeting. They bring their technical expert to Seattle (he is based in Virginia) to participate in a community meeting whose goal is to develop a coherent and unified community response to LDWG's proposed plan. Those meetings are open to anyone, but generally they involve representatives from DRCC's member organizations and members of the most affected community. At the meetings, the expert helps DRCC members and residents understand the technical elements of the plan. The community members help the expert and DRCC leaders understand their everyday experience with and concerns about the site. Ideally, the conversation leads to a collective shaping of a shared response they will make to the approved plan.

At the public meeting then, there is not a mishmash of different individual voices; rather, after LDWG's consulting firm presents the results of their study and the plan they have developed, the DRCC, because it is the Community Advisory Group, is given significant extra time and first opportunity to offer their response. Either their coordinator or their expert offers an equally polished, informed, and coherent presentation of the community's response to the proposed plan. After the DRCC presents, the floor is opened to other speakers. While some offer additional comments, the typical sentiment offered by these remaining speakers is, in the words of one, "the DRCC speaks for me." And the meetings have been full-to-overflowing. Speaker after speaker comes to the microphone to reiterate the DRCC's argument, an argument they participated in shaping. As a result, EPA/Ecology cannot simply dismiss the public response as uninformed, contradictory, or beyond the pale. The public is in fact organized, polished, scientifically sophisticated, and politically savvy. Even though this public input is only advisory, it is so competent and it is coming from such a broad-based and well-organized "community" that EPA/Ecology takes it seriously both because they respect its content and because they suspect there could be significant political repercussions if they brush it aside.

In the Terminal 117 case, the first public meeting followed this script fairly closely. The DRCC's coordinator presented their response. She mostly offered a few critical questions (that the DRCC asked to be evaluated further) and a few alternative suggestions for the actual cleanup. Subsequent speakers supported and added to her comments. On the whole, the meeting was cordial and there was fairly widespread satisfaction with the plan. However, DRCC did make one fairly significant request: they wanted the Port to sample the upland part of the site for PCBs as well. The site is bifurcated by a small river bluff, and the original cleanup plan was to investigate and clean at the bottom of the bluff, in the riverbed (recall that Superfund's mandate is for the river specifically, not its banks). DRCC also wanted the Port to sample on top of the bluff, where the asphalt plant had actually been. And they got their wish. EPA/Ecology approved the Port's riverbank plan, but it required the Port to sample the upland area. When the Port did so, they found alarming concentrations of PCBs. So alarming were the findings that the cleanup was reprioritized, and the Port set about formulating a new plan to clean the upland area first.

That upland plan was met with quite a lot less favor by the community. The PCBs there were physically much closer to residents' everyday routines, and the discovery of PCBs beyond the site, in people's front yards, had made residents particularly concerned. The samples on the site found PCB concentrations as high as 9,200 parts per million, far beyond the legal maximum for industrial sites of 25 ppm (the maximum for residential use is 1 ppm) (Royale, 2006; Sanga, 2006). The Port's plan was to clean up the site to a maximum legal level of 25 ppm, with a zone of 10 ppm at the surface, cap the site with asphalt, and surround it with a fence. That level would make it possible to use the site for an industrial facility, although employees would need to wear protective equipment to work there. At 25/10 ppm, it would not be safe for South Park residents to use, which is why the fence was part of the plan. An amount of 25/10 ppm also would likely preclude other uses, such as commercial, residential, or a public park. The Port's argument, supported by EPA/Ecology, was that such cleanups are designed to return polluted land to its *original* use, which in this case had been as an industrial facility. This argument is consistent with LDWG's more general cleanup imperative we saw above: reduce pollution to maximum levels and sell the property. For the Port, a cleanup to 25/10 ppm would bring the property back inside legal limits, and it could therefore be sold on the market.

For the upland plan, area residents and the DRCC again met in advance of the meeting, and again prepared a cohesive, informed, and articulate response. The outcome of their deliberations was unequivocal: they wanted 1 ppm, not 25/10 ppm. That level would allow all uses at the site, including a riverfront park, which was the preferred vision that emerged from the community meeting. At the EPA's public meeting, the DRCC's technical expert gave their argument against 25/10 ppm and for 1 ppm, and then a chorus of community members came to the microphone to reiterate DRCC's message: the proposed 25/10 ppm plan did not do enough. There were two main thrusts to their comments. The first concerned the use value of the site for inhabitants over and above its exchange value for the Port. While a possible industrial use was good for the Port in that it would allow it to sell the land, and while it *might* benefit some South Park residents in terms of jobs, the health risks to neighborhood inhabitants were too great to ignore. Moreover, the site would be essentially closed to residents, since only those hired by the possible future firm would be able to use it. A far more beneficial option for residents, the community argued, would be a riverfront park that all could use. The second part of the argument was framed in terms of justice. South Park has a long history of bearing a disproportionate share of environmental hazards, of which PCBs in their lawns were only the most recent example. Given that history, they claimed, the Port has an obligation to do *more* than a minimal cleanup. South Park deserves better, they argued. It deserves the best the Port can do. It deserves a maximum cleanup, maximum protection from hazards, and maximum amenities. Representatives from EPA/Ecology continued to stress that Superfund law requires a cleanup to enable a return to "historical uses"—that the Port's plan was in compliance with federal and state law. But South Park residents eloquently claimed that historical uses were part of a long legacy of environmental injustice and that they deserved better than the minimum.

The community's arguments were backed by a measure of political muscle. Seattle City Councilmember Richard Conlin was present at the meeting, and he submitted a letter to EPA/Ecology, signed by the entire City Council, that supported DRCC's position. South Park is in the City of Seattle, and so the residents are Council constituents.[7] Moreover, several Council members have a specific agenda to improve public participation in the city. Conlin is particularly keen on this point. But certainly the most important factor was that the City intends to annex the site once it is cleaned up. The Port currently owns the land, which is unincorporated and therefore under the jurisdiction of King County. Of course, since the Port is paying for the cleanup, the City would prefer that it be as comprehensive as possible so the land the City annexes can be planned for any use. It was a good example of how the different members of LDWG (in this case City and Port) can have different interests and different cleanup agendas and how they can press *each other* for particular outcomes. Such differentiation in the governance structure was exploited by the DRCC to press their claim for a more comprehensive cleanup. However, despite the City-DRCC alliance, the Port representatives and EPA/Ecology clung to the historic uses argument and approved the less comprehensive plan at 25/10 ppm.

But the process was not complete. Yet another layer of governance remained. The Port staff's plan had to be approved by the Port Commission. In Seattle, the Port's governing body is a 5-member commission, each seat of which is elected at large by voters in King County. At the Port Commission hearing on Terminal 117, South Park residents and the DRCC again articulated the argument for 1 ppm, and the Commission was much more receptive than its staff. The DRCC was again backed by the Seattle City Council, who renewed their request for 1 ppm. Also supporting the DRCC was Zach Hudgins, Washington State Representative for the 11th District, in which Terminal 117 is located. Residents intensified their rhetoric. One promised the Commission that South Park residents "will not live quietly with hazardous waste" and intimated that lawsuits were on the horizon (Scott, 2006). In the end, the Port commissioners decided to reject their own staff's plan and instead required a cleanup to a level of 1 ppm. One commissioner, quoted in the local press, felt the Port needed to rebuild its reputation and "to earn back the trust of the community" (Modie, 2006). However, the Port also called on the City to help pay the added cost for a cleanup to 1 ppm since the City stands to benefit directly from the more thorough cleanup. The Commission's 1 ppm plan is where the matter currently stands. EPA/Ecology has promised to try to meet that standard, although new complications could arise at any time.

Conclusion

The case of the DRCC helps us see how neoliberal governance is not monolithic: it is splintered, complex, and continually in motion. Great Society provisions for public participation remain in place. Much Keynesian federal regulation endures as well. Moreover, the active 'flexibilization' of governance under neoliberalism, designed to advance deregulation and foster competitive, free-market relations, can be turned toward other agendas. In the Duwamish case, the very new institutions that neoliberalization has wrought mean there is great uncertainty among those in power. LDWG, for example, is new; it has never done this kind of thing before. It is learning as it goes, governing by trial and error. It does not have an established way to contain and manage a group like the DRCC. LDWG members are continually surprised by the DRCC's intelligence, creativity, and resolve. Neoliberal governance, in other words, can be a very loose, indeterminate mesh. In the governance literature, this complexity often inspires a narrative about how neoliberalism adapts to ensure its own survival. While that analysis is not wrong, there is another layer that is less often stressed: the instability means there are really quite numerous opportunities for mobilized groups to resist neoliberal values and advance alternatives. The governance structure on the Duwamish presents all sorts of democratic opportunities that the DRCC has searched out, exploited, and expanded. They have availed themselves of access to expert knowledge, funds for a professional coordinator, and formal requirements for public participation. On top of that, they have pressed for and won enhanced public comment on draft documents, which has allowed them to organize a much more influential public comment process. Moreover, they have creatively taken advantage of the fissures in the façade of neoliberal governance; they understand LDWG's heterogeneity and have been able to ally with sympathetic elements of LDWG against less sympathetic ones. They have also been skillful in using both the threat of legal action and the ever-present concern of elected officials about electoral retribution. The DRCC's successes have been the result of their insistent searching for existing opportunities to increase popular power and their willful prying open of opportunities that did not yet exist.

But as I have tried to make clear, exploiting those opportunities requires popular mobilization. It requires a broad network linking multiple groups that are able to act in concert effectively. The importance of such mobilized networks raises an issue I have not been able to discuss in detail here: there is something quite promising in this context about the idea of the right to the city. Much of the work on the right to the city, especially that which draws heavily on Henri Lefebvre, argues that one key to the idea is the concept of inhabitance (Purcell, 2002). That is, the right to the city is a demand to prioritize the inhabitants and users of urban space over its owners. It demands that the social use value of urban space be emphasized over and above its exchange value. While the DRCC does not use the term "right to the city" explicitly, their vision for the river as habitat, rather than as a waterway, resonates strongly with the right to the city idea. They envision not simply a waterway that meets the needs of capital and property owners but a river that meets the needs of multiple kinds of inhabitants, both human and non-human. They see the Duwamish as a complex, inhabited ecology rather than as infrastructure for accumulation. While this distinction between inhabitants and property owners is only one element of the right to the city, it is a key one, one that is present in most manifestations of the idea. This idea of an inhabited river has been crucial for the DRCC as they try to coordinate a diverse coalition. Despite having different positionalities and agendas, the various groups in the DRCC cohere around this shared idea of an inhabited river. That coherence is critical for the DRCC to be able to mobilize effectively and to be active and insistent in the decision-making process. And that active insistence is vital to exploiting the political opportunities available in neoliberal governance to increase popular control over the decisions that shape the city.

Clearly the DRCC's achievements are modest. It is not as though they stand at the head of a popular urban revolution. Nevertheless, I think the lessons they teach us are less about the specific outcomes they have achieved than about the political possibilities they are opening up. Their work cracks open the image of cities in the grip of an unassailable neoliberalism. It makes clear the striking indeterminacy that characterizes actually existing neoliberal governance, and it shows us how mobilized coalitions can turn that indeterminacy into political opportunities to increase popular control. Such a reconceptualization of what is possible has always been a catalyst for action. It refocuses our attention away from the closures and toward the openings in neoliberal governance. It conditions us to see not only the barriers to popular power but also the many ways in which that power continually evades capture and creatively reworks the structures designed to tame it. It seems to me that the project of urban democracy today will require seeking out these restless flows of power, sharpening our ability to perceive them, and carving out a space where popular values can flourish and prevail.

Notes

1. This narrative is drawn from an ongoing research study of the cleanup that has spanned the last eight years. Unless a specific source is cited, the information is drawn from field notes, which are based on interview, observation, and archival sources.
2. PRPs is often pronounced "perps."
3. This is particularly true of the Port.
4. Such professionals are generally quite 'Keynesian' in the sense that they are sympathetic to the idea of strong central-government regulation of the environment. They also tend to see themselves as defenders of the 'public interest,' which makes them at best uneasy with the neoliberal agenda of privatization.
5. The grant also pays for outreach activities to broaden membership and participation in the CAG.
6. They have applied for federal recognition, but were denied for what most feel were dubious reasons.
7. Council members are all elected at large, so each member has a citywide constituency. For each council member, therefore, South Park is only a small part of their constituency.

References

Adler, J. (1998). "A New Environmental Federalism: Environmental Policymakers Are Increasingly Turning to the States for Solutions to Today's Environmental Problems." *Forum for Applied Research and Public Policy*, 13(4), 55-61.

Bakker, K. (2007). "The 'Commons' Versus the 'Commodity': Alter-globalization, Anti-privatization, and the Human Right to Water in the Global South." *Antipode*, 39(3), 430-55.

Brenner, N., and N. Theodore. (2002). "Cities and the Geographies of 'Actually Existing Neoliberalism'." *Antipode*, 34(3), 349-79.

Brown, G. (2004). "Sites of Public (Homo)Sex and the Carnivalesque Spaces of Reclaim the Streets." In L. Lees (Ed.), *The Emancipatory City?: Paradoxes and Possibilities* (pp. 91 ff.). Thousand Oaks, CA: Sage.

DeFilippis, J. (2003). *Unmaking Goliath: Community Control in the Face of Global Capital*. New York: Routledge.

Fernandes, E. (2006). "Updating the Declaration of the Rights of Citizens in Latin America: Constructing the 'Right to the City' in Brazil." In UNESCO (Ed.), *International Public Debates: Urban Policies and the Right to the City* (pp. 40-53). Paris: *Editor*.

Gill, S. (1996). "Globalization, Democratization, and the Politics of Indifference." In J. Mittelman (Ed.), *Globalization: Critical Reflections* (pp. 205-28). Boulder, CO: Lynne Rienner.

Giroux, H. (2004). *The Terror of Neoliberalism: Authoritarianism and the Eclipse of Democracy*. New York: Paradigm Publishers.

Hajer, M. (2003). "Policy without Polity? Policy Analysis and the Institutional Void." *Policy Sciences*, 36(2), 175-95.

Harvey, D. (2005). *A Brief History of Neoliberalism*. New York: Oxford University Press.

Heller, C., and G. Perera. (2007). *The Right to the City: Reclaiming Our Urban Centers, Reframing Human Rights, and Redefining Citizenship*. San Francisco: Tides Foundation.

Holifield, R. (2004). "Neoliberalism and Environmental Justice in the United States Environmental Protection Agency: Translating Policy into Managerial Practice in Hazardous Waste Remediation." *Geoforum*, 35(3), 285-97.

International Network for Urban Research and Action (INURA). (2003). "An Alternative Urban World is Possible: A Declaration for Urban Research and Action." *International Journal of Urban and Regional Research*, 27(4), 952-5.

Jessop, B. (2000). "The Crisis of the National Spatio-temporal Fix and the Tendential Ecological Dominance of Globalizing Capitalism." *International Journal of Urban and Regional Research*, 24(2), 323-60.

_____. (2003). "Governance and Meta-governance: On Reflexivity, Requisite Variety, and Requisite Irony." In H. Bang (Ed.), *Governance as Social and Political Communication* (pp. 101-16). Manchester: Manchester University Press.

Keil, R. (2002). "'Common-Sense' Neoliberalism: Progressive Conservative Urbanism in Toronto, Canada." *Antipode*, 34(3), 578-601.

Larner, W. (2000). "Neo-liberalism: Policy, Ideology, Governmentality." *Studies in Political Economy*, 63, 5-25.

Leavitt, J., T. Samara, and M. Brady. (2009). "The Right to the City Alliance: Time to Democratize Urban Governance." *Progressive Planning*, 181, 2-10. Retrieved May 20, 2011, from http://www.plannersnetwork.org/publications/2009_fall/leavitt_samara_brady.html.

Leitner, H., J. Peck, and E. Sheppard (Eds.). (2007). *Contesting Neoliberalism: Urban Frontiers*. New York: Guilford.

Miller, B. (2007). "Modes of Governance, Modes of Resistance: Contesting Neoliberalism in Calgary." In H. Leitner, J. Peck, and E. Sheppard (Eds.), *Contesting Neoliberalism: Urban Frontiers* (pp. 223-49). New York: Guilford.

Mitchell, D. (2003). *The Right to the City: Social Justice and the Fight for Public Space*. New York: Guilford Press.

Modie, N. (2006, Jun 27). "Port Opts to Exceed EPA's South Park Cleanup Plan: Recreational Use Could Be in Duwamish Tract's Future." *Seattle Post-Intelligencer*. Retrieved May 21, 2011, from http://www.seattlepi.com/default/article/Port-opts-to-exceed-EPA-s-South-Park-cleanup-plan-1207422.php.

Office of Emergency and Remedial Response. (2005). *Superfund Community Involvement Handbook*. Washington, DC: US Environmental Protection Agency.

Peck, J., and A. Tickell. (2002). "Neoliberalising Space." *Antipode*, 34(3), 380-404.

Port of Seattle. (2000, Apr 19). "Partnership Forms to Study Lower Duwamish River." Seattle: *Author*. Retrieved May 21, 2011, from http://your.kingcounty.gov/exec/news/2000/041900.htm.

Purcell, M. (2002). "Excavating Lefebvre: The Right to the City and Its Urban Politics of the Inhabitant." *GeoJournal*, 58(2-3), 99-108.

_____. (2008). *Recapturing Democracy: Neoliberalization and the Struggle for Alternative Urban Futures*. New York, Routledge.

Right to the City Alliance. (2007). "Right to the City: Notes from the Inaugural Convening." Los Angeles: Strategic Actions for a Just Economy.

Robbins, P., and A. Luginbuhi. (2005). "The Last Enclosure: Resisting Privatization of Wildlife in the Western United States." *Capitalism Nature Socialism*, 16(1), 45-61.

Royale, R. (2006, Nov 16). "Toxic Avengers: Duwamish Watchdogs Want Port to Be Diligent in Clean Up of PCBs." *Real Change News*. Retrieved May 21, 2011, from http://www.realchangenews.org/old_site/2006/2006_05_24/toxicavengers.html.

Sanga, R. (2006). "T-117 EAA Action Memorandum." Seattle: US Environmental Protection Agency Region 10. Retrieved May 21, 2011, from http://yosemite.epa.gov/R10/CLEANUP.NSF/ddea47a33877982f88256db8007e8049/0cc263002fc96 8fb8825716a0066c0cd/$FILE/Action%20Memo%20for%20a%20Time-Critical%20Removal.pdf.

Sato, M. (1997). *The Price of Taming a River*. Seattle: Mountaineers Books.

Schoenbrod, D. (1996). "Why States, Not EPA, Should Set Pollution Standards." *Regulation: The Review of Business and Government*, 19(4), 18-25.

Scott, A. (2006, Jun 28). "Port OKs $6 Million to Start Cleanup of South Park Site." *Seattle Times*, E1. Retrieved May 21, 2011, from http://community.seattletimes.nwsource.com/archive/?date=20060628&slug=port28.

Staeheli, L., and D. Mitchell. (2008). *The People's Property? Power, Politics, and the Public*. New York: Routledge.

Swyngedouw, E. (2005). "Governance Innovation and the Citizen: The Janus Face of Governance-beyond-the-state." *Urban Studies*, 42(11), 1991-2006.

Swyngedouw, E., F. Moulaert, and A. Rodriguez. (2002). "Neoliberal Urbanization in Europe: Large-scale Urban Development Projects and the New Urban Policy." *Antipode*, 34(3), 542-77.

Torvik, S. (2000). "Duwamish Proposed as Superfund Site." *Seattle Post-Intelligencer*.

US Environmental Protection Agency (USEPA) and Washington State Department of Ecology. (2003, Jun). "Fact Sheet: Lower Duwamish Waterway Site." Seattle: US Environmental Protection Agency Region 10. Retrieved May 21, 2011, from http://www.duwamishcleanup.org/uploads/pdfs/Duwamish_fs_20030627.pdf.

11

Right to the City and the Quiet Appropriations of Local Space in the Heartland

Faranak Miraftab

In the past two decades the discourses and practices of citizenship have departed dramatically from earlier eras. Citizens are disillusioned with the Western liberal promises of automatic social, civil, and political gains based on their legal membership in a nation-state. Rather, they associate their citizenship with the concrete and tangible gains they experience and no longer confine their expectation of such gains to their national belonging. It is in specific localities—the neighborhoods, the towns, the cities—that citizens live their lives and wage their struggles for livelihood and dignity.

The diminished responsibilities of the central state resulting from global capitalist restructuring have contributed to these dramatic changes in people's expectation of their citizenship rights (Miraftab, forthcoming; Purcell, 2003; Turner, 1990). This has highlighted two fallacies of the liberal democratic expectation of citizenship[1]: first, the notion that civil, political, and social rights are accumulative, that one leads to and guarantees the other; and second, that the nation-state is the source and guarantor of citizens' rights and entitlements. Neoliberal processes of privatization of basic public services that erode the public sphere's responsibilities (and hence the links between political and social entitlements) de-link citizens' civil, political, and social rights (Lister, 1997). These processes also de-center the state in the citizens' expectation of rights and wellbeing.

In some instances, restructuring the powers of the national state has invigorated the local and global sites of citizenship contestations—such as in urban and transnational citizenship practices. Subordinate groups, through their local and trans-local practices, have offered an alternative, challenging the assumption that the national state is "the only legitimate source of citizenship rights" (Holston, 1998, p. 39). Undocumented immigrants, legal and illegal residents of squatter settlements, *favelas*, and townships have, in certain instances, taken charge of the local spaces they inhabit. They make their own living space and livelihood not because of, but often in spite of, the state's institutions and laws.

Global accumulation processes where social reproduction of labor is outsourced and performed through transnational families and networks across the globe expose the fallacy of formal citizenship as guarantor of inclusion/exclusion (Miraftab, 2011). A large number of people are better able to secure their wellbeing against social and economic uncertainties outside the national territories where they have formal political membership. The Mexican and Togolese immigrants in the small Illinois town of Beardstown discussed below are instructive. These immigrants are better providers to their families here in the US and across the border than they would be within the territories of their national citizenship. As studies of global remittances show, a large population supports citizen members of national political communities from beyond the national territories where they are located (Ratha, 2005). Poor families increasingly depend on a family member abroad for their safety net. In a strange twist of circumstances, the solution to the problems of disenfranchised citizens and their unfulfilled promise of citizenship has been membership or even non-membership (illegal existence) in another political community. The town of Sokode in the central region of Togo, offers another example; Sokode operated as a stronghold for the opposition against General Gnassingbe Eyadema's dictatorship during the 1990s battle for democracy. Sokode, a town that Piot (2010, p. 4) describes as having a "pure collective fantasy" of living abroad, offered a lifeline to the national struggle for political citizenship. Togolese had fled to Germany as asylees and sent money to Sokode to sustain those who were supporting the opposition in Togo. In this context, where expatriates play a significant role in the mobilization for inclusion in the Togolese national political community, much of the citizenship conception is post-national, even global (Piot, 2010, p. 169).[2]

These realities confirm the new conceptualizations of citizenship that are not tied to the territorial and political bounds of the national state or limited to a set of formalized recognitions. Rather than a bundle of rights granted from above by the state, citizenship is understood as processes constructed from below by people's local, trans-local, and increasingly trans-national practices that secure tangible gains independent of their formal status vis-à-vis a national state. In this alternative conceptualization, which Smith and Guarnizo refer to as the "unsettled terrain of national citizenship" (2009, p. 611), the contestation of citizenship occurs in spaces beyond one's legal status vis-à-vis the state; the content of citizenship is not located in the nation but in the city, the town, the neighborhood—the concrete spaces where inhabitants make their dignified life and livelihood.

In this context, the expectation of social wellbeing has shifted from formal, top-down, and national, to informal, bottom-up, and transnational processes and practices. To fulfill their expectations of a dignified, humane livelihood, people take their interests in their own hands. Whether among minoritized populations of the global North or marginalized residents of the global South, socially excluded people employ direct action; that is, they engage in democratic practices where the defense of their interests is not relinquished to others such as politicians, bureaucrats, or planners. Furthermore, they do not confine their claims-making actions to "invited spaces of citizenship" such as the Senate, the municipal councils, the planning commission's community hearings, citizen review boards, or NGOs. Such citizenship practices occur in self-determined, "invented spaces of citizenship" where people participate through direct action to respond to specific contexts and issues (Miraftab, 2006; 2009).

The discourse of the "right to the city" has increasingly been used to mobilize direct action among disenfranchised and globally mobile citizens. As Mark Purcell (2003) explains, when understood in a radical Lefebvrian sense, this discourse involves the right to appropriate (and thus to use) and the right to participate in (and thus to produce) urban space (Lefebvre, 1996). From this perspective, the urban landscapes of most cities of the global South constitute the material/spatial evidence of citizens' asserting their right to the city—not simply through legal means and bureaucratic channels, but through insurgent citizenship practices by which people appropriate urban spaces, produce their shelter, and use the city to secure a livelihood (Holston, 2008; Irazabal, 2008; Mitchell, 2003).

In the "right to the city" perspective, both as an alternative theoretical construct and as a slogan motivating transnational social movements, "[i]nhabitance becomes a privileged status granting citizens and noncitizens alike a right to participate in public policy-making, as well as in decisions of private corporations affecting urban life chances" (Smith and Guarnizo, 2009, p. 615). Disadvantaged and marginalized inhabitants (who could be either citizens or non-citizens from a formal standpoint) recognize the inadequacy of formal rights and turn to direct participation to achieve justice. They do not hand the advocacy of their interests to others, but directly take part in decisions that affect their lives and shape binding decisions. This formulation of democracy promotes a form of citizenship that is multi-centered and has multiple agencies. Their gains might be trivial, small, and slow, but they are real and tangible.

Citizenship Constructed From Below

To better understand this alternative notion of citizenship as practices grounded in civil society (Friedmann, 2002), I offer a case study from the Midwest of the United States.[3] This example comes from the experience of immigrants, many of them undocumented, whose access to food, shelter, and education has improved despite, and not because of, their status vis-à-vis the state.

In the economically distressed small town of Beardstown, Illinois, with a population of about 6,000 people, Cargill Corporation recruited an immigrant labor force for its meatpacking plant. They first targeted Spanish-speaking Latin Americans in the early 1990s (predominantly Mexicans) and then French-speaking West and Central Africans (predominantly Togolese) in the early 2000s. The town's formal politics of citizen participation in governance comprised an all-white and native-born city council led by an outspoken anti-immigrant mayor. Despite their exclusion from formal political structures, the town's immigrants, estimated to comprise more that 30 percent of the population, have fashioned new forms of citizenship that afford them certain inclusions in public institutions and in public spaces. This has occurred in a town that, until not long ago, remained virtually all white through its municipal policy as a "sundown town" (i.e., a town where blacks had to clear out before sundown).[4]

Today we see high levels of residential integration on almost every block.[5] We also observe a high homeownership rate among Mexican immigrants, with many of them becoming local landlords. In addition, a multi-lingual education system known as the Dual Language Program (DLP) has emerged. Under the DLP students receive half their instruction in Spanish. Lastly, through cultural identity celebrations (e.g., Mexican Independence Day or Africa Day) and through numerous multi-racial soccer clubs playing on outdoor fields, there is a notable presence of immigrants in public space. Let us explore how these developments came about.

In my ethnographic study of community change in this Midwestern town, I have witnessed the importance of informal politics and innovative everyday practices through which subordinate groups renegotiate their social and spatial relations. The gains listed above were not decrees granted by the town's unsupportive local government, nor were they fruits of immigrants' legal citizenship through naturalization. Rather, these are gains built from below by the efforts of immigrants and their allies through everyday practices and informal politics that assert their right to the city. Stripped of the opportunity to participate in state-sanctioned decision-making due to their legal status, immigrants in this town have practiced their right to the city in a radical Lefebvrian sense by producing residential and recreational spaces and, to a certain degree, by appropriating and using public space and institutions. Although they act quietly and unassumingly, immigrants in this town assert their right to the city through everyday practices that have brought them tangible gains. Below I will further discuss the ways in which this quiet appropriation of local space has taken place.

Beyond Formal Politics: Quiet Appropriations of Local Space

Despite the exclusionary formal structures of governance and decision-making that privilege established white residents and their informal networks, Beardstown immigrants have achieved a certain degree of inclusion in public institutions and public spaces.

The first important aspect of the newcomers' achievements is in spatial terms. In 1996, a few years after the recruitment of the first group of Spanish-speaking immigrant workers, violence erupted in the town. This resulted in the killing of a white resident, a subsequent march by the Ku Klux Klan, and the symbolic burning of a 6-foot tall cross in the main plaza of the town.

At this point, a few local, native-born residents joined forces with the immigrants to try to engineer a peaceful transition to a multicultural and multi-racial community. The white Anglophone priest of the Catholic Church instituted weekly services in Spanish and flew in three nuns from Puebla, Mexico; the Nazarene Church brought in a bilingual, US-educated pastor from Jalisco, Mexico; the local realtor signed up for an intensive Spanish course in Springfield; and the school hired a Salvadorian community liaison to facilitate the intercultural relationships at school and between the school and the community. In the early stages of the post-1996 response, these local agents played an important role in the inclusion of immigrants in public institutions and spaces. The nuns worked hard among new arrivals who were struggling with poverty, alienation, and having to live doubled- and tripled-up in run-down rental units. The pastor, the priest, and the school liaison were important as cultural brokers between the new and established residents, and they frequently wrote editorials in the local newspaper to promote a culture of tolerance. The entrepreneurial realtor helped many Mexican tenants to become owners of their own homes, and then the new owners of rental properties began offering more residential options to their fellow newcomers. Schoolteachers (English- and Spanish-speaking) mobilized a campaign for the Dual Language Program. Members of this army of cultural understanding paid a visit to the households of elementary school children in Beardstown.

Much of this took place in the early 2000s while Cargill undertook the recruitment of a new cohort of transnational laborers—immigrants from French-speaking West and Central Africa. Initially the company's concern for further destabilizing the ethno-racial relations prompted local authorities to steer the West Africans toward housing in the adjacent town of Rushville. As one informant explained, the plant managers did not want to risk another explosion (personal interview, 2006). In this light, by the early 2000s a tripartite residential geography evolved in which African Americans lived in larger cities outside of Beardstown (e.g., in Springfield) and commuted to work while Latin Americans and whites resided in Beardstown. Africans stayed in the adjacent town of Rushville.

After 2007 however, following a sharp increase in gas prices that motivated saving transportation time and cost, Africans started moving to Beardstown to be closer to their workplace. Their move was facilitated by a burgeoning market in rental houses owned by Mexican immigrants. Most of these "*nouveaux*" landlords" had arrived in Beardstown more than a decade earlier and had bought and fixed up houses first to live in and later to rent.[6] A randomly sampled survey among Beardstown Hispanics in 2008 indicated that about 40 percent of Latinos in this town had purchased their homes. Many of the new Latino homeowners in Beardstown began to rent units to other immigrants. Today a large proportion of the West and Central

Africans working at the plant have moved to Beardstown. Here they rent from white and Mexican landlords and live side-by-side with other ethnic, linguistic, and social groups. Immigrant groups, relying on the complementarities of their housing needs and interracial rental practices, thus challenged the racialized residential geography.

For immigrants in Beardstown, housing has not been the only means of claiming their right to the city and to making it a new home. The celebration of Mexican Independence Day in Beardstown (since 1998) and the newly instituted annual celebration of Africa Day in Rushville (since 2008) are public events that boldly declare the new immigrants' right to the towns and their public spaces. While the first Africa Day was celebrated indoors, the following ones have been held in the town's public park, starting with a soccer match among Africans and followed by West and Central African music, dance, and food. The celebration of Mexican Independence Day in Beardstown, despite some resentment by native-born locals, has been growing every year with small but increasing participation of diverse local residents. The last celebration was marked by 21 floats parading through the town's streets to the main plaza, where they were greeted by live Mexican music at the gazebo and Mexican food stalls circling the square.

Immigrants in Beardstown have also achieved a notable inclusion in public educational institutions, such as the schools, and the library. Schools were perhaps the town's first public institution to feel the impact of immigration with an enrollment increase within the district of almost 23 percent from 2000 to 2009. These new students have changed the racial and ethnic blend within the district. In 2000, whites compromised more than 84 percent of the student body, with only 14 percent of students within the district identified as Hispanic and only 0.7 percent of students identified as Black. By 2009, Hispanics constituted nearly 35 percent of the student body, while the Black population had increased to over 2 percent, with 5 percent of students identified as multi-racial (Illinois State Board of Education, 2009). This shift in the student body has had significant implications for special programs within the school district. The number of Limited English Proficiency Students, or students who qualify for bilingual education, has increased from 6.5 percent in 2000 to over 27 percent in 2009. The school responded by changing from English as a Second Language (ESL) to a bilingual Dual Language Program (DLP).

By 2006 the elementary school had managed to adopt the DLP. This is a bold program that aims for integration of different linguistic groups in a school by requiring both language groups to receive half of their instruction in the language not spoken at home. For example, every student from an English-speaking family who participates in this program has to do half of his or her curriculum and homework in Spanish; and vice versa for students from a Spanish-speaking family. The school district agreed to adopt the DLP provided that there was parental consent for every participating child. Beardstown teachers then launched what they called "the teachers' movement"—a door-to-door campaign to achieve 100 percent consent among both English- and Spanish-speaking parents. The local teachers—some of them long-standing, native-born local people and others new, Spanish-speaking classroom aides—along with a Central American school-community liaison visited the family of every student in the elementary school and convinced them of the value of multicultural education and DLP. What motivated the local teachers, one teacher said, was "seeing the school yard tensions amongst students reflecting the classroom segregation between linguistically different student bodies. Something had to be done" (personal interview, 2008). Today Beardstown is the only rural school in Illinois with a Dual Language Program. As of November 2008, there were 18 Illinois schools with DL programs; nationwide there were 335 schools (Paciotto and Delany-Barmann, forthcoming).

Beardstown's public library, whose clientele is more than half Spanish- and French-speaking immigrants, has also taken a multi-lingual approach to its services. It offers books and staff services in the three main languages spoken in the town and by its young school-age clientele: English, Spanish, and French.

Today, on a bright Sunday afternoon, visitors reaching Beardstown via Highway 125 encounter scenes that are unusual in the social landscape of the rural Midwest. Where once scenes of racial hatred were on display, one finds at the very entrance to the town large soccer fields filled with racially and linguistically diverse players in colorful outfits. The particularly bold public presence of the town's diverse population is the outcome of a long spatial struggle. My interviews with the soccer league's founders, as well as discussions with players on several of the eleven multi-racial teams, revealed a struggle in which minorities asserted their right to play their sport of choice on proper, public fields—not on clandestine or spatially segregated ones. As one of the interviewees explained, the first immigrants who arrived in Beardstown, almost all of whom were Spanish-speaking, used to play in private spaces like their families' backyards. Even though they tried to be publicly invisible, the interviewee recalled "police cars driving back and forth on the street to check on us...as if we were up to no good" (personal interview, 2008). Then for several years they played soccer on abandoned lands around the town and behind the local school. Such sites were often covered with broken glass and trash. When they were finally kicked out of the field behind the school due to construction, the games moved to the park district fields, which at the time accommodated only baseball. But the regular presence of enthusiastic soccer players and their families occupying the benches and the public park facilities, combined with the tireless efforts of the league president to negotiate with the park district officials, finally gained them the soccer fields they enjoy today; they have a legitimate presence in the town's public space.

The park district's acquisition of land for their soccer teams is indeed a significant achievement in the assertion of immigrants' right to the city. These public fields today are much more than recreational spaces. They are new inclusive spaces of interracial and intercultural interaction among the Francophone West Africans and the Hispanic Latin American immigrants—with increasing numbers of Anglophone residents joining the teams.

While soccer has provided a space for interracial relations among men, childcare has served in a similar role for women. Mexicans, because of their distinct local and trans-local resources and immigration history, are more likely to have their extended families with them than the Africans. The Latinos are also more able to bring in a family member from another state in the US or from across the border to help with childcare. Often within a larger extended family there is one younger or older female member who stays home to provide childcare for other family members, almost all of whom work at Cargill. West African newcomers have a different history of immigration and different trans-local resources and transnational family structures, such that they seldom have their extended families with them in Beardstown or elsewhere in the US.[7] Since West Africans find the Mexicans' expression of affection towards children more akin to their own, Africans with children tend to converge with Mexicans for childcare. "They are like us," was how a West African mother put it when speaking about her Mexican caregiver (personal interview, 2009).

Persistent Creation of a Public Presence through Mediating Sites and Institutions

While the dominant literature on globalization, immigration, and social movements, including the burgeoning writings on the right to the city, offers many insights into the possibilities for emerging transnational spaces like Beardstown, this body of work is still inadequate. The inadequacy lies not only in an urban bias, which regards large metropolitan centers as hotbeds of immigration and immigrants' action, but also in a political bias, with an emphasis on forms of action that are large-scale, collective, and confrontational. Such forms of action are more likely to occur in the relatively open political environments of large cities, which offer anonymity to participants.

In order to understand the differences between Beardstown and major metropolitan areas, we need to examine the role Cargill plays in the economy and politics of the town. Cargill is the source of earnings for the overwhelming majority of local residents and organizations. The company wields virtual monopoly power over all spheres. For example, in 2007 the company had a tax dispute concerning the assessed value of their plant. When the company threatened to leave town after contesting the County Assessment Board's figures, local authorities yielded and cut the assessment in half, saving Cargill more than a million dollars in tax payments (and cutting deeply into the budget of the local authority for schools, libraries, and other services). The company responded with social donations, which, according to their website, came to $150,000. This contributed to an already unequal balance of political power in the community since schools, the park district, and even churches all have become direct recipients of the Cargill community grants; they have become more reliant on corporate donations than on state support. This left them wary of upsetting their relationships with the plant management. In this context, the possibilities for immigrant communities to organize and claim their right to the city are limited. The absence of such forms of action should not be interpreted as passivism on the part of local inhabitants, especially immigrants; many of them are in a precarious situation since they are without legal status in the US.

Subordinate groups in highly restrained political environments, such as those investigated in Beardstown, make claim to the city and to a dignified life through channels and forms of action that bypass the inadequacy and elitism of the formal structures and institutions of urban citizenship. For populations without access to legal or formal channels of citizen inclusion, informal practices offer an unnoticeable but effective means to assert their rights to a dignified livelihood. These insights expand the notion of citizenship from legal and formal entitlements originating with the state to a range of informal and substantive (including spatial) practices constituted from below through people's various forms of action.

Bayat (2010) makes an important intervention in this area of scholarship by expanding the debate on forms of resistance beyond collective forms of action and mobilization. He critiques the social movement literature for its bias towards forms of action more likely to occur in liberal democratic structures. Reflecting on the experience of subordinate groups in highly constrained and contested political environments, he highlights the non-collective forms of action and what he calls the "quiet encroachment of the ordinary."[8] He discusses the struggles by youth, women, and informal traders in Tehran and Cairo whose gains are achieved not through large, media-attracting marches or protests (which will be doomed to instant repression); rather, they are won through potent yet unassuming forms of resistance and under-the-radar politics that are performed quietly and without notice. He calls such actions the "art of presence"—"the courage and creativity to assert collective will in spite of all odds, to circumvent constraints, utilizing what is available and discovering new spaces within which to make oneself heard, seen, felt, and realized" (2010, p. 26). The scholars of popular politics stress the potent force of presence by minoritized and unwanted populations in spaces where they are not wanted. Feminist scholars in particular have stressed the need for such stubborn presence by women in formal politics, coining the term "politics of presence" (Phillips, 1995).

Key to the Beardstown story is the immigrants' persistent creation of a public presence in this former sundown town. Clearly, the celebrations of Mexican Independence Day and of Africa Day, as well as the creation and use of open soccer fields for Sunday soccer games, are not merely recreational events. They assert one's right to the city, the right to be there in that small town where historically only white individuals and families could make a home. For Beardstown, the consideration of its history as a former sundown town is critical. In such a context, the simple presence of immigrants and "others" in previously prohibited spaces counts as an important political achievement. While elsewhere this might not mean much, the sheer presence of non-white bodies and non-English speech in public spaces—from the plaza to the streets and from the sports field to the churches, schools, and libraries—represents enormous political and social gains. In Beardstown, the working of such "art of presence" surfaces in stories that residents shared with me in their interviews. They discuss Mexicans being everywhere, not only in every block of the town as neighbors, but also in every one of their children's classrooms, in the library and grocery stores, and at the barbeque stand that is open on lazy Sunday afternoons. Resistance to being criminalized or made invisible fuels this appropriation of local space.

This persistent presence, however, is not asserted from the top or through formal institutions governing the city. For example, while institutional hierarchies of school and park districts remain dominated by white and English-speaking members, native born and immigrant residents have used local school and soccer fields as significant mediating sites to renegotiate interracial relations. Here I borrow the notion of mediation from Lamphere (1992), who argues that the kind of interrelations emerging between new immigrants and established residents in destination communities are not just a matter of race, ethnicity, and immigration status; they are also influenced by the specificities of those mediating institutions and sites through which they interact. The immigrant labor force recruited to the Beardstown plant arrived in the absence of public and social service agencies experienced in dealing with diverse populations and their needs. Moreover, the pre-existing formal institutions, such as the town council, the Park District, and the School Boards, never opened up to include the new, racially diverse residents amongst them. To renegotiate their inter-racial relations and assert their right to be present in this former sundown town, immigrants and their local native-born allies instead focused on creating a range of local mediating sites. For example, in the absence of pre-existing rental housing complexes to receive immigrants, they promoted residential integration through inter-racial rental practices of refurbished housing units; similarly, in the absence of private, public, and non-profit sector affordable child care services, immigrant women established informal home-based child care services as a site that mediates diverse immigrant groups' relationships.

Whether these mediating sites will make a dent in the formal institutions and hierarchies of city government (school and park districts, city council, policing, or labor and corporate organizations) remains to be seen. The point here is not to assume that grand achievements emerge through these mediating sites, nor is it to romanticize the hardship of immigrant workers in the Midwest and their exploitation in the hazardous meatpacking industry. The intent is not to sketch a rosy picture of optimism, harmony, and a tension-free space of solidarity and cooperation across racialized and socially stratified groups. The social and spatial changes in this town are neither consistent nor stable. They are complex, tentative, and open to future renegotiation. Nevertheless, examples like Beardstown are significant for the ongoing debates on citizenship and the "right to the city" because they bring to light the existence of alternative sites through which immigrants and native-born populations renegotiate their relationships outside formal institutions and formal politics.

The Beardstown case lends a voice to the ongoing conversations on the limitations of formal and liberal democratic formulations of citizenship. It helps to disentangle people's on-the-ground practices of substantive citizenship from the state's legal and formalist citizenship project. Focusing on undocumented immigrants who may not have formal citizenship rights, yet who in practice achieve some of the substantive gains associated with them, pushes the notion of citizenship beyond the limits of its formal construct; moreover, this focus also draws our attention to the mediation between macro- and micro-forces that can occur outside formal institutions.

The Beardstown observations help to push the conceptualization of the "right to the city" beyond the formal means of social and urban mobilization and beyond formal institutional means for mediation of rights. If seen only through the lens of big city marches and their heroic militancy, immigrant inhabitants of Beardstown may seem little more than passive victims of "redneck" Midwestern communities and corporate-infused ethno-racial divisions. Yet, by analyzing transnational processes from below in Beardstown, through opportunities and constraints that the local context offers and imposes (Guarnizo and Smith, 1998), we observe not only exploitation, ethno-racial tension, and animosity, but also the forms of agency from below that otherwise escape attention. This reveals how immigrant groups draw on and construct distinct local and trans-local resources, networks, and meanings; it also reveals how in specific, historically constituted mediating spaces, immigrants' varied constraints and resources converge into social dynamics and forms of action that one would otherwise not expect.

In short, the story of Beardstown immigrants reminds us that the subaltern can speak, but we only recognize their agency if we can hear them in the language in which they speak. In this case the key to recognition of agency among diverse immigrant populations of Beardstown is in recognizing their informal and non-collective forms of action as a valid means of asserting their right to produce and to use local space.

Notes

1. The expectations of liberal democratic citizenship are perhaps best articulated in the writings of T. H. Marshall, where it is argued that formal membership in a nation-state grants national citizens the civil, political, and social rights that automatically guarantee their entitlements (see Marshall, 1977 [1950]).

2. Another point in time is the five-month sit-ins in front of the US embassy in Lome, the capital of Togo, which were held by Togolese applicants for the US Diversity Visa whose applications were rejected. Applicants for the US Diversity Visa, which grants to the recipient a Green Card and a five-year pathway to US citizenship, took part in this enduring sit-in to claim—yes to claim—the visas that were unjustly denied to them by the embassy. In the words of one of the protestors, cited in Piot's extended analysis of the event: "[W]e are here to claim what is rightfully ours" (Piot, 2010, p. 166).

3. This case study is part of larger multi-sited research spanning from 2005 to 2011. Beardstown data were collected through more than 70 semi-structured and in-depth interviews with local, established residents as well as Spanish- and French-speaking immigrants; through three focus group sessions

arranged through ESL classes with mixed groups of Hispanic and African students; through mail-in surveys on housing and households conducted in collaboration with the Illinois Institute of Rural Affairs and the University of Illinois Extension Office, which were complemented by door-to-door follow-up surveys among Spanish- and French-speaking residents (400 English; 69 Spanish; 65 French); through observation of community meetings and celebrations; through review of archival and contemporary newspaper articles from Beardstown and from nearby metropolitan areas; and through analysis of census data. The 2006 field work for this project was conducted in collaboration with Dr. Diaz McConnell, as reflected in our joint publications (2008 and 2009). I acknowledge the support in funding and in kind received from the following units at the University of Illinois, Urbana-Champaign: the Center for Democracy in a Multiracial Society (2004, 2006, and 2007); the Centre for Latin American and Caribbean Studies (2008); the College of Fine and Applied Arts Innovative Research Grant (2010); and the Office of the Vice Chancellor's Research Board (2010).

4. For further discussion of the sundown town phenomenon across the US, see Loewen (2006).

5. In 2000, the white-Hispanic index of dissimilarity for Beardstown was 57.6 compared with 62.1 for Chicago, 63.2 for Los Angeles-Long Beach, and 66.7 for New York (for more see Diaz McConnell and Miraftab, 2009; Miraftab and Diaz McConnell, 2008).

6. Elsewhere with Diaz McConnell (2008 and 2009) I discuss that the high rate of homeownership among Spanish-speaking, predominantly Mexican, immigrants has been made possible by various circumstances. One is the affordability of homeownership in this small town. The house prices are relatively low, the employment at the plant is secure and year-round, and the mortgage market that arose in the early 2000s was favorable to immigrants. The large local and trans-local network of Mexican immigrants was a source of information about the processes and conditions of homeownership. We also discussed in those publications how the absence of zoning and prior planning regulations might have contributed to the residential integration we observe in town today. The absence of any pre-existing residentially segregated spatial structure in town means that newcomers found houses wherever there was a landlord willing to rent or an owner willing to sell.

7. For a detailed discussion of differential local and trans-local histories, resources, and obligations of immigrant groups in Beardstown, see Miraftab (forthcoming) in the *International Journal of Urban and Regional Research*.

8. Bayat defines "quiet encroachment of the ordinary as pertinent to examining the activism of the marginalized groups...[referring] to non-collective but prolonged direct actions of dispersed individuals and families to acquire the basic necessities of their lives...in a quiet and unassuming illegal fashion" (2010, p. 45).

References

Bayat, A. (2010). *Life as Politics: How Ordinary People Change the Middle East*. Palo Alto: Stanford University Press.

Diaz McConnell, E., and F. Miraftab. (2009). "Sundown Town to 'Mexican Town': Newcomers, Old Timers, and Housing in Small Town America." *Rural Sociology*, 74 (4), 605-29.

Friedmann, J. (2002). *The Prospect of Cities*. Minneapolis/London: University of Minnesota Press.

Guarnizo, L. E., and M. P. Smith. (1998). "The Locations of Transnationalism." In M. P. Smith and L. E. Guarnizo (Eds.), *Transnationalism from Below* (pp. 3-34). New Brunswick/London: Transaction Publishers.

Holston, J. (1998). "Spaces of Insurgent Citizenship." In L. Sandercock (Ed.), *Making the Invisible Visible: A Multiracial Planning History* (pp. 37-56). Berkeley/Los Angeles/New York: University of California Press.

———. (2008). *Insurgent Citizenship: Disjunctions of Democracy and Modernity in Brazil*. Princeton/Oxford: Princeton University Press.

Illinois State Board of Education. (2009).

Irazabal, C. (2008). "Citizenship, Democracy and Public Space in Latin America." In C. Irazabal (Ed.), *Ordinary Places/Extraordinary Events: Citizenship, Democracy and Public Space in Latin America* (pp. 11-33). New York: Routledge.

Lamphere, L. (1992). "Introduction: The Shaping of Diversity." In L. Lamphere (Ed.), *Structuring Diversity: Ethnographic Perspective on the New Immigration* (pp. 1-33). Chicago: University of Chicago Press.

Lefevbre, H. (1996). "The Right to the City." In G. Bridge and S. Watson (Eds.), *The Blackwell City Reader* (pp. 367-74). Oxford, UK: Blackwell.

Lister, R. (1997). "Citizenship: Towards a Feminist Synthesis." *Feminist Review*, 57(1), 28-48.

Loewen, J. (2006). *Sundown Towns: A Hidden Dimension of American Racism*. New York: Touchstone.

Marshall, T. H. (1977 [1950]). *Citizenship and Social Class and Other Essays*. Cambridge: Cambridge University Press.

Miraftab, F. (2006). "Feminist Praxis, Citizenship and Informal Politics: Reflections on South Africa's Anti-eviction Campaign." *International Feminist Journal of Politics*, 8(2), 194-218.

_____. (2009). "Insurgent Planning: Situating Radical Planning in the Global South." *Planning Theory*, 8(1), 32-50.

_____. (2011). "Emergent Transnational Spaces: Meat, Sweat and Global (Re)Production in the Heartland." *International Journal of Urban and Regional Research* [in press].

_____. (Forthcoming). "Planning and Citizenship." In R. Weber and R. Crane (Eds.), *Oxford Handbook of Urban Planning*. Oxford University Press.

Miraftab, F., and E. D. McConnell. (2008). "Multiculturalizing Rural Towns: Insights for Inclusive Planning." *International Planning Studies*, 13(4), 343-60.

Mitchell, D. (2003). *The Right to the City: Social Justice and the Fight for Public Space*. New York: Guilford Press.

Paciotto, C., and G. Delany-Barmann. (Forthcoming). "Planning Micro-level Language Education Reform in New Diaspora Sites: Two-Way Immersion Education in the Rural Midwest." *Language Policy*.

Phillips, A. (1995). *The Politics of Presence*. Oxford/New York: Clarendon Press.

Piot, C. (2010). *Nostalgia for the Future: West Africa after the Cold War*. Chicago: The University of Chicago Press.

Purcell, M. (2003). "Citizenship and the Right to the Global City: Reimagining the Capitalist World Order." *International Journal of Urban and Regional Research*, 27(3), 564-90.

Ratha, D. (2005). "Workers' Remittances: An Important and Stable Source of External Development Finance." In S. M. Maimbo and D. Ratha (Eds.), *Remittances: Development Impact and Future Prospects* (pp. 19-52). Washington, DC: The World Bank.

Smith, M. P., and L. E. Guarnizo. (2009). "Global Mobility, Shifting Borders and Urban Citizenship." *Tijdschrift voor Economische en Sociale Geografie*, 100(5), 610–22.

Turner, B. S. (1990). "Outline of a Theory of Citizenship." *Sociology*, 24(2), 189-217.

12

Political Moments with Long-term Consequences*

Debbie Becher

This chapter is about one way that poor, urban residents claim their rights to cities. I call this specific type of organizing "political moments." The word "moment" indicates impermanence. Political signals something more. Residents create political moments by mobilizing around very specific issues affecting them. Political moments contrast with other kinds of organizing that are often privileged in studies of social movements. Political moments are intentionally short-lived and small scale. Resident leaders do not seek to create lasting organizations. They expect any organizations they form to dissolve once the immediate issue is addressed. Residents rarely refer to rights or other abstract ideals when they frame their claims. Their work is somewhat isolated from other struggles for rights or justice. They demand resolutions to specific problems affecting them. I thus use the term political moments to refer to intentionally temporary, grassroots organizing around small-scale, specific claims. In this chapter, I elaborate on what distinguishes this kind of collective action and why it deserves special attention. I demonstrate how city residents secure change—indeed how they secure rights to cities—through political moments.

One of the reasons that political moments deserve notice is that they promise long-term impacts. The very characteristics that distinguish political moments as organizing—that they are small-scale and temporary—suggest that their impacts will be the same: limited and short-term. I argue that, on the contrary, political moments can secure durable changes that give a wide range of poor people access to city resources. Political moments are fleeting and narrowly focused, and even somewhat isolated, yet through them, poor urban residents create enduring control over their parts of the city in ways that other forms of politics may not make possible. The kind of organizing I call political moments is especially likely to mobilize people accustomed to being disengaged from politics. The experience can change both the individuals and the institutions that become involved. The organizing experience develops the actors' personal commitments and skills to access political power. It also alters established local institutions, which sometimes unwittingly open their doors to long-term local resident involvement through a temporary issue. In these ways, through political moments, poor, urban residents establish control over city resources.

In what follows, I elaborate each of the issues just mentioned above, first theoretically and second through a case study. I divide the first half of the chapter into four subsections to make my primary analytical points. I first detail the conditions that create opportunities for political moments and then the kind of organizing that comprises them. I then explain how these kinds of opportunities and organizing combine powerfully to mobilize poor communities and secure short- and long-term gains. I then illustrate these arguments through the specific conflict that made me recognize them: a redevelopment plan for a poor Philadelphia neighborhood at the turn of the millennium. I present the case in the same order as the analytical points presented in the first half of the chapter, beginning with the conditions that became opportunities for organizing, followed by the details of the organizing and mobilization around those opportunities (which constitute what I call a political moment), and ending with the short- and long-term consequences of the moment.

Theorizing Political Moments

Opportunities in Problems

Conditions that might foreshadow doom can become opportunities. A serious threat that might strip community power can help do the opposite. Often, massive changes to neighborhoods become imminent, and residents fear they have little voice in that change. Ideas to develop a big-box store or a casino, to reroute a highway or public transportation, or to assemble large plots of land for housing redevelopment can be kicked around for years by developers and politicians with residents paying little attention. However, once those ideas look like real plans, the potential for quick and dramatic change catches people's attention. Even people who would otherwise ignore development planning, for instance, will focus on significant plans for change.

Individuals and organizations become politically active when they stand to win or lose a great deal. The specter of an unusually serious change to land development concentrates interests in space and time. *Specific* plans to significantly reroute traffic, build sidewalks, or construct a large residential or commercial development (as occurs in the case explored later in this chapter) are all likely to draw the undivided attention of the particular people they will impact most seriously. Plans focus interests when they make clear exactly which people and which addresses will be significantly affected and when.

Individuals and organizations marshal their resources around an issue when their interests are large, immediate, and apparent. Countless ideas and plans for urban change are usually being tossed around at kitchen tables, on street corners, and in executive offices. The expectation that one of those issues is going to be realized soon motivates action.[1] The anticipation of a massive change, concentrated in space and time, can draw the attention of those who would otherwise ignore political struggles. Put simply, even if we are accustomed to being quiet or losing fights with power, we will stand up and pay attention when issues seem big, affect us, and are happening now. We already know this much, but scholars have not considered how shriveling neighborhood organizations can combine with these conditions to create an even greater opening for change.

Established organizations provide crucial resources to any collective action. Even a highly motivated and skilled group of individuals will struggle without them. Novice or one-time political activists need meeting space, publicity channels, political experience, and personal connections. People with little financial wealth and formal education might have trouble accessing these resources quickly to respond to a threat or opportunity. A range of local organizations exists in most neighborhoods. Churches, social clubs, schools, day-care centers, settlement houses, corner stores, barbershops, and other community institutions hold physical, human, political, and organizational resources crucial to the success of collective action.[2] Yet these organizations can sometimes be more of a barrier than an opportunity. As neighborhoods have changed over time, many older organizations have lost their original connections to the neighborhood residents.

A disjuncture between neighborhoods and organizations is especially likely when neighborhood wealth has declined and racial makeup has shifted. Many churches and settlement houses in the older neighborhoods of postindustrial cities, for example, continue to say they are committed to a neighborhood, but their actions betray only a shallow connection. Churches often continue to serve the same congregants even after they have moved out of the neighborhood. Church leadership may resist welcoming newer residents who usually differ from the old ones by race, class, nationality, language, and more (McRoberts, 2003). Settlement houses, once established to assist immigrant incorporation into particular neighborhoods, lose direction once migration patterns change. Organizations persist, but with different activities at their core. Many have changed themselves into providers of social services, with fewer grassroots connections than they once had (Lasch-Quinn, 1993).

Often, these community organizations struggle to survive in changing neighborhoods. Organizations may endure for a time with their original members, even after those members move away. Over time, however, as these members die or otherwise leave, the organizations suffer. Churches with disappearing congregations find themselves responsible for maintaining ambitious programming and large buildings designed for more people than currently attend. Their responsibilities to their buildings overwhelm their declining membership. Organizations' failure to incorporate new neighbors can thus become a problem for their very survival.

Older organizations struggling to retain members may therefore be particularly poised to benefit from involvement in political moments. Publicity about their involvement in political moments promises to increase hopes for their own, somewhat endangered survival. Established local organizations that have become sick and distant from the people who surround them, therefore, can have their own reasons to want to get involved in eye-catching neighborhood issues. Becoming committed to organizing around an important neighborhood issue can help older, established organizations create new, necessary community ties.

A Particular Kind of Organizing

The opportunities or conditions I described give birth to what I call political moments when a particular kind of organizing emerges. For reasons I will discuss below, this kind of organizing might be motivated by the relatively disenfranchised neighborhood conditions just mentioned. But the conditions just mentioned by no means guarantee that a political moment will emerge. At the most basic level, turning a moment political, in the sense I mean it, requires the development of a contentious politics. That is, people must take action collectively in opposition to a defined target. But the collective action that comprises political moments, as I define them, has a particular character.

Political moments involve intentionally temporary, grassroots organizing around clearly specified issues. Neighborhood efforts to stop or to relocate specific development projects typify these small-scale, specific, and short-term organizing efforts. First, the people most directly affected by the issue at hand significantly direct the mobilization. Second, the claims around which people organize and the way they frame their issues are drawn into particular focus. That is, people make claims about very specific issues, people, places, and events. They rarely explicitly connect their local claims to other struggles or even to claims about rights or justice for larger groups than themselves. They seldom invoke abstract or general claims. During political moments, people might draw attention to the concerns identified by scholars and activists as comprising a right to the city, but they almost never use the words "right to the city" or connect to collective action reaching beyond their neighborhoods' boundaries.

Third, political moments are intentionally and explicitly temporary. People are not, at least not intentionally, joining ongoing campaigns. The specific issues around which claims are made are expected to end in the foreseeable future. It is likely that people even expect the organizations they form to dissolve once the issue is addressed. This is something different from joining issue-based campaigns led by established organizations. In this case, leaders expect that the organizing will be temporary, that its structures will disband, and that people will terminate their political activity and return home when the issue dies.

We should already expect episodes of small-scale, specific, and short-term organizing to be not only prevalent but fundamental to large-scale social movements. Social movement scholars recognize the importance of episodic collective action. Such activity can create and cement social networks and community organizations that become resources in future bouts of activity (Tarrow, 1998). Recent studies highlighting the particular importance of churches and social networks in the building of the American Civil Rights Movement suggest that large-scale social movements are built on these small-scale events (McAdam, 1988; Morris, 1986). Scholarship on community organizing has consistently paid attention to these seemingly smaller forms of action (Alinsky, 1971; Kretzmann and McKnight, 1997; Warren, 2001), and some scholars of social movements also understand specific and temporary organizing to be a type of social movement activity (Flacks, 2005; Snow, Soule, and Kriesi, 2004; Staggenborg, 2011). In fact, Snow, *et al.* (2004) claim that this kind of organizing may be more common and may engage more people than the more formal, large-scale, long-term networks and organizations typically queried by social movement researchers.

Even though particular scholars have probed or acknowledged this kind of organizing, scholarship on social movements has generally downplayed its significance in comparison to more explicitly permanent and ideological forms of organizing. Long-term, rights-oriented organizing is usually more visible to researchers of urban-based and other social movements. Writers about urban movements, for example, tend to privilege lasting, citywide, national, and global organizing with abstract claims and goals, such as the right to housing, living wages, and environmental justice (Brenner and Theodore, 2002; Marcuse, 2009). To deserve consideration as urban social movements, Manuel Castells (1983, p. xvi) insists organizing should consciously articulate a program for change. Mayer Zald (2000) similarly requires that collective action be "ideologically structured" in order for it to count for researchers of social movements, whether inside or outside of the city.

The social movement scholars who recognize the importance of short-term specific organizing also realize that this activity has taken the backseat in research. The very things that characterize what I call political moments can lead scholars of cities and social movements to overlook them and characterize them as forms of rebellion or contentious politics with short-term impacts at best. There is, perhaps, even a bit of disdain among progressives for organizing that is local and short-lived, as the example Snow (2004) use suggests—that is, of not-in-my backyard (NIMBY) organizing. Sidney Tarrow (1998) distinguishes social movements as those collective actions that last over time and extend across space. Still, his theories of social change appreciate the importance of enduring ties among actors that can be accessed at crucial moments. He also lauds flexible rather than rigid structures for the development of social movements. By characterizing social movements by their extension over space and time, Tarrow rightly calls attention to a distinct form of social action. The problem with this focus, however, is that it can lead scholars to privilege these distinct forms of collective action and to miss other important forms.

The reasons for the oversight may largely be methodological: researchers can more easily locate large-scale, rights-based organizing. If not methodological, the reasons may be more theoretical. Perhaps political moments seem too little, fleeting, specific, and disconnected. Perhaps they appear important only to the few people directly involved or to studies of community organizations, but not to larger movements for social change. Whatever the reason, the result is that organizing of the type I call political moments too rarely informs theory of how the rights demanded in social movements are won and institutionalized.[3] Scholars of social movements and the right to the city have not discovered the benefits of *not* making abstract claims and of focusing on organizations and mobilizations that are *not* intended to last.

The Long Arm of Mobilization

Political moments' specific and fleeting nature can make it possible to mobilize individuals and organizations that might be hesitant to engage in politics. Claims about an issue related to a specific place, rather than a more general political struggle, can actually broaden the potential for mobilizing people and organizations near that space. An expectation that the collective action will be temporary can further extend the likelihood that a broader spectrum of people will become involved. The specific framing and short-term time frame, therefore, have actual, often positive, consequences for who is mobilized.

Residents of poor, American neighborhoods are particularly *un*likely to think of themselves as involved in "politics." Poor urban residents in the United States often turn away from issues because they are defined as political. By contrast, issues that seem relevant to their "community" engage them. They organize collectively around concrete issues related to their own neighborhoods. Issues that either promise to build or threaten to distress their local community can inspire them to join forces (Naples, 1998; Warren, 2001). Residents of poor, urban neighborhoods will become involved in what they consider community issues rather than political issues.

Place creates connections among people and organizations and makes allies of directly affected residents. Because they share a place, nearby individuals and organizations may feel a responsibility and affinity for one another. Physical proximity not only makes neighbors likely to help; it can make those primarily affected more likely to ask them for help. And asking is often an important precursor to participation. Framing an issue around a place increases the likelihood that nearby organizations will consider themselves uniquely available, capable, and responsible for helping. The professed commitment to place of older organizations that have lost their local ties makes involvement logical, if not recently typical. When an issue is focused on a specific change to a place, reticent people and organizations may speak out.

Ironically, residents may avoid some organizations explicitly dedicated to their neighborhood or community. The community organizations that regularly engage in politics, specifically in development issues, may seem particularly *ill* served to assist with grassroots mobilization. Neighborhood associations, community development corporations, and housing and social service providers directly engage in local politics and often represent community residents (Marwell, 2007; McQuarrie, 2010; McQuarrie and Marwell, 2009); however, because these organizations have primary interests in their own survival and development projects, residents faced with a particular challenge may avoid alliances with them.

The expectation of *temporary* involvement in politics can and does help motivate other, less overtly political organizations and individuals to step up. The temporary nature of the organizing breaks down barriers to mobilization for individuals and for institutions like churches and cultural centers. One can engage in a short-lived and unique issue with little threat to an identity that usually keeps him or her on the sidelines. Residents and organizations that typically eschew politics will be more likely to see their role in a political moment rather than a movement. In addition, political moments can create a way for established organizations that have become estranged from their communities to test new modes of engagement. They can become involved in the neighborhood on a singular issue without making long-term commitments. Though an issue's overt connection to government might give pause to some apolitical community organizations and individuals, its temporary nature might reduce that barrier.

Beyond Mobilization: Short- and Long-term Gains

Specifically framed and short-term organizing may be crucially important for securing wins for residents. The strategies of political moments, in and of themselves, may help residents win concessions from government and other large, powerful organizations. Temporary organizing around issues that are framed as unique encourages concessions. Politicians and bureaucrats worry about setting examples that will cost them. If they give in this time, the next group of residents will hear about it and understand the concession as their right. Therefore, they are more likely to give in to claims that are framed as distinct, since they are less likely to serve as examples of anything that will occur again.

A win on the particular issue can be an extremely significant accomplishment; critics may assume, however, that the effects of political moments seem to stop soon after the moment subsides. Those who overlook political moments might worry that individuals' and organizations' participation in emergent associations may last only as long as a particular issue. Perhaps, they would say, these political moments remain important as isolated and promising instances of issue-based organizing, but no more. Perhaps no other lasting or general impacts, such as increased political consciousness, political participation, or organizational capacity, will result. Perhaps political moments do not deserve to be considered a part or a type of social movement building or of rights institutionalization because they do not promise the same results (Giugni, 1998). Through political moments, participants do not (by definition) develop ties to established, political organizations that might mobilize them around later campaigns. Individuals probably remain involved in politics only until the particular event is over. Their organizations only exist as long as the situation requires. Therefore, one reason right to the city and social movement scholars may have neglected political moments is that they do not seem to win particularly sizeable gains beyond the local issues at hand.

On the contrary, changes beyond the immediate issue can and do result. Focused, short-lived collective action creates broad and long-lasting changes. Participants in political moments institutionalize gains that they do not demand or anticipate—and that they may not even notice.

Organizing around a particular situation potentially builds local capacity by increasing a sense of power and ties among people and organizations. Involvement in political moments, like any participation in contentious politics, promises to build individual consciousness and interpersonal relationships, especially when groups are victorious. These changes are particularly notable for people who usually eschew political action. Thus, through political moments, urban residents can transform local political culture (feelings of efficacy) and networks (interpersonal ties), both of which are important impacts and building blocks of social movements (Staggenborg, 2011).

These moments promise long-term impacts even beyond personal beliefs and interpersonal ties. They transform the established organizations that become involved. Political moments can recharge the dedication of organizations like churches to their immediate neighborhoods. Through political moments, established local institutions can become more available and responsive to their surrounding neighborhoods. Such adjustments might serve not only the neighborhoods' residents but also the organizations' survival. Temporary practices can spill over into how organizations approach more permanent issues like membership, leadership, and programming. Through the temporary activities of political moments, leaders might redirect the attention of established organizations to the neighborhoods surrounding them for years to come. By helping local residents during especially trying times in a visible way, established organizations can build positive local reputations. Thus, temporary and specifically focused organizing can transform organizational infrastructures, another important impact by which any social movement might be deemed a success (Andrews, 2004).

A Political Moment: A Case Study

The conflict over Jefferson Square in Philadelphia, Pennsylvania, from 1998 to 2000 exemplified a political moment that established rights to a city. First District City Councilperson Frank DiCicco's ideas for the redevelopment of a portion of a south Philadelphia neighborhood in the late 1990s incensed the area's residents. The white city councilperson, a hospital owner, and other non-residents had dreamed up a plan for the city to acquire ownership of about five blocks of privately owned land, including where over 30 families lived, to be razed and redeveloped into a new parking lot for a hospital and new, market-rate housing—complete with fences, driveways, and garages—to appeal to middle-class buyers.

African American residents made up the majority of those in the immediate path of the plan. They were angry, but they were not organized. They were in a city with highly racialized politics and in a neighborhood historically populated by white ethnic residents (though less so recently). Italian Americans and African Americans had moved into the area throughout the early decades of the century when jobs were plentiful. After the jobs and many residents had left, more African American families moved in. But local power did not shift as quickly as jobs and populations did. One particularly important site of local power was the district city council position, to which men who ethnically identified as Italian regularly won elections. In the late 1990s, the city councilman's plans to redevelop what is now called Jefferson Square seemed to replicate a familiar picture. Residents knew that they would resist, but they expected a repetition of the familiar American story in which poor, African American residents are displaced by someone with more power who wants their land.

Residents organized themselves into a focused group that spoke as a collective voice and won concrete victories. Residents living in the center of the targeted area—people who usually avoided official politics—allied themselves with neighbors, relatives, a church, and a settlement house to form a temporary organization. Through this organization, they lobbied politicians, engaged the mass media, mobilized allies, and negotiated with city officials about the plans for neighborhood change. As a result, the city adopted a revitalization plan that the residents approved, a plan that looked much different from the one Councilman DiCicco originally proposed. Residents won major concessions on the issue at hand. They also secured long-lasting interpersonal ties and established institutional commitments to the neighborhood.

Opportunities in Problems

By at least the early 1990s, many of the people living in the bull's-eye of the city councilman's "Jefferson Square Revitalization Plan" believed they had a right to their small place in the city. The area that Councilman DiCicco dubbed "Jefferson Square" was becoming increasingly poor after decades of decline. Poverty rates, rents, and the proportion of renters to homeowners rose. Median household incomes and home prices, adjusted for inflation, continued to drop, and many buildings were simply abandoned. A once-thriving hospital, where many neighbors were born and had worked, bought up some of the leftover buildings and demolished them with plans to eventually rebuild. But the hospital slowly declined and filed for bankruptcy, leaving vacant its own campus and the scattered lots it had purchased.

In spite of, and sometimes taking advantage of, this devastation, some families established their homes there. Residents came and stayed. One family had a particularly significant claim. The Stones[4] owned several of the houses in the redevelopment's way. The African American family had moved into the neighborhood as others abandoned it. They had patiently acquired property over the years. The parents bought individual houses from their neighbors who left, and their adult children and other relatives moved in. Just before the family patriarch died years earlier, he reminded his wife and children to think about the land they owned and occupied as a pot of gold. He reminded them that those houses were *theirs*. The Stones and other mostly African American neighbors talked about how they had come and stayed during the hard times, when jobs and families left but drugs arrived (Becher, 2009).

The Stones and some of their neighbors believed that, through the time and effort they had given, they had established a right to the space beyond their privately owned plots. They established claims to the area surrounding and connecting their houses. For example, residents held regular block parties in the middle of the street and in the empty lots. Neighbors knew to go to the 1400 block of South Leithgow Street for good times every Fourth of July and every time Mrs. Stone's birthday rolled around. Locals informally referred to that section of Leithgow as "Stone Street." The Stones and many of their neighbors understood their right to use neighborhood land that extended beyond what they privately owned. Their history there and their commitment to the place, they thought, had earned them a right to control their houses and their neighborhood. Problems and all, the neighborhood was theirs.

City government's attention to redevelopment of the area scared many of these residents. It threatened their control over that space and thus hit a collective nerve. Once they heard that the city was moving on something, neighbors started talking. They were angry and fearful, and they knew that if they had a chance of winning any fight against being pushed around they needed to channel that anger into collective action. They believed government should and could respect their rights, but they knew they did not know how to make that happen. They knew they had claims that would draw public sympathy, but they realized that they lacked the political experience or the organizational resources to capitalize on their assets.

Longtime residents of this particular area were not typically engaged in neighborhood politics and saw this redevelopment planning as one more policy arena where they lacked power. But they saw this plan as so drastically disruptive and unfair that they would not take it lying down. At first, between 1993 and 1998, when residents received flyers about planning meetings, they did not react. Throughout the 1990s, managers of the local hospital, nearby neighborhood leaders, and the city council office had been discussing revitalization plans for the residential area north of the hospital. Some of the neighbors in the targeted area attended early meetings, voiced their opinions, and went home to continue on with their lives. Even an immense threat of dislocation and the loss of property would mean little if it went no further than the meeting rooms.

Mobilization around the Jefferson Square plan began only after people saw evidence that government was really going to do something. The Jefferson Square Revitalization Plan sparked community organizing when it became specific and immediate, that is, when residents learned which properties were in the footprint for redevelopment and when they came to believe that city government was seriously pursuing this plan. In 1998, the plan suddenly seemed imminent. Official, bright orange signs from the city's Department of Licenses and Inspections appeared on the front doors of a small group of properties the city thought were vacant. The signs stated that the properties were dangerous and thus condemned. Because these signs were posted throughout an area only a few city blocks long and wide, residents decided that somebody was actually moving on a plan for their neighborhood. They soon learned that the city councilperson's official plan for Jefferson Square's redevelopment threatened to forcibly take thirty owner-occupied homes, displace renters, and confiscate the property from landlords and absentee owners. The city's plan was dramatic. It concentrated on a small area of about five city blocks that had between one and two hundred privately owned properties. About 30 of the properties were occupied by homeowners and a few by business owners. Most of the owners were non-resident owners of both vacant and occupied properties. If owners would not sell, the city would invoke eminent domain, the power to take property for urban redevelopment in return for just compensation. Residents became convinced that the city was actually doing something. Specific people were targeted, and the proposed change was drastic.

Neighborhood residents, largely African American, heard white Councilman DiCicco saying in public meetings that the plan's main purpose was to bring the middle class back to live in an area he wanted to dub "Jefferson Square." Residents watched their representative on city council, the owners of the neighborhood hospital, and even the heads of nearby neighborhood organizations strategize about what they called "revitalization." When they got wind of this plan, residents were mad, but they did not know if they could fight the city and win. Though residents were enraged and believed they had a right to control the neighborhood's change, they also believed they did not have the skills to claim their rights. They knew they did not know how to win a fight with the city. They knew they would be on shaky ground even if they could take their stories public. Their houses were in bad shape. Some of them had not paid property taxes. Some were probably running drugs and guns.

At first, there was no organized voice, no particular leader or group of leaders to represent the affected individuals. The question of who spoke for "the community" frustrated early advocacy on this issue. Who should or could the councilman listen to? Whose wishes would and should matter as the final plan was drawn up? Homeowners who wanted to stay had different interests from those who wanted to leave; tenants felt differently from homeowners and landlords. Absentee investors had their own approaches.

Constituting a Political Moment: Organizing and Mobilization

Homeowners, neighbors, relatives, a local church, and a neighborhood settlement house banded together to create a temporary organization to fight and then negotiate with the city over the redevelopment plan. The St. John's Leadership Team represented residents who wanted to stay. Their stated goals involved this redevelopment plan and nothing more. The group never organized around this event as an example for or in order to connect with others. They did not frame their fight around an ideological issue or connect themselves to other issue-based organizations. Residents could have allied themselves, for example, with local and national anti-eminent domain activism that was growing at the time. Or they could have accessed other longstanding social movement organizations dedicated to the poor, to cities, to issues of race, or to other issues. They probably would have received resources, but for the most part they did not do this.[5] Most of the work of the St. John's Leadership Team was focused on gathering specific information, convincing specific people to support them, and, eventually, finding specific plans for redevelopment that they could agree to. Eventually, members of the group unanimously signed a dramatically revised Jefferson Square Revitalization Plan, and the group dissolved once the plan was implemented.

That residents in the footprint of the redevelopment plan devoted themselves to the issue over a long period of two years was crucial to their success, but they are quick to attribute their eventual wins to the support of other individuals and groups. Looking at how the residents organized others' support can teach us about a political moment's potential for mobilization, even beyond the immediately affected individuals. In Jefferson Square, the core people affected pulled others—who could have remained nothing more than bystanders—into the struggle.

Neighbors joined a struggle they perceived as different from the usual politics, one that was centered on a decidedly local and immense issue. Residents requested help from individuals and organizations located within a few blocks of the plan's footprint. One nearby resident named Ellen, who took on a leadership role, usually turned away from political meetings in South Philadelphia because she had seen that they were full of screaming and ended up nowhere. She saw that this time it was different. The people yelling at each other were not the usual characters, and what the city was planning to do was just too horrendous for her to ignore. In addition, the meetings seemed to her like they might actually get somewhere. People were not just blowing off steam and arguing to argue; they were trying to solve a real problem. Tammy, another participant, did not live in the immediate footprint of the plan either, but she committed herself to helping with the organizing. As a new member of the St. John's congregation, she heard about the neighborhood development conflict and kept attending meetings, taking notes, and helping out however she could. An issue singularly affecting their little place in the city drew neighbors in to help with the fight, even when they had little particular interest in the event and no prior personal relationship with the people involved. For guidance about what to do, residents first looked to neighbors who seemed to have learned to work the system for help. At first, they followed the advice of a pair of men who had grown up in the neighborhood and eventually left. One had his own construction business; the other had worked with the city on official community recreational activities. But residents still needed resources like physical meeting space that these individuals could not provide.

At first, it seemed like neighborhood organizations and associations might offer little help to the residents resisting the councilman's plan. They turned to the preacher of the closest church with an African American congregation. Eventually, the most active resident-organizers abandoned this preacher because they thought he was acting more in his own interests than in theirs. The area had no formal neighborhood association or community development corporation, unlike most other Philadelphia neighborhoods. Some churches and other associations sat in the neighborhood physically and were originally sustained by mostly local members. Over time, their members had moved away. Many of the older members returned for services and meetings, keeping the organizations afloat. The organizations' programs became increasingly detached from local concerns. The predominately white ethnic organizations formed early in the century had retained their ethno-racial identity and membership, even as the African American population greatly increased in the surrounding neighborhood. Residents eventually asked some of these predominantly white churches if they could hold their meetings there. They also asked for and received help from Marcella, the community organizer for a nearby settlement house, whom they had met months earlier when she was knocking on neighborhood doors to find out what concerns people might have. The support of one of these churches and the settlement house became crucial to the successful campaign to make the revitalization plan serve the existing residents.

The decision to get involved with the conflict over Jefferson Square was hard for both the church and settlement house. At first, leaders of both resisted. It was unclear to them how relevant the issue of local development was to their organizations. They also worried about antagonizing their city councilperson and state senator. Like the individual neighbors mentioned above, these neighborhood organizations would have probably declined involvement in an issue framed around abstract political principles and enduring issues. Members of both boards recommended against getting involved in this issue precisely because it was so political, but they were in the minority. It scared the leaders of the church and settlement house that the development plan directly engaged a city councilperson. If the residents had framed this issue as more abstract or permanent, the organization leaders who wanted to steer clear of politics might have won the argument.

In addition, disengagement from the neighborhood, especially at the church, was partially intentional. Internal conflicts over the organizations' responsibilities to nearby residents had been brewing for years. These issues were rarely debated explicitly. Some leaders and members fought programmatic changes that would shift the mix of members from white to black. Others wanted to increase membership from their immediate neighborhood. Without a particular issue to force their hand, members and leaders would continue disagreeing and make only slow changes, if any at all. By making explicit decisions about whether and how to support neighborhood organizers, the church would have to deal with longstanding but often unacknowledged questions about how the church's mission and congregation should respond to neighborhood changes.

The two individuals who pushed for involvement understood that this struggle could help their organizations to survive. Marcella, the community organizer working with a settlement house, and Pastor Rick of nearby St. John Evangelist Church, realized that the redevelopment plan was unusual precisely because it had caught residents' attention as no other common issue had. Most neighbors had paid little attention to St. John Evangelist Church or the settlement house. St. John's had recently hired Pastor Rick to help the organization survive dwindling numbers of congregants and rising operational costs. He saw the Jefferson Square redevelopment issue as a way to help the church turn toward its local community and, in turn, enlarge its congregation. Similarly, Marcella saw this conflict as an opportunity for the nearby settlement house where she was working as a community organizer. Her agency—formed almost a hundred years earlier to help European immigrants adapt—had been struggling to keep up interest and support and to provide needed services as the neighborhood changed. The organizations could earn recognition, respect, and membership by helping with the issue that had motivated even the most private of neighbors to become involved in community affairs.

Short- and Long-term Gains

As a result of their own tenacity, their mobilization of individual and organizational support, and many other factors, residents who organized around the Jefferson Square Revitalization Plan won a great deal. After two years of struggle, the redevelopment plans became much more amenable to resident wishes than in their first instantiations. Instead of a new parking lot for the imaginary new owner of the bankrupt hospital, a full street of new houses replaced the blocks where older homes were scattered. Instead of having to move to other neighborhoods and possibly worse living conditions, homeowners could move into new houses within the footprint of the project at no extra cost to them. Instead of being relocated twice—once so that the redevelopment could happen and a second time to move back—construction was staged so that people could move directly from old houses to new ones. They had not been worried about moving twice; they worried that the first move would happen but the second one would not. By staging the construction they were guaranteed not to give up their old homes until they had new keys in hand. It was a dramatic victory, then, that instead of being pushed out of the neighborhood, homeowners could get keys to new homes a few blocks from their original ones without incurring any costs. Other low-income families who wanted to move into the neighborhood would also receive subsidies to buy new houses. In addition, many of the surrounding row-homes were renovated for new and existing owners.

Circumstances related and unrelated to their efforts helped residents broker such a significantly improved deal. Residents engaged other council members who forced DiCicco to negotiate, and once DiCicco started talking to residents he seemed to develop a personal commitment. The councilman and his aide seemed to want to find a better solution once they got to know the Stones and others as invested residents rather than as slumlords. Private interest in the original plan of rehabilitating or expanding the hospital fell through. The hospital went bankrupt and closed in 1997, and the next private developer who showed interest withdrew—perhaps because of a visit from protesting residents. DiCicco subsequently accessed government funding for senior and low-income housing through his powerful ally in the state senate.

The most notable element of the organizing, however, is that residents helped themselves secure this agreement by pursuing an issue specific to their neighborhood without tying it to larger political concerns or to similar struggles in other places. The city government, on the other hand, was concerned that large concessions would end up increasing the cost of relocations and development in other areas; this concern even threatened the viability of the councilman's agreement with the residents. Indeed, insiders are quite sure that the Philadelphia Mayor held up the implementation of the Jefferson Square project for over a year out of concern that the generous relocation arrangement would set a costly precedent. This suggests that, if Jefferson Square's residents had joined forces with other neighborhoods or more permanent organizing drives, they might have ended up sacrificing the ample concessions that they won. Though the lack of apparent growth of a larger movement may be disappointing to justice-minded outside observers, poor urban residents might gain power over particular issues by avoiding such connections.

At first glance, it seems this isolated win is the only reason for celebration of the mobilization around Jefferson Square. A more durable shift in political participation or organizational resources was not readily apparent. The direct participation and formal organization dedicated to the issue dissolved with the resolution of the specific problem. Even during the struggle, direct resident participation fizzled. Some people stopped coming to meetings once they worked out solutions that suited them individually, even if others were still fighting. Many professionals, neighbors, family, and friends who took part in this struggle confessed hopes that the residents who persevered and won the battle for the group would stay involved in the war for their neighborhood and for the poor. They hoped the residents, at the very least, would form new neighborhood associations and organize themselves around new issues.

Yet, by definition, when people engage in what I am calling a political moment they organize around temporary, discrete issues. Thus much to the chagrin of many observers and participants, even the most involved residents went home after the battle was won. The St. John's Leadership Team disbanded, and its core group of residents went and stayed home once the general issue was resolved. By 2009, the residents who had been in the eye of the storm had not taken on any new political issues or campaigns. Thus, longer lasting transformations of political voice seemed to remain out of reach. It seemed like the private and isolated win would have little if any long-lasting effect beyond individual homeowners who avoided displacement.

Once we look a bit more closely, however, we find some long-lasting effects of the organizing. First of all, through this political moment, residents created their own newly powerful orientation to city politics. The people who dedicated so much of their time and energy to the struggle felt vindicated, dignified, and empowered. They began the struggle with a sense of entitlement to their little piece of the city, but they had little faith that they could actually affect city government plans. The people involved with St. John's Leadership Team testify that they now expect greater attention to their voices in future issues. The experience taught them that they could fight the city and win.

More than one of the Stones said the fight made their family proud. Considering how the struggle strained their time and energy, I assumed that residents would have preferred to have avoided it. I thought they would have liked to turn the clock back, if they could, and have the city begin by offering them the solution eventually reached after more than two years of conflict. To my surprise, the woman who took the most intense leadership role and talked about how exhausting it was told me she is glad they had to struggle for what they won. It was worth it to her to have learned that they could and did succeed in budging seemingly unmovable powers. Residents who struggled over Jefferson Square expect to fight again if necessary and say they would tell others in similar situations to stick up for what they believe—and that they can win too.

Second, the people who mobilized in Jefferson Square developed new interpersonal ties. For many, the new relationships they built—and not just the political victories—made the energy they put into organizing worthwhile. Core members of the St. John's Leadership Team talk about how they formed new friendships through the organizing. They attribute their own staying power in the struggle and their continued feelings of community to those new friendships. One of the women who had taken a leadership role as a neighbor stopped me in the middle of an interview to make sure I understood what she (rightly) sensed I was not getting: that to her, the relationships built from the organizing were as important as the obvious political gains. Even if we do only care about political outcomes, the new friendships she told me about may serve these residents well the next time they want to claim access to power. In addition, people developed familiarity not just with individuals but with local organizations. They can now access these new relationships if they, or anyone else they know, are threatened or see an opportunity they want to pursue.

Third, two established neighborhood institutions became more locally available and responsive. Through their involvement in the Jefferson Square conflict, the church and the settlement house shifted their agendas, their leadership, and their membership to be more *of* the neighborhood rather than just *in* the neighborhood. As a result of the decision to support the residents through the redevelopment struggle, the church and settlement house lost members and leaders who had resisted more neighborhood-oriented policies. A few longtime board members left the church, and a key staff member left the settlement house. The organizations gained new devotees and a reputation for engagement with their neighborhood. In the years following the Jefferson Square redevelopment, even after Rick and Marcella had moved on to jobs elsewhere, the church developed and maintained new, neighborhood-oriented programs. Both organizations made temporary public decisions about their relationships to the neighborhood, and those decisions had long-term impacts.

Having to make a solid decision on a dramatic local issue forced these organizations to choose how they would adapt to neighborhood change. The decisions made at St. John the Evangelist Church and the settlement house could have gone the other way; in fact, at least one other established church passed up the opportunity to support the organizing. Still, the request to get involved in this issue created an opportunity for these organizations to turn towards the neighborhood. Many of the organizations in changing neighborhoods struggle over who their constituency is and plod along without making any major adjustments. When a dramatic political situation comes to their front door, they might be forced to choose sides. A temporary alliance with the neighbors can pull the established organizations more permanently in their direction. Publicly visible and specific issues may offer established organizations' progressive tendencies an opening to manifest themselves and earn a positive reputation with neighbors.

Conclusion

In this chapter I have articulated and illustrated a particular form of organizing that I call political moments. Political moments are comprised of intentionally short-term collective action directed toward very specific goals. These moments of organizing emerge, in large part, from the conditions that residents of poor, urban neighborhoods face periodically; they do not emerge from the initiative of widespread or long-term political campaigns. Conditions typically experienced as problems become opportunities for organizing. A drastic plan threatening local control over development, local residents preferring participation in community over politics, and organizations facing dwindling rates of local membership can come together to form a volatile concoction. When this combination gives birth to a political action that is specifically focused and temporary, it promises to mobilize unlikely suspects. Furthermore, the political action promises to win short- and long-term control over resources.

Undoubtedly there are limits to where political moments can mobilize and secure short- and long-term change, and we need more research to know what those limits are. I hope that by proposing the concept of political moments in this essay I will encourage others to develop it further. We need to know more about how temporary organizing around specific events emerges and what the tradeoffs are. More research comparing political moments to other kinds of organizing can answer additional questions. Whose support is gained and lost by specific framing? Who might be motivated or excluded if large-scale organizations take leadership? Would more explicitly political or large-scale organizations push harder for bigger wins? Would established, local organizations encourage earlier compromises with power? With this research, we will be better equipped to understand how political moments can contribute to theories on winning political claims, including the right to the city. Most interestingly for the discussion in this volume, political moments suggest how residents can, somewhat surreptitiously, engage local organizations in a way that secures their commitments to neighborhoods in the long run. This opportunity for organizational involvement and change is especially likely to prevail in older neighborhoods with significant histories of demographic change. Through participation in political moments, older local organizations, such as churches that have strayed from having neighborhood-based membership, can reinvigorate their neighborhood connections and commitment. Political moments may secure established organizations' survival by forcing needed adaptations to changing neighborhoods, securing in turn the organization's attention to the neighborhood. Residents can thus win greater power over the organizations in their midst. The organizations' participation can reignite a dedication to the neighborhood and even help the organizations survive and grow.

Experienced organizers are very likely to be crucial to the formation and success of political moments. Professional organizers take on a particular role. They do not expect to recruit members for the organizations that employ them. Rather, they prioritize service in the moment. Though they certainly may seek long-term gains for their organizations (e.g., enhancing their reputation), they do not expect individuals who are mobilized to become long-term participants. In the Jefferson Square conflict, several outsiders took on this role. Most significant were Marcella, the professional community organizer connected to the settlement house, and Pastor Rick, the preacher at St. John Evangelist Church. An experienced neighbor and an attorney from Community Legal Services of Philadelphia also provided considerable support. Resident leaders attest that these individuals were vital to the campaign's success.

As they mount successful challenges to power in political moments, people need and transform established organizations. But these organizations look different from those dedicated to political change or social movements. Organizations that typically turn away from political issues may be the most useful to local residents in both the short and the long term. Organizations like churches and cultural centers typically identify as apolitical, except perhaps on occasions when an issue about place lands on their lap. The long-term changes that can arise from temporary partnerships may mean different things to local residents than the growth of an organization dedicated to political or development issues. During political moments, these organizations offer some of the same resources, such as space, equipment, and connections, that others dedicated to social movements can. Because these partnerships occur with any number of kinds of organizations, they can secure resources for many different areas of life. Thus the results of political moments may be, in some ways, more widespread than those of the more traditionally studied social movements.

Under this model of organizing, what can we say is institutionalized? Sociologists know that institutionalization can refer to a wide range of structures, from concepts and norms to laws and organizations. Still, we may tend to think of the institutionalization of rights to the city through the establishment of social movement organizations explicitly dedicated to those rights (or components of them) and not through local churches and settlement houses. Yet the very organizations that can seem peripheral to right to the city movements may be central. Their involvement in politics may be sporadic, but their ability to make resources available to poor neighborhoods in the long term may be much more significant than that of movement organizations. These organizational changes may build networks and resources to be accessed by larger-scale movements, but they may also comprise rights to the city in and of themselves.

Notes

I would like to thank the many people who opened their hearts, minds, and offices to my research. In the scholarly world, I owe a great debt to Michael Peter Smith and Michael McQuarrie for their careful and astute editing of this chapter. I also thank Emily Zackin and Caryn Carpenter for their extremely helpful comments. The research for this chapter was completed with support from the National Science Foundation (Dissertation Improvement Grant, Law and Social Sciences), the Department of Housing and Urban Development (Office of University Partnerships, Grant Number H-21536SG), the Horowitz Foundation for Social Policy, and Princeton University. Points of views or opinions in this document are those of the author and do not necessarily represent the official position or policies of any of these supporting organizations.

1. Government bureaucrats and politicians, non-profit organizations, for-profit companies, and individuals standing around street corners or sitting at kitchen tables are constantly dreaming up ideas about how to change a little piece of a neighborhood. Many of those plans even make it onto paper, but they usually go no further. At some point, however, concrete actions on behalf of the plan can make it seem like someone's idea might actually materialize. The initiator might start buying up property or put up a significant amount of money, for instance. Actions like this can make a concentrated threat or opportunity seem pressing.

2. Many local organizations, such as barbershops and hair salons, day-care centers, and recreation centers play a more central role in residents' daily life but have not been as closely analyzed for their political impact (Sanchez-Janowski, 2008; Small, 2009).

3. This kind of activity is more likely to be covered in research on organizing or activism in contrast to social movements; see for example Hart (2001) and Warren (2001). Neither are political moments adequately captured by scholarship on what is called everyday resistance, which connotes even more short-term and hidden forms of action (Scott, 1985). What I call political moments involves open and public resistance.

4. Names of individuals are fictitious, but names of organizations and places are real.

5. This is a matter of emphasis; the resources they did access were, of course, not developed or maintained in isolation. An attorney from Community Legal Services of Philadelphia assisted. The organizer at the settlement house was supported by a program that placed such professionals throughout the city. St. John the Evangelist Church was connected to larger organizations.

References

Alinsky, S. D. (1971). *Rules for Radicals: A Practical Primer for Realistic Radicals*. New York: Random House.

Andrews, K. T. (2004). *Freedom Is a Constant Struggle: The Mississippi Civil Rights Movement and Its Legacy*. Chicago: University of Chicago Press.

Becher, D. (2009). *Valuing Property: Eminent Domain for Urban Redevelopment, Philadelphia 1992-2007* (Doctoral dissertation). Princeton University.

Brenner, N., and N. Theodore. (2002). "Preface: From the 'New Localism' to the Spaces of Neoliberalism." *Antipode*, 34(3), 341-7.

Castells, M. (1983). *The City and the Grassroots: A Cross-cultural Theory of Urban Social Movements*. London/Berkeley: E. Arnold/University of California Press.

Flacks, R. (2005). "The Question of Relevance in Social Movement Studies." In D. Croteau, W. Hoynes, and C. Ryan (Eds.), *Rhyming Hope and History: Activists, Academics, and Social Movement Scholarship* (pp. 3-19). Minneapolis: University of Minnesota Press.

Giugni, M. G. (1998). "Was It Worth the Effort? The Outcomes and Consequences of Social Movements." *Annual Review of Sociology*, 24, 371-93.

Hart, S. (2001). *Cultural Dilemmas of Progressive Politics: Styles of Engagement among Grassroots Activists*. Chicago: University of Chicago Press.

Harvey, D. (2003). "The Right to the City." *International Journal of Urban and Regional Research*, 27(4), 939-41.

Kretzmann, J. P., and J. McKnight. (1997). *Building Communities from the Inside Out: A Path Toward Finding and Mobilizing a Community's Assets*. Evanston, IL: ACTA Publications.

Lasch-Quinn, E. (1993). *Black Neighbors: Race and the Limits of Reform in the American Settlement House Movement, 1890-1945*. Chapel Hill: University of North Carolina Press.

Lefebvre, H. (2003). *The Urban Revolution*. Minneapolis, MN/London: University of Minnesota Press.

Marwell, N. P. (2007). *Bargaining for Brooklyn: Community Organizations in the Entrepreneurial City*. Chicago: University of Chicago Press.

McQuarrie, M. (2010). "Nonprofits and the Reconstruction of Urban Governance: Housing Production and Community Development in Cleveland, 1975-2005." In E. S. Clemens and D. Guthrie (Eds.), *Politics and Partnerships: The Role of Voluntary Associations in America's Political Past and Present* (pp. 237 ff.). Chicago: University of Chicago Press.

McQuarrie, M., and N. P. Marwell. (2009). "The Missing Organizational Dimension in Urban Sociology." *City and Community*, 8(3), 247-68.

Marcuse, P. (2009). "Beyond the Just City to the Right to the City." In P. Marcuse (Ed.), *Searching for the Just City: Debates in Urban Theory and Practice* (pp. 240-54). London/New York: Routledge.

McAdam, D. (1988). *Freedom Summer*. New York: Oxford University Press.

McRoberts, O. M. (2003). *Streets of Glory: Church and Community in a Black Urban Neighborhood*. Chicago: University of Chicago Press.

Morris, A. D. (1986). *The Origins of the Civil Rights Movement: Black Communities Organizing for Change*. New York/Toronto: Free Press/Maxwell Macmillan Canada/Maxwell Macmillan International.

Naples, N. A. (1998). *Grassroots Warriors: Activist Mothering, Community Work, and the War on Poverty*. New York: Routledge.

Sánchez-Jankowski, M. (2008). *Cracks in the Pavement: Social Change and Resilience in Poor Neighborhoods*. Berkeley: University of California Press.

Scott, J. C. (1985). *Weapons of the Weak: Everyday Forms of Peasant Resistance*. New Haven: Yale University Press.

Small, M. L. (2009). *Unanticipated Gains: Origins of Network Inequality in Everyday Life*. Oxford/New York: Oxford University Press.

Snow, D. A., S. A. Soule, and H. Kriesi. (2004). "Mapping the Terrain." In D. A. Snow, S. A. Soule, and H. Kriesi *The Blackwell Companion to Social Movements* (pp. 3-16). Malden, MA: Blackwell Publishing Ltd.

Staggenborg, S. (2011). *Social Movements*. New York: Oxford University Press.

Tarrow, S. G. (1998). *Power in Movement: Social Movements and Contentious Politics*. Cambridge, UK/New York: Cambridge University Press.

Warren, M. R. (2001). *Dry Bones Rattling: Community Building to Revitalize American Democracy*. Princeton, NJ: Princeton University Press.

Zald, M. N. (2000). "Ideologically Structured Action: An Enlarged Agenda for Social Movement Research." *Mobilization*, 5(1), 1-36.

Contributors

Debbie Becher is Assistant Professor in the Department of Sociology at Barnard College, Columbia University. Her research links political culture to legal, urban, and economic sociology. She is currently writing a book titled *The Investment State* on the legitimacy of government investment in private markets based on her investigation of Philadelphia property taking. It is the first comprehensive study of a city's eminent-domain acquisitions. Dr. Becher has published articles in the *International Journal of Urban and Regional Research* and *Poetics* and has received fellowships from the American Academy of Arts and Sciences, the Brookings Institution's Metropolitan Policy Program, the American Association of University Women, the Mellon Foundation, and the Arthur Liman Public Interest Law Program. She earned her BA in mathematics from the University of Virginia in 1991 and her PhD in Sociology from Princeton University in 2009. In addition to her academic work, she has a decade of professional experience in social work and neighborhood development. She teaches classes on law, urban studies, and social theory.

Irene Bloemraad is Associate Professor of Sociology at the University of California, Berkeley, and a Scholar with the Canadian Institute for Advanced Research. Her work examines the intersection of immigration and politics, with emphasis on citizenship, immigrants' political and civic participation, and multiculturalism. Her research has appeared in academic journals spanning the fields of sociology, history, political science, and ethnic studies. Her books include *Rallying for Immigrant Rights: The Fight for Inclusion in 21st Century America* (edited with Kim Voss, 2011), *Civic Hopes and Political Realities: Immigrants, Community Organizations, and Political Engagement* (edited with Karthick Ramakrishnan, 2008), and *Becoming a Citizen: Incorporating Immigrants and Refugees in the United States and Canada* (2006), which won an honorable mention for the Thomas and Znaniecki Award for best book published in the previous two years from the American Sociological Association's International Migration section. Professor Bloemraad believes that excellence in research and teaching go hand-in-hand; in 2008 she was honored to receive UC Berkeley's Sarlo Distinguished Mentoring Award for her work with graduate students.

Ernesto Castañeda received his doctorate in Sociology from Columbia University. He is Assistant Professor of Sociology in the Department of Sociology and Anthropology at the University of Texas at El Paso, which is located at the US/Mexico border. He was a visiting scholar at the Sorbonne and the Institute of Political Studies in Paris. He has conducted ethnographic fieldwork in New York City, Paris, Barcelona, and many cities and communities in Algeria, Mexico, and Morocco. His work takes a transnational perspective and compares Latino and Muslim immigrants in the US and Europe. It analyzes the relationship between the contexts of reception, including the avenues available for political voice, and the political inclusion of immigrants and minorities.

Els de Graauw is Assistant Professor of Political Science at Baruch College, the City University of New York. Her teaching and research interests lie at the intersection of immigration studies, (sub)urban politics, civic organizations, and public policy. Her book manuscript analyzes the role of community-based nonprofit organizations as public policy advocates on behalf of disadvantaged immigrants in San Francisco. De Graauw also has underway a project on municipal identification cards and undocumented immigrants and research on local bureaucracies and immigrant integration, with a focus on mayoral offices of immigrant affairs. De Graauw received her PhD in Political Science from the University of California, Berkeley, and previously was a post-doctoral researcher at the Harvard Kennedy School of Government. Currently, she is an immigration research associate at Cornell University.

Shannon Gleeson is Assistant Professor of Latin American and Latino Studies at the University of California, Santa Cruz. She received her PhD in 2008 in Sociology and Demography from the University of California, Berkeley. Dr. Gleeson's research focuses on immigrant civic engagement, the workplace experiences of immigrants, and processes of legal mobilization. Her recent articles on these topics have been published in the *Law and Society Review* (2009), *Law & Social Inquiry* (2010), *Latino Studies* (2010), and *International Migration* (forthcoming, with Roberto G. Gonzales). Her book manuscript is an institutional analysis of the process of enforcing immigrant rights through the lens of government bureaucrats, local governments, civil society, and foreign consulates in San Jose, California, and Houston, Texas.

Luis Eduardo Guarnizo is Professor of Sociology and Community Studies and Development in the Department of Human and Community Development at the University of California, Davis. His work has been published in the *Journal of Economic and Social Geography*, the *American Journal of Sociology*, the *American Sociological Review*, the *International Migration Review*, *The Annals of the American Academy of Political and Social Science*, and *Ethnic and Racial Studies*. His most recent book is *Londres Latina: La presencia colombiana en la capital británica*.

Michael McQuarrie is Assistant Professor of Sociology at the University of California, Davis. His work examines urban organizations and transformations in urban governance and authority. He is currently writing a book manuscript on the organization of urban political authority in the neoliberal era. He has published work on urban governance, low-income housing production, community-based organizations, and the role of organizational analysis in urban sociology.

Faranak Miraftab is Associate Professor of Urban and Regional Planning at the University of Illinois, Urbana-Champaign. She joined the department in 1999 with a PhD from the University of California, Berkeley. Her work seeks to understand the global and local development processes and contingencies involved in the formation of the city and citizens' struggles to access urban space and socio-economic resources. Her publications cross the terrains of several fields, including planning, geography, and feminist and transnational studies. Her inter-disciplinary work explores three interconnected themes: neoliberal governance and the ways in which state-society relations are managed and governed; grassroots mobilizations and the ways in which they claim rights to urban livelihood and resources; and transnational and trans-local practices that shape globalization from below. She has taught and researched in several countries, including Chile, Mexico, Canada, Australia, South Africa, and the US. Her most recent research project concerns transnational networks of care and work that make for the development of the US heartland.

Walter Nicholls received his PhD in Urban Planning from the University of California, Los Angeles. He is currently an Assistant Professor of Sociology at the University of Amsterdam. His research focuses on urban sociology, social movements, and immigration politics. His work on cities and social movements appears in *Transactions of the Institute of British Geographers*, *City and Community*, the *International Journal of Urban and Regional Research*, *Space and Polity*, *Urban Studies*, *Environment and Planning A*, *European Urban and Regional Studies*, and *Compass*. His work on immigration politics is forthcoming in *Ethnic and Racial Studies* and *Citizenship Studies*. He is the co-editor (with Byon Miller and Justin Beaumont) of the forthcoming book *Spatialities of Social Movements*. He is currently performing research on undocumented immigrant rights movements in the United States and France.

Mark Purcell teaches in the Department of Urban Design and Planning at the University of Washington. He writes about urban and political theory, and his work has appeared in journals such as the *International Journal of Urban and Regional Research*, *Urban Studies*, *Environment and Planning A*, *Political Geography*, the *Review of International Political Economy*, *Rue Descartes*, *Progress in Human Geography*, *Geoforum*, *Urban Geography*, and *Antipode*. His book *Recapturing Democracy*, published in 2008, argues that the struggle against neoliberalism in cities should be a struggle for democratization. He is currently at work on a book that draws on post-1968 political theory to develop a radical new conception of democracy.

Xuefei Ren is Assistant Professor of Sociology and Global Urban Studies at Michigan State University and a 2011 fellow at the Woodrow Wilson International Center for Scholars in Washington, DC. Her research focuses on development, urban governance, and political economy. She is the author of *Building Globalization: Transnational Architecture Production in Urban China* (2011).

Tony Roshan Samara is Associate Professor of Sociology at George Mason University. Currently he is involved with two major projects, both of which are concerned with the relationship between socio-spatial transformation and emergent political forms. The first project, from which his chapter in this volume is drawn, examines emergent political subjectivities and forms of counter-governance across US cities. The second is a comparative study of transnational networks of governance and the reconfigurations of urban spaces in Shanghai, New Delhi, and Cape Town. Both projects are driven by an interest in identifying and drawing attention to new developments in the deployment of power against marginal populations and the opportunities for renewed democratic struggles that these inevitably present.

William Sites is Associate Professor at the School of Social Service Administration of the University of Chicago and the author of *Remaking New York: Primitive Globalization and the Politics of Urban Community* (2003). His doctorate in Sociology is from the City University of New York Graduate Center, and he has published in a number of journals, including the *Urban Affairs Review*, *Sociological Theory*, *Politics and Society*, the *Journal of Urban Affairs*, and *Environment and Planning A*. His research interests include urban political economy, welfare states, social movements, racial inequality, and the politics of immigration.

Michael Peter Smith is Distinguished Research Professor in Community Studies at the University of California, Davis. His research focuses on the relationship between cities, the state, globalization, and transnationalism. He is co-author of the award-winning book *Citizenship across Borders* (2008). His other major books include *Transnational Urbanism* (2001), *City State, & Market* (1988), and *The City and Social Theory* (1979, 1980). His research has been published in a wide array of interdisciplinary social science journals including *Theory and Society*, *Politics & Society*, *Social Text*, *Political Geography*, *Global Networks*, the *Journal of Ethnic and Migration Studies*, *Ethnic and Racial Studies*, the *International Journal of Urban and Regional Research*, *City & Society*, and the *Urban Affairs Review*. Smith is the series editor of Transaction's *Comparative Urban and Community Research* book series.

Floris Vermeulen is Assistant Professor in the Department of Political Science and co-director of the Institute for Migration and Ethnic Studies at the University of Amsterdam. His research focuses on different themes, including the civic and political participation of immigrants at the local level and the development of populations of immigrant organizations. He has studied local integration policies and their effects on different domains by looking, for instance, at local policies that target violent extremism. He has also studied the effects of ethnic diversity on social capital at the neighborhood level. He is currently involved in a European research project on the governance of religious diversity. His work is published in several international volumes and journals such as the *Journal of Ethnic and Migration Studies*, *Turkish Studies*, and the *Urban Studies Journal*.

Rebecca Vonderlack-Navarro is a Post-Doctoral Research Affiliate at the Loyola University Graduate School of Social Work's Institute for Migration and International Social Work. She received her doctorate at the School of Social Service Administration at the University of Chicago where she focused on the community organizing and bi-national political incorporation of Mexican immigrants in Chicago. Rebecca has cultivated extensive fieldwork connections with emergent transnational migrant hometown associations in Chicago along with several Illinois state government and Chicago-based Mexican consular officials who interact with local immigrant communities. She has both practical and academic experience working with Latino populations in their countries of origin. Before beginning her doctoral studies, she worked at a community development agency located in a marginalized area of Honduras' capital, Tegucigalpa. While in Honduras, she was awarded a Fulbright scholarship to support qualitative research that explored the economic and political impacts of a microcredit program on its participants. Rebecca is also currently a Research Associate at the Latino Policy Forum, which conducts research on K-12 education issues for Latino youth in Illinois.

Index

CPSIA information can be obtained at www.ICGtesting.com
Printed in the USA
BVOW081847210312

285698BV00004B/1/P

9 781412 846189